Teen Titans

CHILD'S PLAY

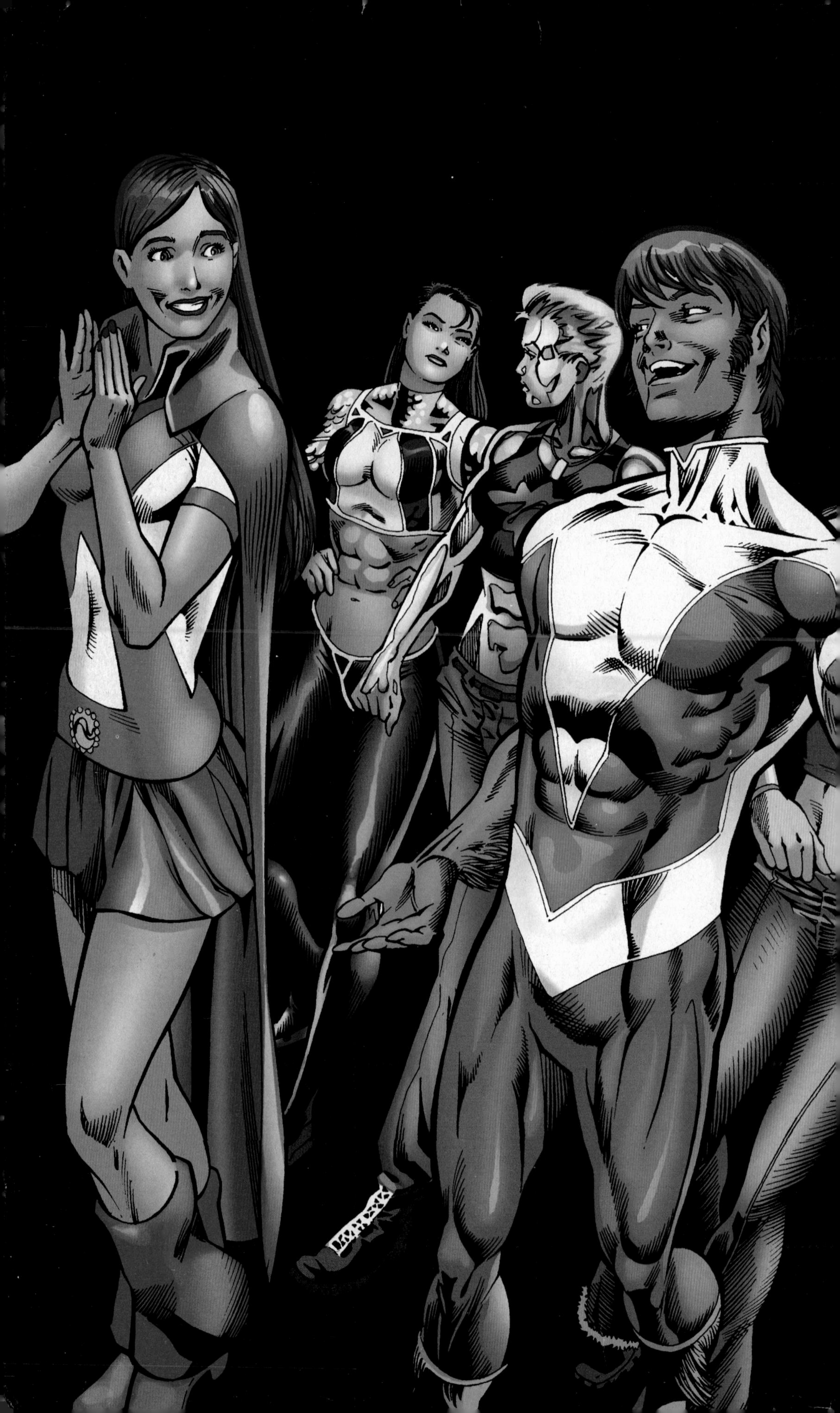

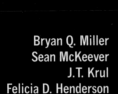

Bryan Q. Miller
Sean McKeever
J.T. Krul
Felicia D. Henderson
Writers

Joe Bennett
Yildiray Cinar
Pencillers

Jack Jadson
Julio Ferreira
Ruy José
Inkers

Rod Reis
Pete Pantazis
Colorists

Sal Cipriano
Letterer

CHILD'S PLAY

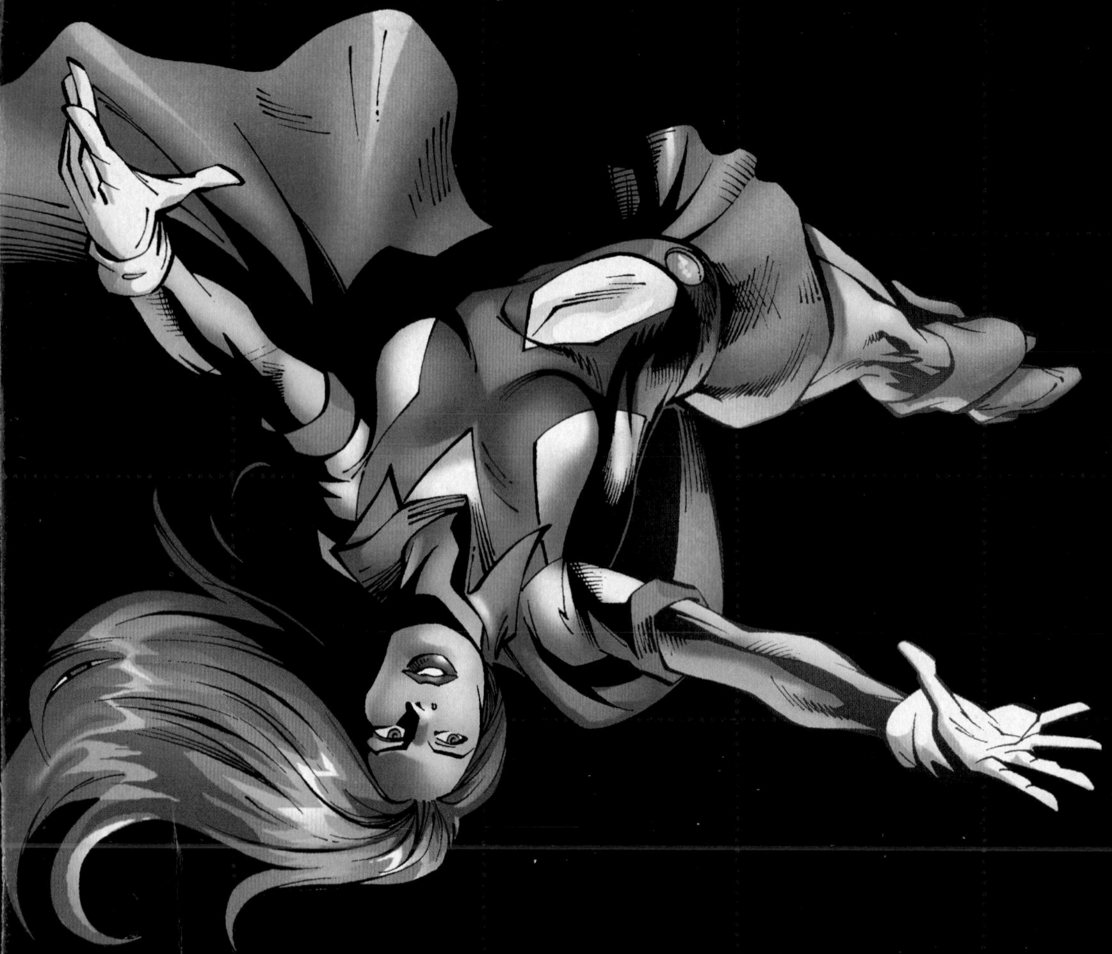

Dan DiDio SVP-Executive Editor
Brian Cunningham Editor-original series
Rex Ogle Assistant Editor-original series
Georg Brewer VP-Design & DC Direct Creative
Bob Harras Group Editor-Collected Editions
Bob Joy Editor
Robbin Brosterman Design Director-Books

DC COMICS

Paul Levitz President & Publisher
Richard Bruning SVP-Creative Director
Patrick Caldon EVP-Finance & Operations
Amy Genkins SVP-Business & Legal Affairs
Jim Lee Editorial Director-WildStorm
Gregory Noveck SVP-Creative Affairs
Steve Rotterdam SVP-Sales & Marketing
Cheryl Rubin SVP-Brand Management

Cover art by **Joe Bennett** and **Jack Jadson** with **Rod Reis**

TEEN TITANS: CHILD'S PLAY
Published by DC Comics.

DC Comics, 1700 Broadway, New York, NY 10019
A Warner Bros. Entertainment Company
Printed by World Color Press, Inc.
St-Romuald, QC, Canada. 3/10/2010
First Printing.
ISBN: 978-1-4012-2641-1

WONDER GIRL

Cassie Sandsmark is the daughter of the Greek god Zeus. Gifted with amazing powers from the gods themselves, Wonder Girl leads the Teen Titans

MISS MARTIAN

Megan Morse is a changeling and telepath from the planet Mars. Naive in the ways of Earth, Miss Martian lives with and fights alongside the Titans while learning about her new planet.

EDDIE BLOOMBERG

The former demon-powered Red Devil recently lost his super abilities. His enthusiasm and knowledge of the team's equipment makes Eddie a valuable member of the group.

BLUE BEETLE

Jamie Reyes shares his body with an alien scarab that gives him fantastic powers.

STATIC SHOCK

Virgil Hawkins has the ability to generate and manipulate electromagnetism.

AQUAGIRL

Lorena Marquez gained her underwater breathing powers in an experiment gone horribly wrong.

KID ETERNITY

This nameless orphan has the power to resurrect the dead — for a limited time.

BOMBSHELL

Amy Allen has quantum metal skin, which makes her invulnerable as well as giving her the power to fly and fire energy blasts.

RAVAGER

Rose Wilson is an ex-Teen Titan and daughter of the team's archnemesis — Deathstroke the Terminator. She recently joined her former teammates to defeat her brother, Jericho...

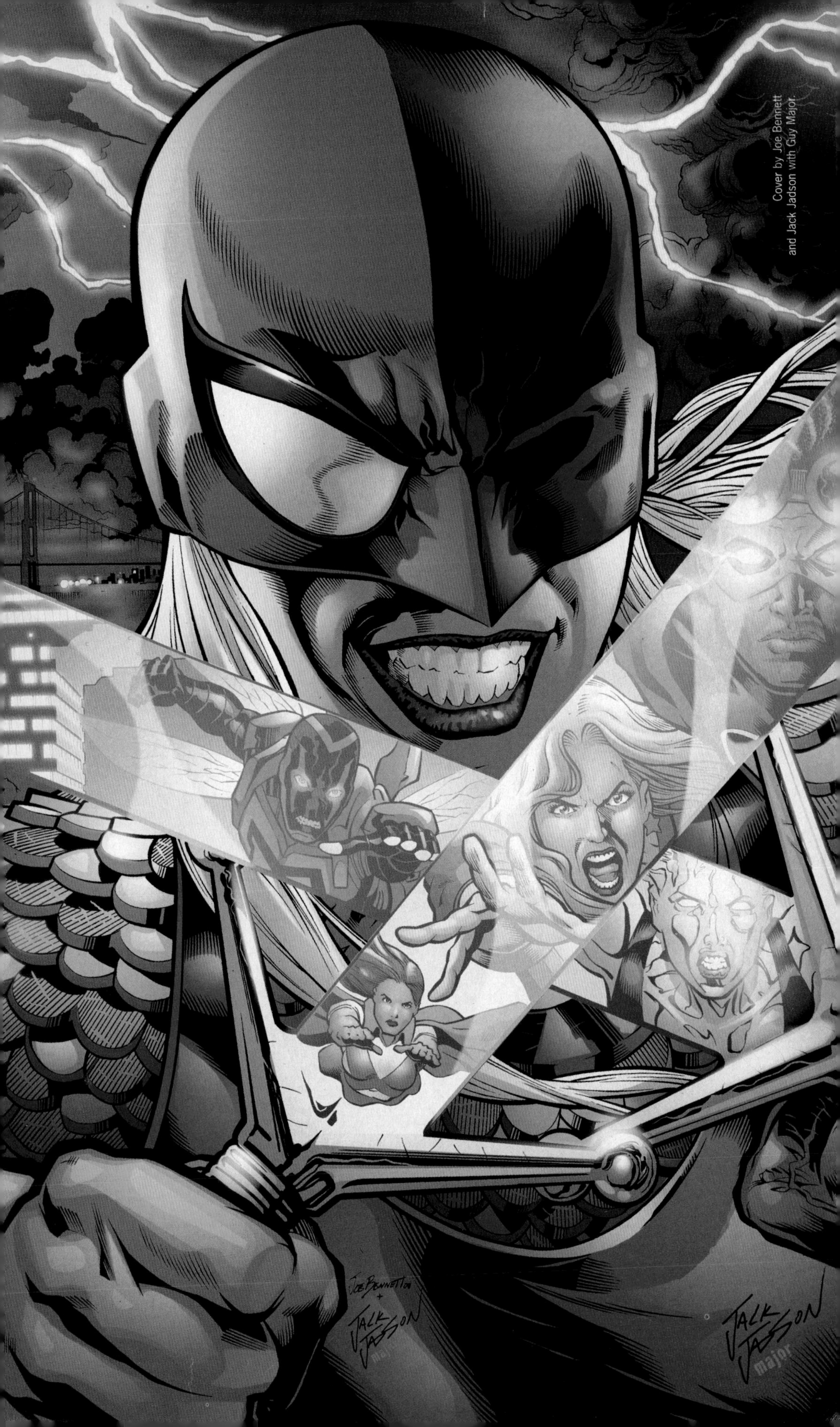
Cover by Joe Bennett
and Jack Jadson with Guy Major

HOMECOMING

Sean McKeever
Story

Yildiray Cinar
Pencils

Júlio Ferreira
Inks

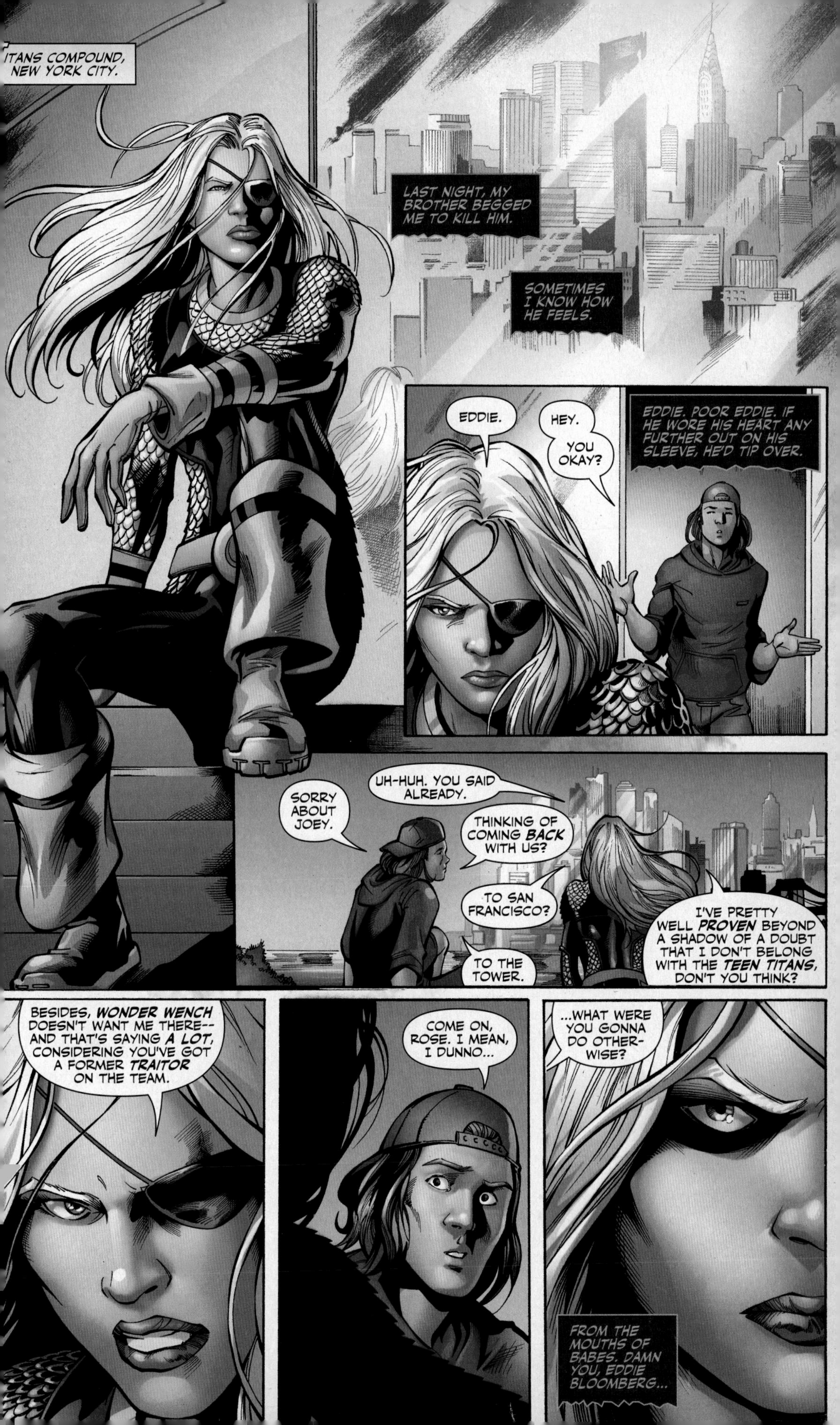

ITANS COMPOUND, NEW YORK CITY.
LAST NIGHT, MY BROTHER BEGGED ME TO KILL HIM.
SOMETIMES I KNOW HOW HE FEELS.
EDDIE.
HEY.
YOU OKAY?
EDDIE. POOR EDDIE. IF HE WORE HIS HEART ANY FURTHER OUT ON HIS SLEEVE, HE'D TIP OVER.
SORRY ABOUT JOEY.
UH-HUH. YOU SAID ALREADY.
THINKING OF COMING BACK WITH US?
TO SAN FRANCISCO?
TO THE TOWER.
I'VE PRETTY WELL PROVEN BEYOND A SHADOW OF A DOUBT THAT I DON'T BELONG WITH THE TEEN TITANS, DON'T YOU THINK?
BESIDES, WONDER WENCH DOESN'T WANT ME THERE-- AND THAT'S SAYING A LOT, CONSIDERING YOU'VE GOT A FORMER TRAITOR ON THE TEAM.
COME ON, ROSE. I MEAN, I DUNNO...
...WHAT WERE YOU GONNA DO OTHER-WISE?
FROM THE MOUTHS OF BABES. DAMN YOU, EDDIE BLOOMBERG...

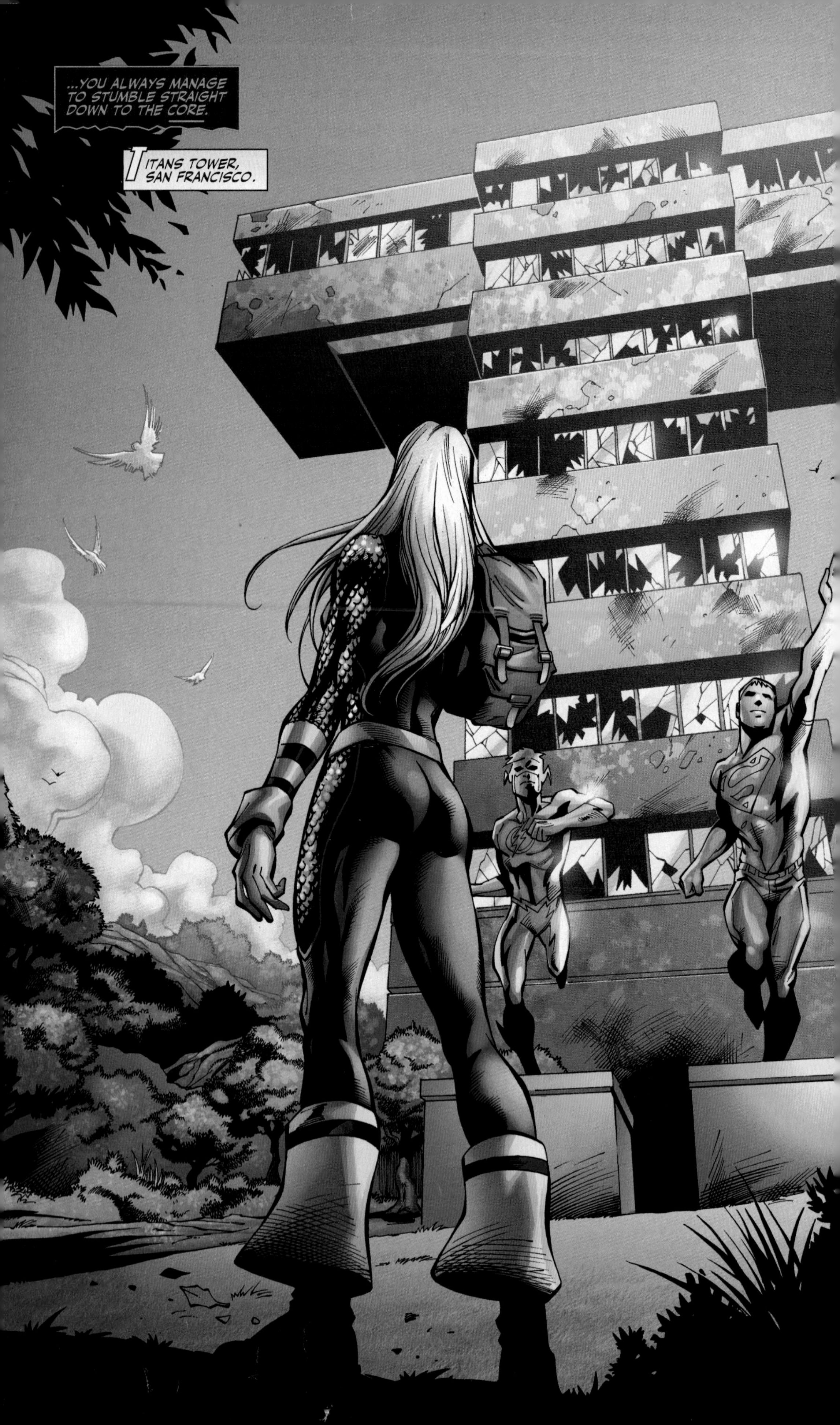
...YOU ALWAYS MANAGE TO STUMBLE STRAIGHT DOWN TO THE CORE.
TITANS TOWER, SAN FRANCISCO.

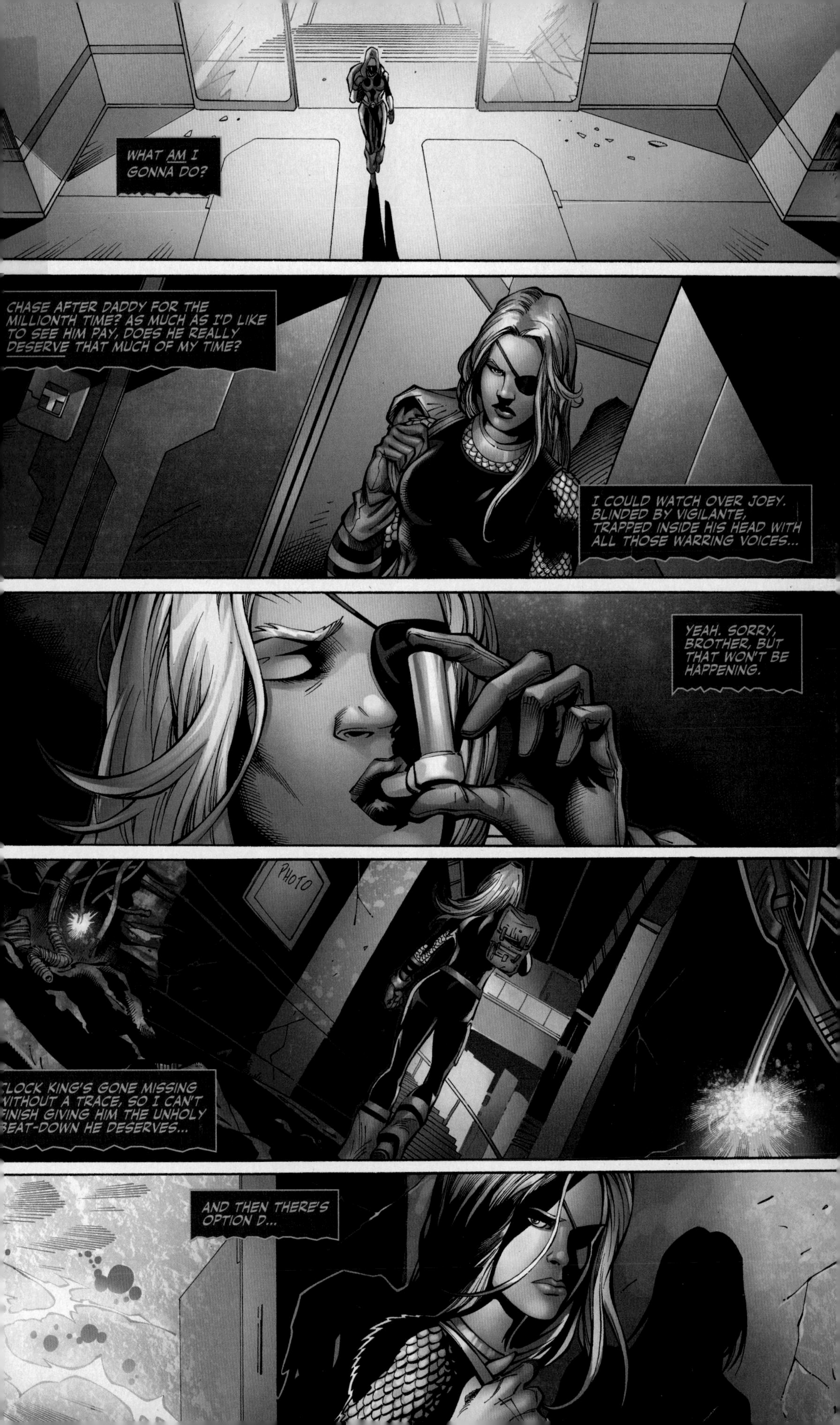

WHAT AM I GONNA DO?
CHASE AFTER DADDY FOR THE MILLIONTH TIME? AS MUCH AS I'D LIKE TO SEE HIM PAY, DOES HE REALLY DESERVE THAT MUCH OF MY TIME?
I COULD WATCH OVER JOEY. BLINDED BY VIGILANTE, TRAPPED INSIDE HIS HEAD WITH ALL THOSE WARRING VOICES...
YEAH. SORRY, BROTHER, BUT THAT WON'T BE HAPPENING.
PHOTO
CLOCK KING'S GONE MISSING WITHOUT A TRACE, SO I CAN'T FINISH GIVING HIM THE UNHOLY BEAT-DOWN HE DESERVES...
AND THEN THERE'S OPTION D...

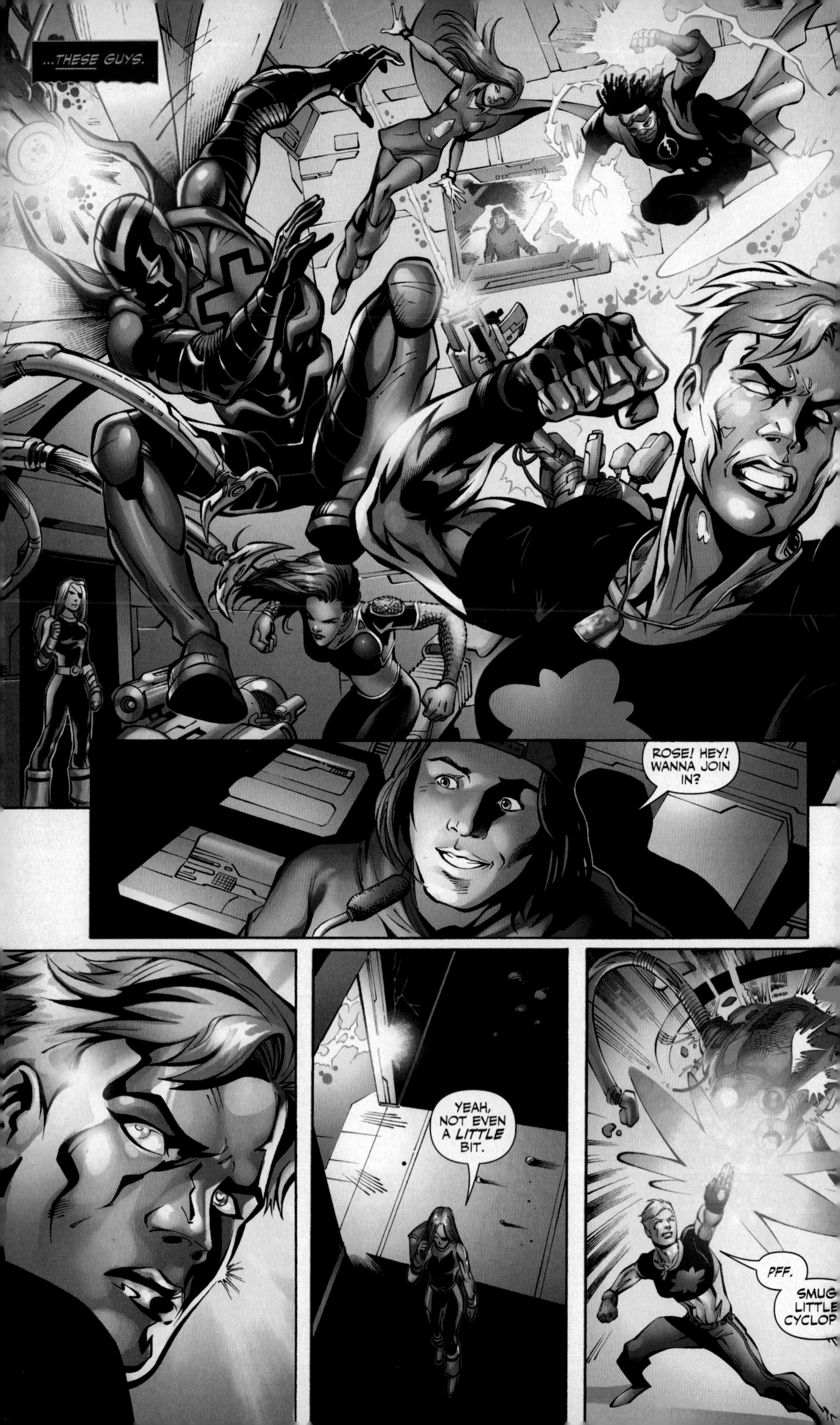
...THESE GUYS.
ROSE! HEY! WANNA JOIN IN?
YEAH, NOT EVEN A LITTLE BIT.
PFF.
SMUG LITTLE CYCLOP

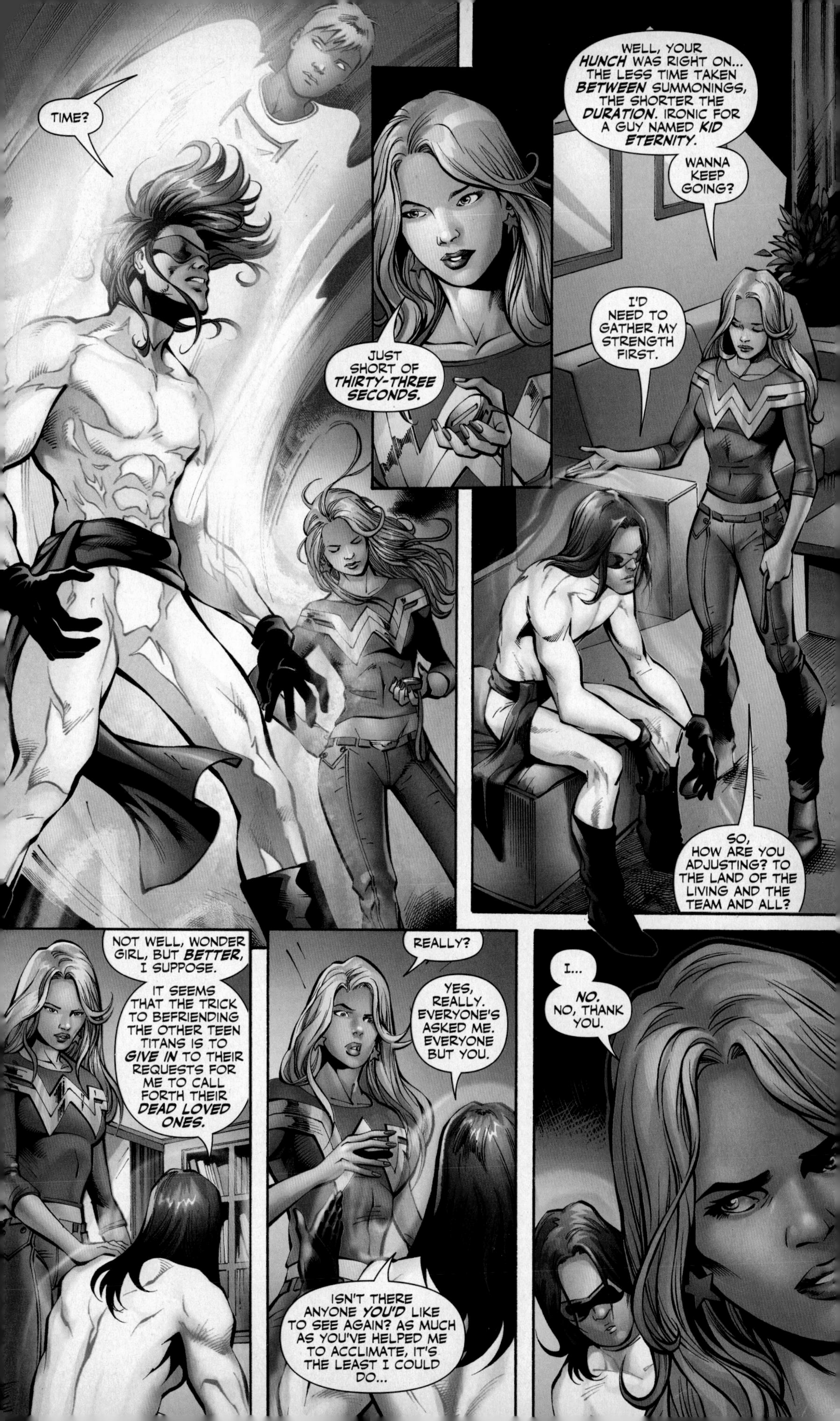
TIME?
JUST SHORT OF THIRTY-THREE SECONDS.
WELL, YOUR HUNCH WAS RIGHT ON... THE LESS TIME TAKEN BETWEEN SUMMONINGS, THE SHORTER THE DURATION. IRONIC FOR A GUY NAMED KID ETERNITY.
WANNA KEEP GOING?
I'D NEED TO GATHER MY STRENGTH FIRST.
SO, HOW ARE YOU ADJUSTING? TO THE LAND OF THE LIVING AND THE TEAM AND ALL?
NOT WELL, WONDER GIRL, BUT BETTER, I SUPPOSE.
IT SEEMS THAT THE TRICK TO BEFRIENDING THE OTHER TEEN TITANS IS TO GIVE IN TO THEIR REQUESTS FOR ME TO CALL FORTH THEIR DEAD LOVED ONES.
REALLY?
YES, REALLY. EVERYONE'S ASKED ME. EVERYONE BUT YOU.
ISN'T THERE ANYONE YOU'D LIKE TO SEE AGAIN? AS MUCH AS YOU'VE HELPED ME TO ACCLIMATE, IT'S THE LEAST I COULD DO...
I...
NO. NO, THANK YOU.

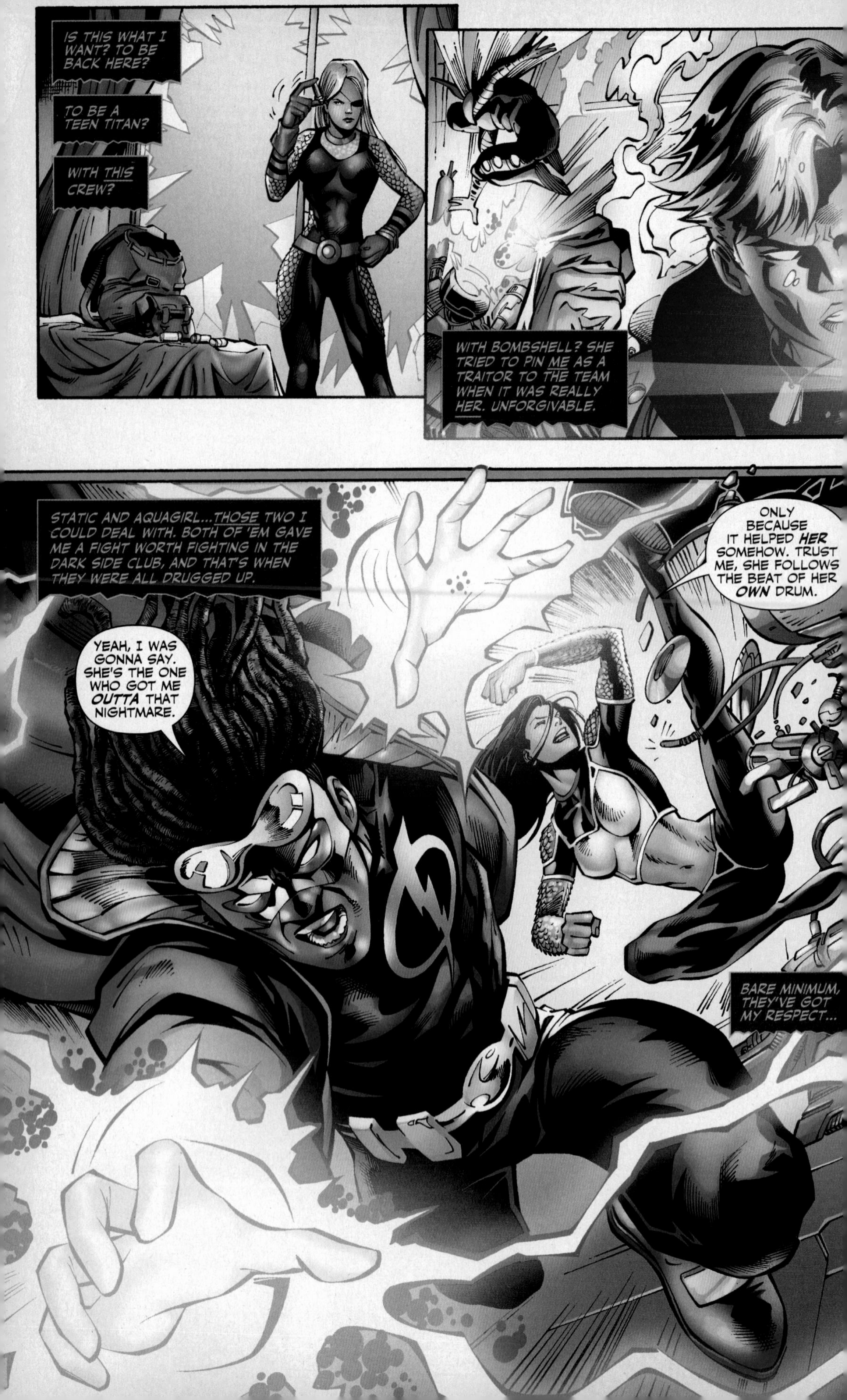
IS THIS WHAT I WANT? TO BE BACK HERE?
TO BE A TEEN TITAN?
WITH THIS CREW?
WITH BOMBSHELL? SHE TRIED TO PIN ME AS A TRAITOR TO THE TEAM WHEN IT WAS REALLY HER. UNFORGIVABLE.
STATIC AND AQUAGIRL...THOSE TWO I COULD DEAL WITH. BOTH OF 'EM GAVE ME A FIGHT WORTH FIGHTING IN THE DARK SIDE CLUB, AND THAT'S WHEN THEY WERE ALL DRUGGED UP.
ONLY BECAUSE IT HELPED HER SOMEHOW. TRUST ME, SHE FOLLOWS THE BEAT OF HER OWN DRUM.
YEAH, I WAS GONNA SAY. SHE'S THE ONE WHO GOT ME OUTTA THAT NIGHTMARE.
BARE MINIMUM, THEY'VE GOT MY RESPECT...

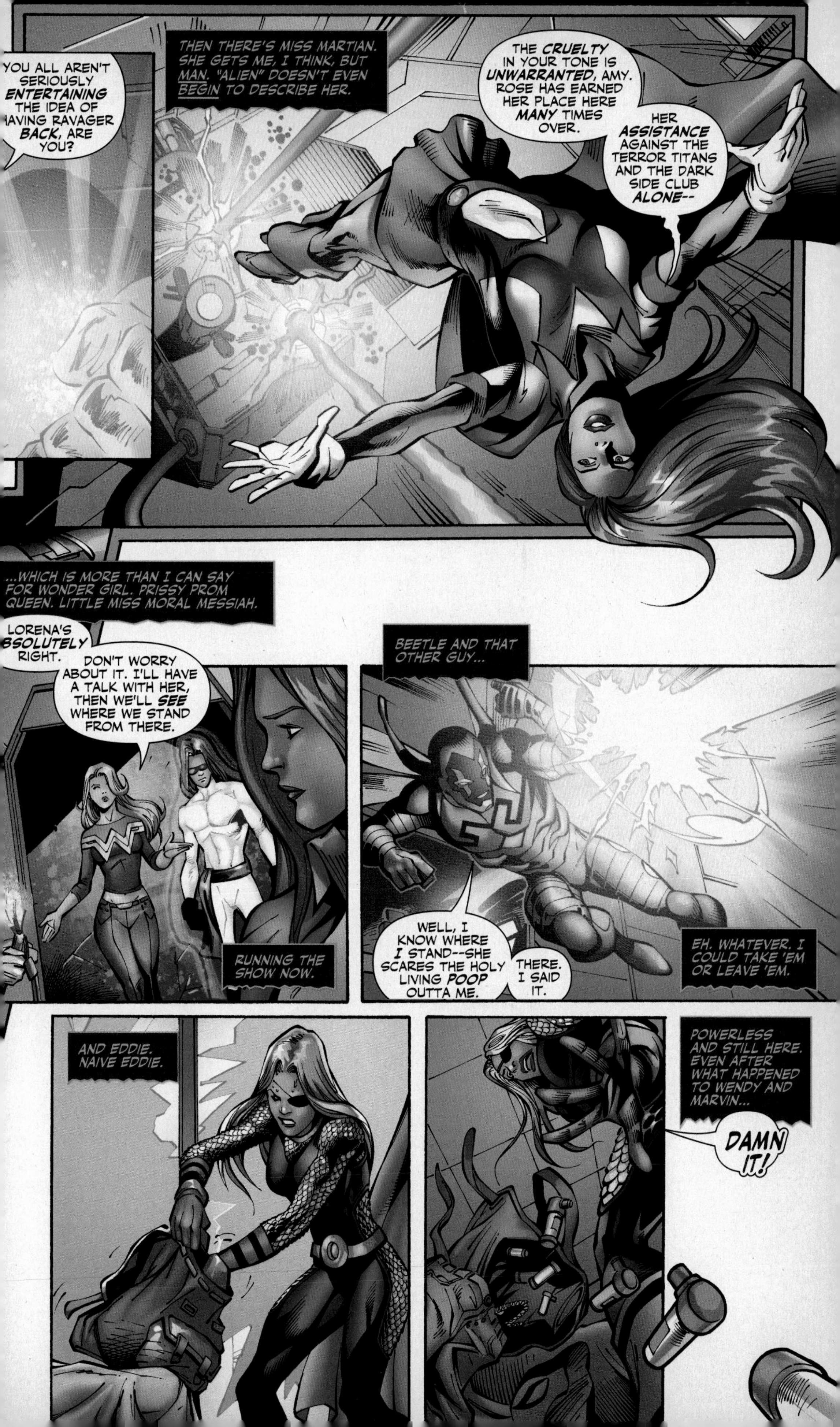

YOU ALL AREN'T SERIOUSLY ENTERTAINING THE IDEA OF HAVING RAVAGER BACK, ARE YOU?
THEN THERE'S MISS MARTIAN. SHE GETS ME, I THINK, BUT MAN. "ALIEN" DOESN'T EVEN BEGIN TO DESCRIBE HER.
THE CRUELTY IN YOUR TONE IS UNWARRANTED, AMY. ROSE HAS EARNED HER PLACE HERE MANY TIMES OVER.
HER ASSISTANCE AGAINST THE TERROR TITANS AND THE DARK SIDE CLUB ALONE--
...WHICH IS MORE THAN I CAN SAY FOR WONDER GIRL. PRISSY PROM QUEEN. LITTLE MISS MORAL MESSIAH.
LORENA'S BSOLUTELY RIGHT.
DON'T WORRY ABOUT IT. I'LL HAVE A TALK WITH HER, THEN WE'LL SEE WHERE WE STAND FROM THERE.
RUNNING THE SHOW NOW.
BEETLE AND THAT OTHER GUY...
WELL, I KNOW WHERE I STAND--SHE SCARES THE HOLY LIVING POOP OUTTA ME.
THERE. I SAID IT.
EH. WHATEVER. I COULD TAKE 'EM OR LEAVE 'EM.
AND EDDIE. NAIVE EDDIE.
POWERLESS AND STILL HERE. EVEN AFTER WHAT HAPPENED TO WENDY AND MARVIN...
DAMN IT!

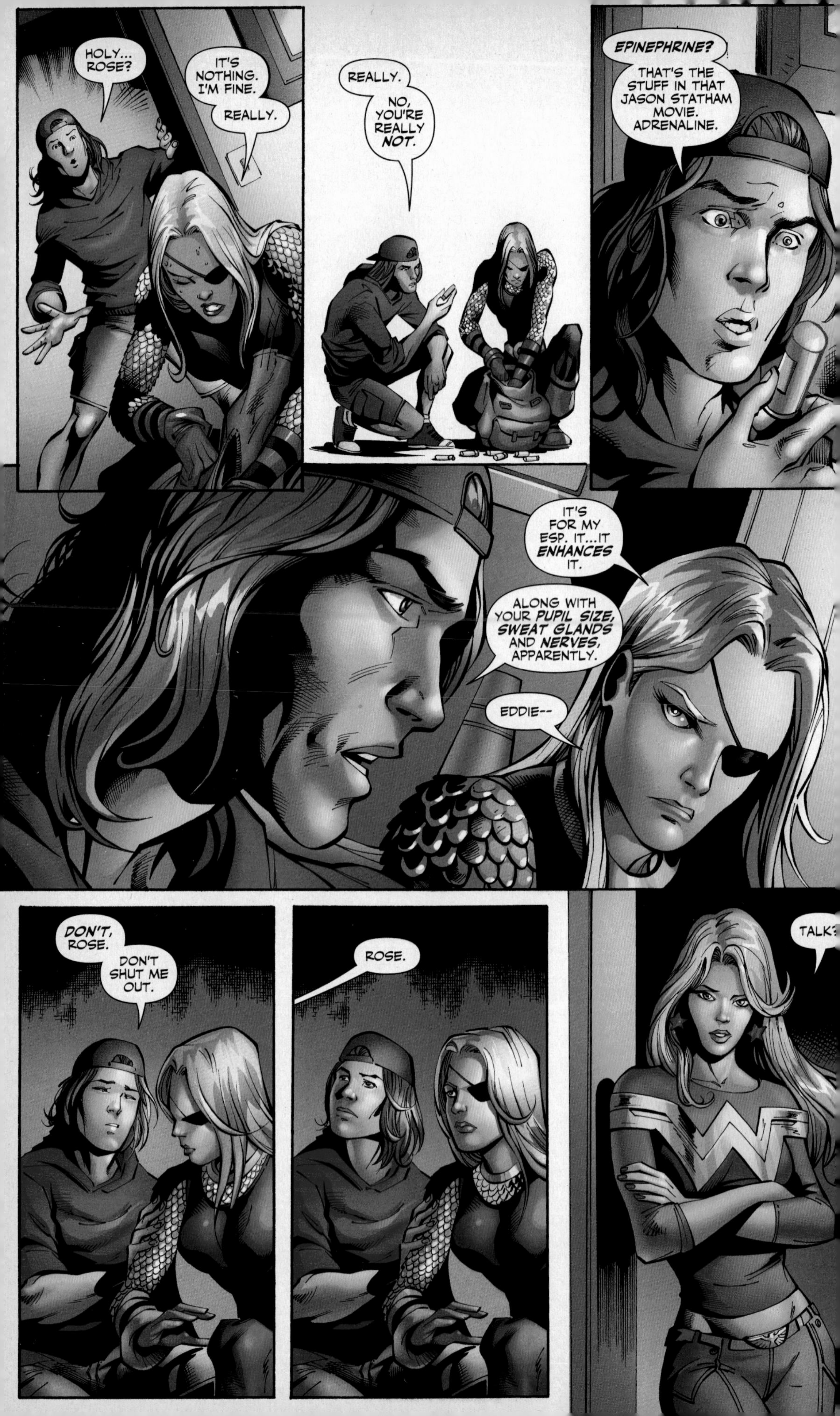
HOLY... ROSE?
IT'S NOTHING. I'M FINE.
REALLY.
REALLY.
NO, YOU'RE REALLY *NOT*.
EPINEPHRINE?
THAT'S THE STUFF IN THAT JASON STATHAM MOVIE. ADRENALINE.
IT'S FOR MY ESP. IT...IT *ENHANCES* IT.
ALONG WITH YOUR *PUPIL SIZE, SWEAT GLANDS* AND *NERVES,* APPARENTLY.
EDDIE--
DON'T, ROSE.
DON'T SHUT ME OUT.
ROSE.
TALK?

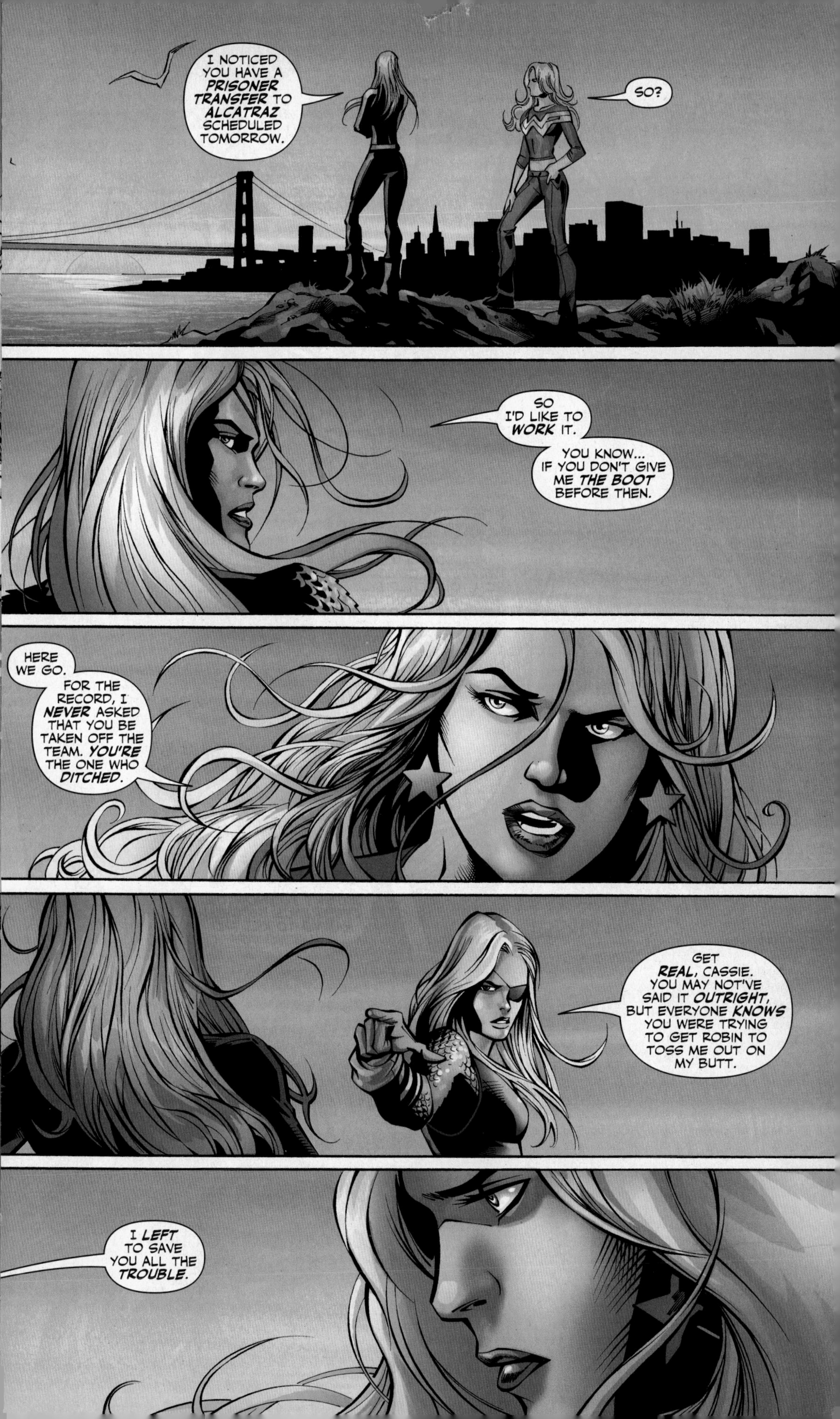
I NOTICED YOU HAVE A PRISONER TRANSFER TO ALCATRAZ SCHEDULED TOMORROW.
SO?
SO I'D LIKE TO WORK IT.
YOU KNOW... IF YOU DON'T GIVE ME THE BOOT BEFORE THEN.
HERE WE GO.
FOR THE RECORD, I NEVER ASKED THAT YOU BE TAKEN OFF THE TEAM. YOU'RE THE ONE WHO DITCHED.
GET REAL, CASSIE. YOU MAY NOT'VE SAID IT OUTRIGHT, BUT EVERYONE KNOWS YOU WERE TRYING TO GET ROBIN TO TOSS ME OUT ON MY BUTT.
I LEFT TO SAVE YOU ALL THE TROUBLE.

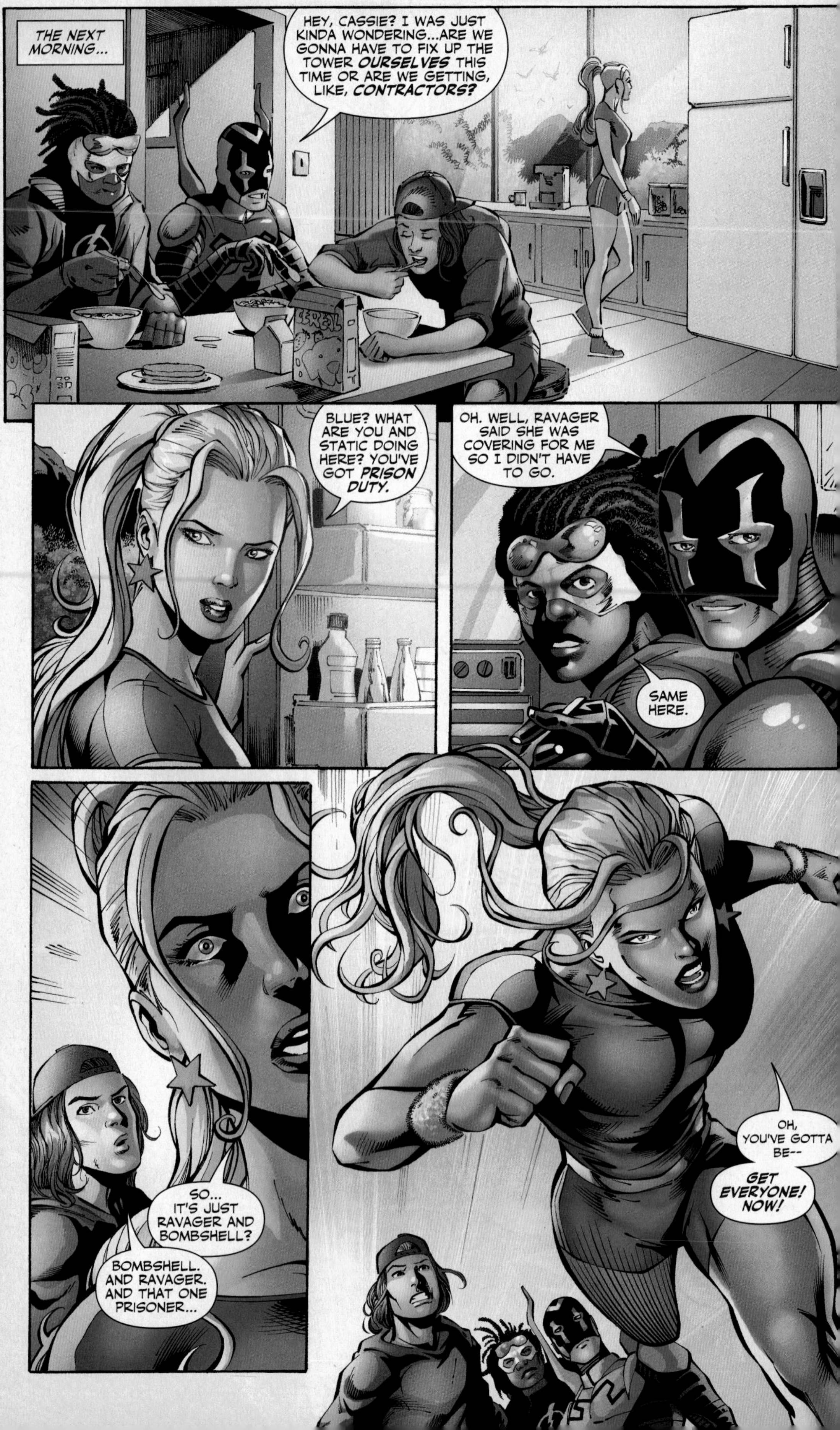
THE NEXT MORNING...
HEY, CASSIE? I WAS JUST KINDA WONDERING...ARE WE GONNA HAVE TO FIX UP THE TOWER OURSELVES THIS TIME OR ARE WE GETTING, LIKE, CONTRACTORS?
BLUE? WHAT ARE YOU AND STATIC DOING HERE? YOU'VE GOT PRISON DUTY.
OH. WELL, RAVAGER SAID SHE WAS COVERING FOR ME SO I DIDN'T HAVE TO GO.
SAME HERE.
SO... IT'S JUST RAVAGER AND BOMBSHELL?
BOMBSHELL. AND RAVAGER. AND THAT ONE PRISONER...
OH, YOU'VE GOTTA BE--
GET EVERYONE! NOW!

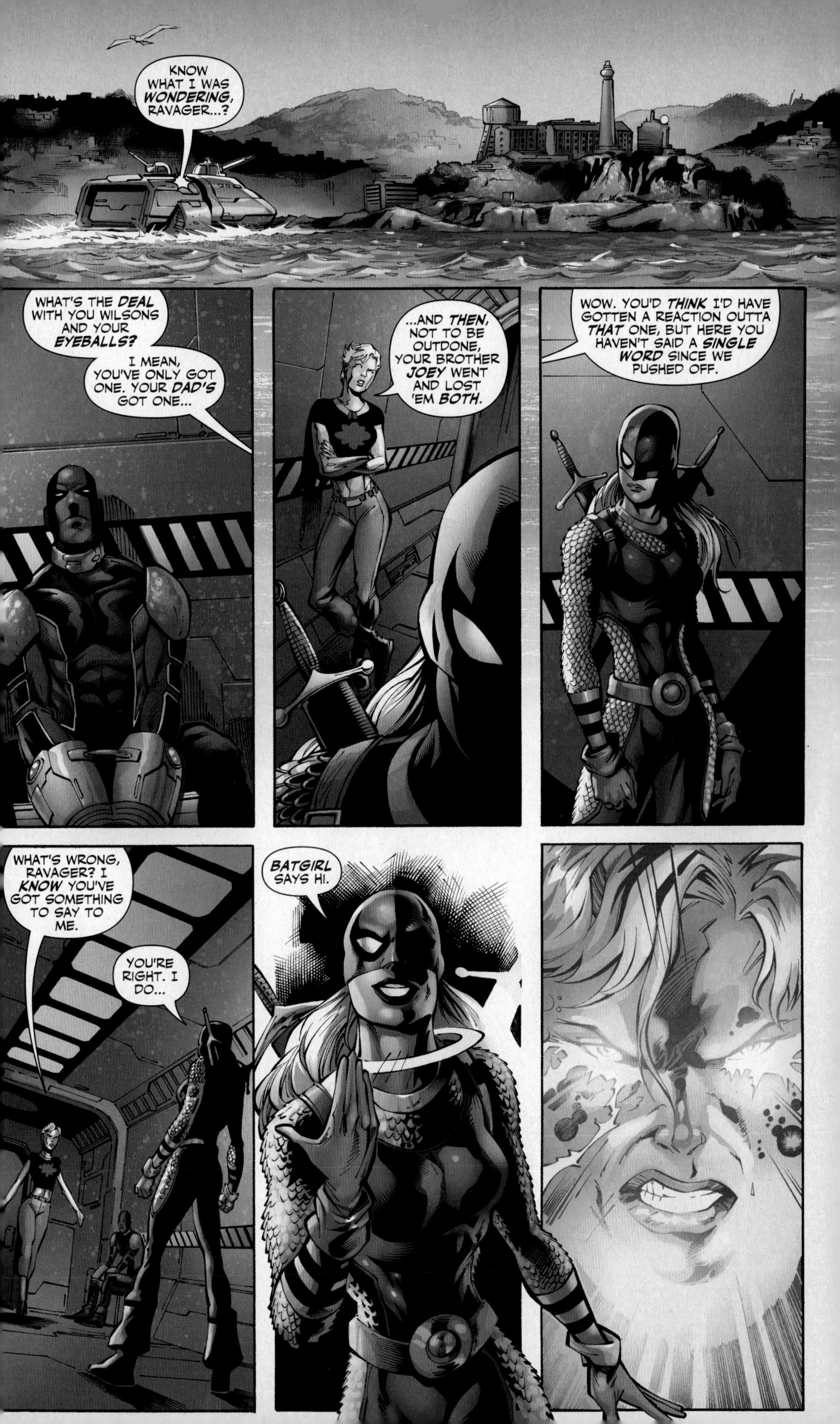
KNOW WHAT I WAS WONDERING, RAVAGER...?
WHAT'S THE DEAL WITH YOU WILSONS AND YOUR EYEBALLS?
I MEAN, YOU'VE ONLY GOT ONE. YOUR DAD'S GOT ONE...
...AND THEN, NOT TO BE OUTDONE, YOUR BROTHER JOEY WENT AND LOST 'EM BOTH.
WOW. YOU'D THINK I'D HAVE GOTTEN A REACTION OUTTA THAT ONE, BUT HERE YOU HAVEN'T SAID A SINGLE WORD SINCE WE PUSHED OFF.
WHAT'S WRONG, RAVAGER? I KNOW YOU'VE GOT SOMETHING TO SAY TO ME.
YOU'RE RIGHT. I DO...
BATGIRL SAYS HI.

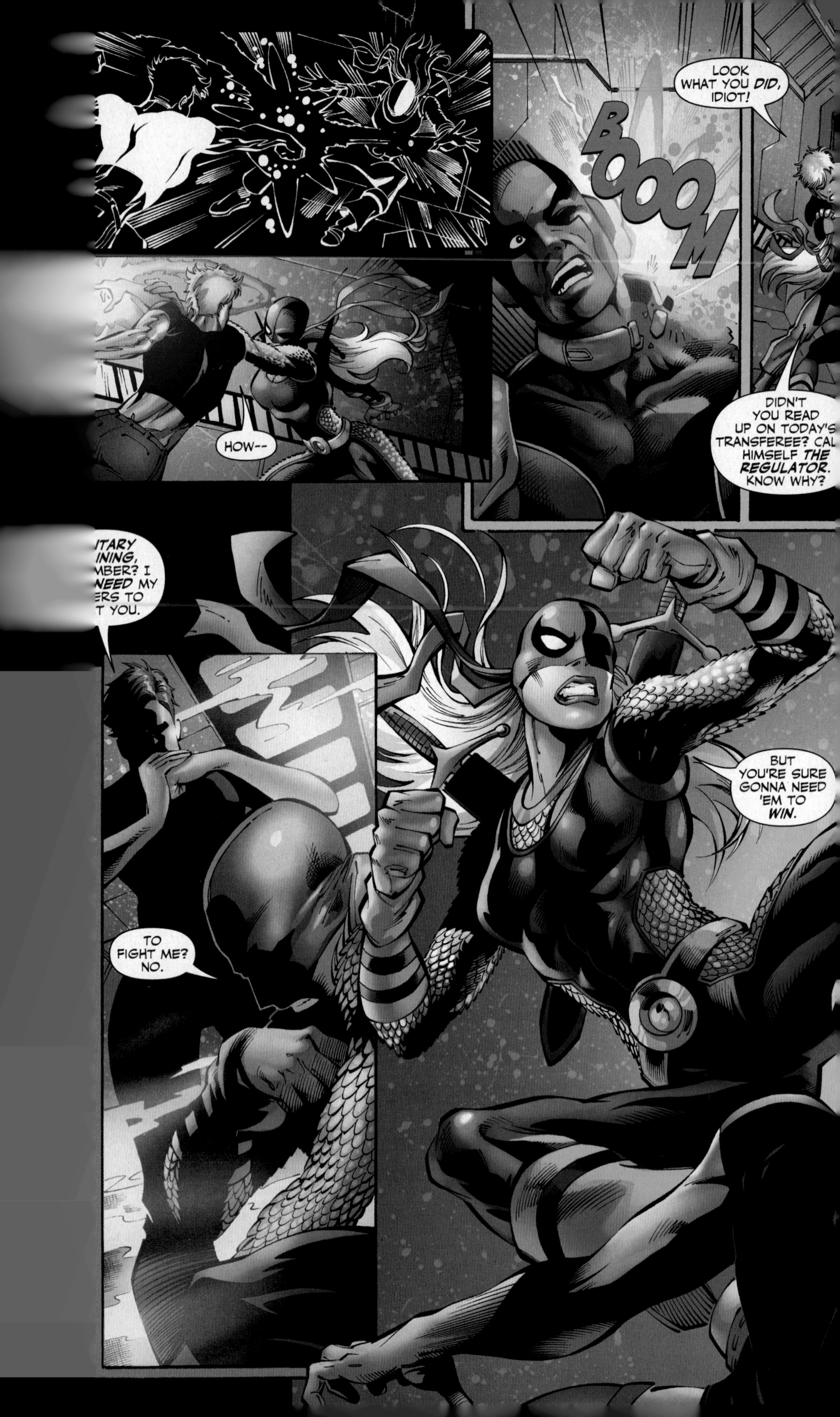
HOW--
LOOK WHAT YOU *DID*, IDIOT!
BOOOOM
DIDN'T YOU READ UP ON TODAY'S TRANSFEREE? CAL HIMSELF ***THE REGULATOR***. KNOW WHY?
ITARY *INING,* MBER? I *NEED* MY ERS TO T YOU.
TO FIGHT ME? NO.
BUT YOU'RE SURE GONNA NEED 'EM TO *WIN*.

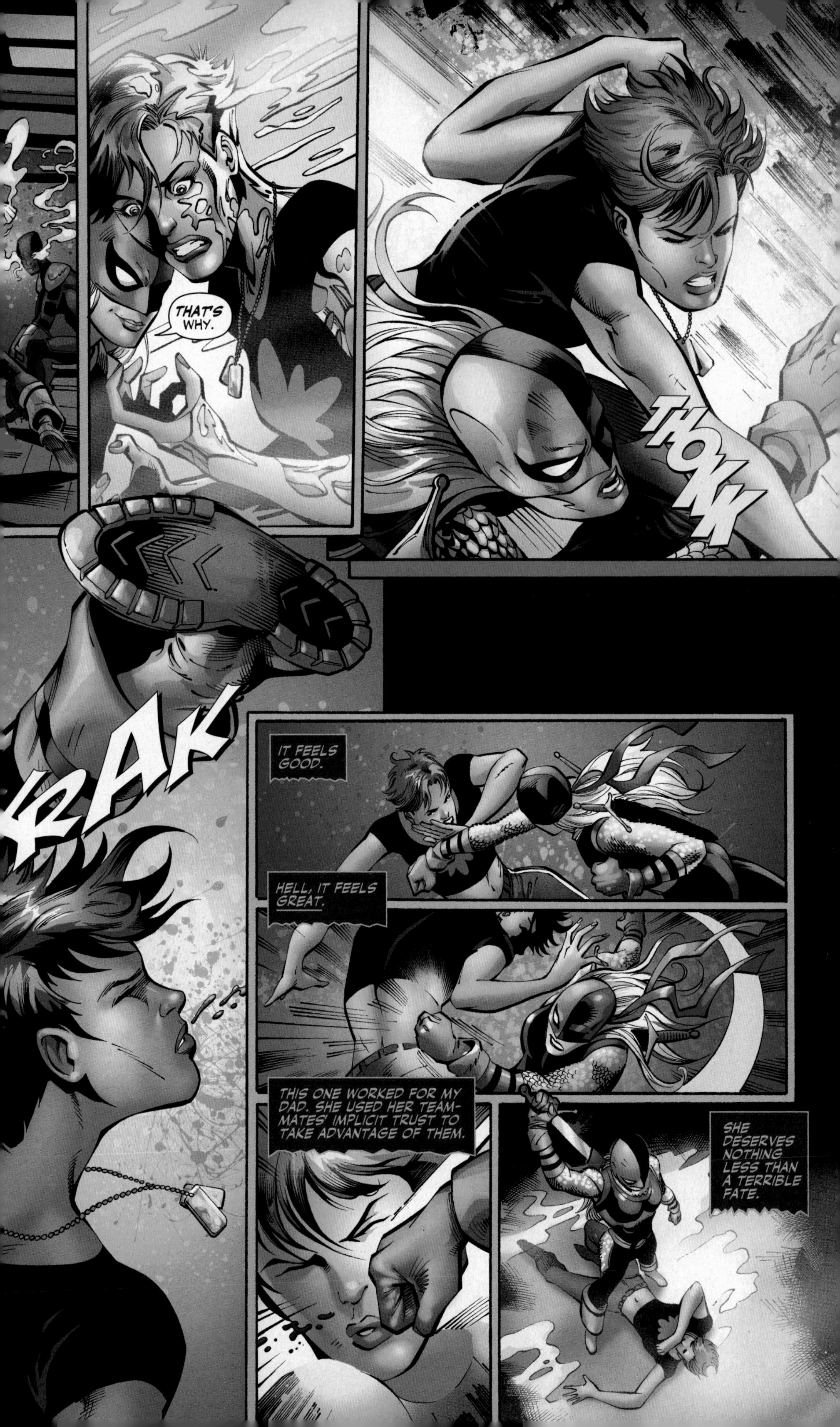

THAT'S WHY.
THONK
KRAK
IT FEELS GOOD.
HELL, IT FEELS GREAT.
THIS ONE WORKED FOR MY DAD. SHE USED HER TEAM-MATES' IMPLICIT TRUST TO TAKE ADVANTAGE OF THEM.
SHE DESERVES NOTHING LESS THAN A TERRIBLE FATE.

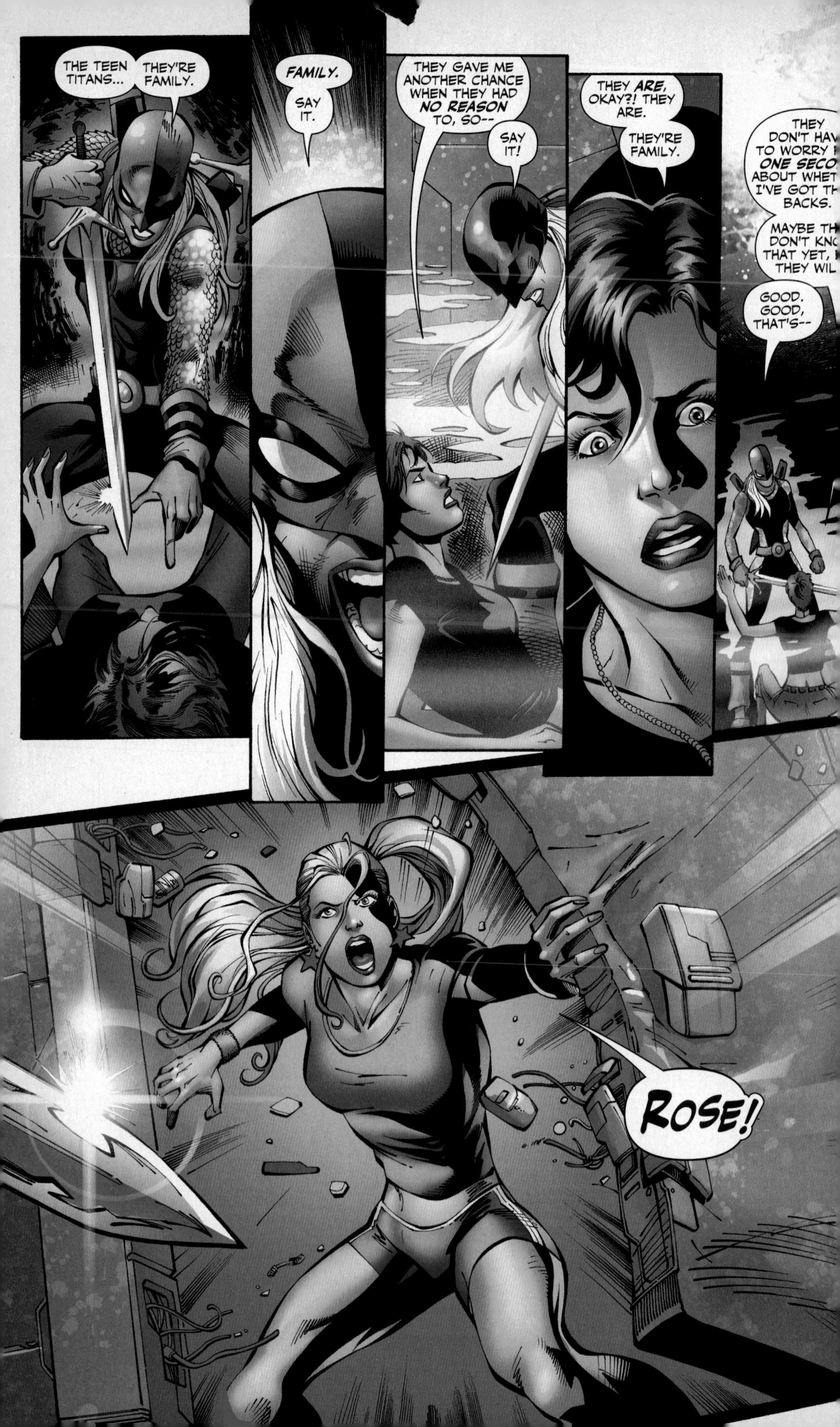

THE TEEN TITANS...
THEY'RE FAMILY.
FAMILY.
SAY IT.
THEY GAVE ME ANOTHER CHANCE WHEN THEY HAD NO REASON TO, SO--
SAY IT!
THEY ARE, OKAY?! THEY ARE.
THEY'RE FAMILY.
THEY DON'T HAV TO WORRY ONE SECO ABOUT WHET I'VE GOT TH BACKS.
MAYBE TH DON'T KN THAT YET, THEY WIL
GOOD. GOOD, THAT'S--
ROSE!

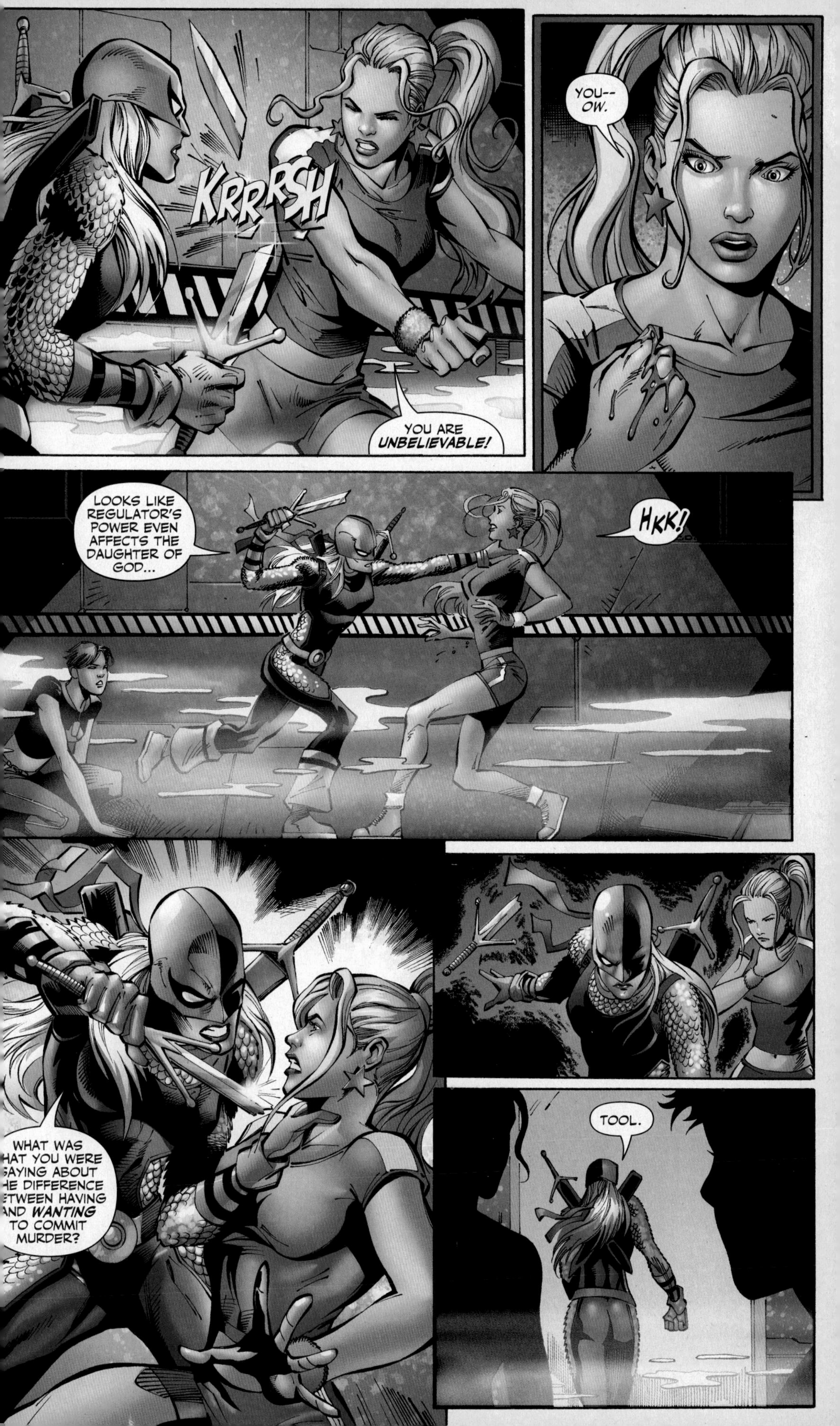
KRRRSH
YOU ARE UNBELIEVABLE!
YOU--OW.
LOOKS LIKE REGULATOR'S POWER EVEN AFFECTS THE DAUGHTER OF GOD...
HKK!
WHAT WAS THAT YOU WERE SAYING ABOUT THE DIFFERENCE BETWEEN HAVING AND WANTING TO COMMIT MURDER?
TOOL.

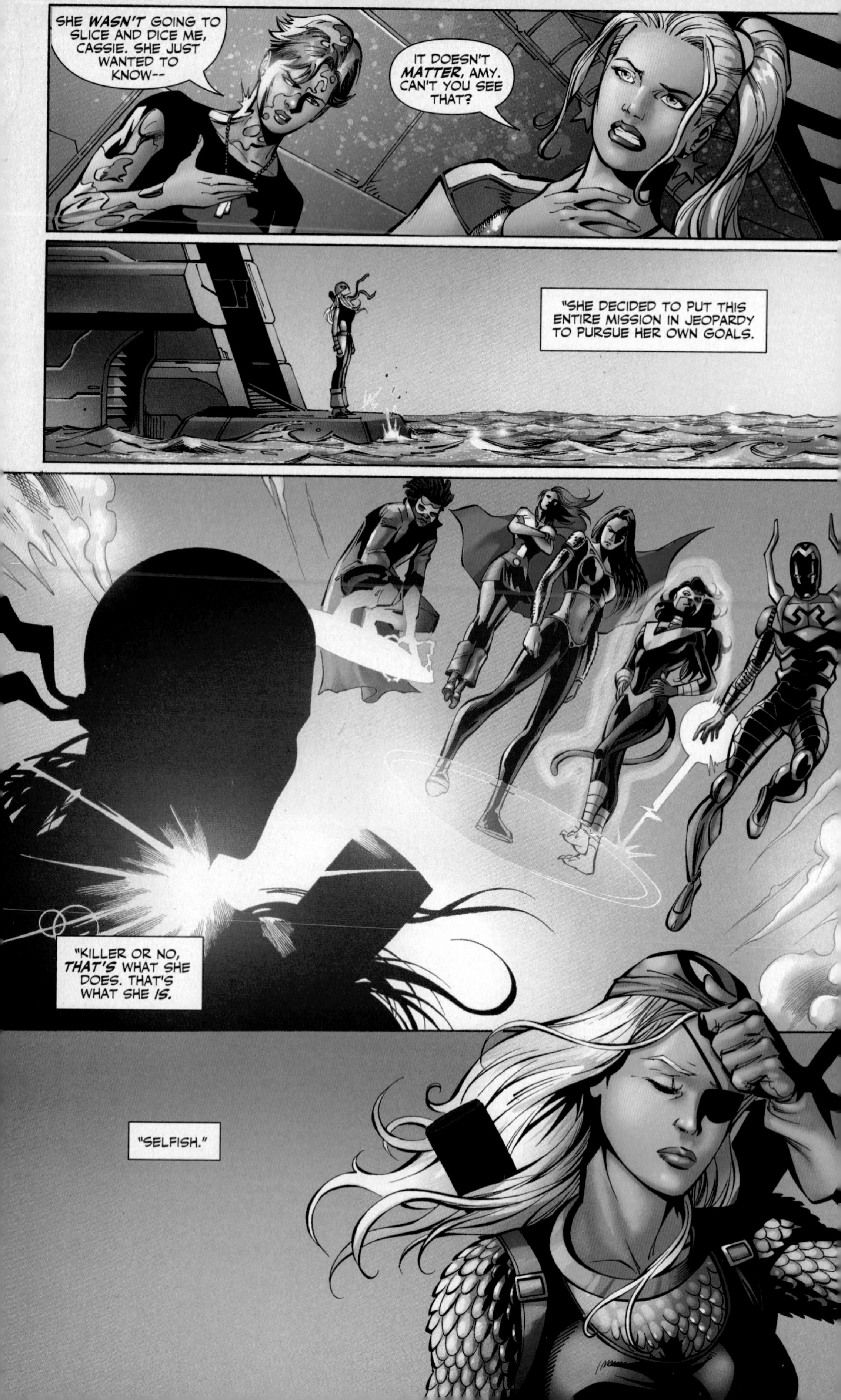
SHE WASN'T GOING TO SLICE AND DICE ME, CASSIE. SHE JUST WANTED TO KNOW--
IT DOESN'T MATTER, AMY. CAN'T YOU SEE THAT?
"SHE DECIDED TO PUT THIS ENTIRE MISSION IN JEOPARDY TO PURSUE HER OWN GOALS.
"KILLER OR NO, THAT'S WHAT SHE DOES. THAT'S WHAT SHE IS.
"SELFISH."

FOUND ME.

FIGURED YOU MIGHT BE UP HERE.

YOU ALWAYS LIKED THIS SPOT, DIDN'T YOU? THE VIEW. THE PRIVACY.

WHAT ABOUT YOU? STILL COME UP HERE TO THINK?

NOT REALLY. NOT ANYMORE.

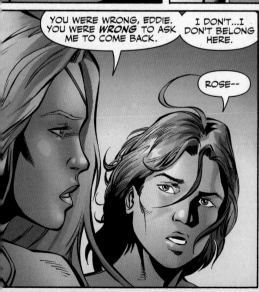

YOU WERE WRONG, EDDIE. YOU WERE *WRONG* TO ASK ME TO COME BACK.

I DON'T...I DON'T BELONG HERE.

ROSE--

AND NEITHER DO YOU.

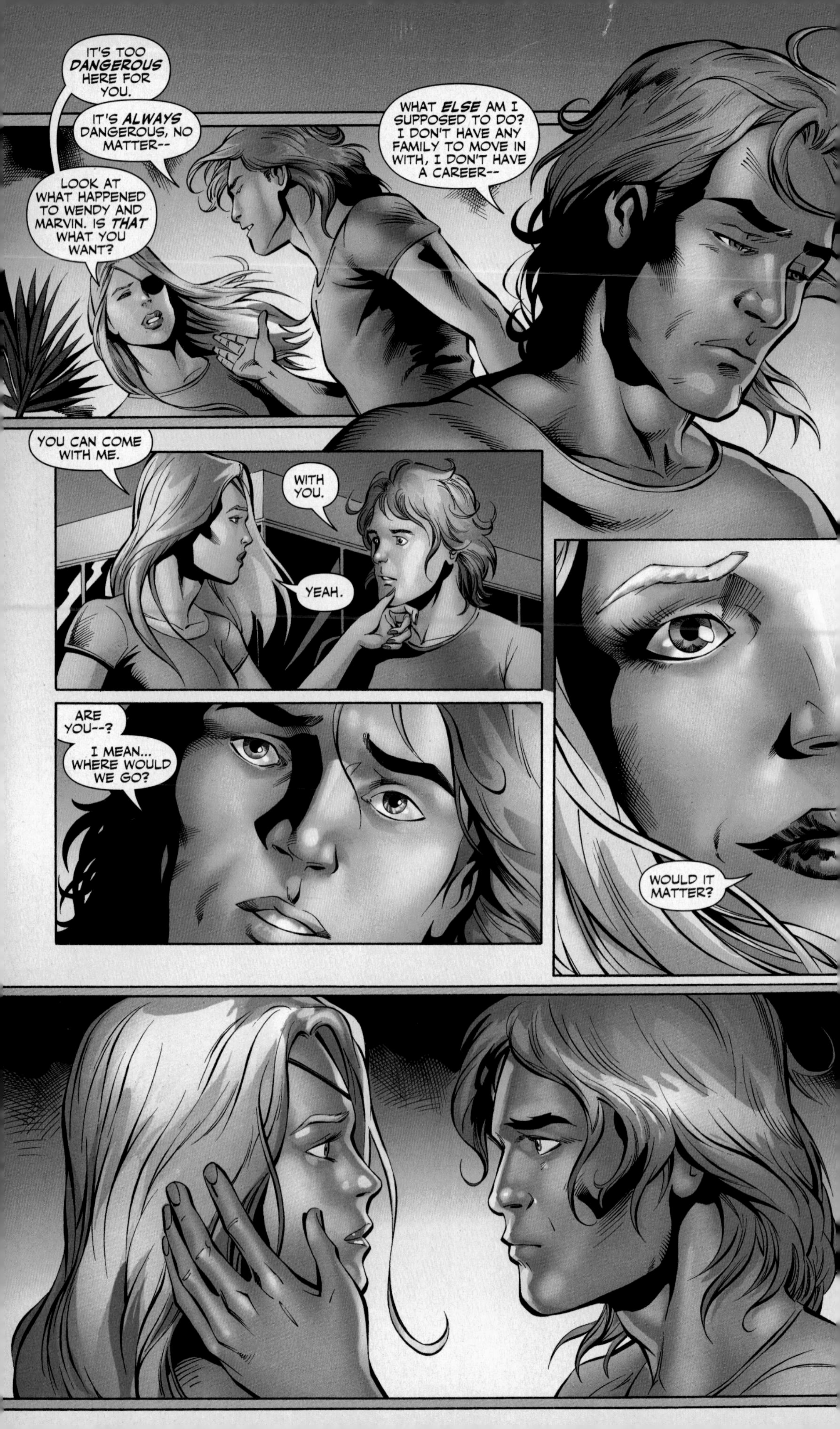
IT'S TOO DANGEROUS HERE FOR YOU.
IT'S ALWAYS DANGEROUS, NO MATTER--
LOOK AT WHAT HAPPENED TO WENDY AND MARVIN. IS THAT WHAT YOU WANT?
WHAT ELSE AM I SUPPOSED TO DO? I DON'T HAVE ANY FAMILY TO MOVE IN WITH, I DON'T HAVE A CAREER--
YOU CAN COME WITH ME.
WITH YOU.
YEAH.
ARE YOU--?
I MEAN... WHERE WOULD WE GO?
WOULD IT MATTER?

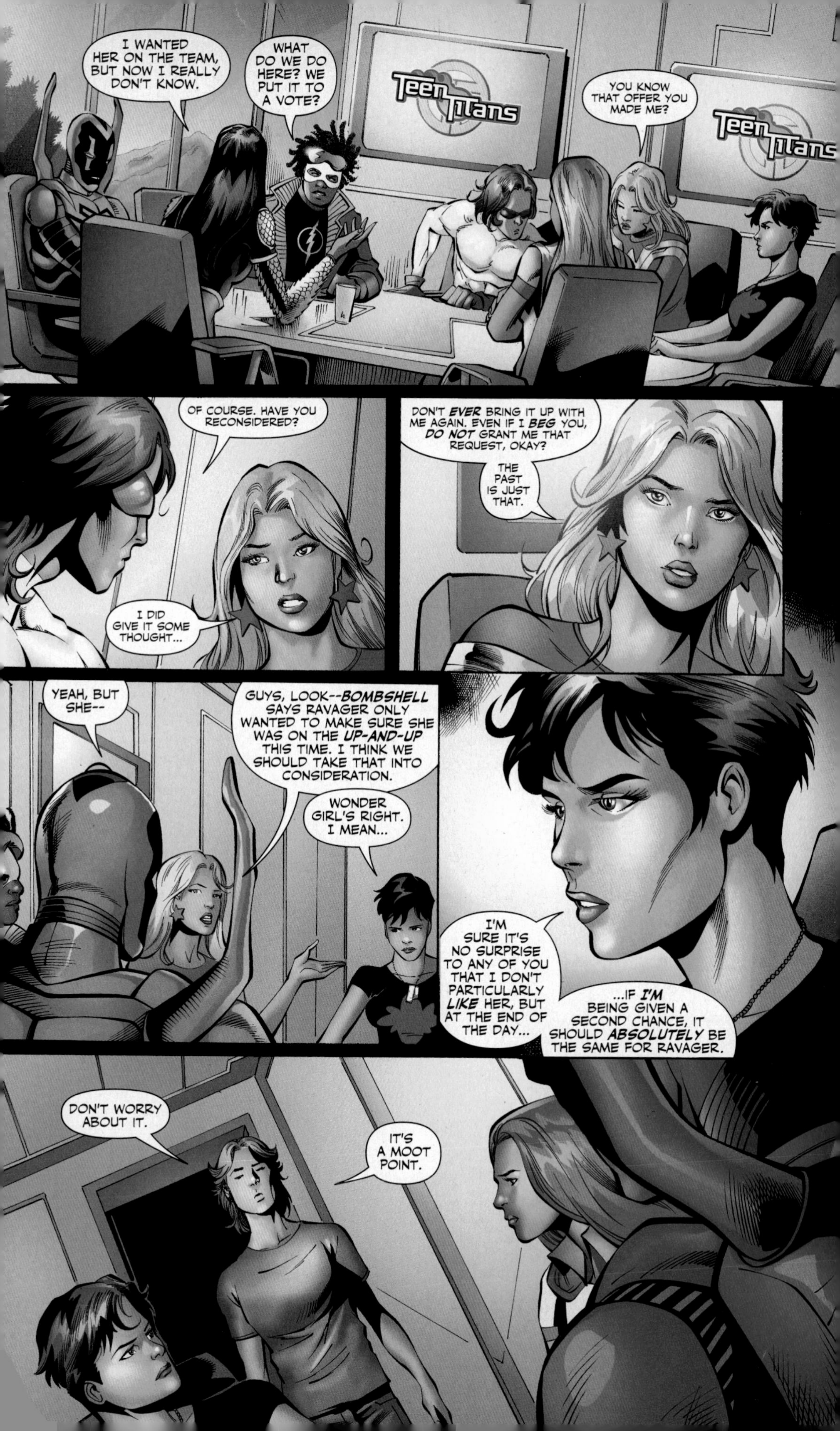
I WANTED HER ON THE TEAM, BUT NOW I REALLY DON'T KNOW.
WHAT DO WE DO HERE? WE PUT IT TO A VOTE?
TEEN TITANS
YOU KNOW THAT OFFER YOU MADE ME?
TEEN TITANS
OF COURSE. HAVE YOU RECONSIDERED?
I DID GIVE IT SOME THOUGHT...
DON'T *EVER* BRING IT UP WITH ME AGAIN. EVEN IF I *BEG* YOU, *DO NOT* GRANT ME THAT REQUEST, OKAY?
THE PAST IS JUST THAT.
YEAH, BUT SHE--
GUYS, LOOK--*BOMBSHELL* SAYS RAVAGER ONLY WANTED TO MAKE SURE SHE WAS ON THE *UP-AND-UP* THIS TIME. I THINK WE SHOULD TAKE THAT INTO CONSIDERATION.
WONDER GIRL'S RIGHT. I MEAN...
I'M SURE IT'S NO SURPRISE TO ANY OF YOU THAT I DON'T PARTICULARLY *LIKE* HER, BUT AT THE END OF THE DAY...
...IF *I'M* BEING GIVEN A SECOND CHANCE, IT SHOULD *ABSOLUTELY* BE THE SAME FOR RAVAGER.
DON'T WORRY ABOUT IT.
IT'S A MOOT POINT.

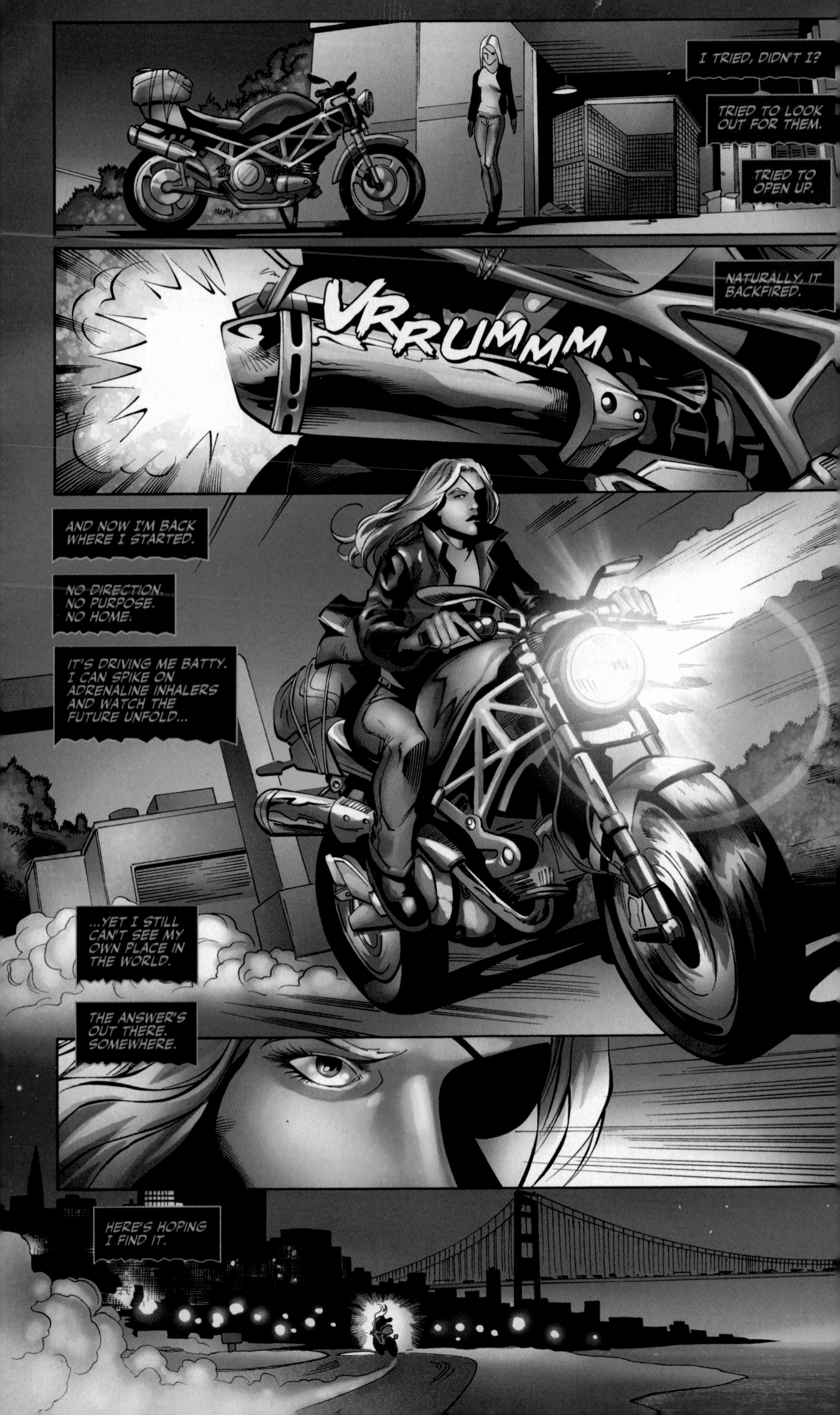
I TRIED, DIDN'T I?
TRIED TO LOOK OUT FOR THEM.
TRIED TO OPEN UP.
VRRUMMM
NATURALLY, IT BACKFIRED.
AND NOW I'M BACK WHERE I STARTED.
NO DIRECTION. NO PURPOSE. NO HOME.
IT'S DRIVING ME BATTY. I CAN SPIKE ON ADRENALINE INHALERS AND WATCH THE FUTURE UNFOLD...
...YET I STILL CAN'T SEE MY OWN PLACE IN THE WORLD.
THE ANSWER'S OUT THERE. SOMEWHERE.
HERE'S HOPING I FIND IT.

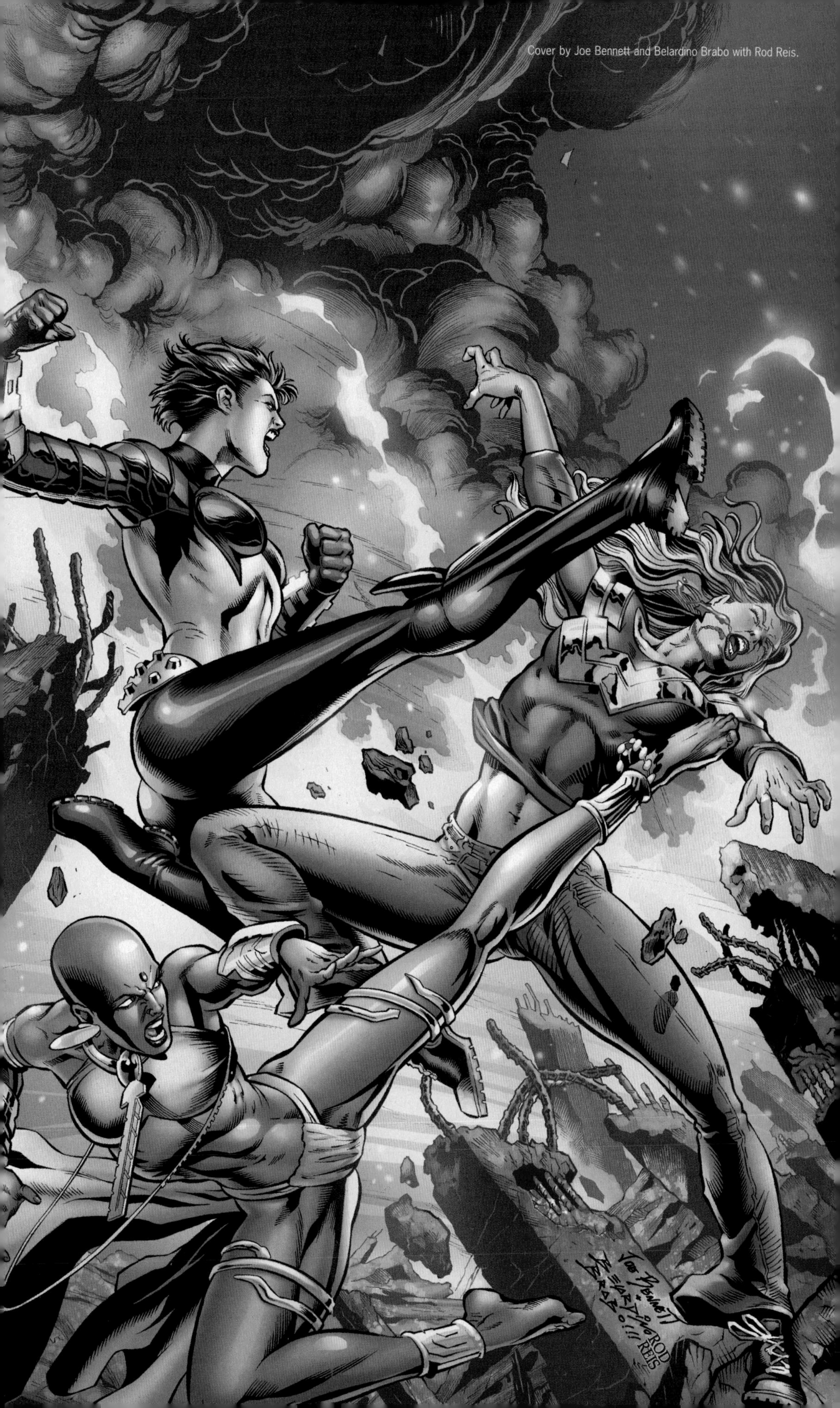

Cover by Joe Bennett and Belardino Brabo with Rod Reis.

CHILD'S PLAY PART 1: RING AROUND THE ROSIE

Bryan Q. Miller
Writer

Joe Bennett
Pencils

Jack Jadson
Inks

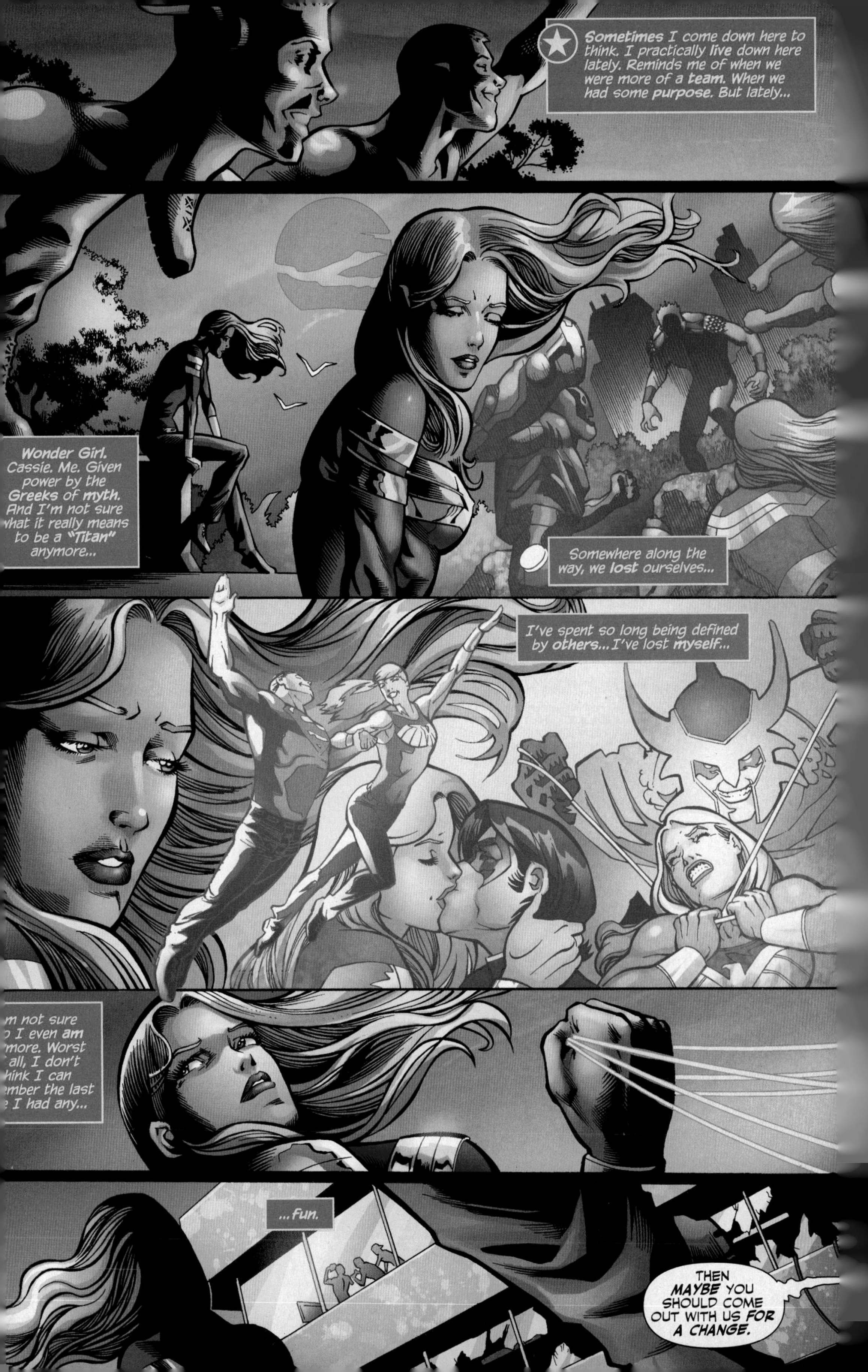
Sometimes I come down here to think. I practically live down here lately. Reminds me of when we were more of a team. When we had some purpose. But lately...
Wonder Girl. Cassie. Me. Given power by the Greeks of myth. And I'm not sure what it really means to be a "Titan" anymore...
Somewhere along the way, we lost ourselves...
I've spent so long being defined by others... I've lost myself...
m not sure o I even am ymore. Worst all, I don't hink I can ember the last e I had any...
...fun.
THEN MAYBE YOU SHOULD COME OUT WITH US FOR A CHANGE.

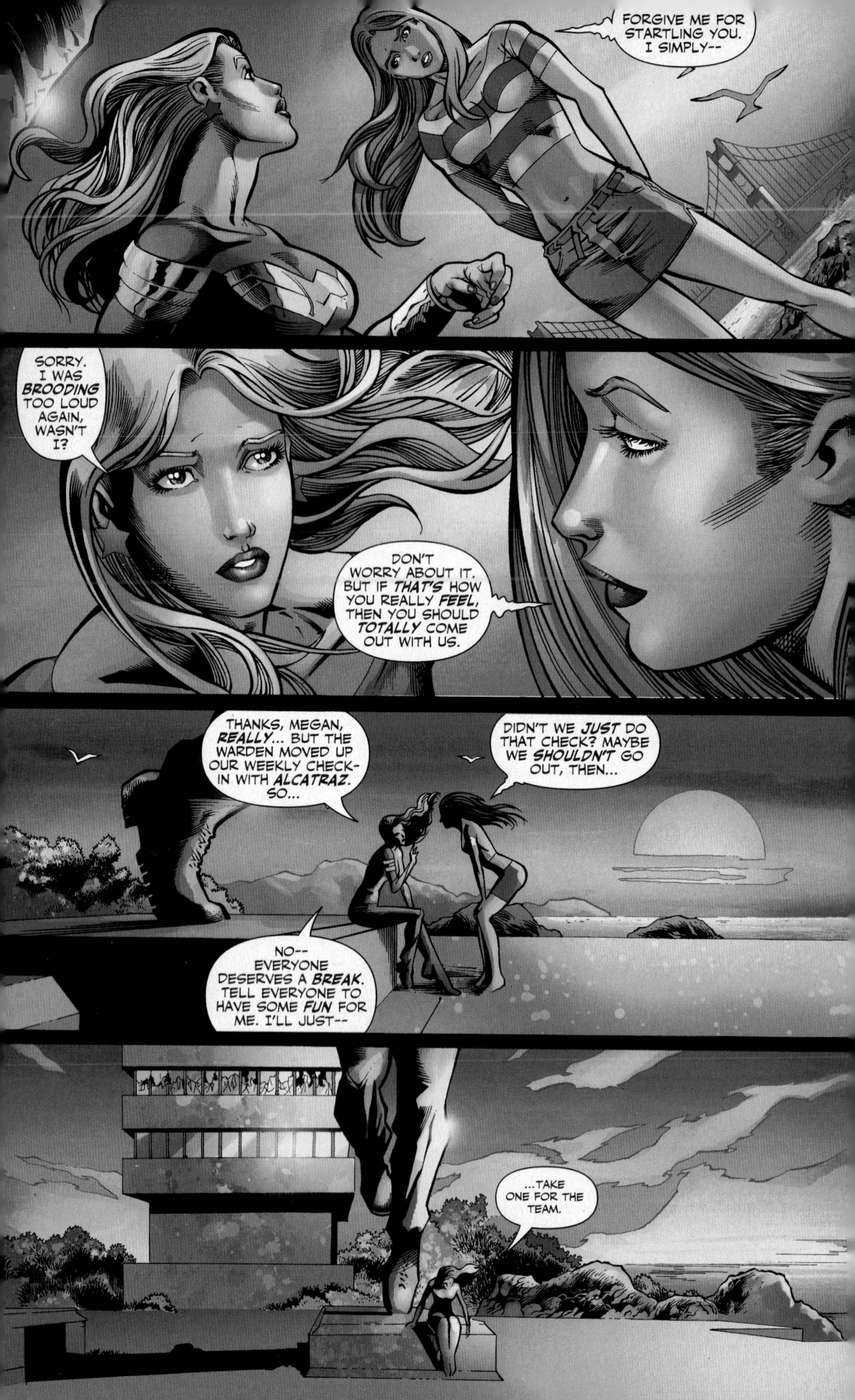
FORGIVE ME FOR STARTLING YOU. I SIMPLY--
SORRY. I WAS BROODING TOO LOUD AGAIN, WASN'T I?
DON'T WORRY ABOUT IT. BUT IF THAT'S HOW YOU REALLY FEEL, THEN YOU SHOULD TOTALLY COME OUT WITH US.
THANKS, MEGAN, REALLY... BUT THE WARDEN MOVED UP OUR WEEKLY CHECK-IN WITH ALCATRAZ. SO...
DIDN'T WE JUST DO THAT CHECK? MAYBE WE SHOULDN'T GO OUT, THEN...
NO-- EVERYONE DESERVES A BREAK. TELL EVERYONE TO HAVE SOME FUN FOR ME. I'LL JUST--
...TAKE ONE FOR THE TEAM.

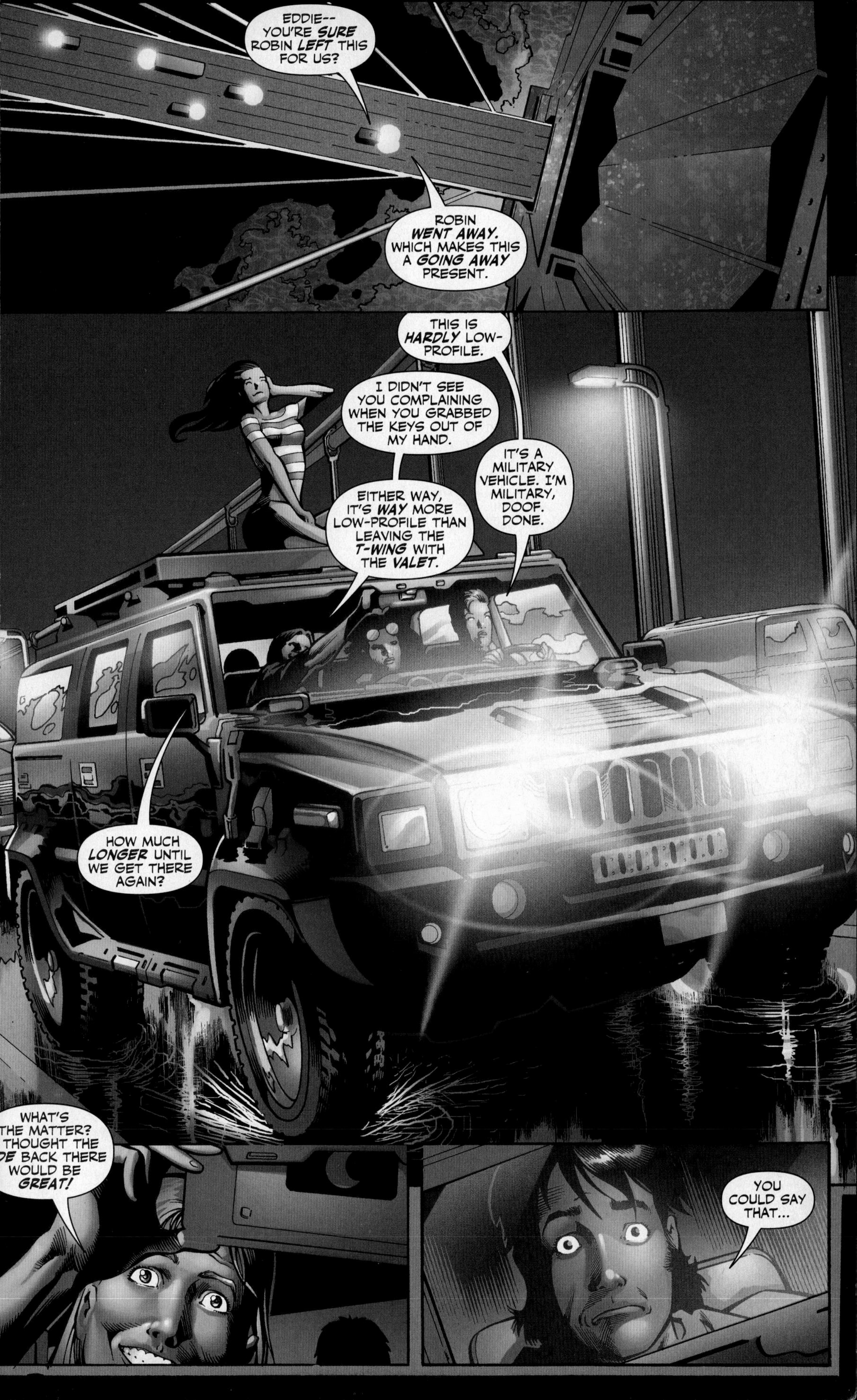
EDDIE-- YOU'RE SURE ROBIN LEFT THIS FOR US?
ROBIN WENT AWAY. WHICH MAKES THIS A GOING AWAY PRESENT.
THIS IS HARDLY LOW-PROFILE.
I DIDN'T SEE YOU COMPLAINING WHEN YOU GRABBED THE KEYS OUT OF MY HAND.
IT'S A MILITARY VEHICLE. I'M MILITARY, DOOF. DONE.
EITHER WAY, IT'S WAY MORE LOW-PROFILE THAN LEAVING THE T-WING WITH THE VALET.
HOW MUCH LONGER UNTIL WE GET THERE AGAIN?
WHAT'S THE MATTER? THOUGHT THE DE BACK THERE WOULD BE GREAT!
YOU COULD SAY THAT...

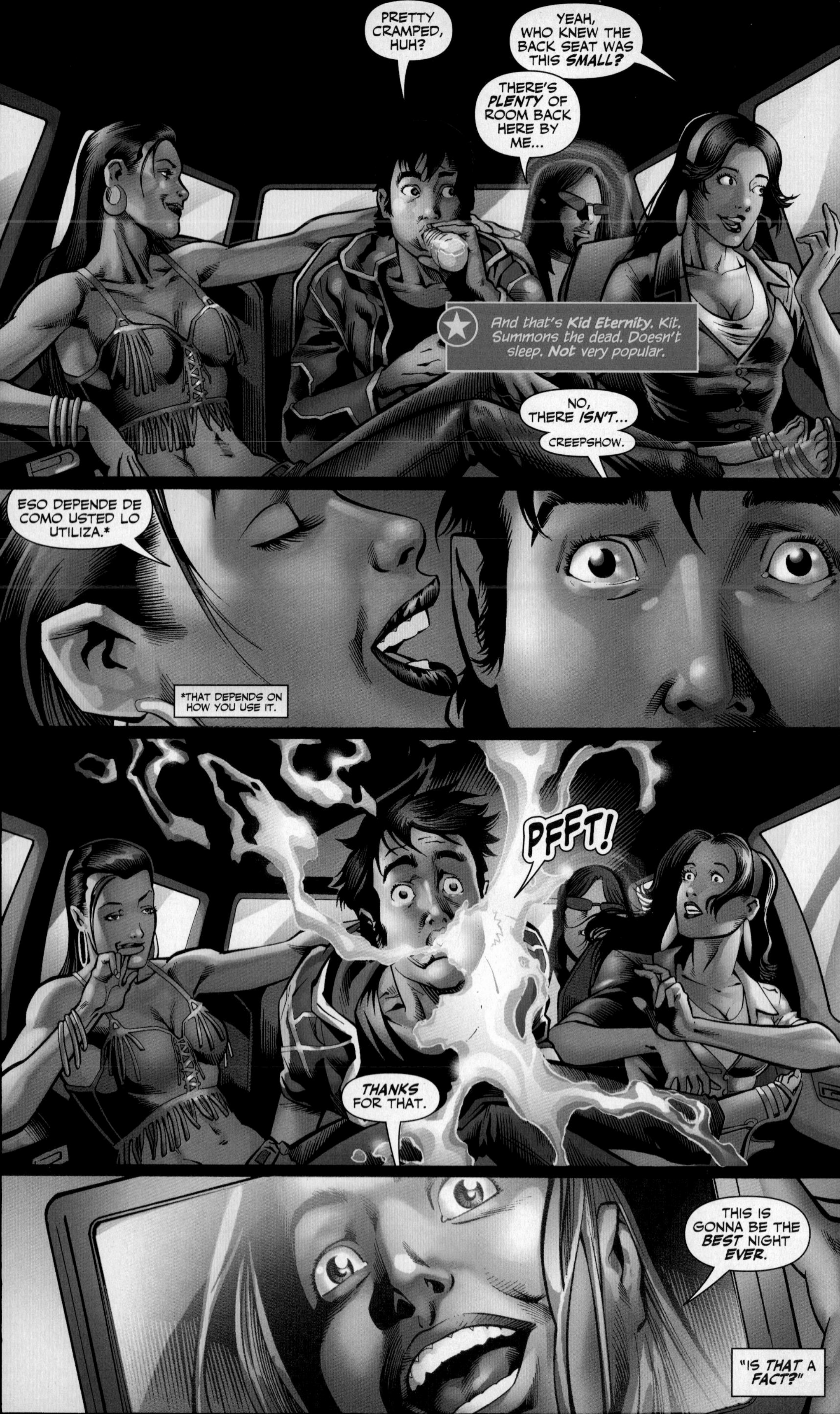
PRETTY CRAMPED, HUH?
YEAH, WHO KNEW THE BACK SEAT WAS THIS SMALL?
THERE'S PLENTY OF ROOM BACK HERE BY ME...
And that's Kid Eternity. Kit. Summons the dead. Doesn't sleep. Not very popular.
NO, THERE ISN'T...
CREEPSHOW.
ESO DEPENDE DE COMO USTED LO UTILIZA.*
*THAT DEPENDS ON HOW YOU USE IT.
PFFT!
THANKS FOR THAT.
THIS IS GONNA BE THE BEST NIGHT EVER.
"IS THAT A FACT?"

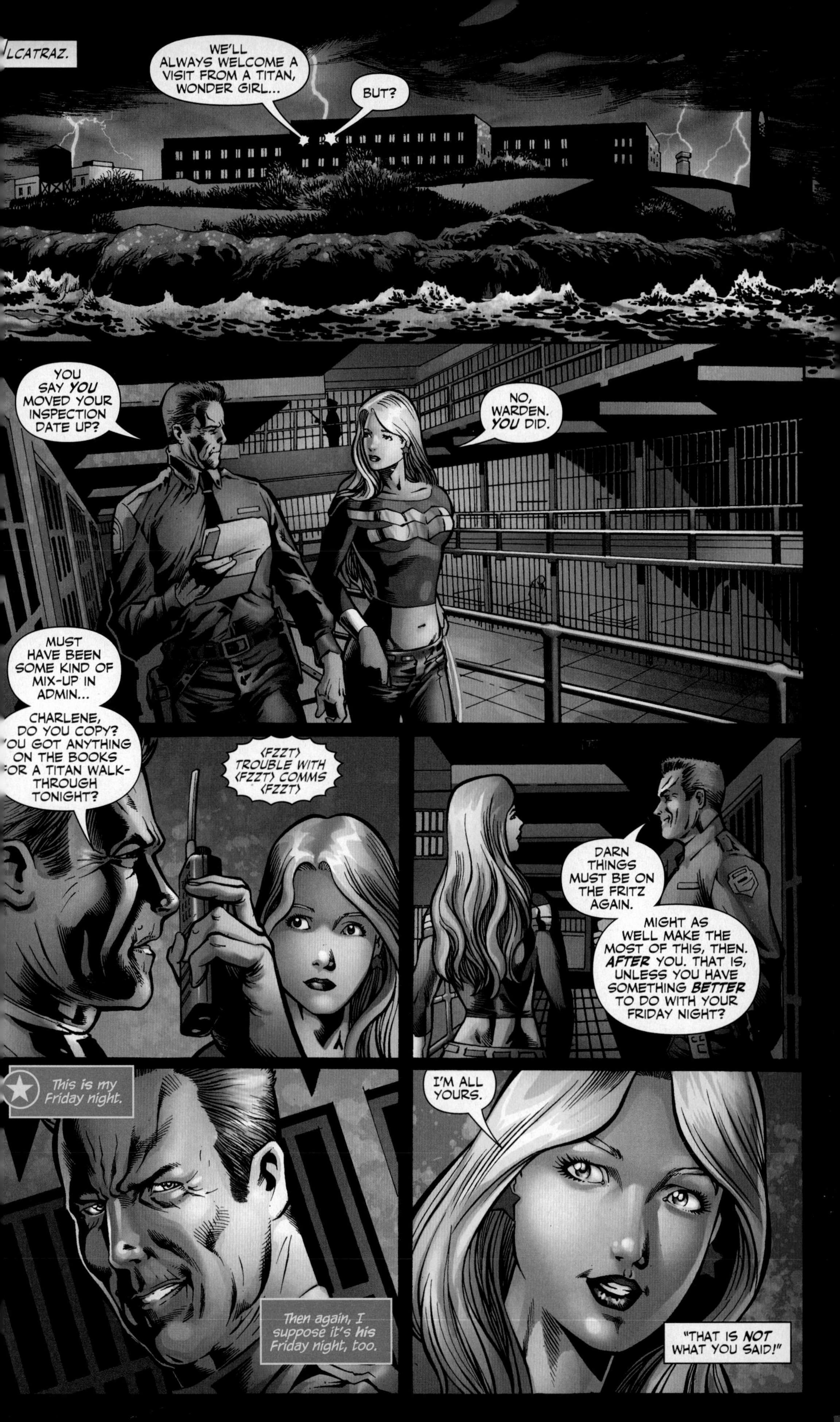
LCATRAZ.
WE'LL ALWAYS WELCOME A VISIT FROM A TITAN, WONDER GIRL...
BUT?
YOU SAY YOU MOVED YOUR INSPECTION DATE UP?
NO, WARDEN. YOU DID.
MUST HAVE BEEN SOME KIND OF MIX-UP IN ADMIN...
CHARLENE, DO YOU COPY? YOU GOT ANYTHING ON THE BOOKS FOR A TITAN WALK-THROUGH TONIGHT?
<FZZT> TROUBLE WITH <FZZT> COMMS <FZZT>
DARN THINGS MUST BE ON THE FRITZ AGAIN.
MIGHT AS WELL MAKE THE MOST OF THIS, THEN. AFTER YOU. THAT IS, UNLESS YOU HAVE SOMETHING BETTER TO DO WITH YOUR FRIDAY NIGHT?
This is my Friday night.
Then again, I suppose it's his Friday night, too.
I'M ALL YOURS.
"THAT IS NOT WHAT YOU SAID!"

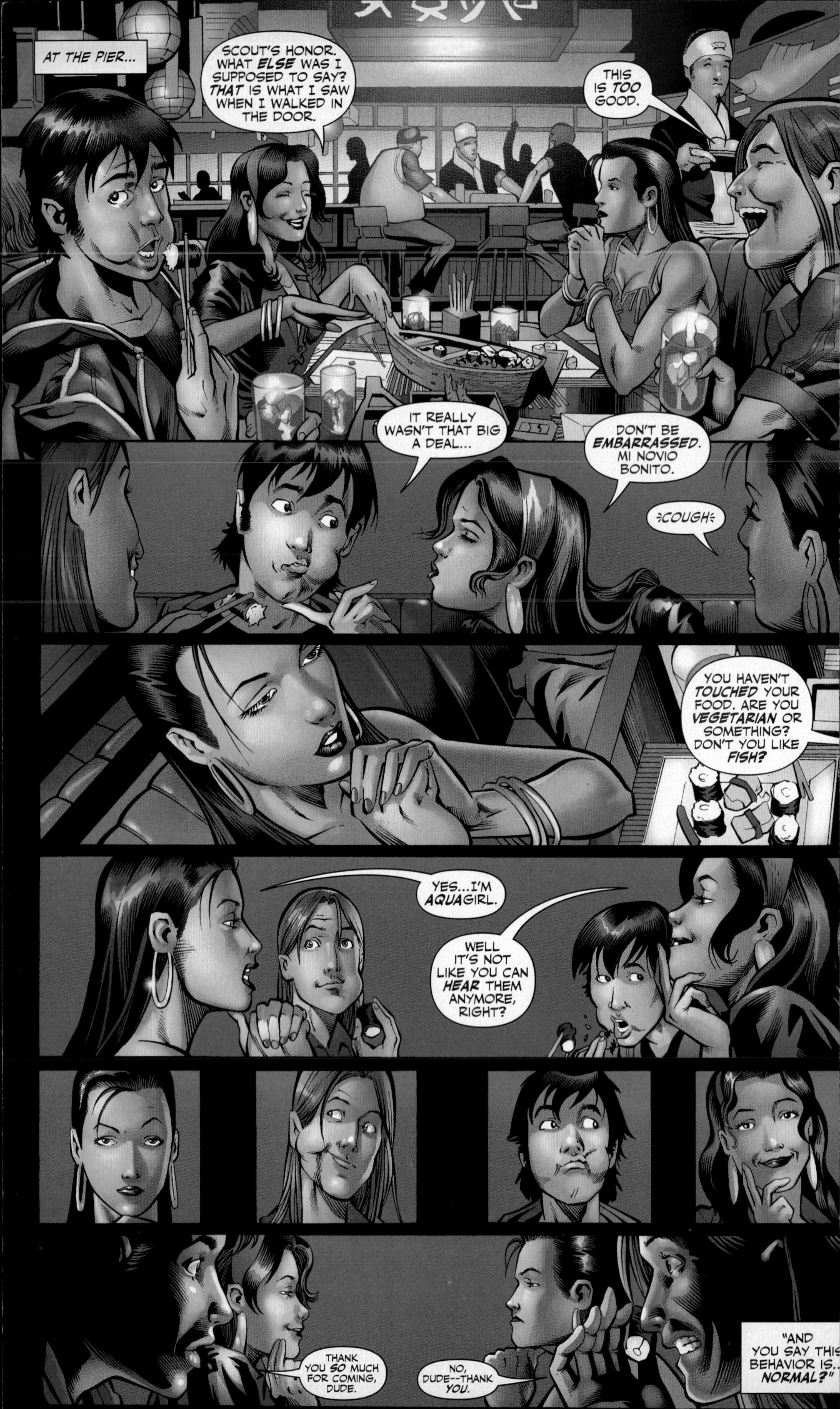

AT THE PIER...
SCOUT'S HONOR. WHAT ELSE WAS I SUPPOSED TO SAY? THAT IS WHAT I SAW WHEN I WALKED IN THE DOOR.
THIS IS TOO GOOD.
IT REALLY WASN'T THAT BIG A DEAL...
DON'T BE EMBARRASSED. MI NOVIO BONITO.
COUGH
YOU HAVEN'T TOUCHED YOUR FOOD. ARE YOU VEGETARIAN OR SOMETHING? DON'T YOU LIKE FISH?
YES...I'M AQUAGIRL.
WELL IT'S NOT LIKE YOU CAN HEAR THEM ANYMORE, RIGHT?
THANK YOU SO MUCH FOR COMING, DUDE.
NO, DUDE--THANK YOU.
"AND YOU SAY THIS BEHAVIOR IS... NORMAL?"

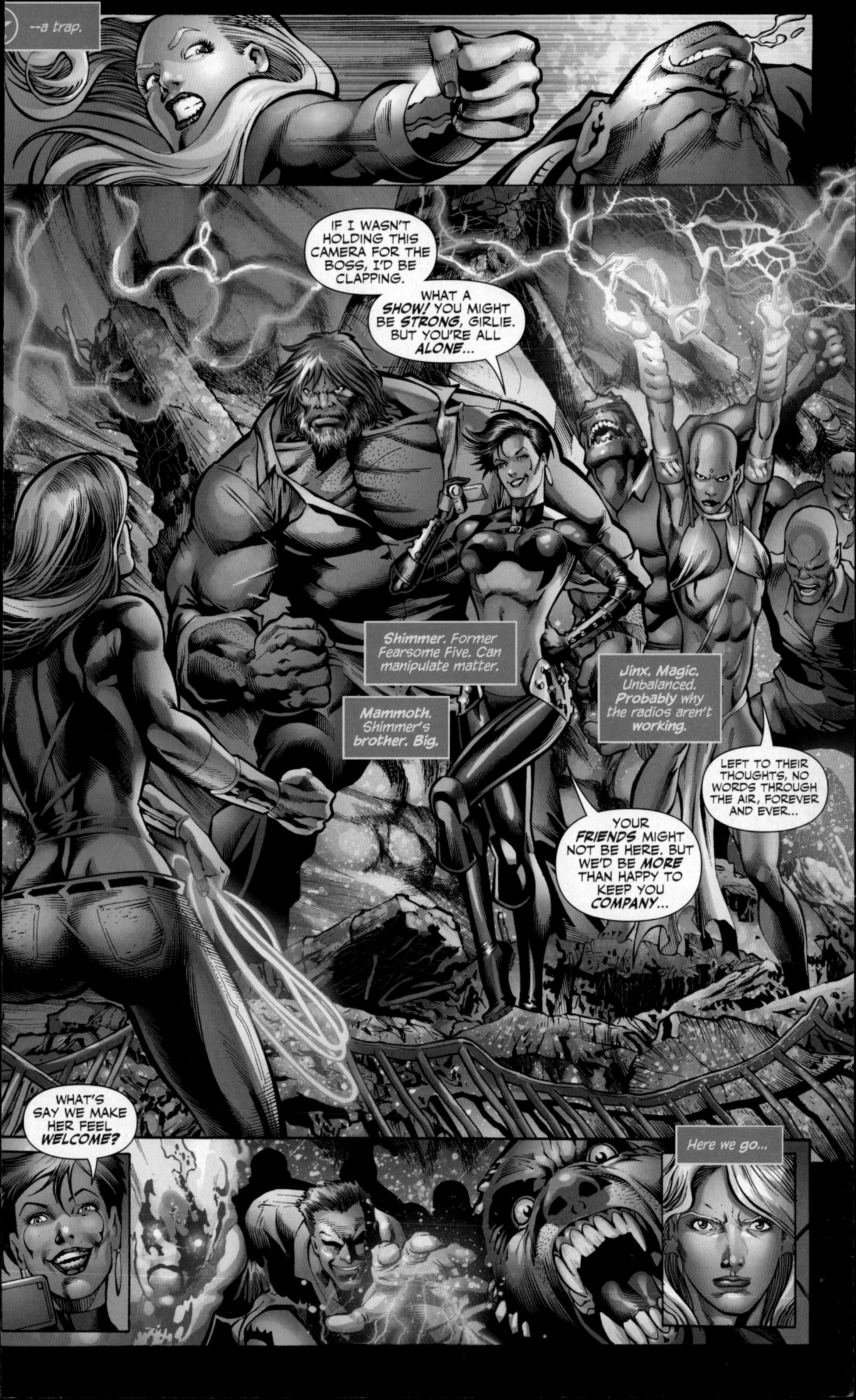

--a trap.
IF I WASN'T HOLDING THIS CAMERA FOR THE BOSS, I'D BE CLAPPING.
WHAT A SHOW! YOU MIGHT BE STRONG, GIRLIE. BUT YOU'RE ALL ALONE...
Shimmer. Former Fearsome Five. Can manipulate matter.
Mammoth. Shimmer's brother. Big.
Jinx. Magic. Unbalanced. Probably why the radios aren't working.
LEFT TO THEIR THOUGHTS, NO WORDS THROUGH THE AIR, FOREVER AND EVER...
YOUR FRIENDS MIGHT NOT BE HERE. BUT WE'D BE MORE THAN HAPPY TO KEEP YOU COMPANY...
WHAT'S SAY WE MAKE HER FEEL WELCOME?
Here we go...

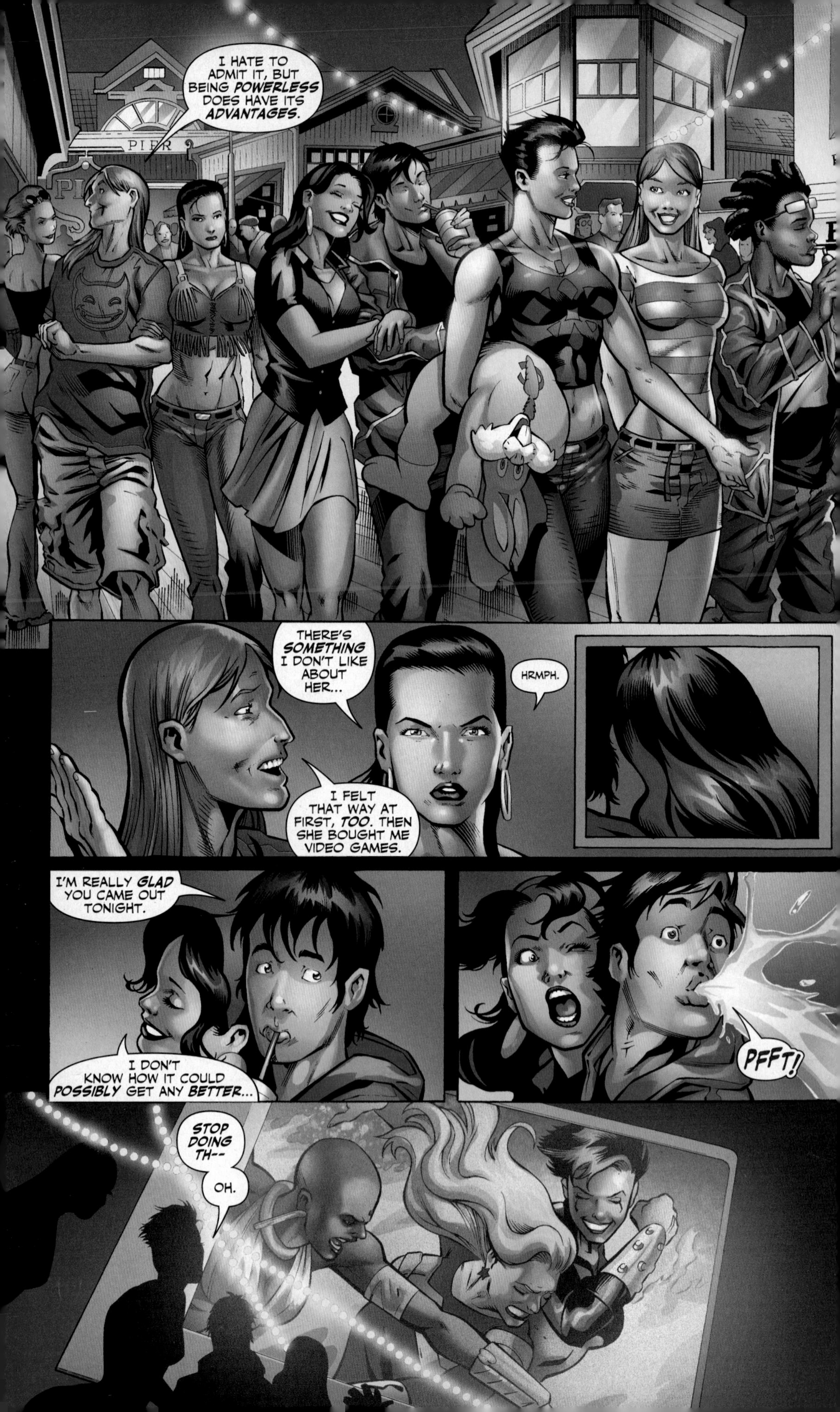

PIER
I HATE TO ADMIT IT, BUT BEING POWERLESS DOES HAVE ITS ADVANTAGES.
THERE'S SOMETHING I DON'T LIKE ABOUT HER...
I FELT THAT WAY AT FIRST, TOO. THEN SHE BOUGHT ME VIDEO GAMES.
HRMPH.
I'M REALLY GLAD YOU CAME OUT TONIGHT.
I DON'T KNOW HOW IT COULD POSSIBLY GET ANY BETTER...
PFFT!
STOP DOING TH--
OH.

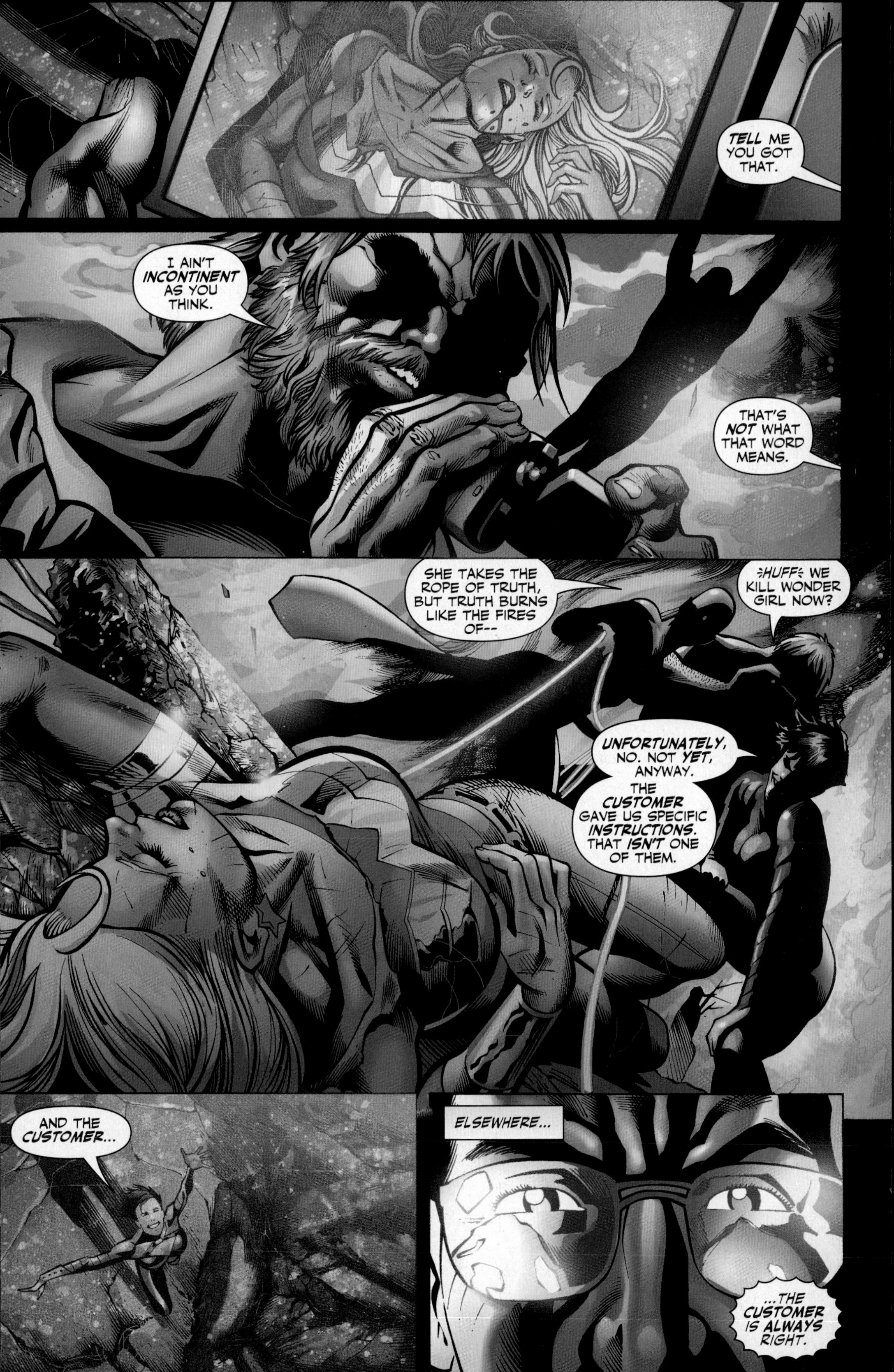

TELL ME YOU GOT THAT.
I AIN'T INCONTINENT AS YOU THINK.
THAT'S NOT WHAT THAT WORD MEANS.
SHE TAKES THE ROPE OF TRUTH, BUT TRUTH BURNS LIKE THE FIRES OF--
HUFF WE KILL WONDER GIRL NOW?
UNFORTUNATELY, NO. NOT YET, ANYWAY.
THE CUSTOMER GAVE US SPECIFIC INSTRUCTIONS. THAT ISN'T ONE OF THEM.
AND THE CUSTOMER...
ELSEWHERE...
...THE CUSTOMER IS ALWAYS RIGHT.

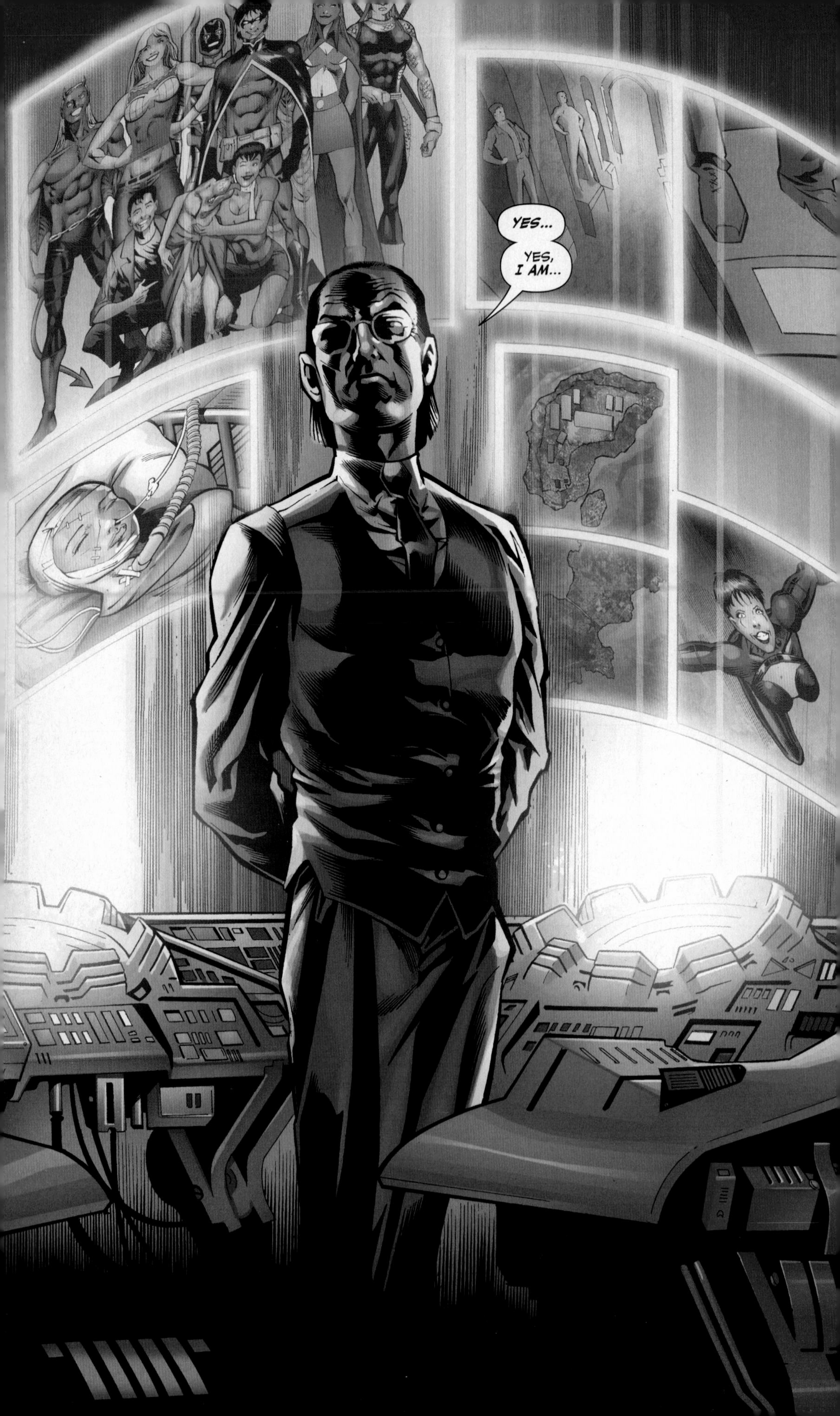
YES...
YES, I AM...

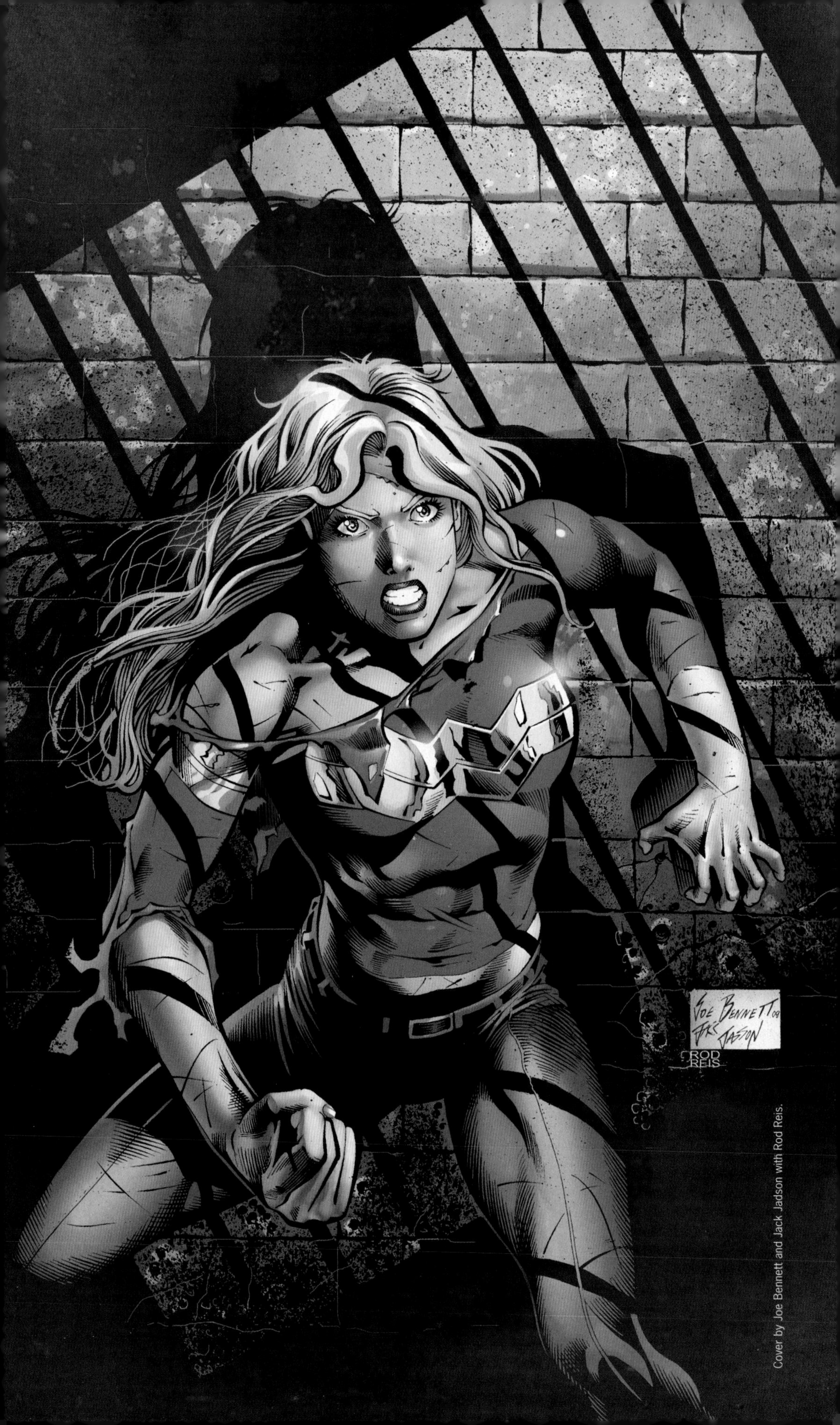

Cover by Joe Bennett and Jack Jadson with Rod Reis.

CHILD'S PLAY PART 2: UPSTAIRS, DOWNSTAIRS...

Bryan Q. Miller

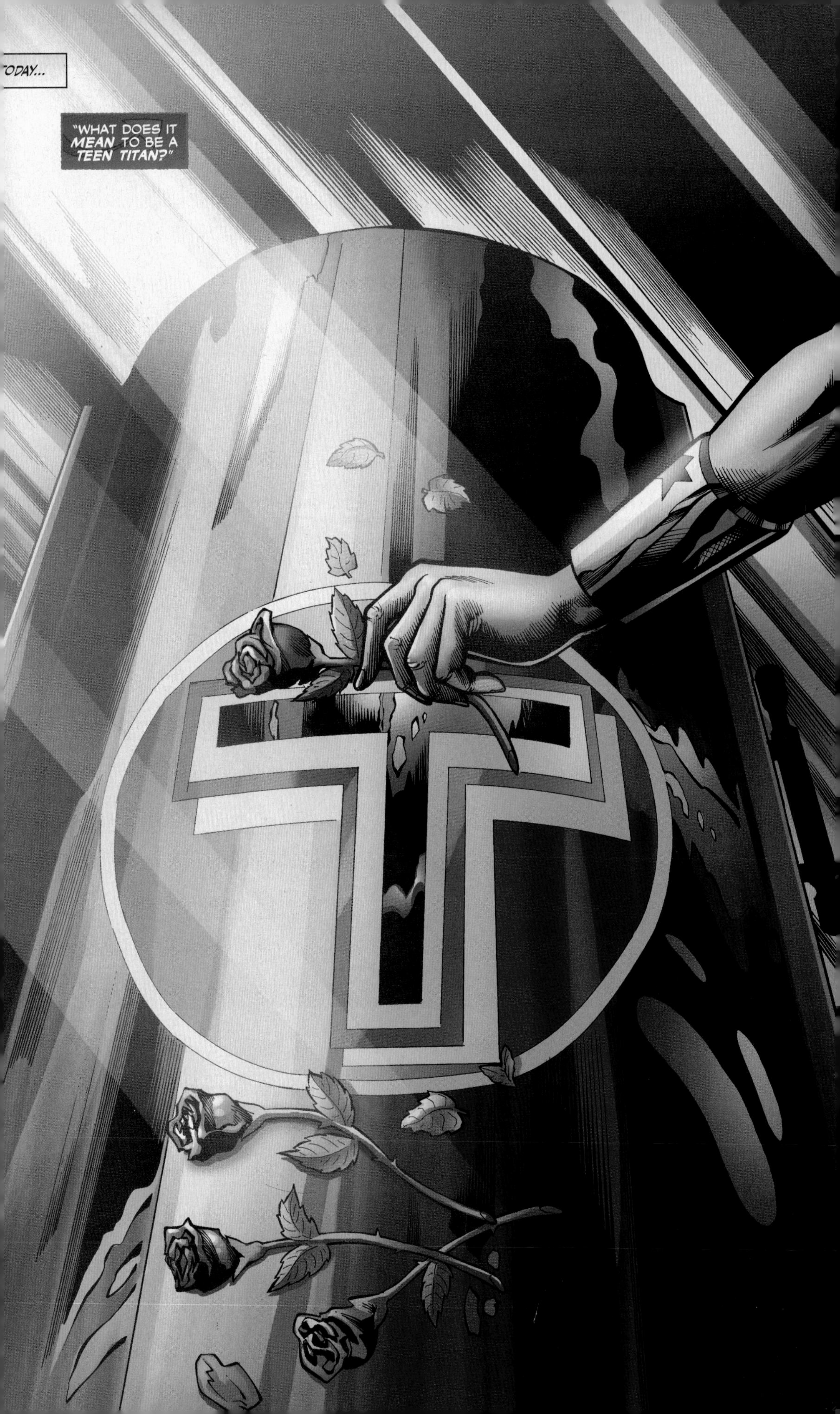

TODAY...
"WHAT DOES IT MEAN TO BE A TEEN TITAN?"

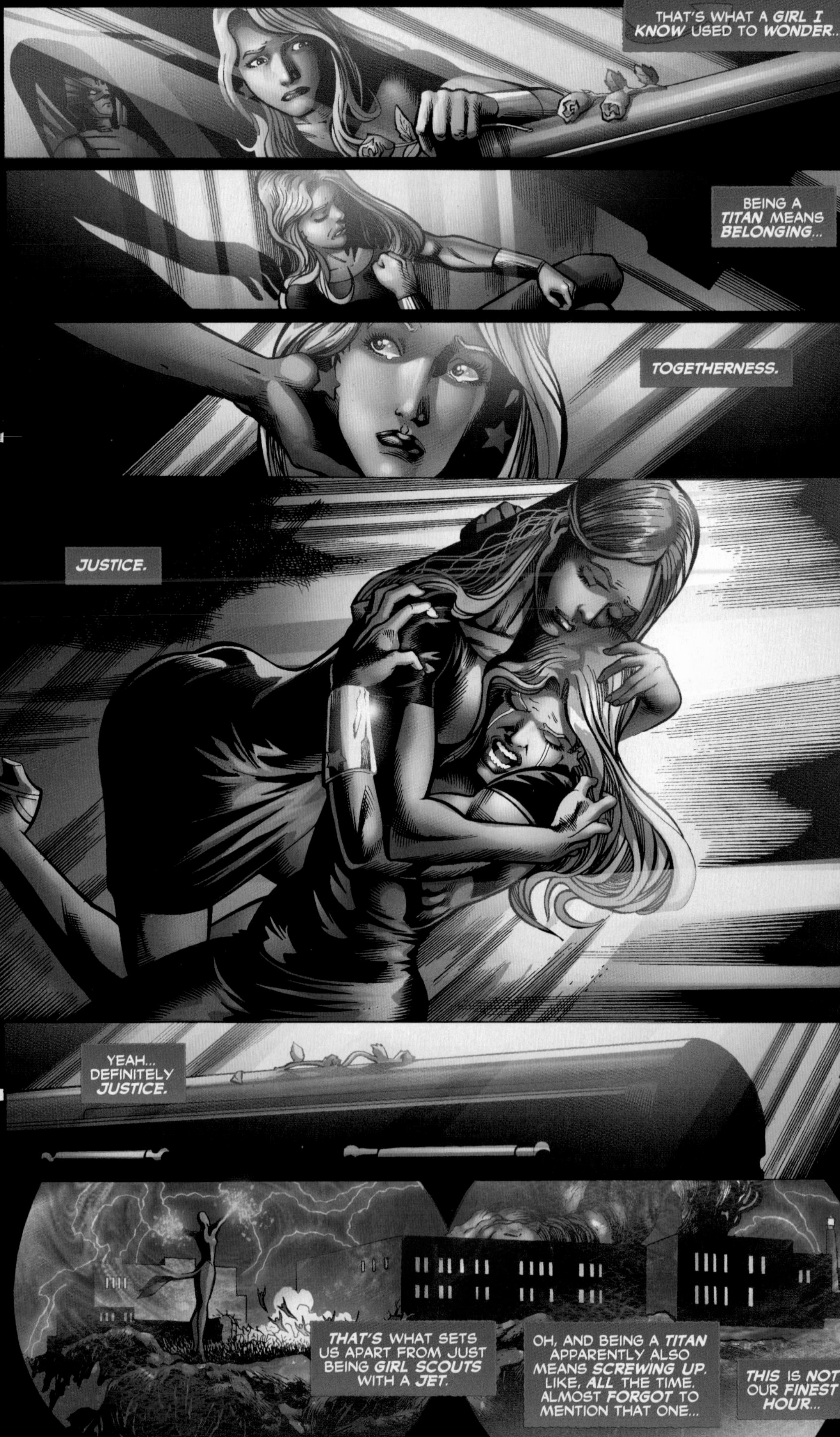

THAT'S WHAT A GIRL I KNOW USED TO WONDER...
BEING A TITAN MEANS BELONGING...
TOGETHERNESS.
JUSTICE.
YEAH... DEFINITELY JUSTICE.
THAT'S WHAT SETS US APART FROM JUST BEING GIRL SCOUTS WITH A JET.
OH, AND BEING A TITAN APPARENTLY ALSO MEANS SCREWING UP. LIKE, ALL THE TIME. ALMOST FORGOT TO MENTION THAT ONE...
THIS IS NOT OUR FINEST HOUR...

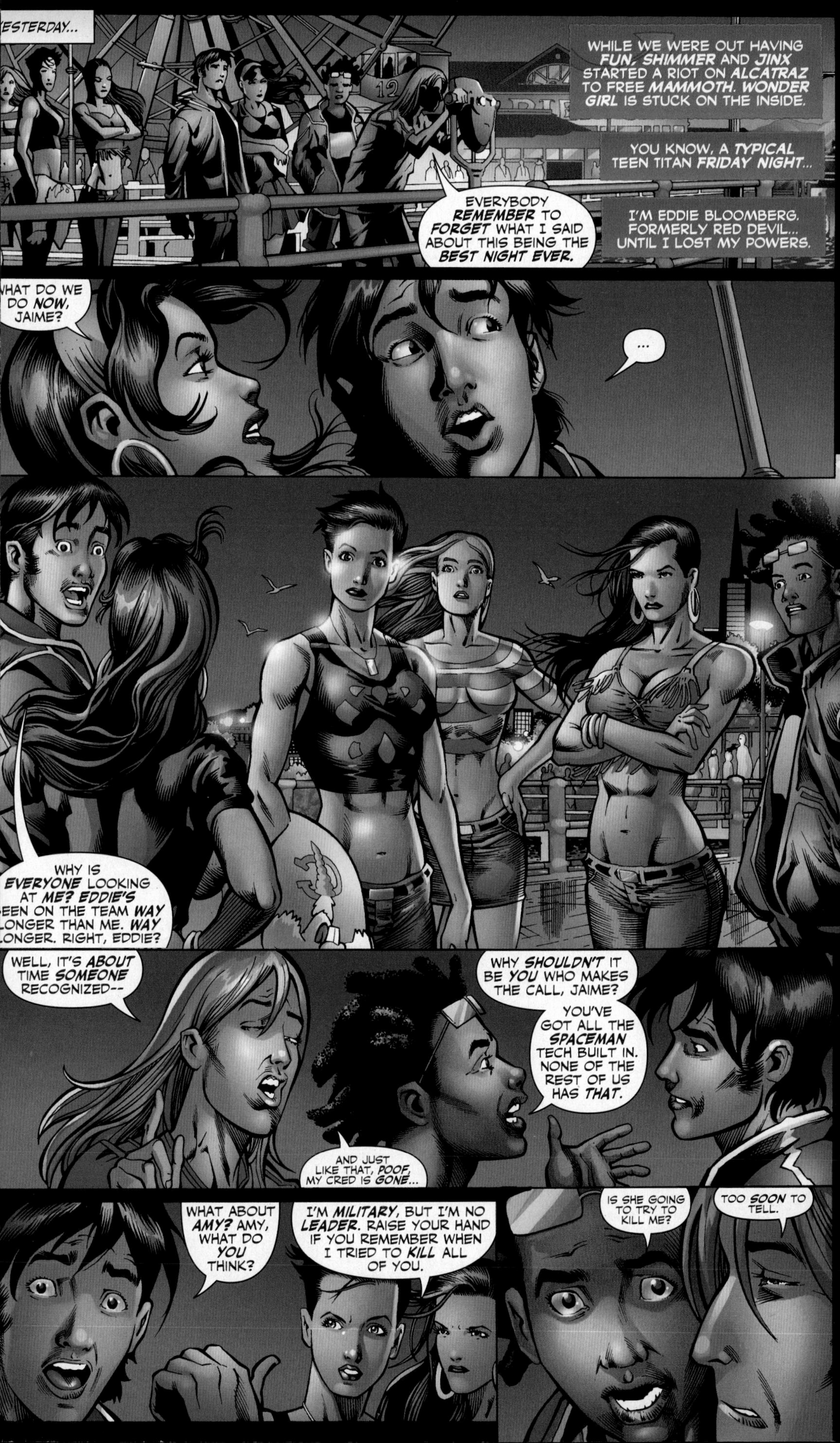

YESTERDAY...
WHILE WE WERE OUT HAVING FUN, SHIMMER AND JINX STARTED A RIOT ON ALCATRAZ TO FREE MAMMOTH. WONDER GIRL IS STUCK ON THE INSIDE.
YOU KNOW, A TYPICAL TEEN TITAN FRIDAY NIGHT...
I'M EDDIE BLOOMBERG. FORMERLY RED DEVIL... UNTIL I LOST MY POWERS.
EVERYBODY REMEMBER TO FORGET WHAT I SAID ABOUT THIS BEING THE BEST NIGHT EVER.
WHAT DO WE DO NOW, JAIME?
...
WHY IS EVERYONE LOOKING AT ME? EDDIE'S BEEN ON THE TEAM WAY LONGER THAN ME. WAY LONGER. RIGHT, EDDIE?
WELL, IT'S ABOUT TIME SOMEONE RECOGNIZED--
WHY SHOULDN'T IT BE YOU WHO MAKES THE CALL, JAIME?
YOU'VE GOT ALL THE SPACEMAN TECH BUILT IN. NONE OF THE REST OF US HAS THAT.
AND JUST LIKE THAT, POOF, MY CRED IS GONE...
WHAT ABOUT AMY? AMY, WHAT DO YOU THINK?
I'M MILITARY, BUT I'M NO LEADER. RAISE YOUR HAND IF YOU REMEMBER WHEN I TRIED TO KILL ALL OF YOU.
IS SHE GOING TO TRY TO KILL ME?
TOO SOON TO TELL.

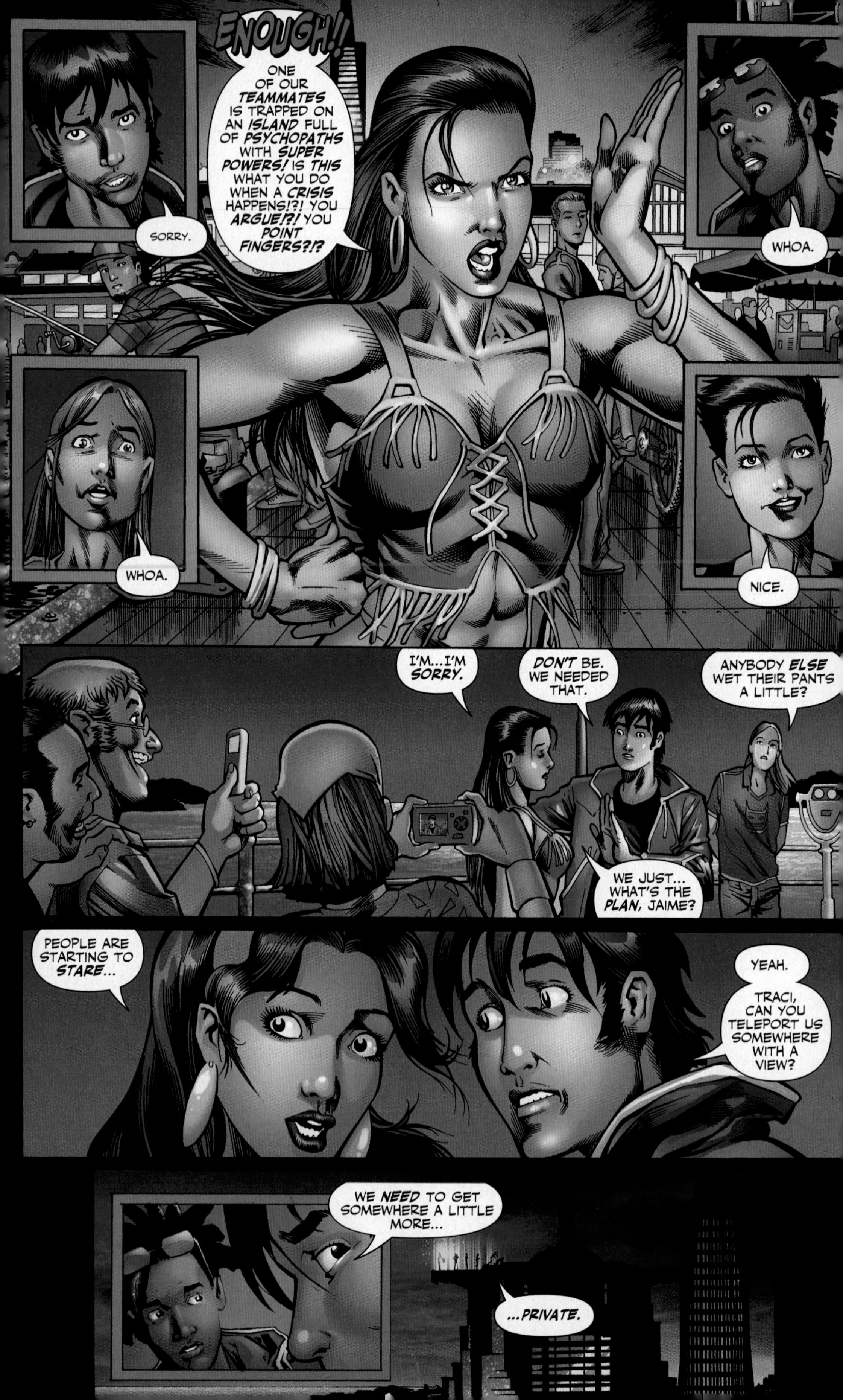

ENOUGH!!
ONE OF OUR TEAMMATES IS TRAPPED ON AN ISLAND FULL OF PSYCHOPATHS WITH SUPER POWERS! IS THIS WHAT YOU DO WHEN A CRISIS HAPPENS!?! YOU ARGUE!?! YOU POINT FINGERS?!?
SORRY.
WHOA.
WHOA.
NICE.
I'M...I'M SORRY.
DON'T BE. WE NEEDED THAT.
ANYBODY ELSE WET THEIR PANTS A LITTLE?
WE JUST... WHAT'S THE PLAN, JAIME?
PEOPLE ARE STARTING TO STARE...
YEAH.
TRACI, CAN YOU TELEPORT US SOMEWHERE WITH A VIEW?
WE NEED TO GET SOMEWHERE A LITTLE MORE...
...PRIVATE.

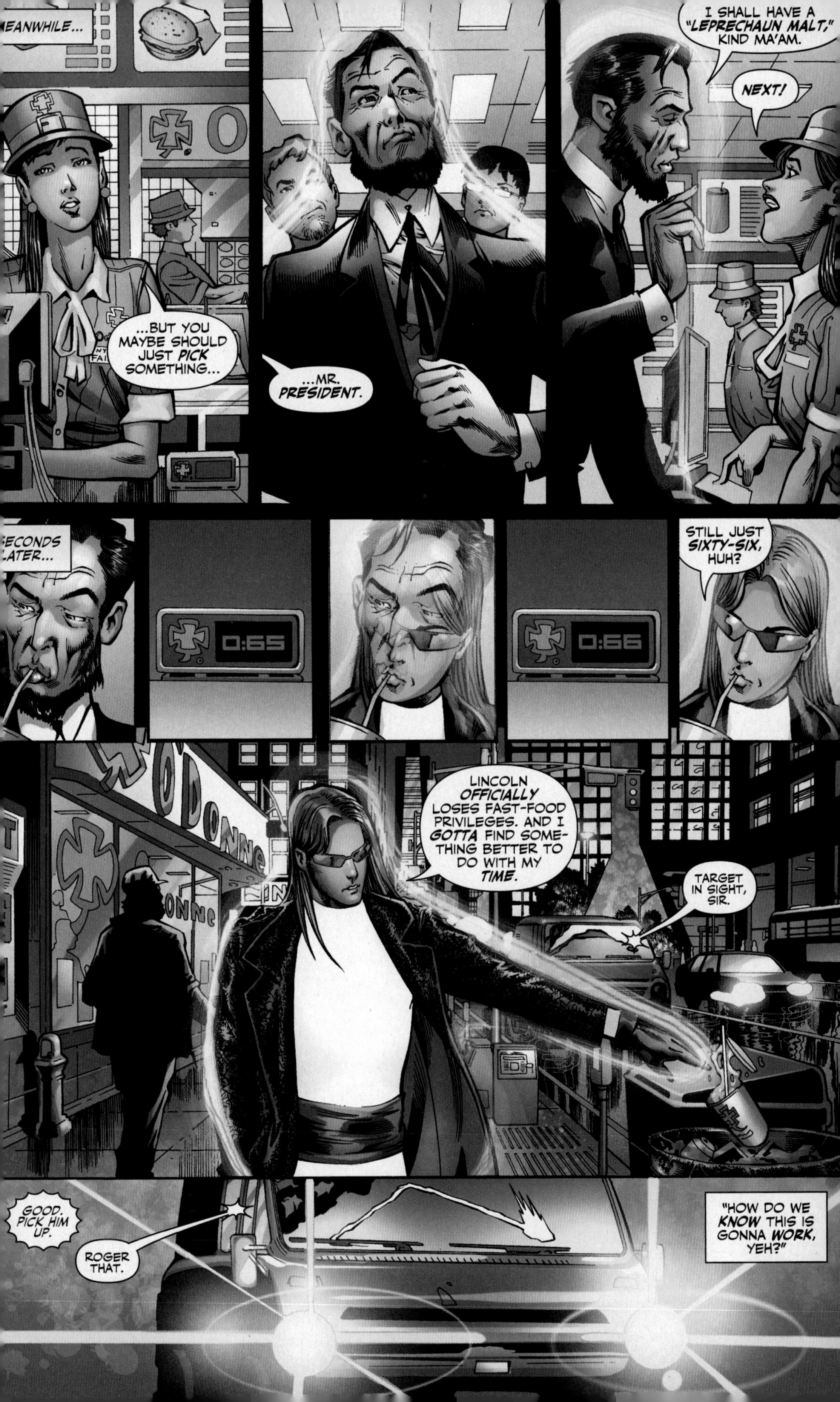

EANWHILE...
...BUT YOU MAYBE SHOULD JUST PICK SOMETHING...
...MR. PRESIDENT.
I SHALL HAVE A "LEPRECHAUN MALT," KIND MA'AM.
NEXT!
ECONDS LATER...
0:65
0:66
STILL JUST SIXTY-SIX, HUH?
LINCOLN OFFICIALLY LOSES FAST-FOOD PRIVILEGES. AND I GOTTA FIND SOME-THING BETTER TO DO WITH MY TIME.
TARGET IN SIGHT, SIR.
GOOD. PICK HIM UP.
ROGER THAT.
"HOW DO WE KNOW THIS IS GONNA WORK, YEH?"

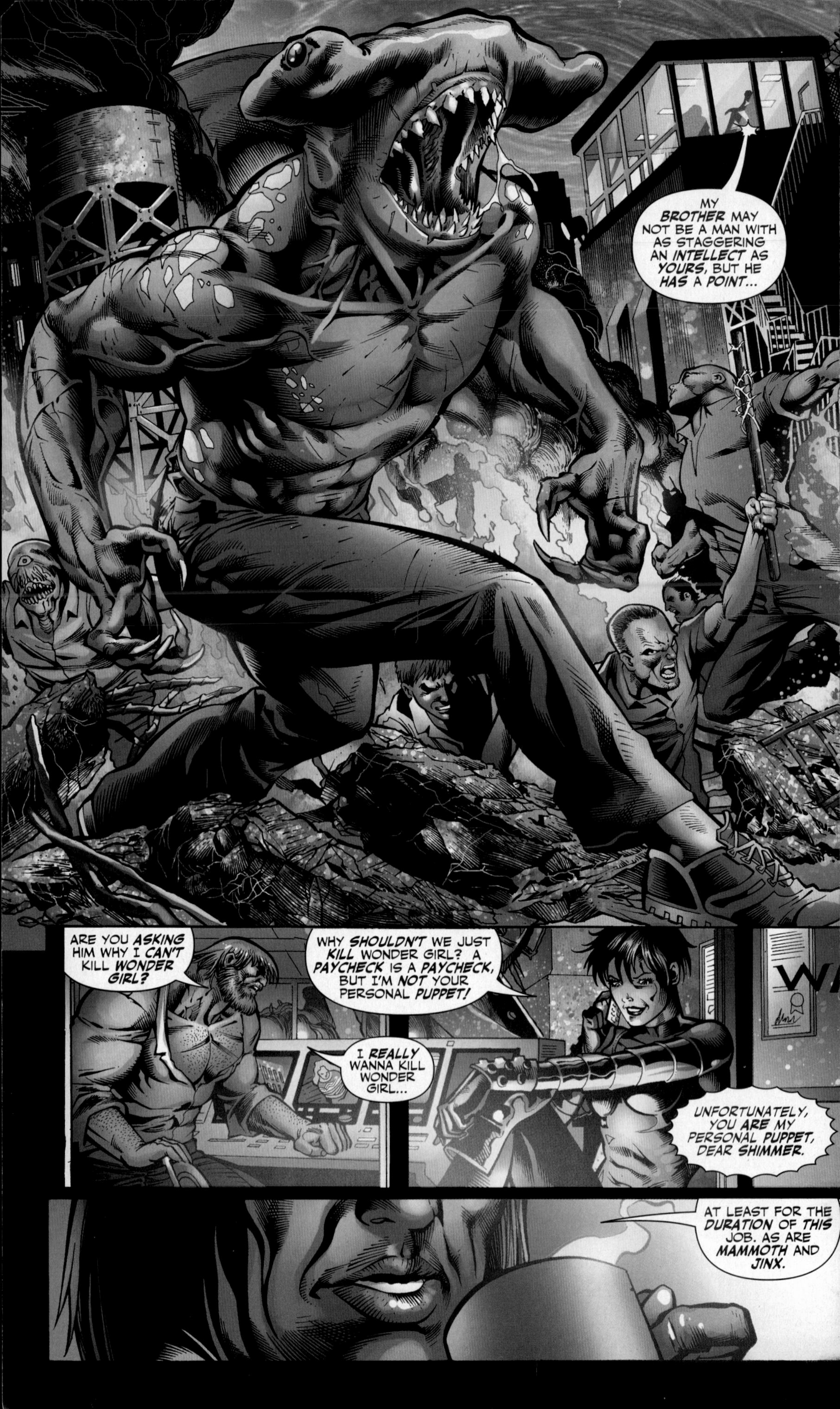

MY BROTHER MAY NOT BE A MAN WITH AS STAGGERING AN INTELLECT AS YOURS, BUT HE HAS A POINT...
ARE YOU ASKING HIM WHY I CAN'T KILL WONDER GIRL?
WHY SHOULDN'T WE JUST KILL WONDER GIRL? A PAYCHECK IS A PAYCHECK, BUT I'M NOT YOUR PERSONAL PUPPET!
I REALLY WANNA KILL WONDER GIRL...
UNFORTUNATELY, YOU ARE MY PERSONAL PUPPET, DEAR SHIMMER.
AT LEAST FOR THE DURATION OF THIS JOB. AS ARE MAMMOTH AND JINX.

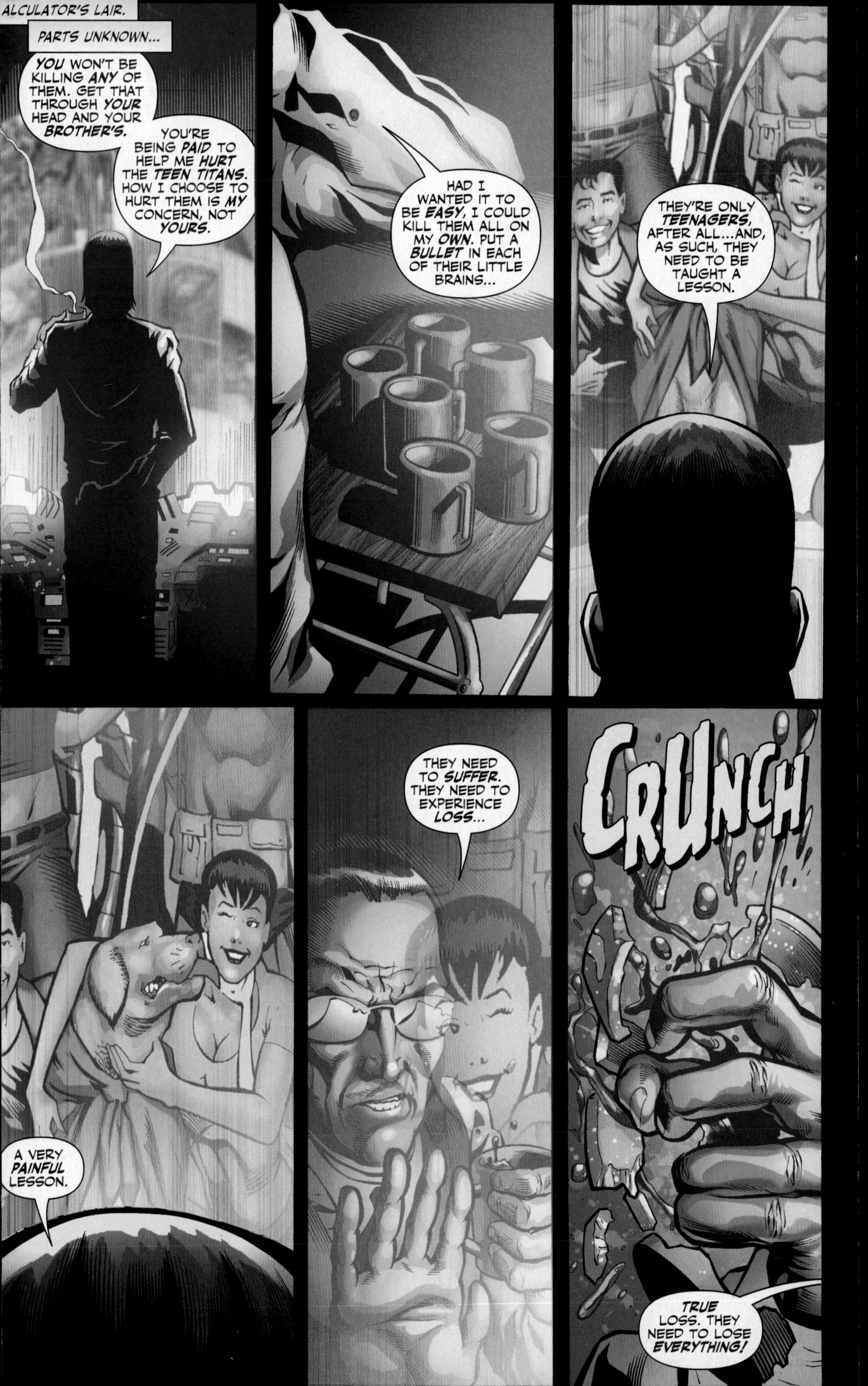
ALCULATOR'S LAIR.
PARTS UNKNOWN...
YOU WON'T BE KILLING ANY OF THEM. GET THAT THROUGH YOUR HEAD AND YOUR BROTHER'S.
YOU'RE BEING PAID TO HELP ME HURT THE TEEN TITANS. HOW I CHOOSE TO HURT THEM IS MY CONCERN, NOT YOURS.
HAD I WANTED IT TO BE EASY, I COULD KILL THEM ALL ON MY OWN. PUT A BULLET IN EACH OF THEIR LITTLE BRAINS...
THEY'RE ONLY TEENAGERS, AFTER ALL...AND, AS SUCH, THEY NEED TO BE TAUGHT A LESSON.
A VERY PAINFUL LESSON.
THEY NEED TO SUFFER. THEY NEED TO EXPERIENCE LOSS...
CRUNCH
TRUE LOSS. THEY NEED TO LOSE EVERYTHING!

I THINK YOU'VE WASTED ENOUGH OF MY TIME. ACQUIRE THE ASSET, THEN PROCEED TO THE NEXT LOCATION. TIMING IS CRITICAL. DON'T CALL THIS NUMBER AGAIN.

CLICK

I JUST *WANTED* TO KILL HER...

I KNOW. I KNOW. MAYBE ON THE *NEXT* GO 'ROUND, YEH?

NOW CHEER UP...

NOT SURE WHAT THE LITTLE *BRATS* DID TO *WHOEVER* THE *CLIENT* IS...

...YOU STILL GET TO KILL *HIM.*

INMATE #10170_
GEIGER.
METAHUMAN

...ns and creates explosive fie
y, high-speed electrons or
s of radioactive nuclei su
mma radiation(electroma
produced by subatomic
positron annihilation, n
fusion, fission or inve
physical processes). Th
f ionizing radiation a
particle
eek
d
os

WHAT ABOUT *YOU?*

THINK I'M GONNA MAKE US SOME *NEW* FRIENDS...

INMATE #102408.
VIRGIL ADAMS.
NANO.

INMATE #1120_
JOHN DOE.
RUMBLE

"COULD YOU *NOT* LOOK AT ME WHILE I DO THIS?"

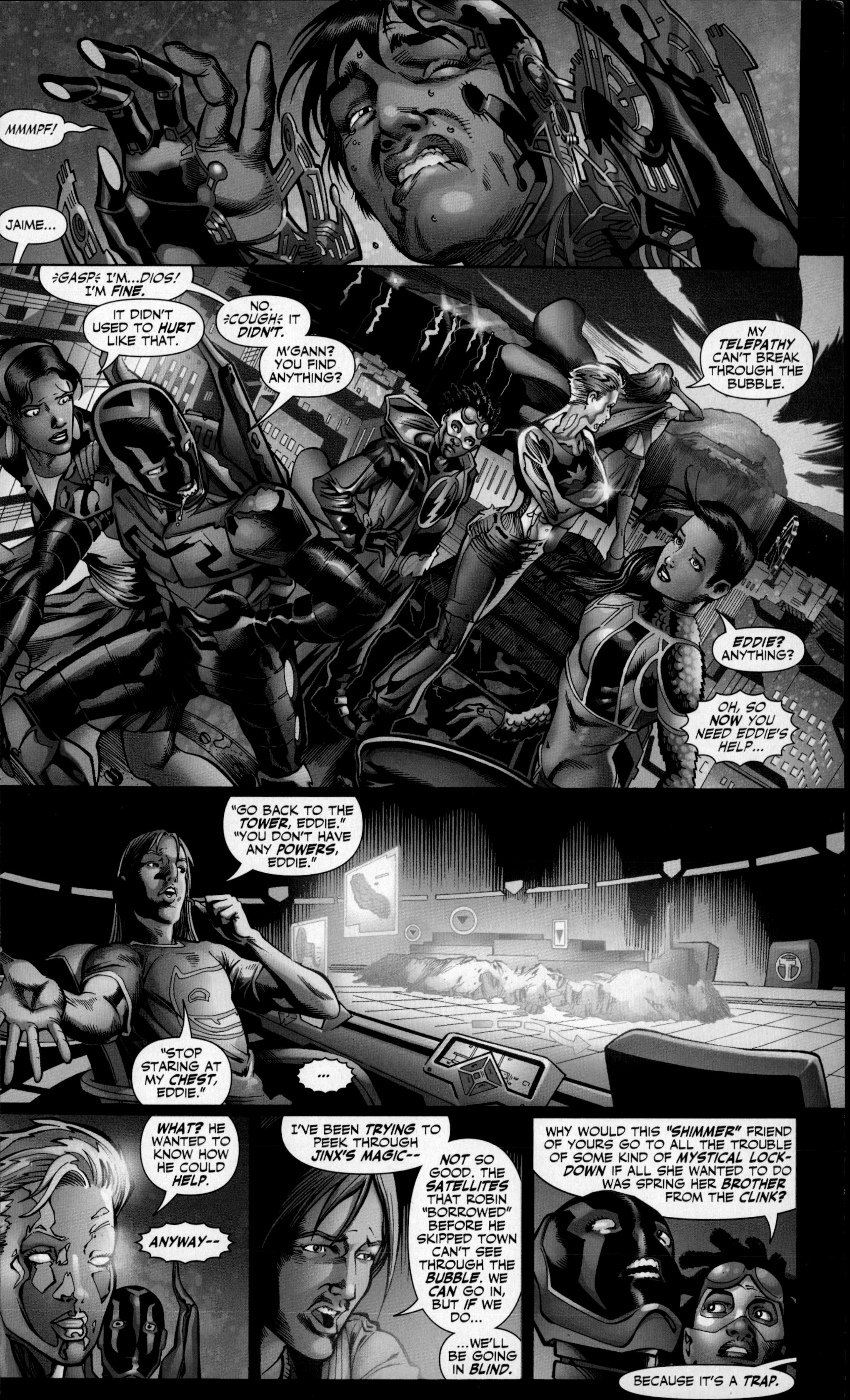
MMMPF!
JAIME...
≠GASP≠ I'M...DIOS! I'M FINE.
IT DIDN'T USED TO HURT LIKE THAT.
NO. ≠COUGH≠ IT DIDN'T.
M'GANN? YOU FIND ANYTHING?
MY TELEPATHY CAN'T BREAK THROUGH THE BUBBLE.
EDDIE? ANYTHING?
OH, SO NOW YOU NEED EDDIE'S HELP...
"GO BACK TO THE TOWER, EDDIE." "YOU DON'T HAVE ANY POWERS, EDDIE."
"STOP STARING AT MY CHEST, EDDIE."
...
WHAT? HE WANTED TO KNOW HOW HE COULD HELP.
ANYWAY--
I'VE BEEN TRYING TO PEEK THROUGH JINX'S MAGIC--
NOT SO GOOD. THE SATELLITES THAT ROBIN "BORROWED" BEFORE HE SKIPPED TOWN CAN'T SEE THROUGH THE BUBBLE. WE CAN GO IN, BUT IF WE DO...
...WE'LL BE GOING IN BLIND.
WHY WOULD THIS "SHIMMER" FRIEND OF YOURS GO TO ALL THE TROUBLE OF SOME KIND OF MYSTICAL LOCK-DOWN IF ALL SHE WANTED TO DO WAS SPRING HER BROTHER FROM THE CLINK?
BECAUSE IT'S A TRAP.

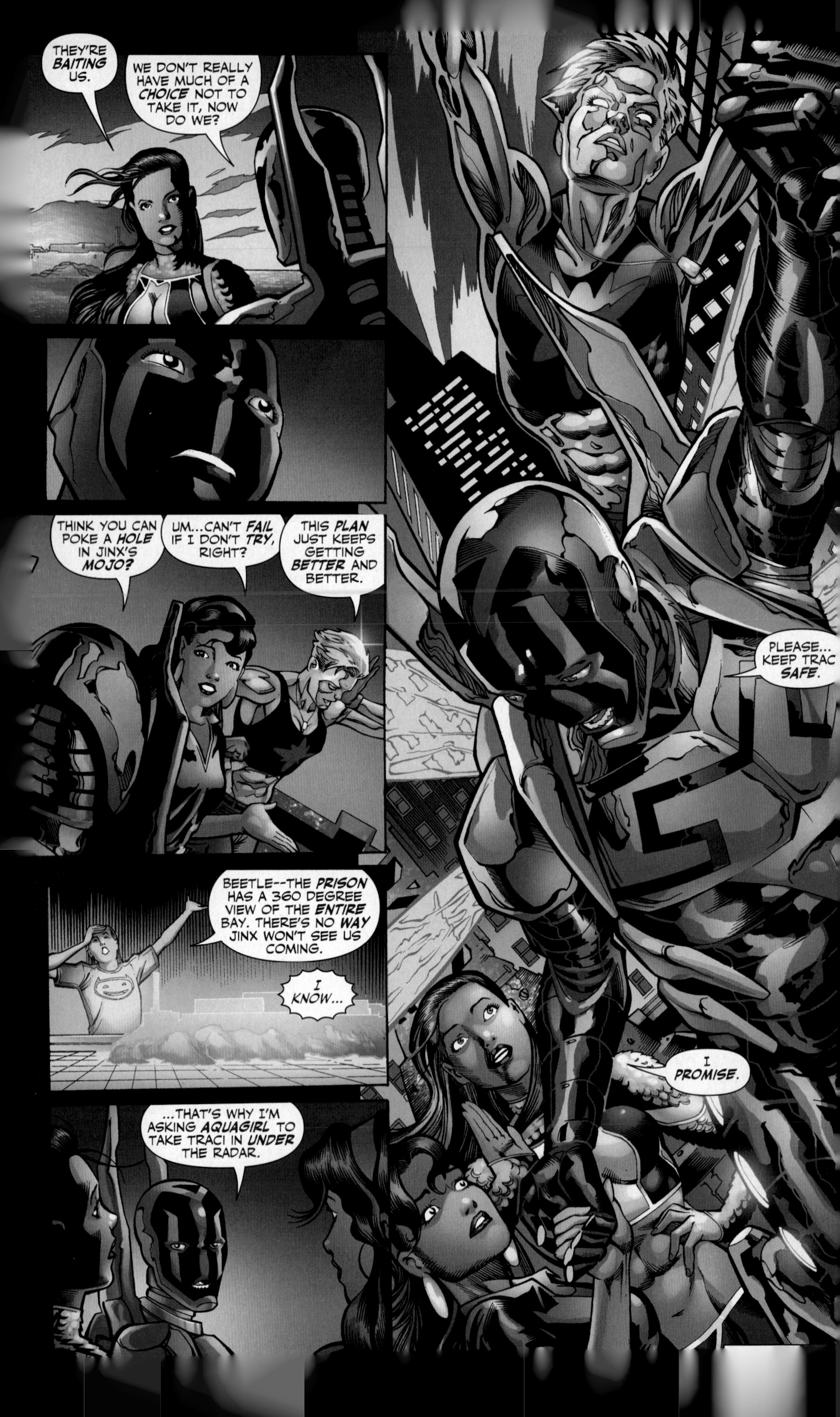

THEY'RE BAITING US.
WE DON'T REALLY HAVE MUCH OF A CHOICE NOT TO TAKE IT, NOW DO WE?
THINK YOU CAN POKE A HOLE IN JINX'S MOJO?
UM...CAN'T FAIL IF I DON'T TRY, RIGHT?
THIS PLAN JUST KEEPS GETTING BETTER AND BETTER.
BEETLE--THE PRISON HAS A 360 DEGREE VIEW OF THE ENTIRE BAY. THERE'S NO WAY JINX WON'T SEE US COMING.
I KNOW...
...THAT'S WHY I'M ASKING AQUAGIRL TO TAKE TRACI IN UNDER THE RADAR.
PLEASE... KEEP TRAC SAFE.
I PROMISE.

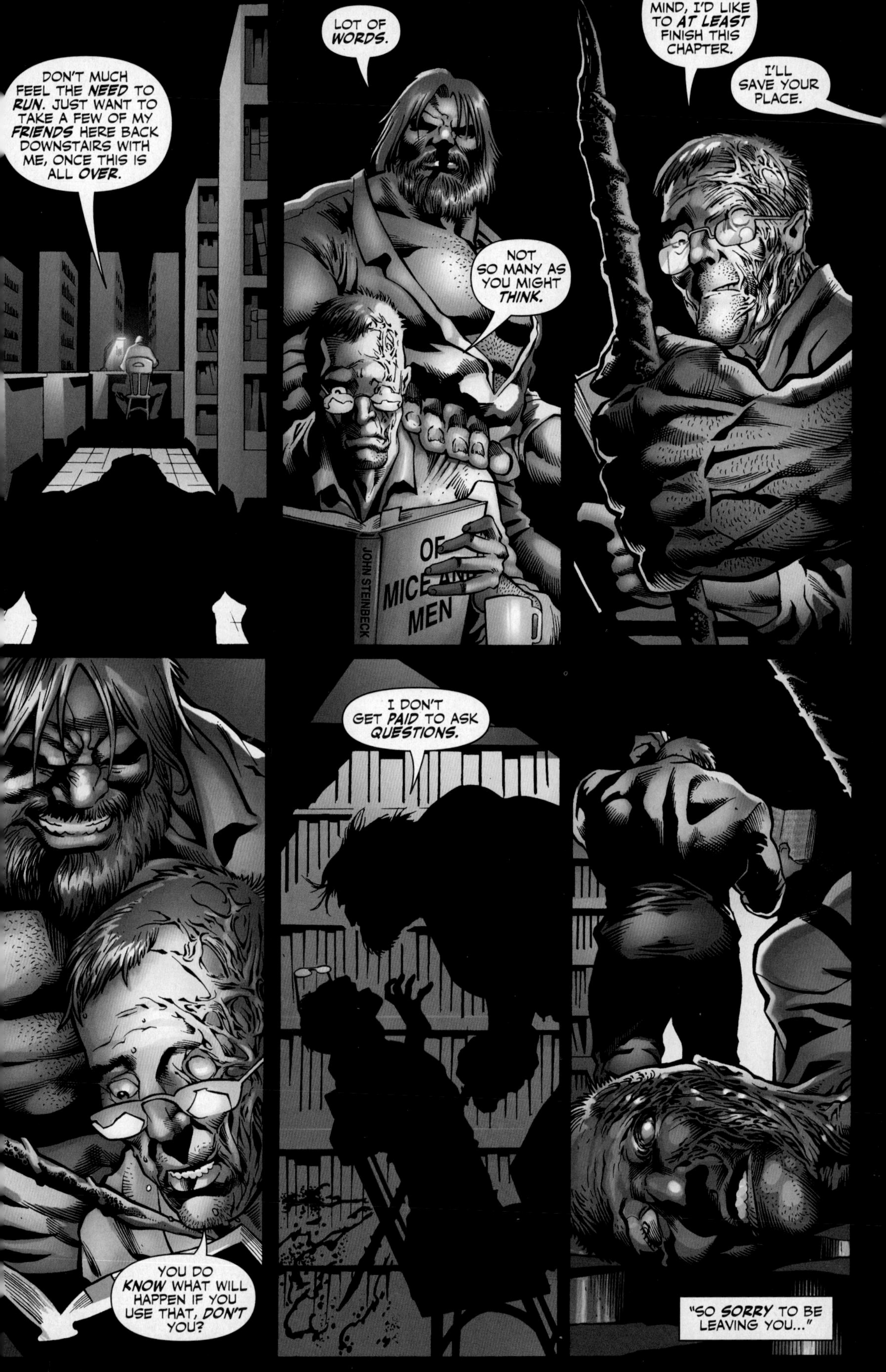
DON'T MUCH FEEL THE NEED TO RUN. JUST WANT TO TAKE A FEW OF MY FRIENDS HERE BACK DOWNSTAIRS WITH ME, ONCE THIS IS ALL OVER.
LOT OF WORDS.
NOT SO MANY AS YOU MIGHT THINK.
JOHN STEINBECK
OF MICE AND MEN
I SEE. IF YOU DON'T MIND, I'D LIKE TO AT LEAST FINISH THIS CHAPTER.
I'LL SAVE YOUR PLACE.
YOU DO KNOW WHAT WILL HAPPEN IF YOU USE THAT, DON'T YOU?
I DON'T GET PAID TO ASK QUESTIONS.
"SO SORRY TO BE LEAVING YOU..."

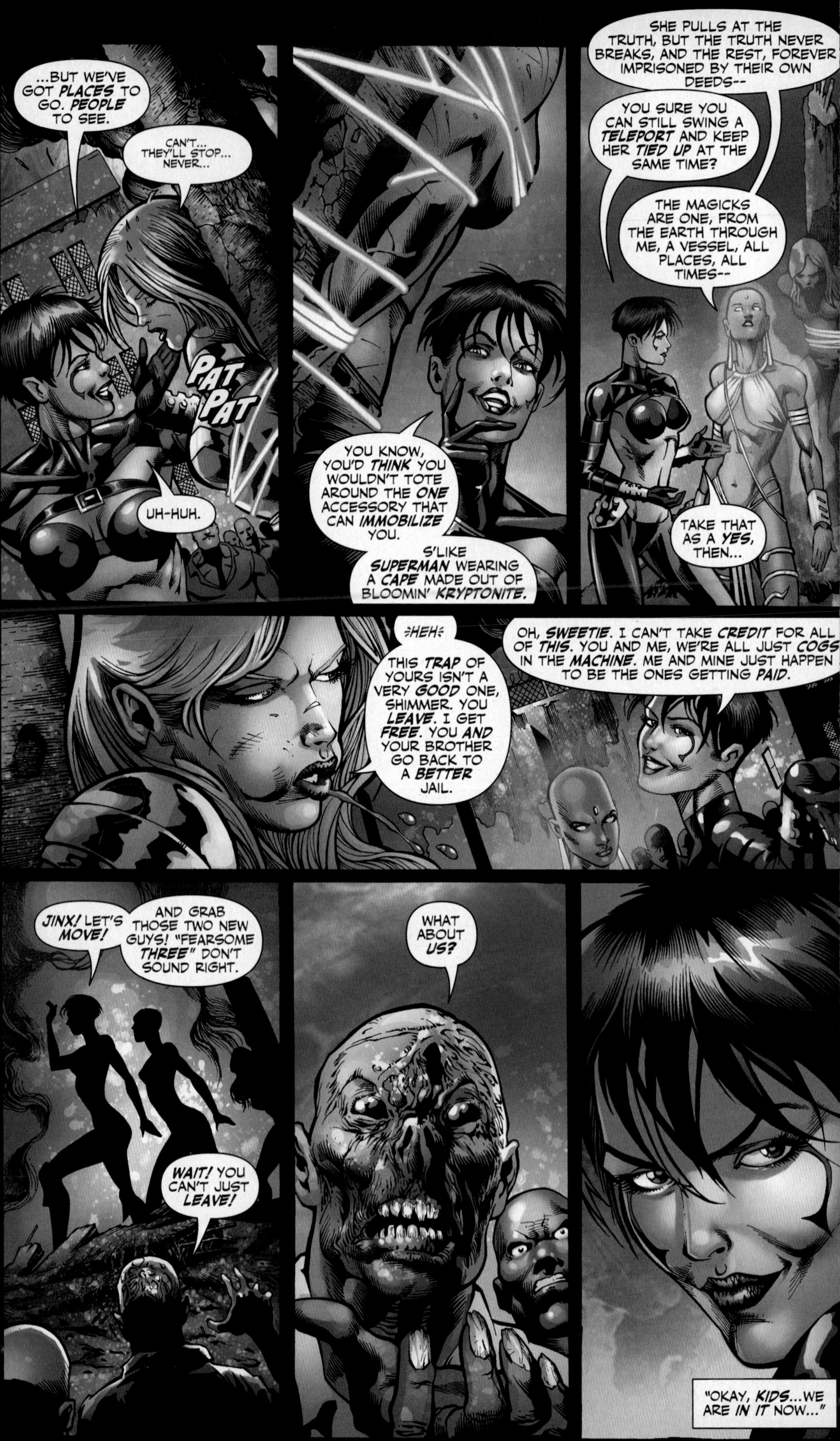
...BUT WE'VE GOT PLACES TO GO. PEOPLE TO SEE.
CAN'T... THEY'LL STOP... NEVER...
PAT PAT
UH-HUH.
YOU KNOW, YOU'D THINK YOU WOULDN'T TOTE AROUND THE ONE ACCESSORY THAT CAN IMMOBILIZE YOU.
S'LIKE SUPERMAN WEARING A CAPE MADE OUT OF BLOOMIN' KRYPTONITE.
SHE PULLS AT THE TRUTH, BUT THE TRUTH NEVER BREAKS, AND THE REST, FOREVER IMPRISONED BY THEIR OWN DEEDS--
YOU SURE YOU CAN STILL SWING A TELEPORT AND KEEP HER TIED UP AT THE SAME TIME?
THE MAGICKS ARE ONE, FROM THE EARTH THROUGH ME, A VESSEL, ALL PLACES, ALL TIMES--
TAKE THAT AS A YES, THEN...
HEH
THIS TRAP OF YOURS ISN'T A VERY GOOD ONE, SHIMMER. YOU LEAVE. I GET FREE. YOU AND YOUR BROTHER GO BACK TO A BETTER JAIL.
OH, SWEETIE. I CAN'T TAKE CREDIT FOR ALL OF THIS. YOU AND ME, WE'RE ALL JUST COGS IN THE MACHINE. ME AND MINE JUST HAPPEN TO BE THE ONES GETTING PAID.
JINX! LET'S MOVE!
AND GRAB THOSE TWO NEW GUYS! "FEARSOME THREE" DON'T SOUND RIGHT.
WAIT! YOU CAN'T JUST LEAVE!
WHAT ABOUT US?
"OKAY, KIDS...WE ARE IN IT NOW..."

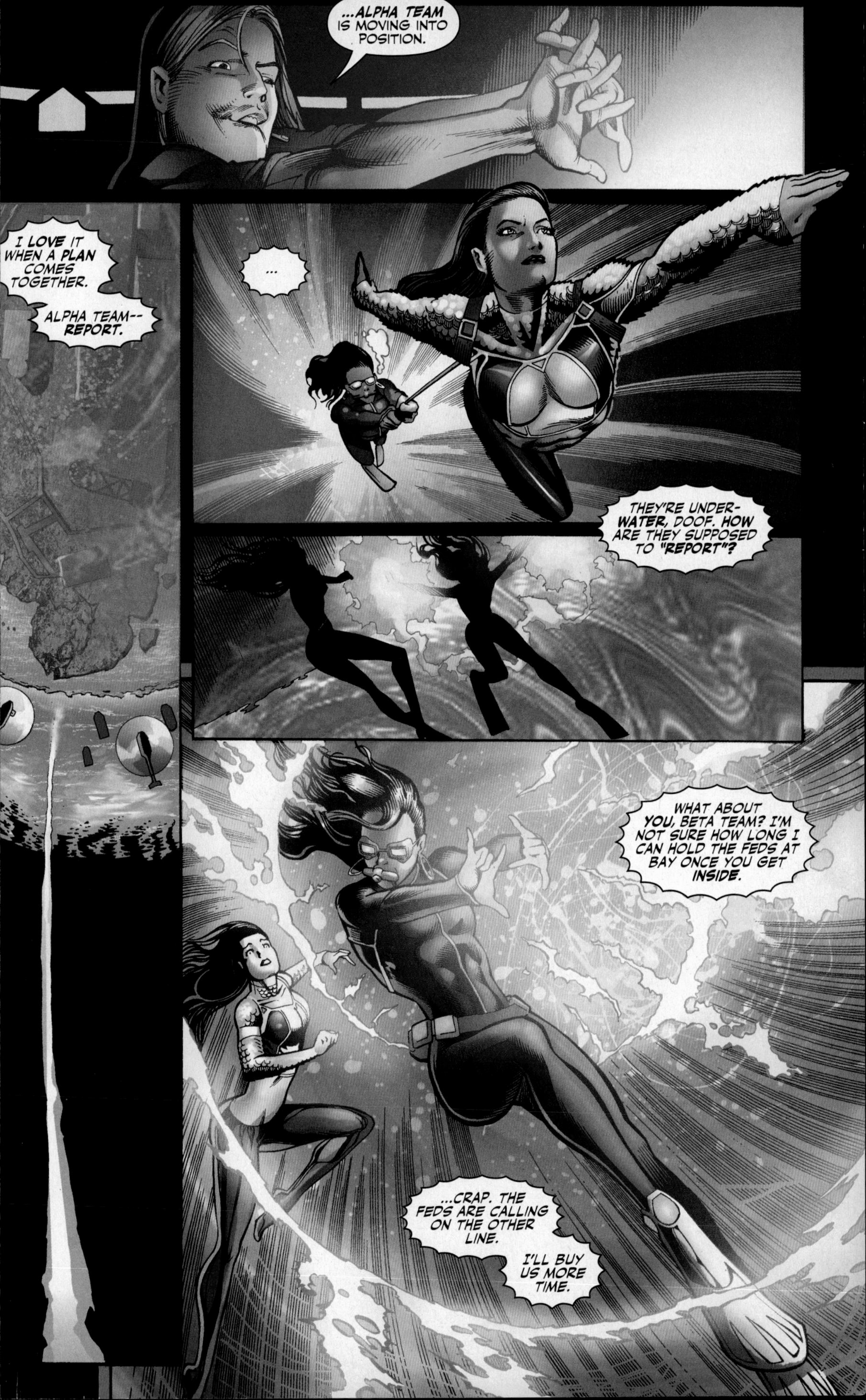
...ALPHA TEAM IS MOVING INTO POSITION.
I LOVE IT WHEN A PLAN COMES TOGETHER.
ALPHA TEAM-- REPORT.
...
THEY'RE UNDER-WATER, DOOF. HOW ARE THEY SUPPOSED TO "REPORT"?
WHAT ABOUT YOU, BETA TEAM? I'M NOT SURE HOW LONG I CAN HOLD THE FEDS AT BAY ONCE YOU GET INSIDE.
...CRAP. THE FEDS ARE CALLING ON THE OTHER LINE.
I'LL BUY US MORE TIME.

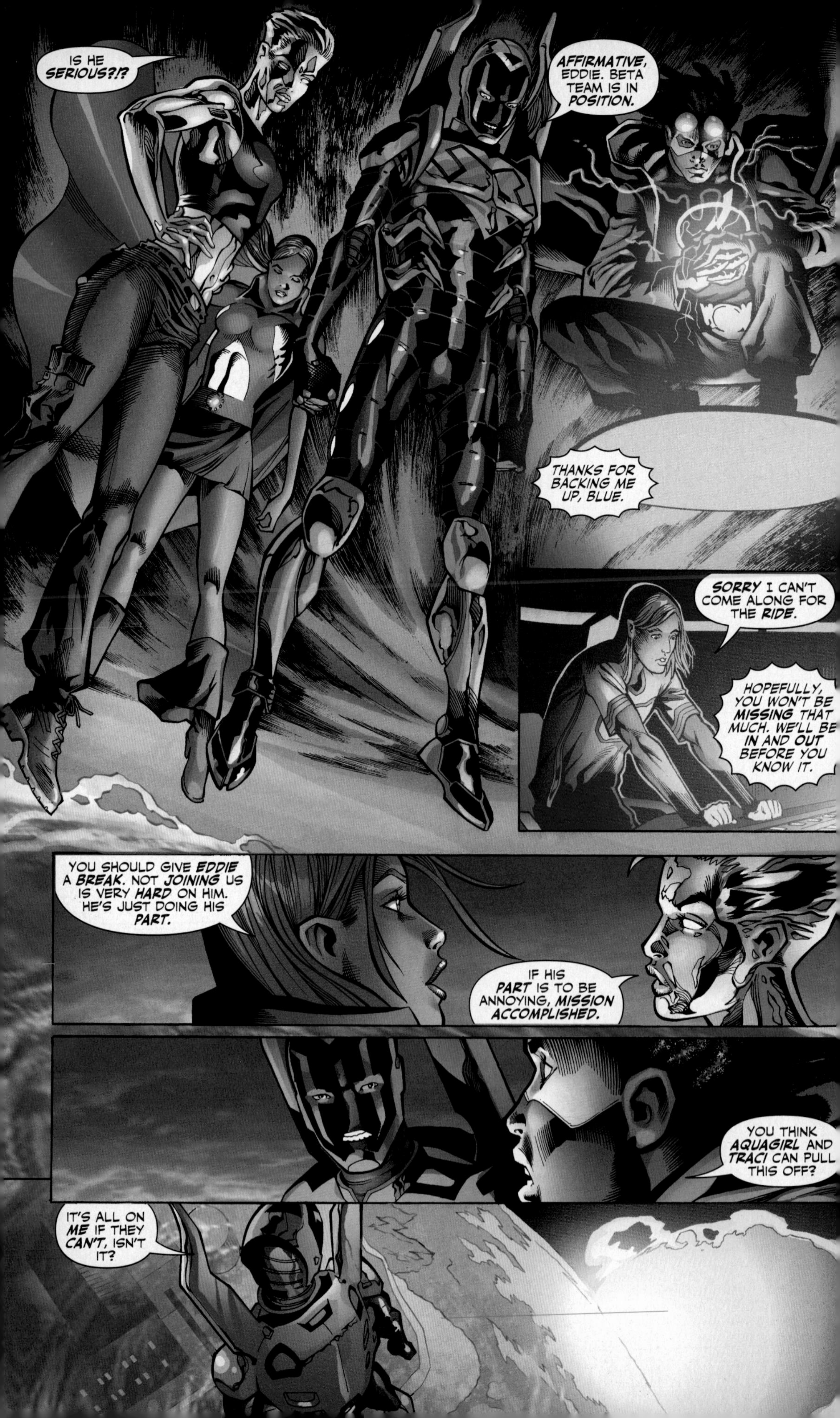
IS HE SERIOUS?!?
AFFIRMATIVE, EDDIE. BETA TEAM IS IN POSITION.
THANKS FOR BACKING ME UP, BLUE.
SORRY I CAN'T COME ALONG FOR THE RIDE.
HOPEFULLY, YOU WON'T BE MISSING THAT MUCH. WE'LL BE IN AND OUT BEFORE YOU KNOW IT.
YOU SHOULD GIVE EDDIE A BREAK. NOT JOINING US IS VERY HARD ON HIM. HE'S JUST DOING HIS PART.
IF HIS PART IS TO BE ANNOYING, MISSION ACCOMPLISHED.
YOU THINK AQUAGIRL AND TRACI CAN PULL THIS OFF?
IT'S ALL ON ME IF THEY CAN'T, ISN'T IT?

JINX?! WHAT'S HAPPENING?!

TOOMUCHTOO MANYSOMUCH ALLATONCE!

AGGHHH!!!

THIS ISN'T FAR ENOUGH *AWAY*, JINX! WE NEED TO KEEP *MOVING!* NOW!

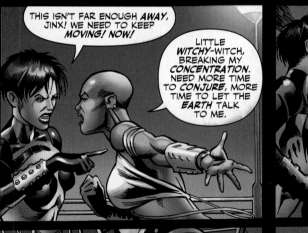

LITTLE *WITCHY*-WITCH, BREAKING MY *CONCENTRATION.* NEED MORE TIME TO *CONJURE*, MORE TIME TO LET THE *EARTH* TALK TO ME.

UM...WHERE YA GOIN', BROTHER?

IF I'M A DEAD MAN--

--I'LL AT LEAST DIE *HAPPY.*

WHAT SAY WE GO OUT IN *STYLE*, YEH?

"MUST BE MY *LUCKY* DAY!"

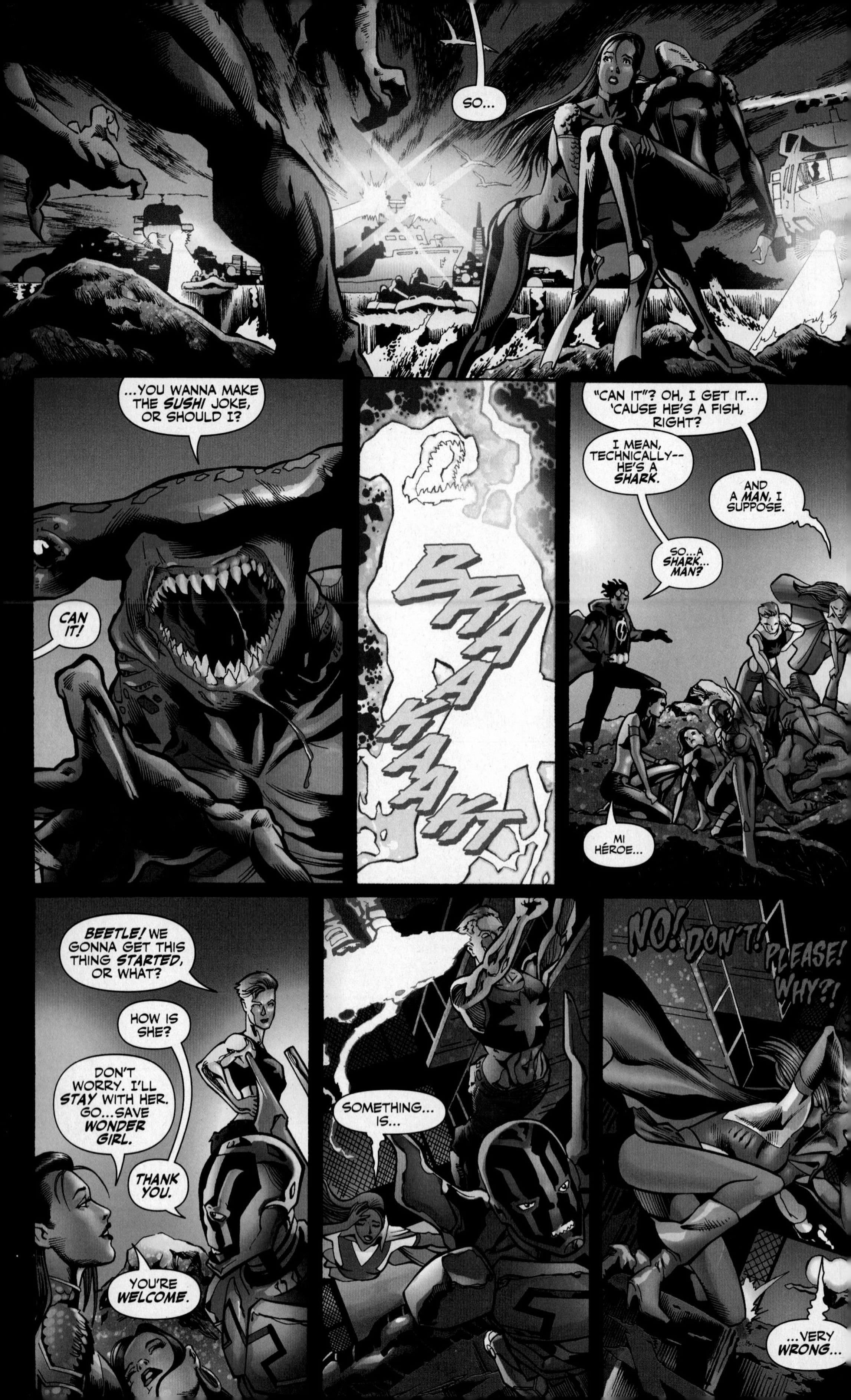
SO...
...YOU WANNA MAKE THE SUSHI JOKE, OR SHOULD I?
CAN IT!
BRRAKKAKANT
"CAN IT"? OH, I GET IT... 'CAUSE HE'S A FISH, RIGHT?
I MEAN, TECHNICALLY-- HE'S A SHARK.
AND A MAN, I SUPPOSE.
SO...A SHARK... MAN?
MI HÉROE...
BEETLE! WE GONNA GET THIS THING STARTED, OR WHAT?
HOW IS SHE?
DON'T WORRY. I'LL STAY WITH HER. GO...SAVE WONDER GIRL.
THANK YOU.
YOU'RE WELCOME.
SOMETHING... IS...
NO! DON'T! PLEASE! WHY?!
...VERY WRONG...

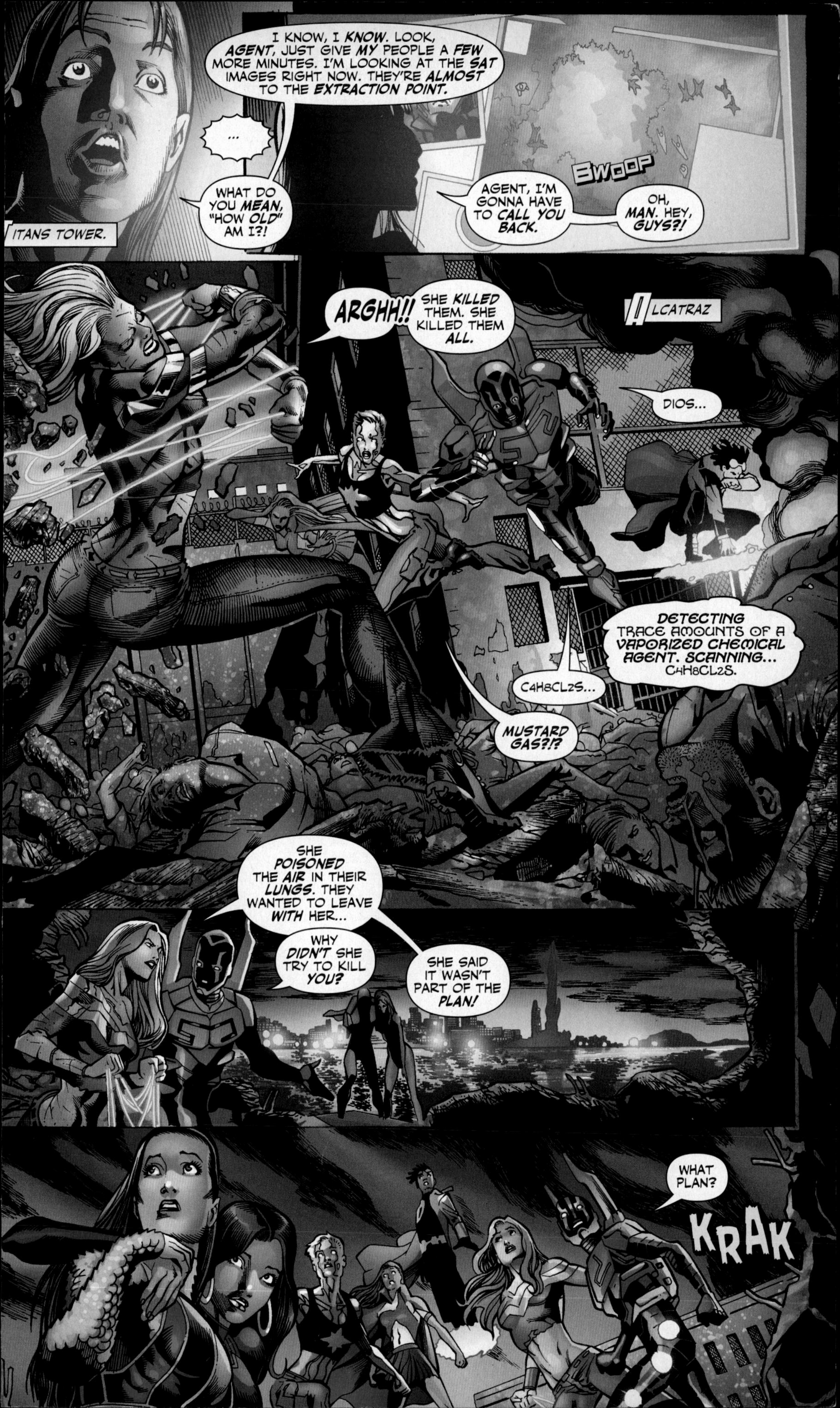
TITANS TOWER.
I KNOW, I KNOW. LOOK, AGENT, JUST GIVE MY PEOPLE A FEW MORE MINUTES. I'M LOOKING AT THE SAT IMAGES RIGHT NOW. THEY'RE ALMOST TO THE EXTRACTION POINT.
...
WHAT DO YOU MEAN, "HOW OLD" AM I?!
BWOOP
AGENT, I'M GONNA HAVE TO CALL YOU BACK.
OH, MAN. HEY, GUYS?!
ALCATRAZ
ARGHH!!
SHE KILLED THEM. SHE KILLED THEM ALL.
DIOS...
DETECTING TRACE AMOUNTS OF A VAPORIZED CHEMICAL AGENT. SCANNING... C4H8CL2S.
C4H8CL2S...
MUSTARD GAS?!?
SHE POISONED THE AIR IN THEIR LUNGS. THEY WANTED TO LEAVE WITH HER...
WHY DIDN'T SHE TRY TO KILL YOU?
SHE SAID IT WASN'T PART OF THE PLAN!
WHAT PLAN?
KRAK

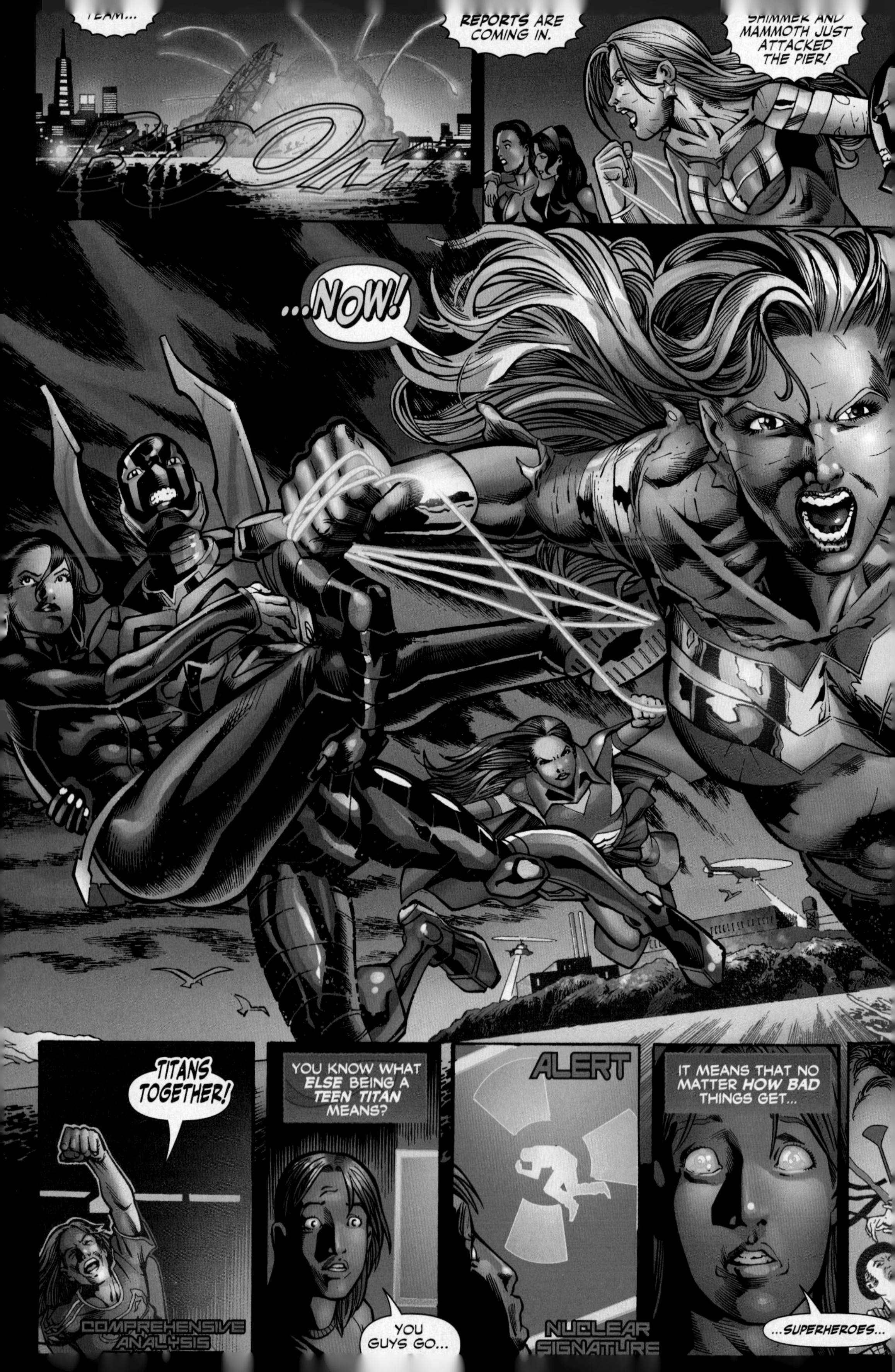
TEAM...
BROOM
REPORTS ARE COMING IN.
SHIMMER AND MAMMOTH JUST ATTACKED THE PIER!
...NOW!
TITANS TOGETHER!
COMPREHENSIVE ANALYSIS
YOU KNOW WHAT ELSE BEING A TEEN TITAN MEANS?
YOU GUYS GO...
ALERT
NUCLEAR SIGNATURE
IT MEANS THAT NO MATTER HOW BAD THINGS GET...
...SUPERHEROES...

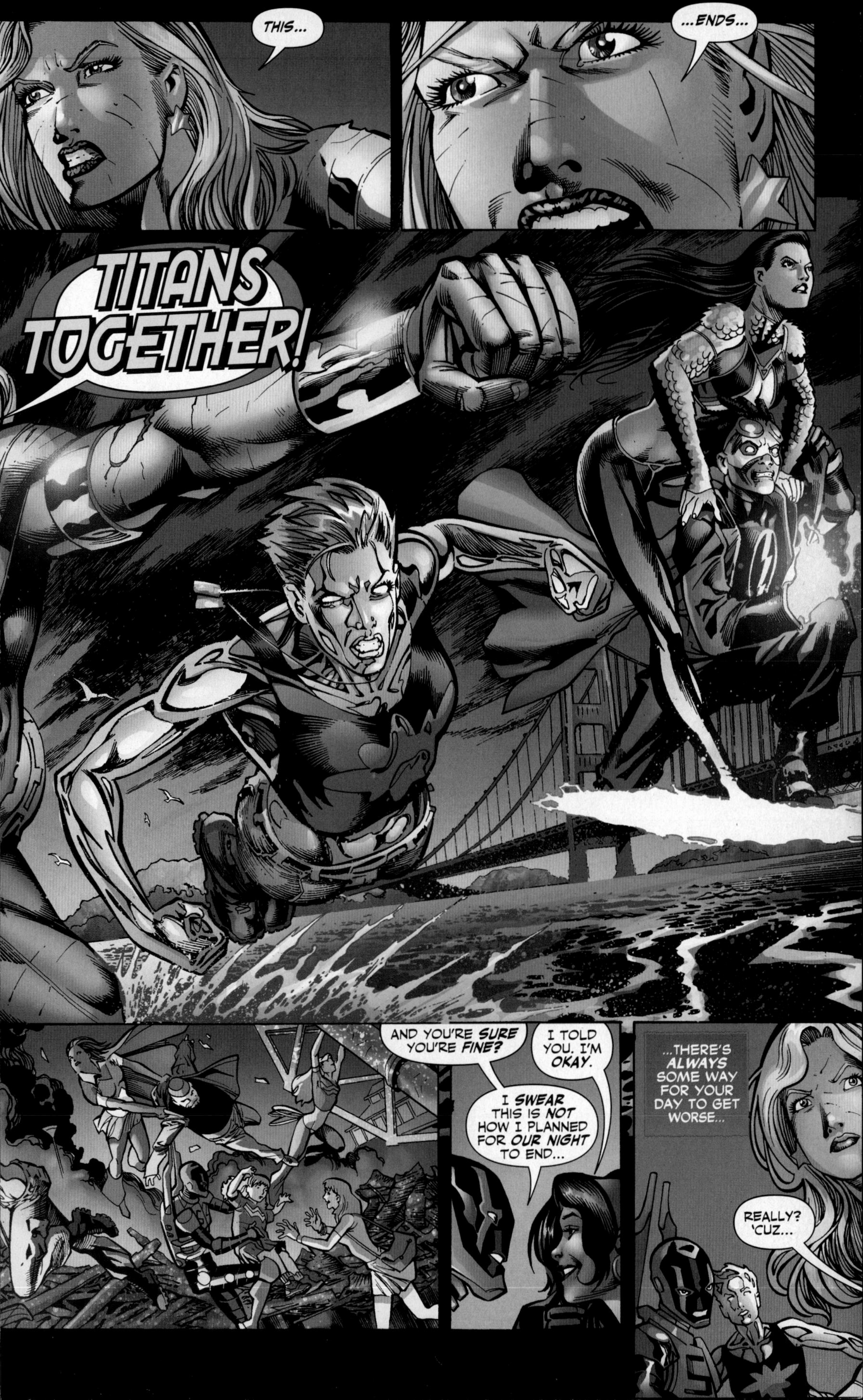
THIS...
...ENDS...
TITANS TOGETHER!
AND YOU'RE SURE YOU'RE FINE?
I TOLD YOU. I'M OKAY.
I SWEAR THIS IS NOT HOW I PLANNED FOR OUR NIGHT TO END...
...THERE'S ALWAYS SOME WAY FOR YOUR DAY TO GET WORSE...
REALLY? 'CUZ...

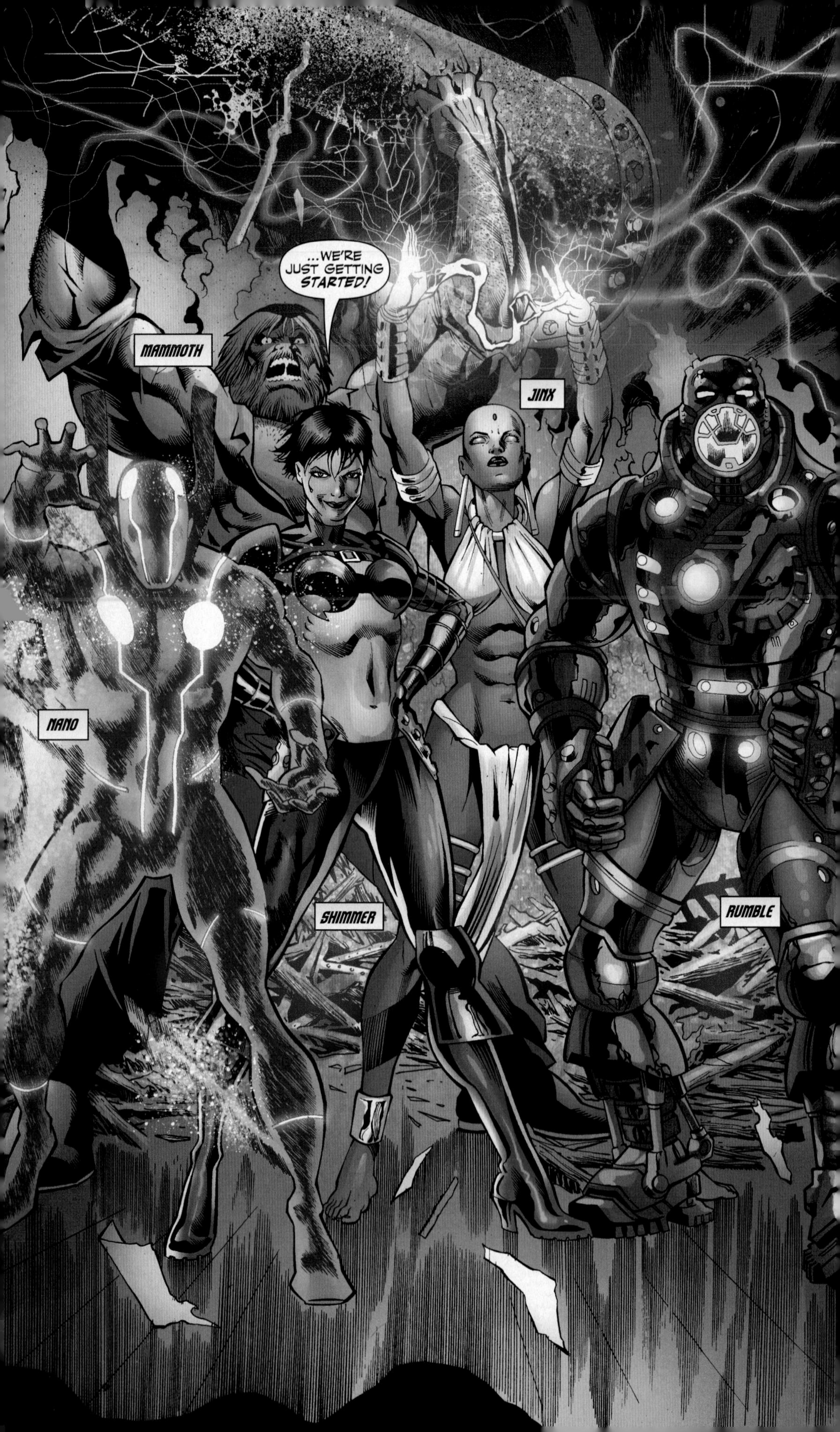
...WE'RE JUST GETTING STARTED!
MAMMOTH
JINX
NANO
SHIMMER
RUMBLE

Cover by Joe Bennett and Jack Jadson with Rod Reis

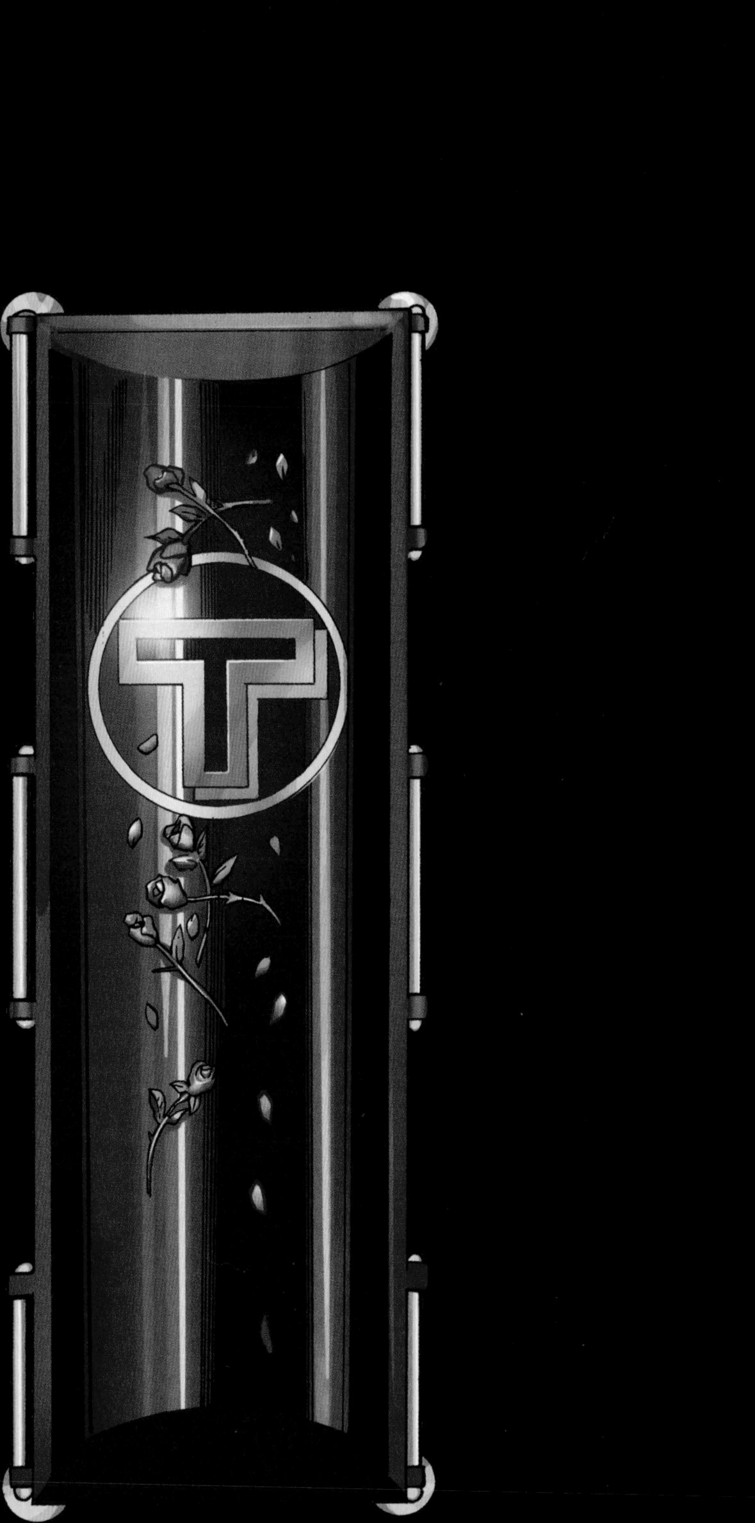

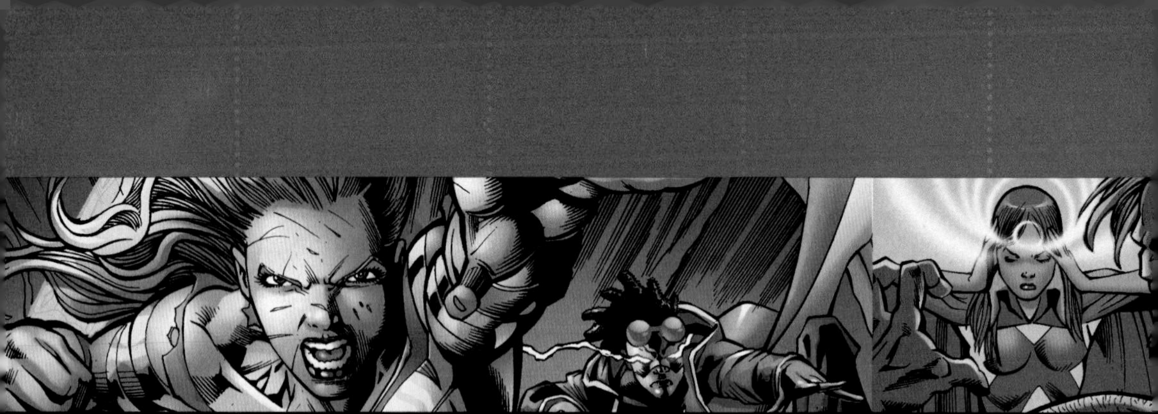

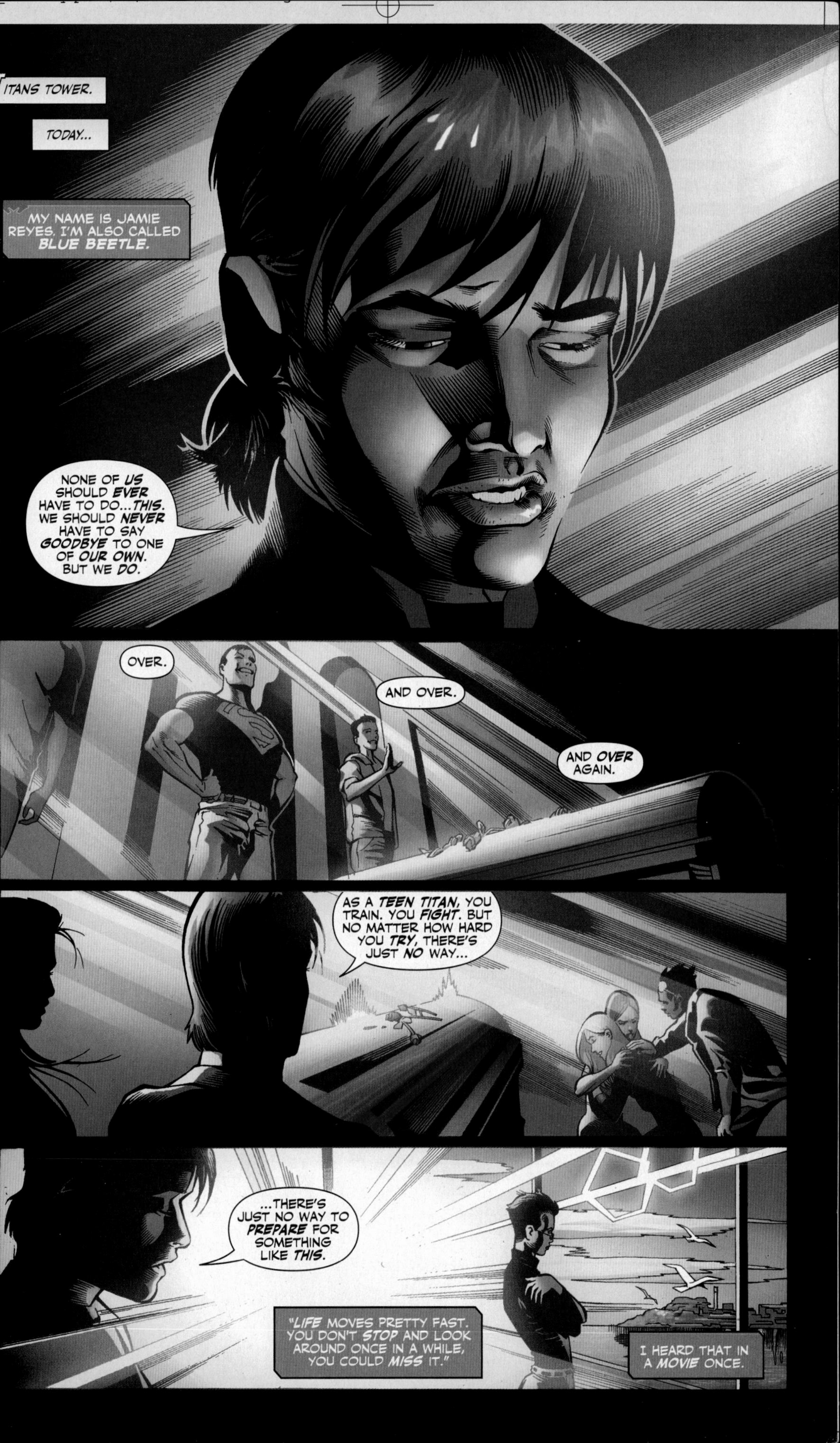

ITANS TOWER.
TODAY...
MY NAME IS JAMIE REYES. I'M ALSO CALLED BLUE BEETLE.
NONE OF US SHOULD EVER HAVE TO DO...THIS. WE SHOULD NEVER HAVE TO SAY GOODBYE TO ONE OF OUR OWN. BUT WE DO.
OVER.
AND OVER.
AND OVER AGAIN.
AS A TEEN TITAN, YOU TRAIN. YOU FIGHT. BUT NO MATTER HOW HARD YOU TRY, THERE'S JUST NO WAY...
...THERE'S JUST NO WAY TO PREPARE FOR SOMETHING LIKE THIS.
"LIFE MOVES PRETTY FAST. YOU DON'T STOP AND LOOK AROUND ONCE IN A WHILE, YOU COULD MISS IT."
I HEARD THAT IN A MOVIE ONCE.

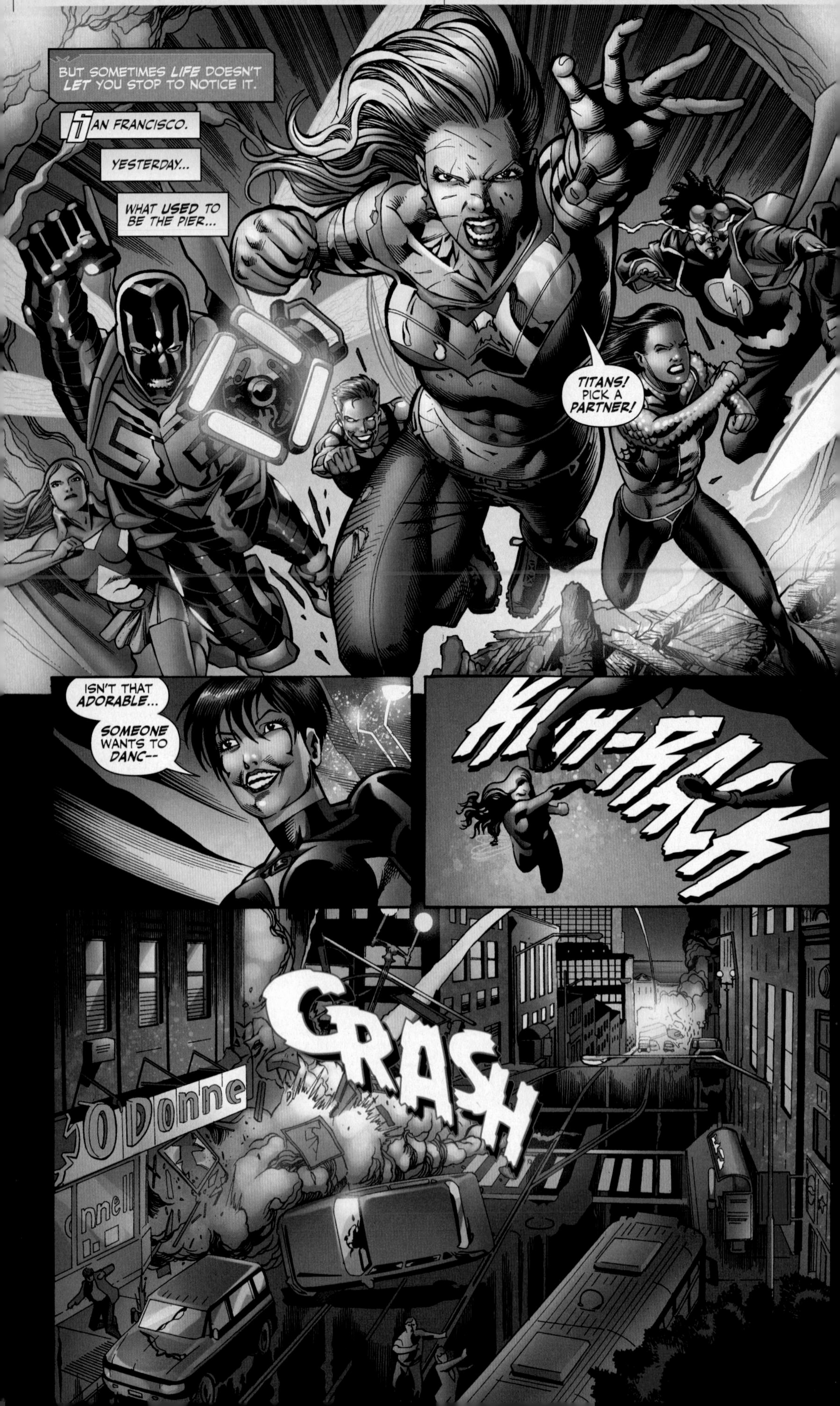
BUT SOMETIMES LIFE DOESN'T LET YOU STOP TO NOTICE IT.
SAN FRANCISCO.
YESTERDAY...
WHAT USED TO BE THE PIER...
TITANS! PICK A PARTNER!
ISN'T THAT ADORABLE... SOMEONE WANTS TO DANC--
CRASH
ODonne
nnell

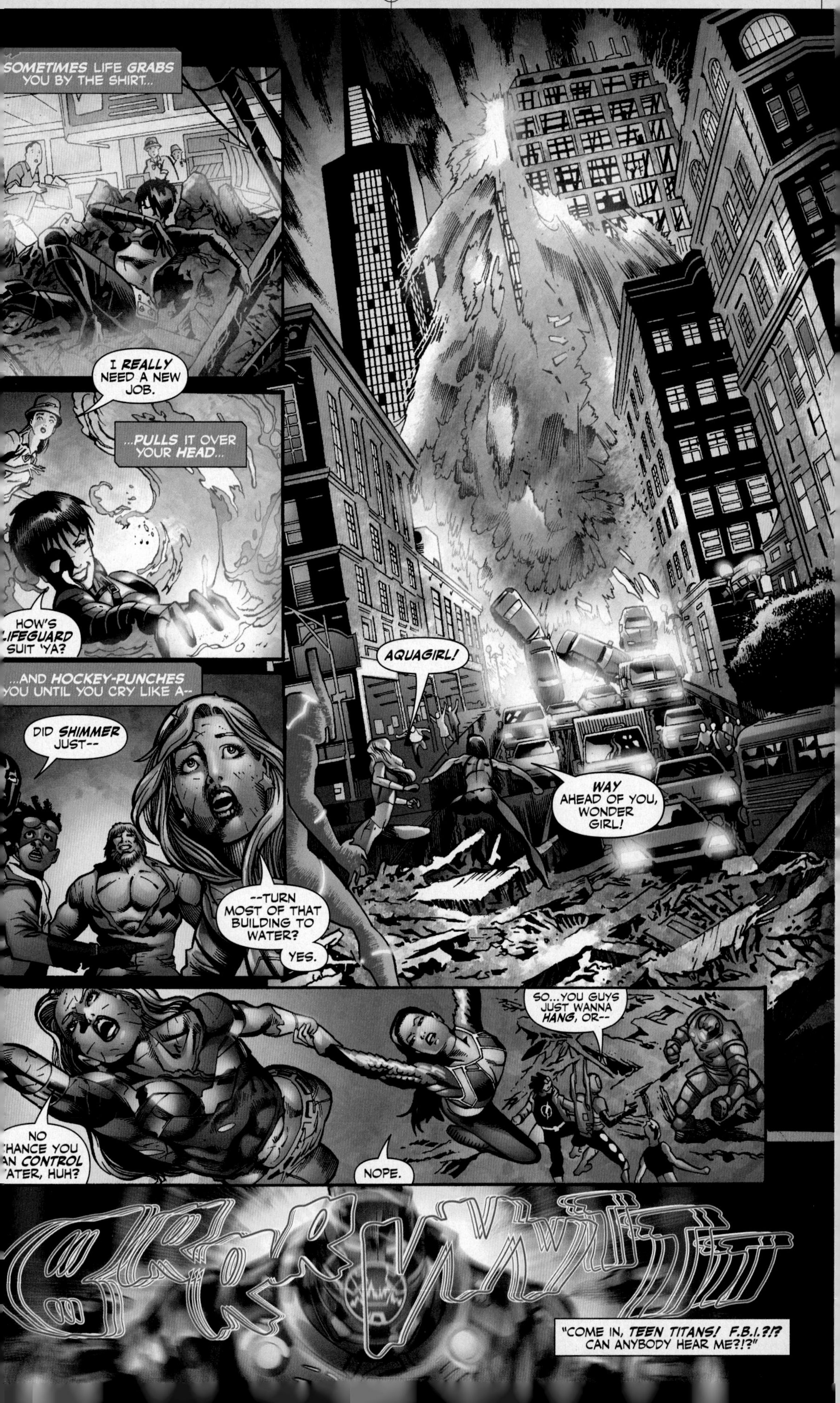
SOMETIMES LIFE GRABS YOU BY THE SHIRT...
I REALLY NEED A NEW JOB.
...PULLS IT OVER YOUR HEAD...
HOW'S LIFEGUARD SUIT 'YA?
...AND HOCKEY-PUNCHES YOU UNTIL YOU CRY LIKE A--
AQUAGIRL!
DID SHIMMER JUST--
WAY AHEAD OF YOU, WONDER GIRL!
--TURN MOST OF THAT BUILDING TO WATER?
YES.
NO CHANCE YOU CAN CONTROL WATER, HUH?
NOPE.
SO...YOU GUYS JUST WANNA HANG, OR--
"COME IN, TEEN TITANS! F.B.I.?!? CAN ANYBODY HEAR ME?!?"

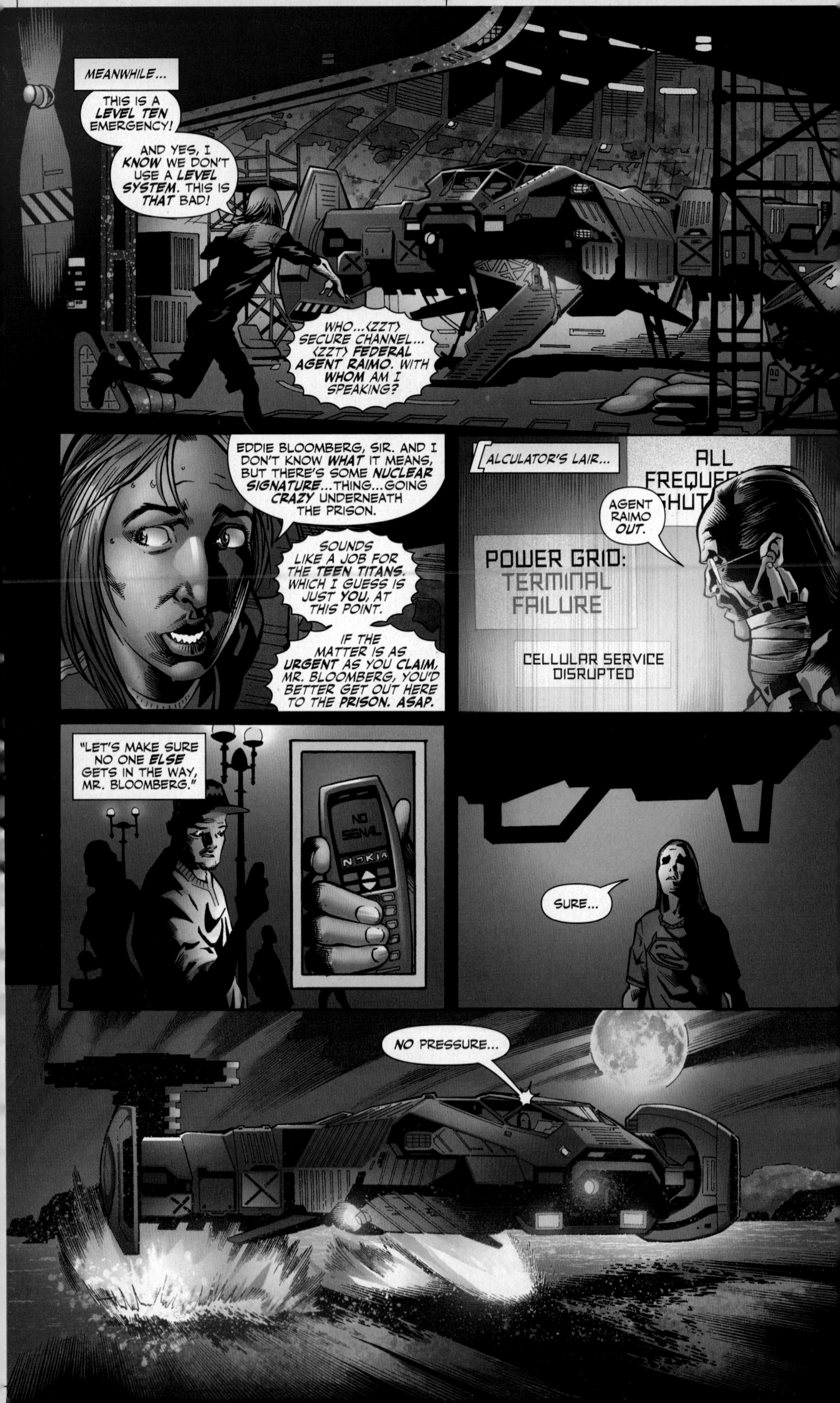
MEANWHILE...
THIS IS A LEVEL TEN EMERGENCY!
AND YES, I KNOW WE DON'T USE A LEVEL SYSTEM. THIS IS THAT BAD!
WHO...⟨ZZT⟩ SECURE CHANNEL... ⟨ZZT⟩ FEDERAL AGENT RAIMO. WITH WHOM AM I SPEAKING?
EDDIE BLOOMBERG, SIR. AND I DON'T KNOW WHAT IT MEANS, BUT THERE'S SOME NUCLEAR SIGNATURE...THING...GOING CRAZY UNDERNEATH THE PRISON.
SOUNDS LIKE A JOB FOR THE TEEN TITANS. WHICH I GUESS IS JUST YOU, AT THIS POINT.
IF THE MATTER IS AS URGENT AS YOU CLAIM, MR. BLOOMBERG, YOU'D BETTER GET OUT HERE TO THE PRISON. ASAP.
ALCULATOR'S LAIR...
ALL
AGENT RAIMO OUT.
POWER GRID: TERMINAL FAILURE
CELLULAR SERVICE DISRUPTED
"LET'S MAKE SURE NO ONE ELSE GETS IN THE WAY, MR. BLOOMBERG."
NO SIGNAL
NOKIA
SURE...
NO PRESSURE...

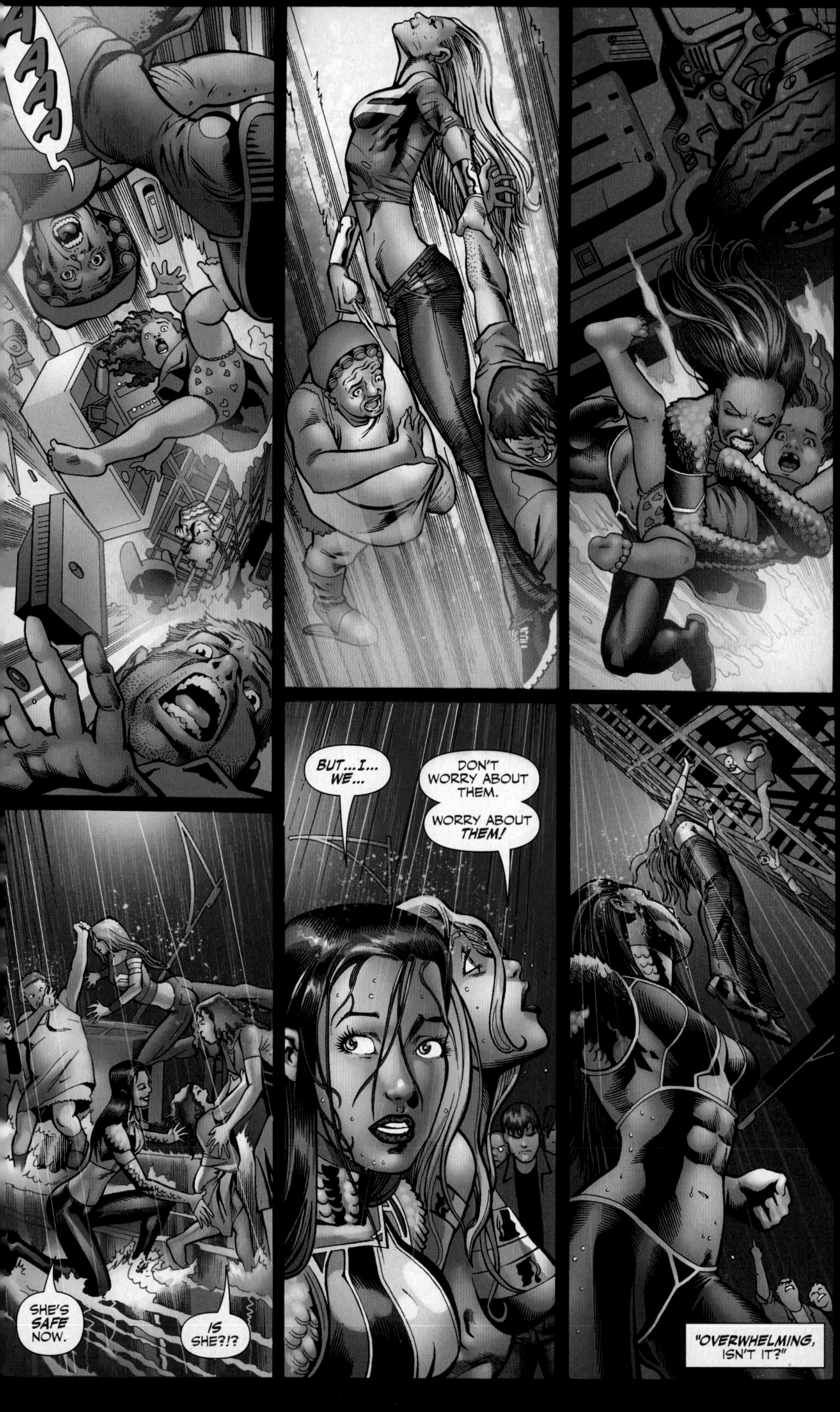
AAAAA
BUT... I... WE...
DON'T WORRY ABOUT THEM.
WORRY ABOUT THEM!
SHE'S SAFE NOW.
IS SHE?!?
"OVERWHELMING, ISN'T IT?"

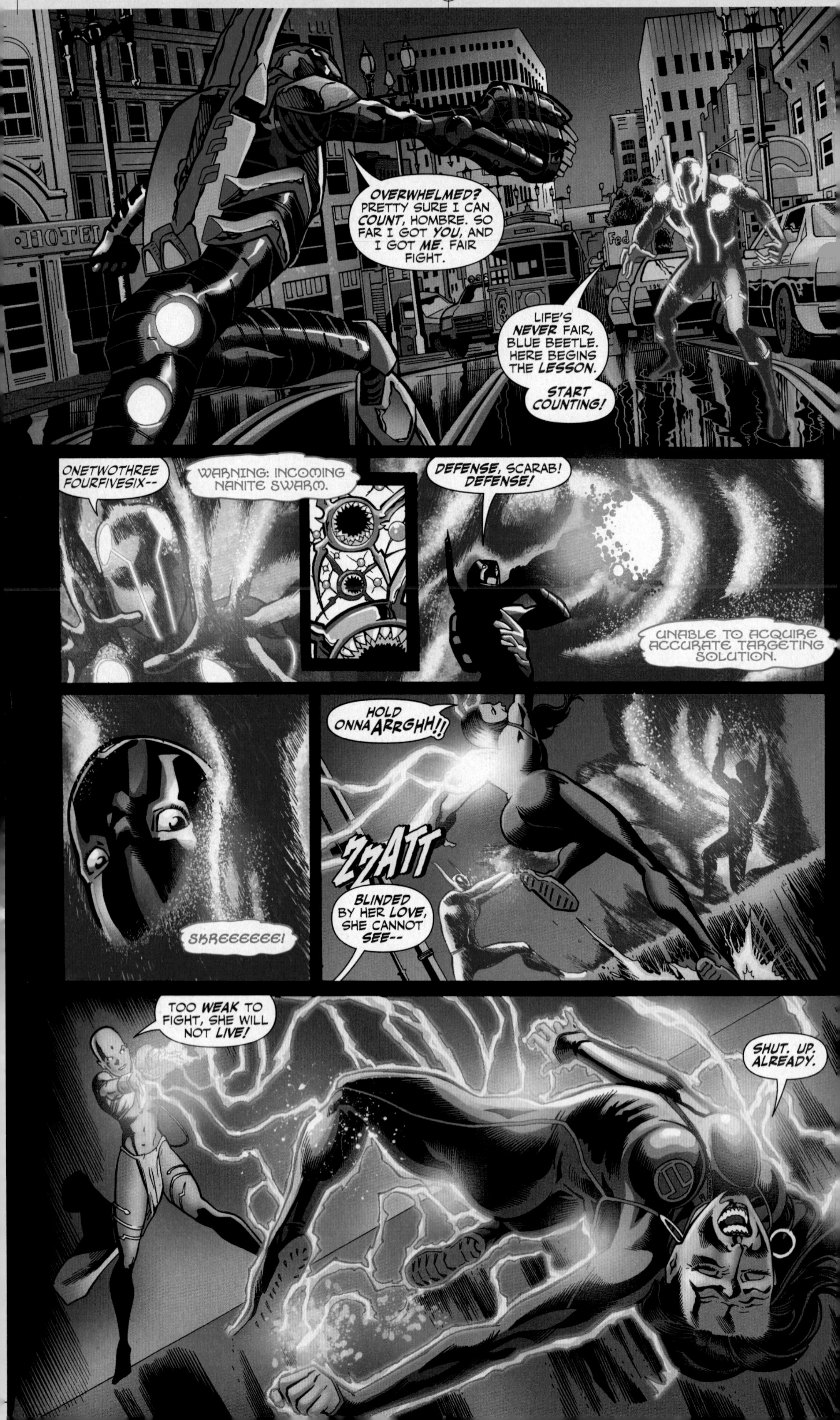
OVERWHELMED? PRETTY SURE I CAN COUNT, HOMBRE. SO FAR I GOT YOU, AND I GOT ME. FAIR FIGHT.
LIFE'S NEVER FAIR, BLUE BEETLE. HERE BEGINS THE LESSON.
START COUNTING!
ONETWOTHREE FOURFIVESIX--
WARNING: INCOMING NANITE SWARM.
DEFENSE, SCARAB! DEFENSE!
UNABLE TO ACQUIRE ACCURATE TARGETING SOLUTION.
SKREEEEEEE!
HOLD ONNA ARRGHH!!
ZZATT
BLINDED BY HER LOVE, SHE CANNOT SEE--
TOO WEAK TO FIGHT, SHE WILL NOT LIVE!
SHUT. UP. ALREADY.

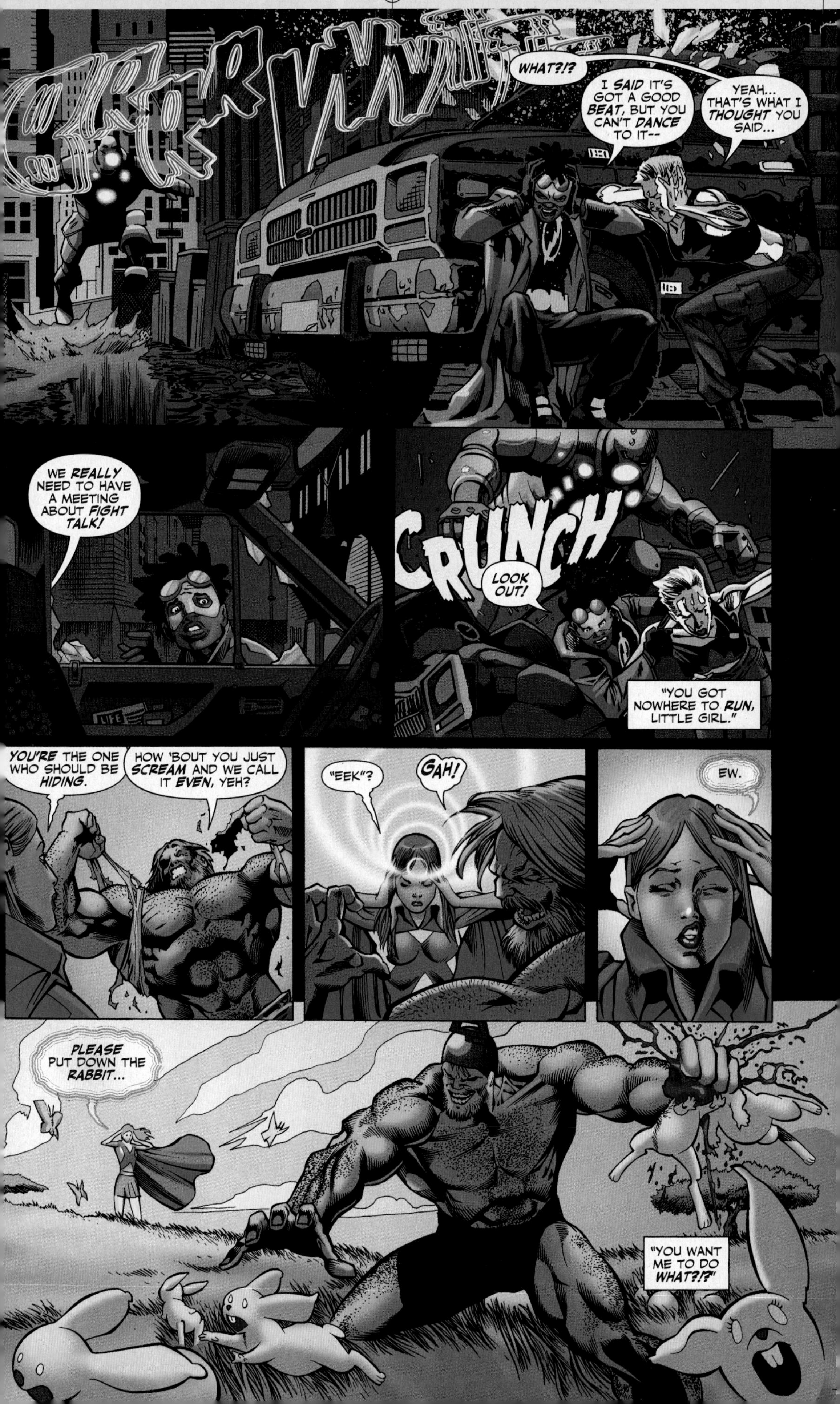
WHAT?!?
I SAID IT'S GOT A GOOD BEAT, BUT YOU CAN'T DANCE TO IT--
YEAH... THAT'S WHAT I THOUGHT YOU SAID...
WE REALLY NEED TO HAVE A MEETING ABOUT FIGHT TALK!
CRUNCH
LOOK OUT!
"YOU GOT NOWHERE TO RUN, LITTLE GIRL."
YOU'RE THE ONE WHO SHOULD BE HIDING.
HOW 'BOUT YOU JUST SCREAM AND WE CALL IT EVEN, YEH?
"EEK"?
GAH!
EW.
PLEASE PUT DOWN THE RABBIT...
"YOU WANT ME TO DO WHAT?!?"

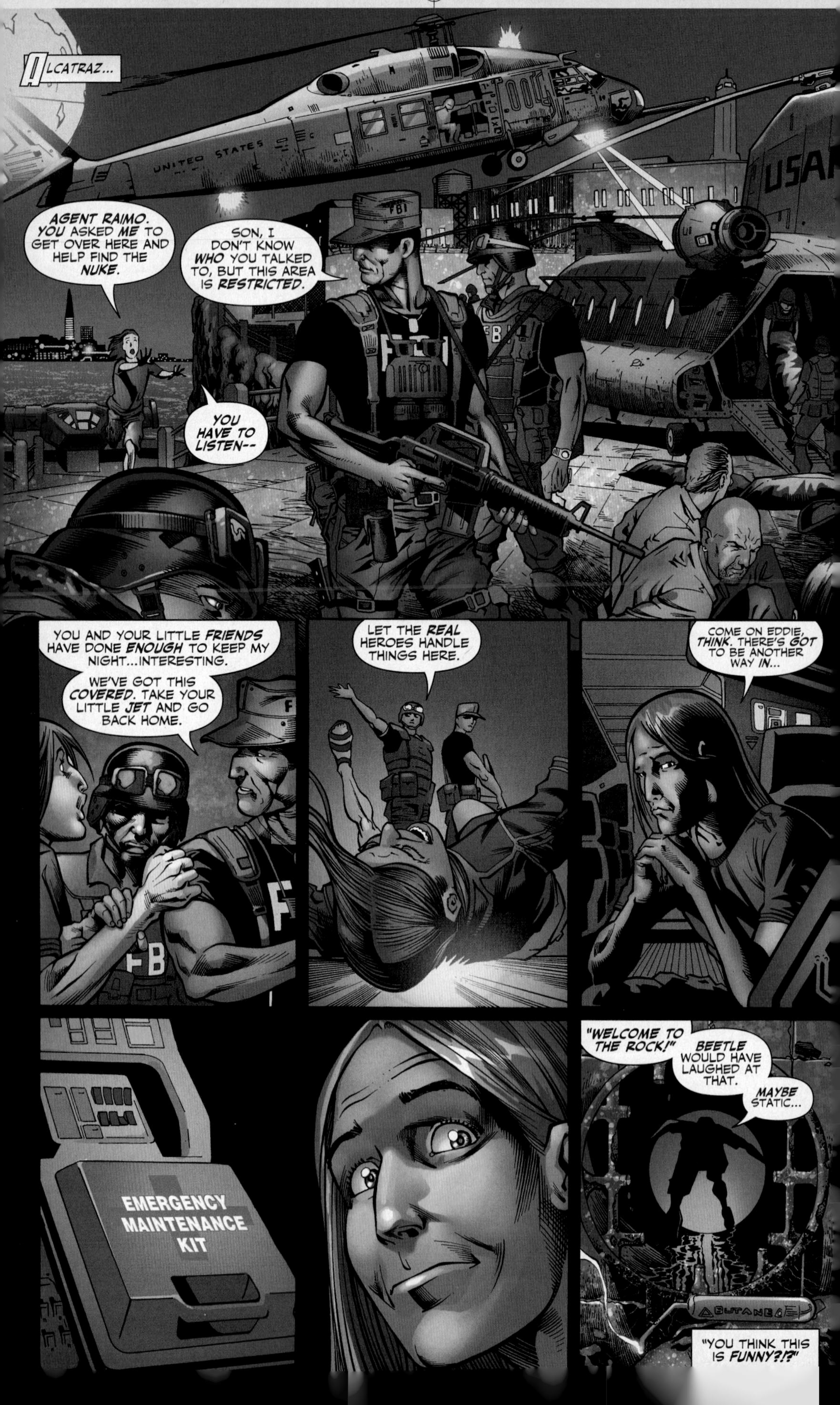

ALCATRAZ...
AGENT RAIMO. YOU ASKED ME TO GET OVER HERE AND HELP FIND THE NUKE.
SON, I DON'T KNOW WHO YOU TALKED TO, BUT THIS AREA IS RESTRICTED.
YOU HAVE TO LISTEN--
UNITED STATES
USA
FBI
YOU AND YOUR LITTLE FRIENDS HAVE DONE ENOUGH TO KEEP MY NIGHT...INTERESTING.
WE'VE GOT THIS COVERED. TAKE YOUR LITTLE JET AND GO BACK HOME.
LET THE REAL HEROES HANDLE THINGS HERE.
COME ON EDDIE, THINK. THERE'S GOT TO BE ANOTHER WAY IN...
EMERGENCY MAINTENANCE KIT
"WELCOME TO THE ROCK!"
BEETLE WOULD HAVE LAUGHED AT THAT.
MAYBE STATIC...
BUTANE
"YOU THINK THIS IS FUNNY?!?"

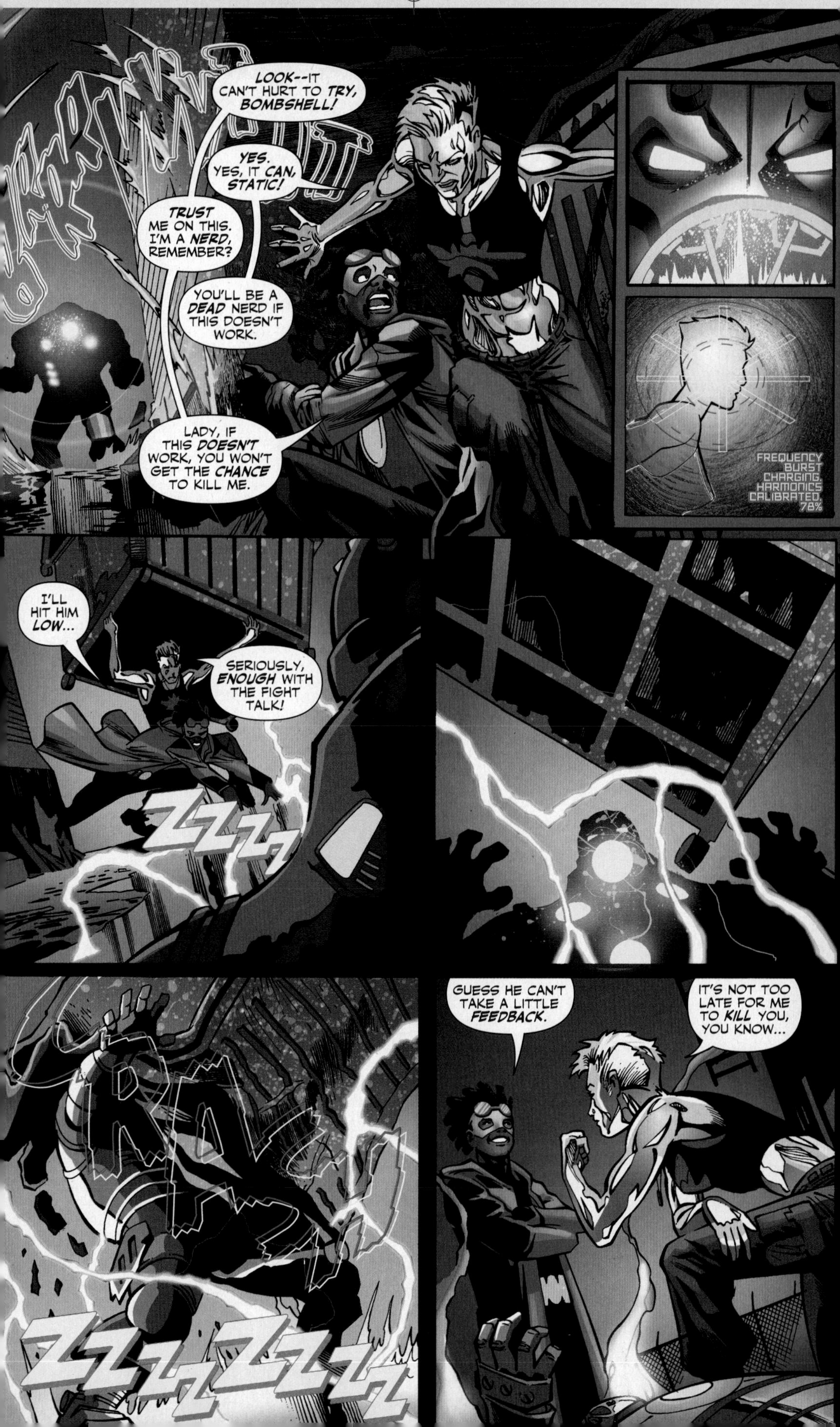
LOOK--IT CAN'T HURT TO TRY, BOMBSHELL!
YES. YES, IT CAN, STATIC!
TRUST ME ON THIS. I'M A NERD, REMEMBER?
YOU'LL BE A DEAD NERD IF THIS DOESN'T WORK.
LADY, IF THIS DOESN'T WORK, YOU WON'T GET THE CHANCE TO KILL ME.
FREQUENCY BURST CHARGING. HARMONICS CALIBRATED. 78%
I'LL HIT HIM LOW...
SERIOUSLY, ENOUGH WITH THE FIGHT TALK!
GUESS HE CAN'T TAKE A LITTLE FEEDBACK.
IT'S NOT TOO LATE FOR ME TO KILL YOU, YOU KNOW...

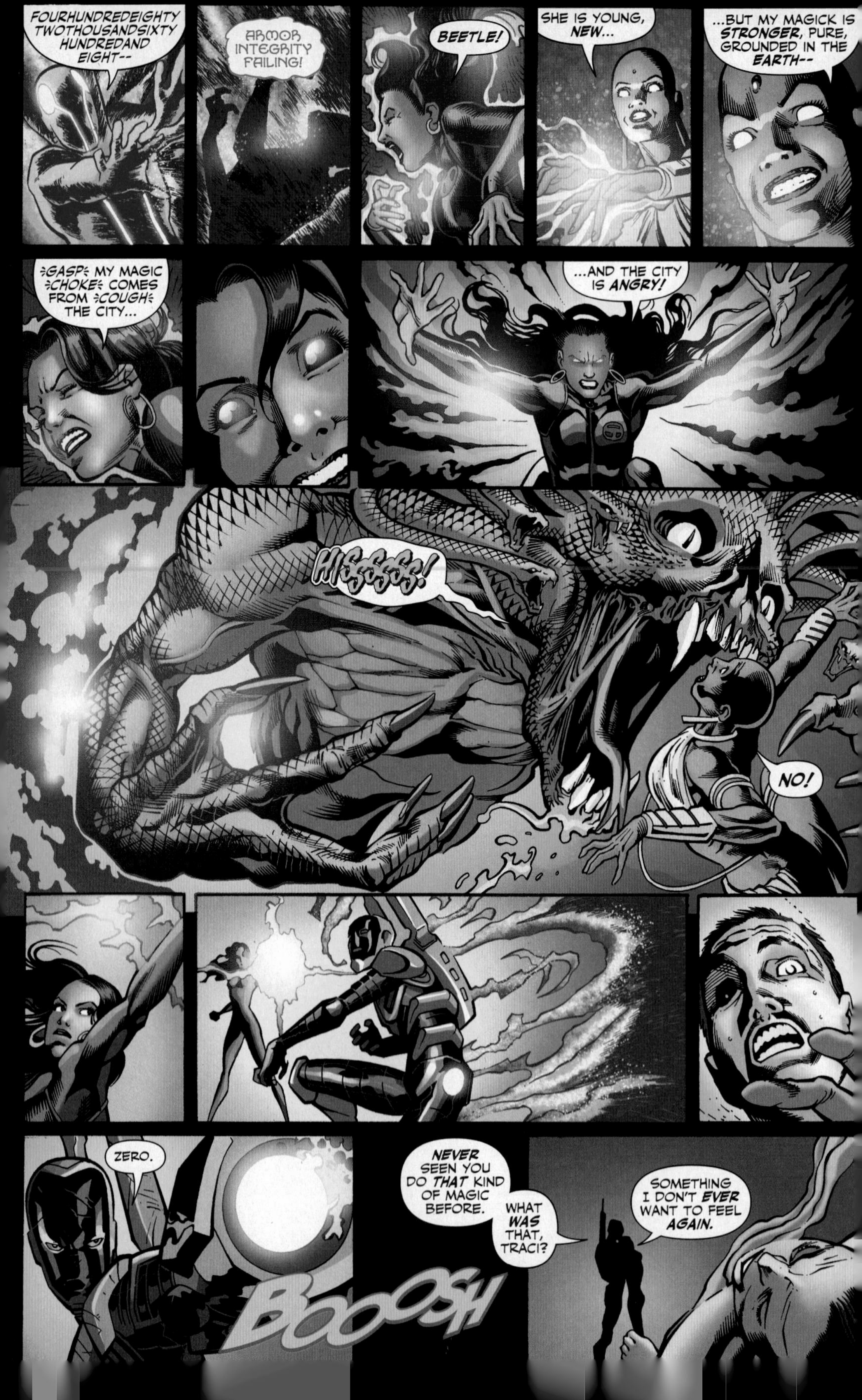
FOURHUNDREDEIGHTY TWOTHOUSANDSIXTY HUNDREDAND EIGHT--
ARMOR INTEGRITY FAILING!
BEETLE!
SHE IS YOUNG, NEW...
...BUT MY MAGICK IS STRONGER, PURE, GROUNDED IN THE EARTH--
GASP MY MAGIC *CHOKE* COMES FROM *COUGH* THE CITY...
...AND THE CITY IS ANGRY!
HISSSSSS!
NO!
ZERO.
BOOOSH
NEVER SEEN YOU DO THAT KIND OF MAGIC BEFORE.
WHAT WAS THAT, TRACI?
SOMETHING I DON'T EVER WANT TO FEEL AGAIN.

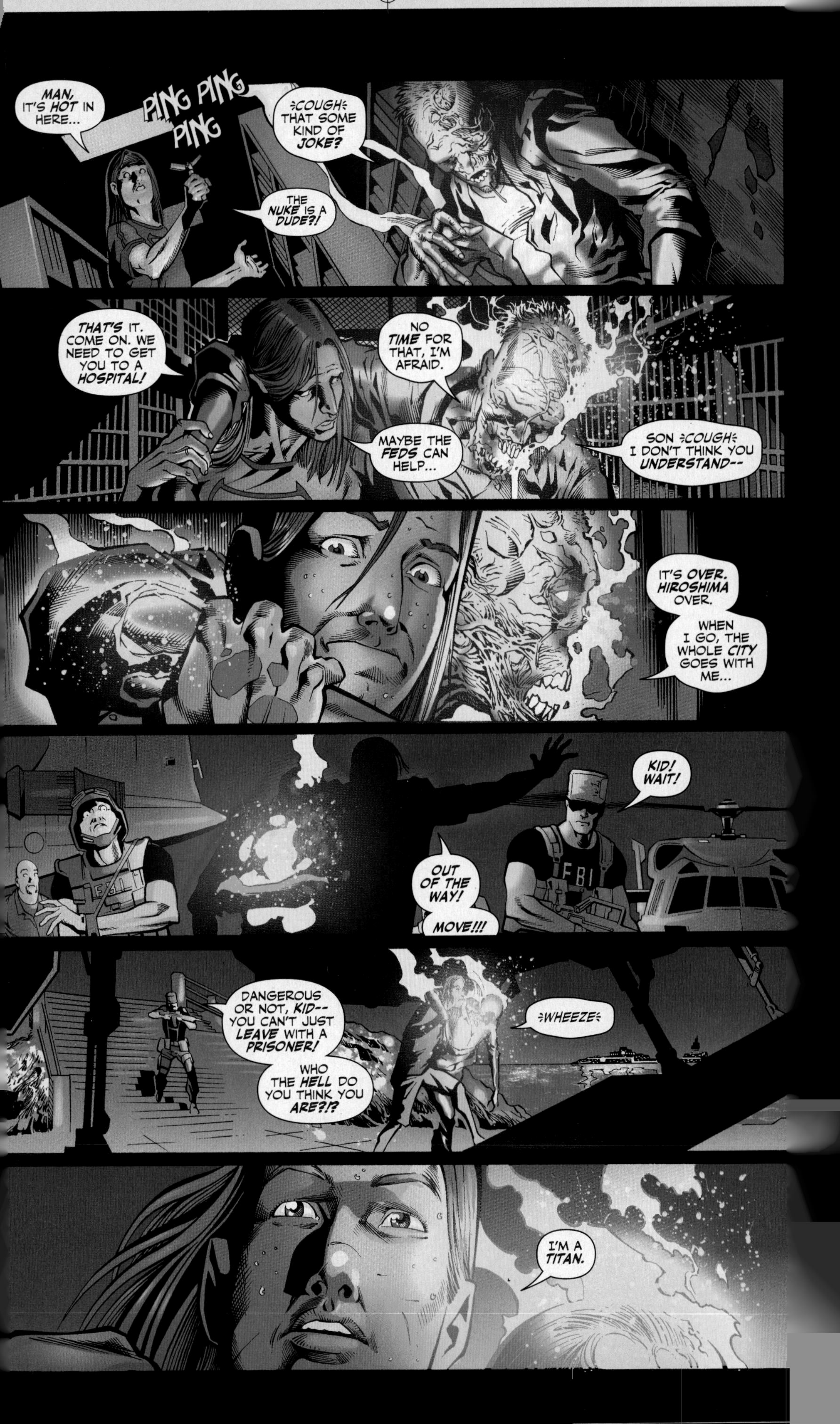

MAN, IT'S HOT IN HERE...
PING PING PING
≷COUGH≶ THAT SOME KIND OF JOKE?
THE NUKE IS A DUDE?!
THAT'S IT. COME ON. WE NEED TO GET YOU TO A HOSPITAL!
NO TIME FOR THAT, I'M AFRAID.
MAYBE THE FEDS CAN HELP...
SON ≷COUGH≶ I DON'T THINK YOU UNDERSTAND--
IT'S OVER. HIROSHIMA OVER.
WHEN I GO, THE WHOLE CITY GOES WITH ME...
KID! WAIT!
OUT OF THE WAY!
MOVE!!!
FBI
FBI
DANGEROUS OR NOT, KID-- YOU CAN'T JUST LEAVE WITH A PRISONER!
WHO THE HELL DO YOU THINK YOU ARE?!?
≷WHEEZE≶
I'M A TITAN.

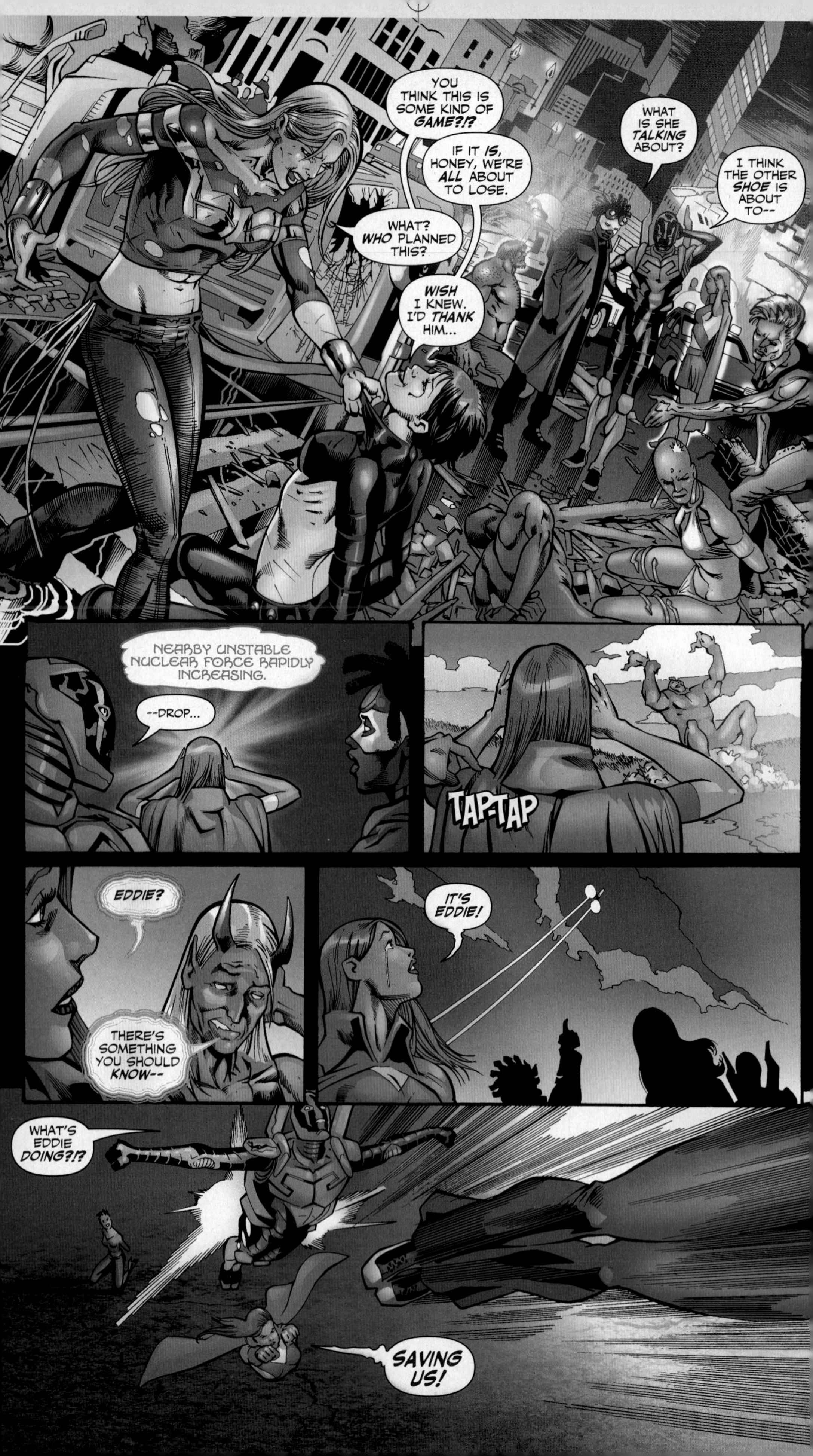

YOU THINK THIS IS SOME KIND OF GAME?!?
IF IT IS, HONEY, WE'RE ALL ABOUT TO LOSE.
WHAT? WHO PLANNED THIS?
WISH I KNEW. I'D THANK HIM...
WHAT IS SHE TALKING ABOUT?
I THINK THE OTHER SHOE IS ABOUT TO--
NEARBY UNSTABLE NUCLEAR FORCE RAPIDLY INCREASING.
--DROP...
TAP-TAP
EDDIE?
THERE'S SOMETHING YOU SHOULD KNOW--
IT'S EDDIE!
WHAT'S EDDIE DOING?!?
SAVING US!

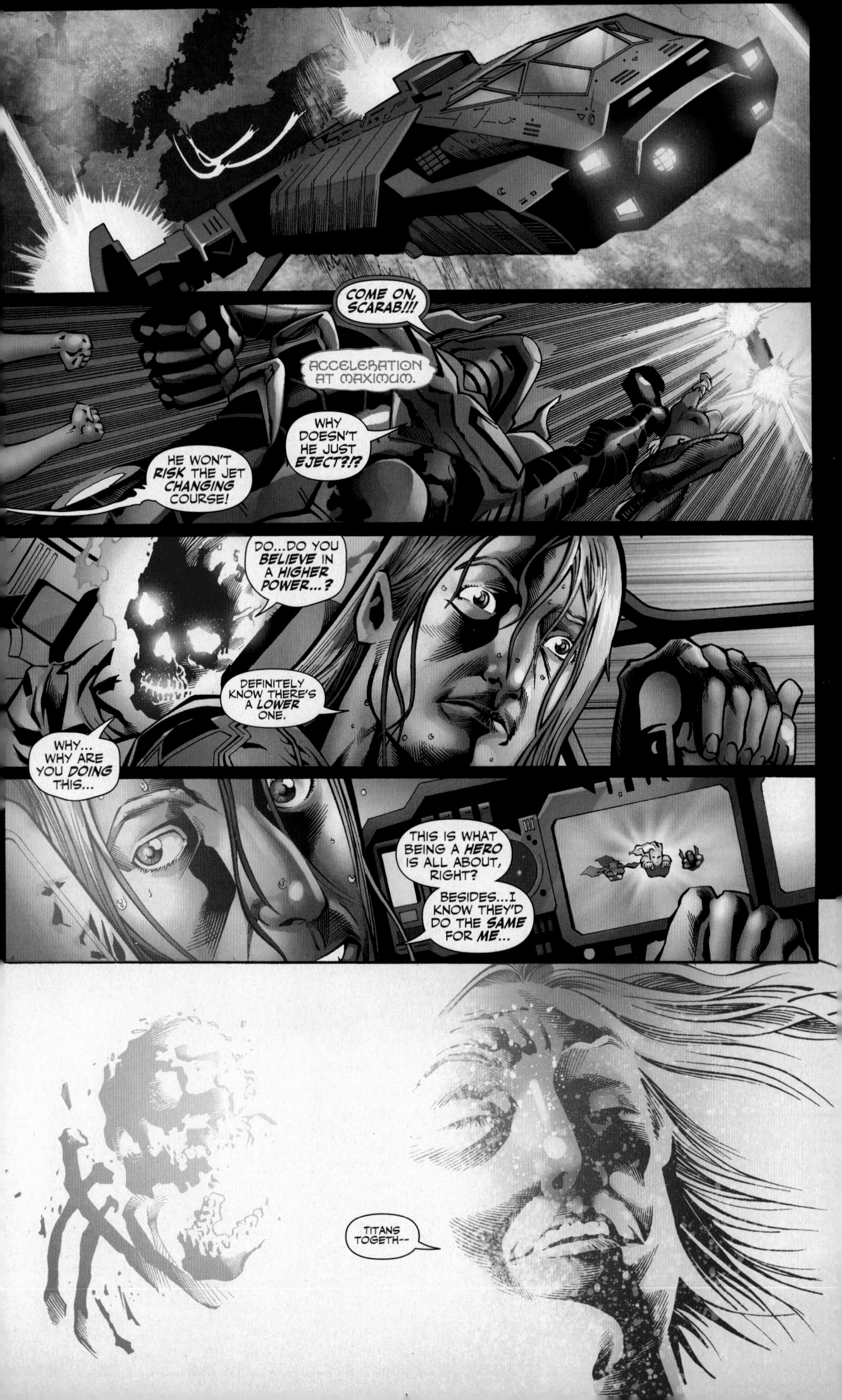
COME ON, SCARAB!!!
ACCELERATION AT MAXIMUM.
WHY DOESN'T HE JUST EJECT?!?
HE WON'T RISK THE JET CHANGING COURSE!
DO...DO YOU BELIEVE IN A HIGHER POWER...?
DEFINITELY KNOW THERE'S A LOWER ONE.
WHY... WHY ARE YOU DOING THIS...
THIS IS WHAT BEING A HERO IS ALL ABOUT, RIGHT?
BESIDES...I KNOW THEY'D DO THE SAME FOR ME...
TITANS TOGETH--

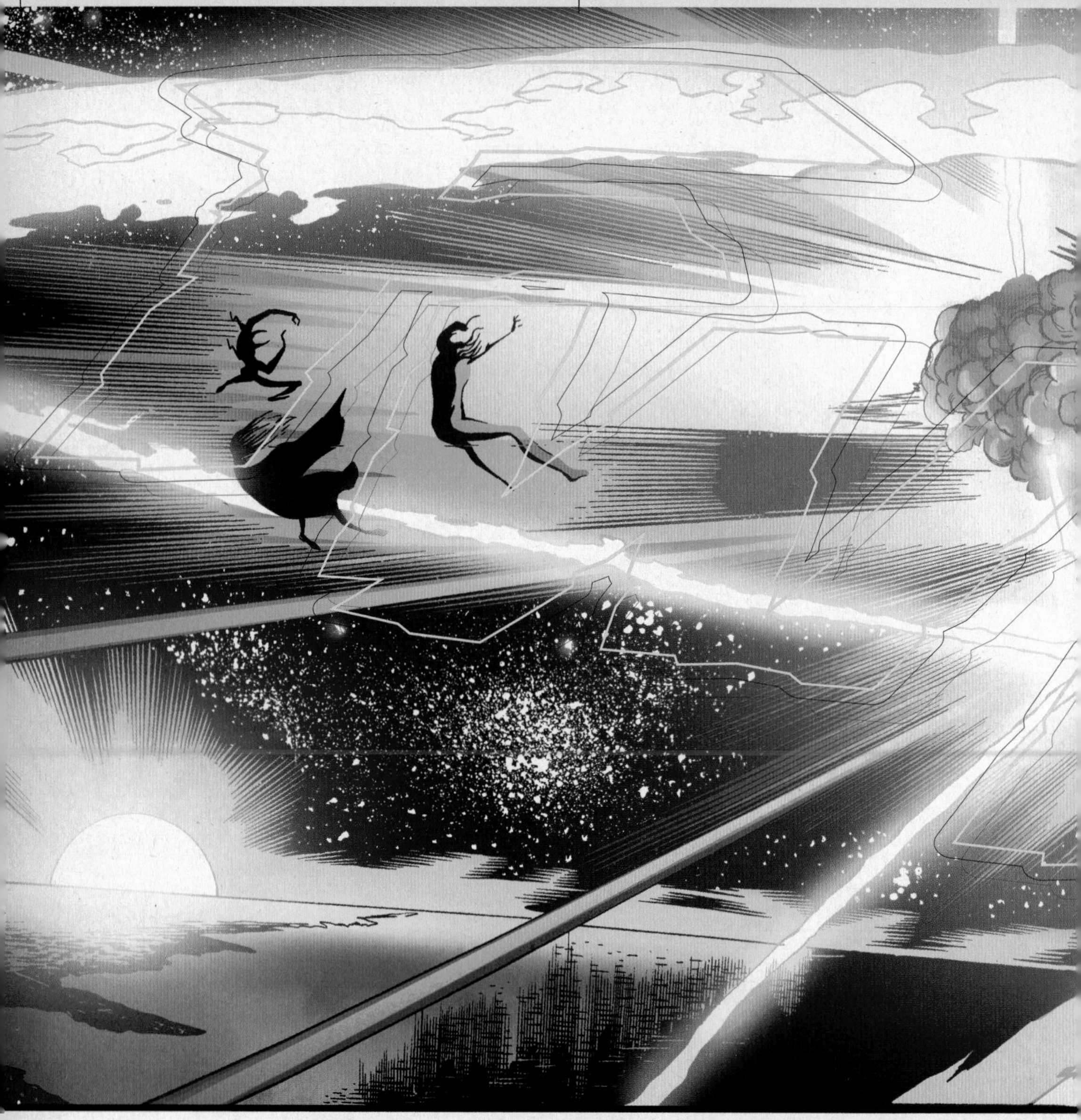

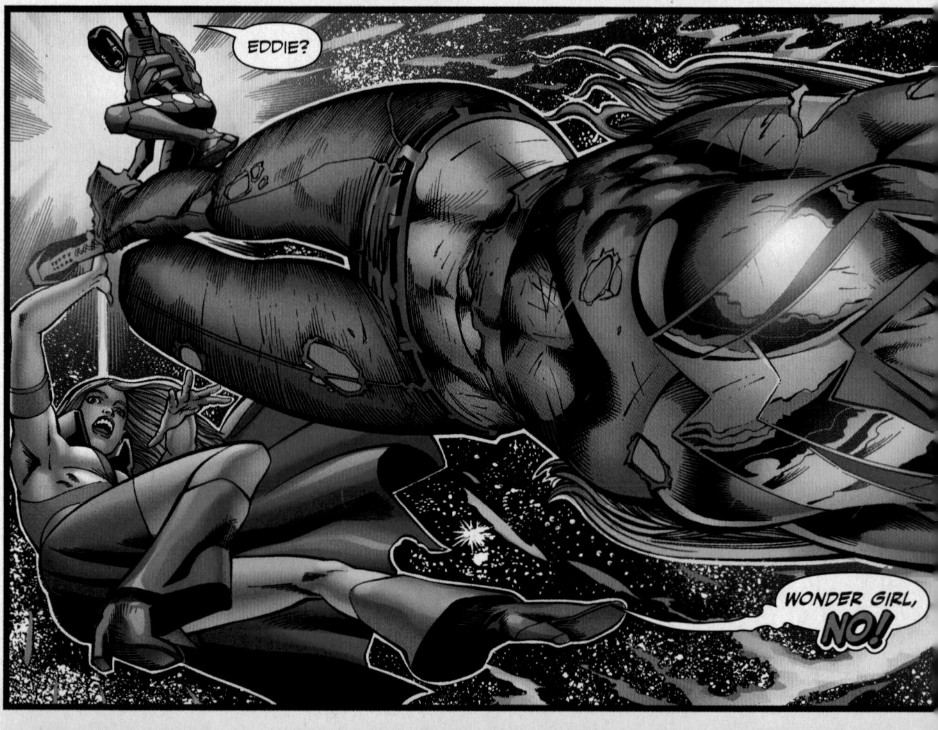
EDDIE?
WONDER GIRL, NO!

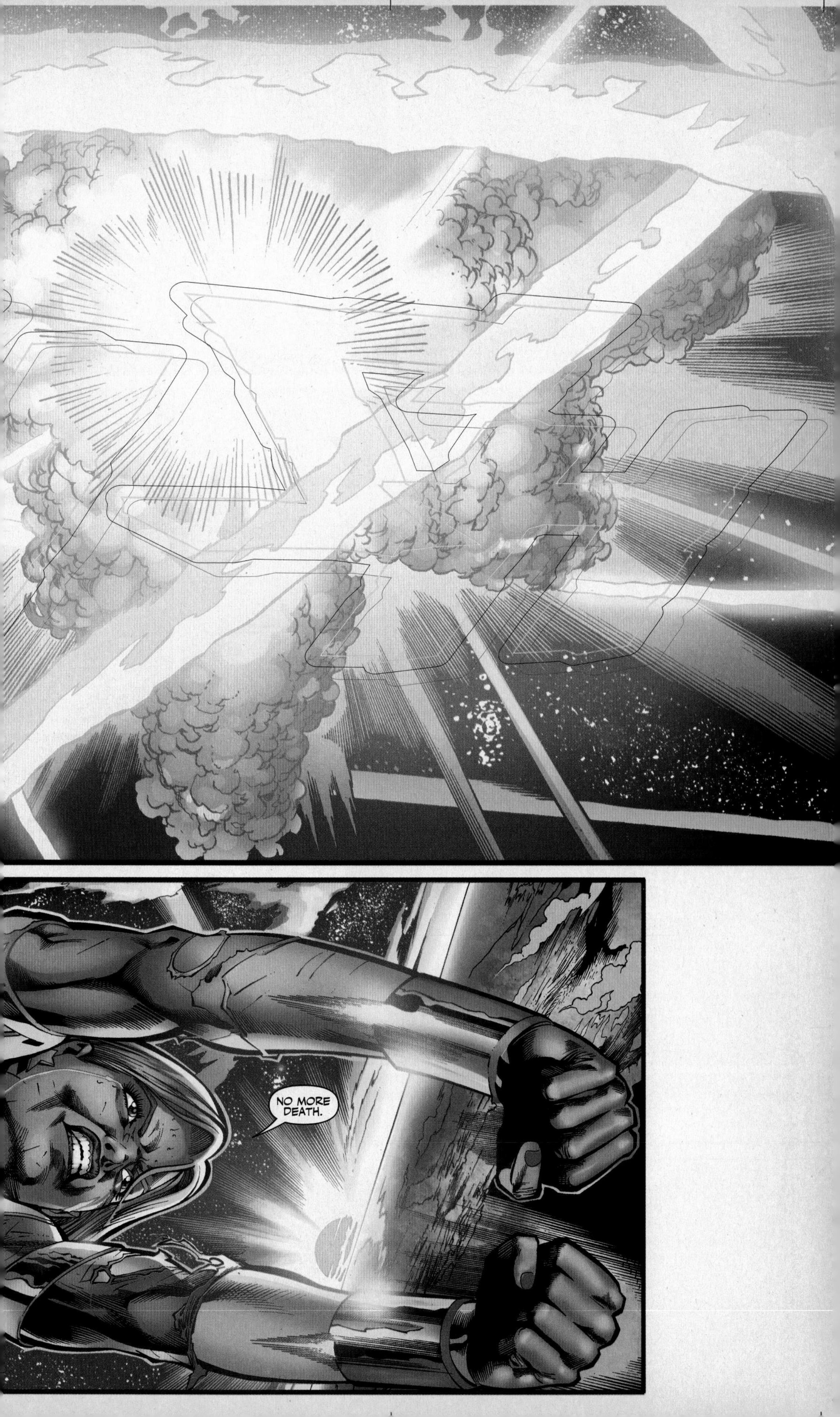
NO MORE DEATH.

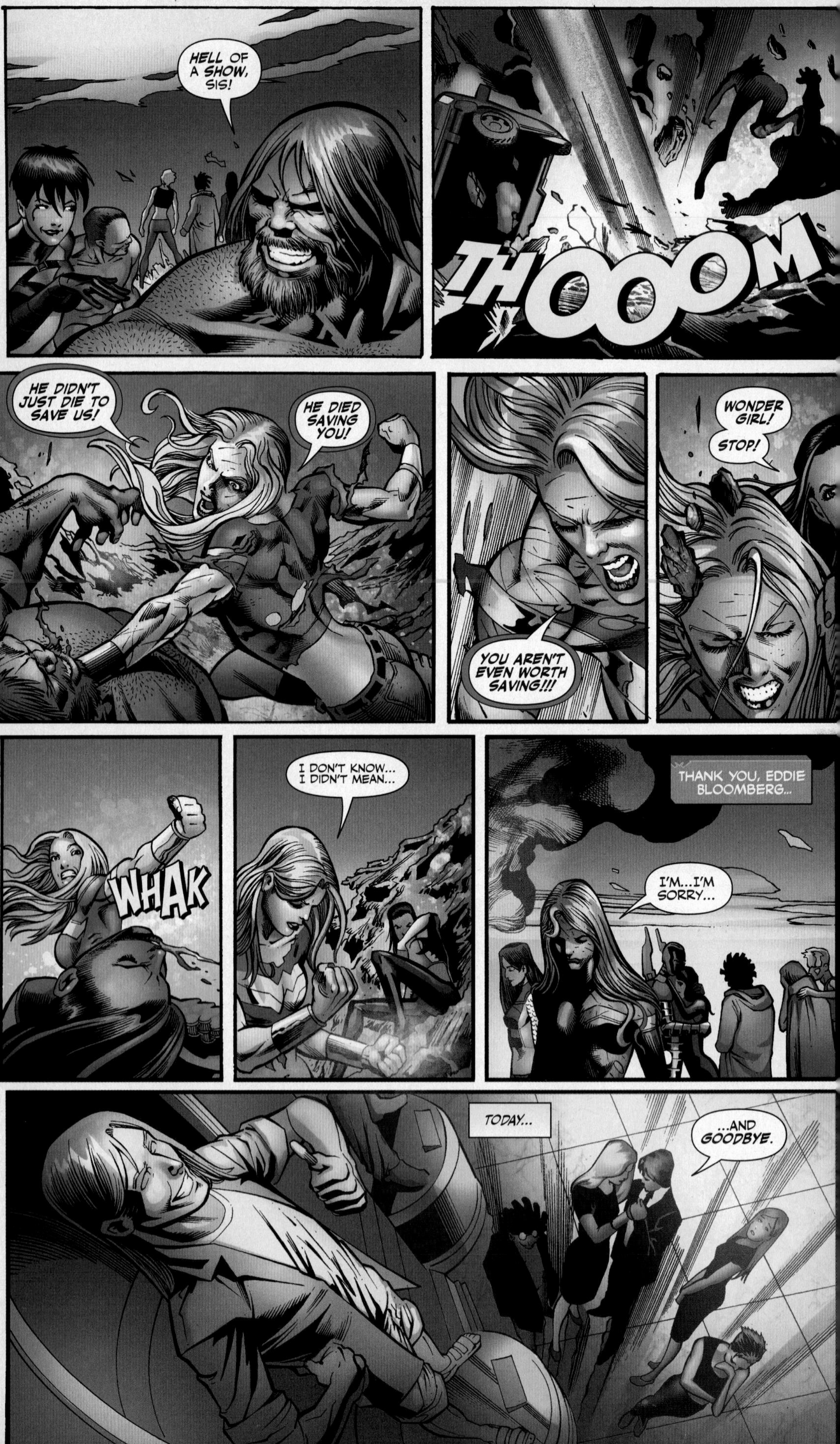
HELL OF A SHOW, SIS!
THOOOM
HE DIDN'T JUST DIE TO SAVE US!
HE DIED SAVING YOU!
YOU AREN'T EVEN WORTH SAVING!!!
WONDER GIRL!
STOP!
WHAK
I DON'T KNOW... I DIDN'T MEAN...
THANK YOU, EDDIE BLOOMBERG...
I'M...I'M SORRY...
TODAY...
...AND GOODBYE.

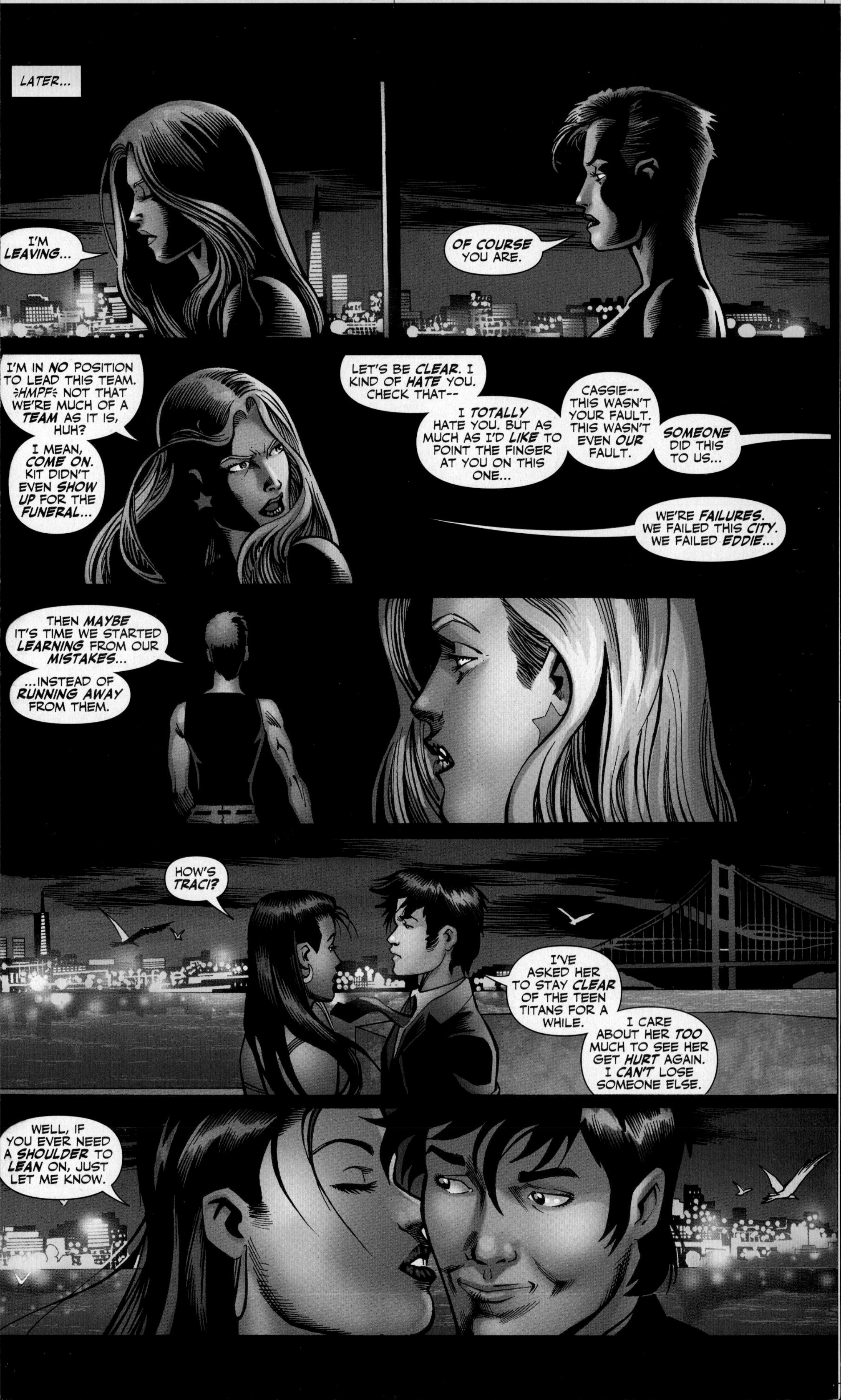
LATER...
I'M LEAVING...
OF COURSE YOU ARE.
I'M IN NO POSITION TO LEAD THIS TEAM. *HMPF* NOT THAT WE'RE MUCH OF A TEAM AS IT IS, HUH?
I MEAN, COME ON. KIT DIDN'T EVEN SHOW UP FOR THE FUNERAL...
LET'S BE CLEAR. I KIND OF HATE YOU. CHECK THAT--
I TOTALLY HATE YOU. BUT AS MUCH AS I'D LIKE TO POINT THE FINGER AT YOU ON THIS ONE...
CASSIE-- THIS WASN'T YOUR FAULT. THIS WASN'T EVEN OUR FAULT.
SOMEONE DID THIS TO US...
WE'RE FAILURES. WE FAILED THIS CITY. WE FAILED EDDIE...
THEN MAYBE IT'S TIME WE STARTED LEARNING FROM OUR MISTAKES...
...INSTEAD OF RUNNING AWAY FROM THEM.
HOW'S TRACI?
I'VE ASKED HER TO STAY CLEAR OF THE TEEN TITANS FOR A WHILE.
I CARE ABOUT HER TOO MUCH TO SEE HER GET HURT AGAIN. I CAN'T LOSE SOMEONE ELSE.
WELL, IF YOU EVER NEED A SHOULDER TO LEAN ON, JUST LET ME KNOW.

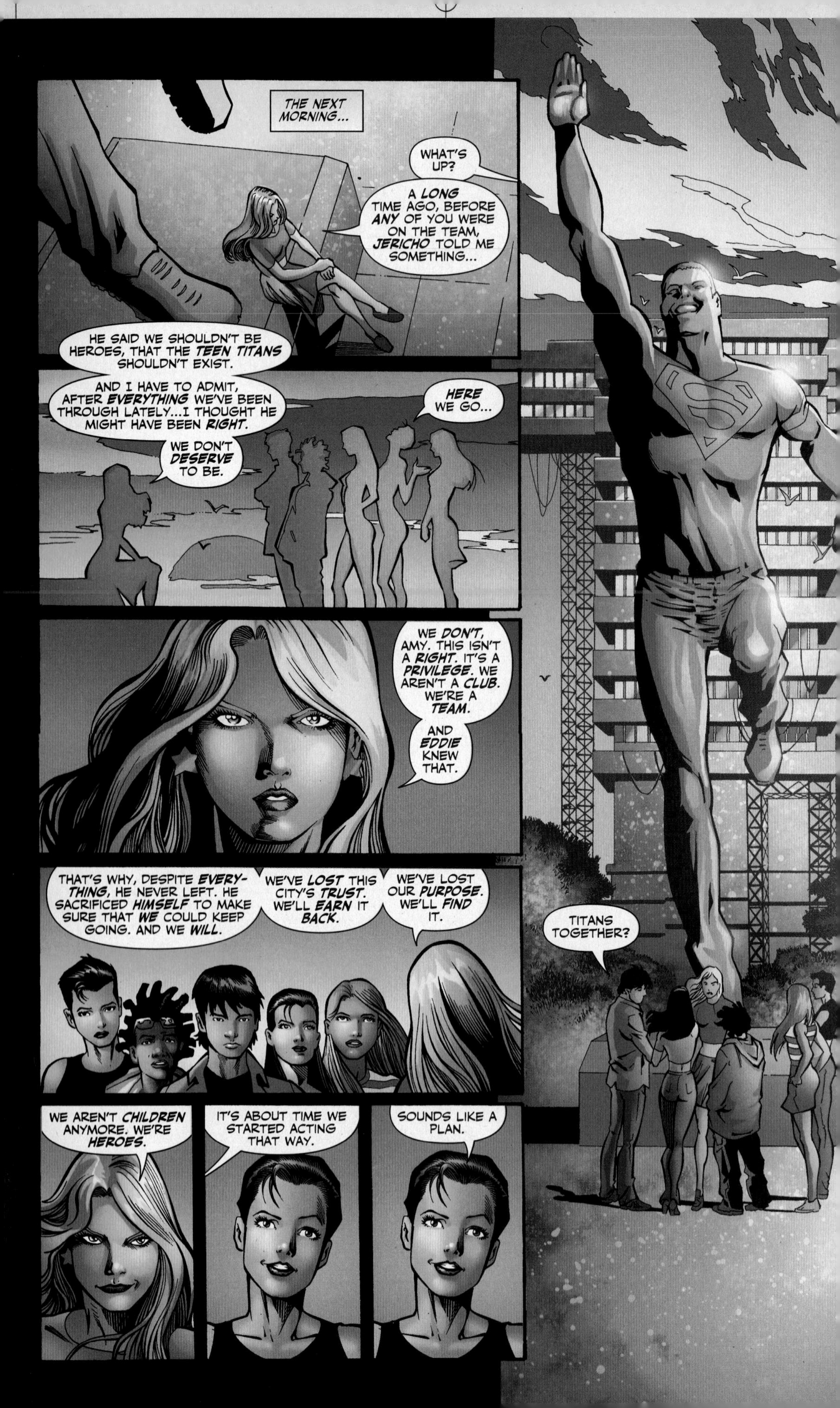
THE NEXT MORNING...
WHAT'S UP?
A LONG TIME AGO, BEFORE ANY OF YOU WERE ON THE TEAM, JERICHO TOLD ME SOMETHING...
HE SAID WE SHOULDN'T BE HEROES, THAT THE TEEN TITANS SHOULDN'T EXIST.
AND I HAVE TO ADMIT, AFTER EVERYTHING WE'VE BEEN THROUGH LATELY...I THOUGHT HE MIGHT HAVE BEEN RIGHT.
HERE WE GO...
WE DON'T DESERVE TO BE.
WE DON'T, AMY. THIS ISN'T A RIGHT. IT'S A PRIVILEGE. WE AREN'T A CLUB. WE'RE A TEAM.
AND EDDIE KNEW THAT.
THAT'S WHY, DESPITE EVERY-THING, HE NEVER LEFT. HE SACRIFICED HIMSELF TO MAKE SURE THAT WE COULD KEEP GOING. AND WE WILL.
WE'VE LOST THIS CITY'S TRUST. WE'LL EARN IT BACK.
WE'VE LOST OUR PURPOSE. WE'LL FIND IT.
WE AREN'T CHILDREN ANYMORE. WE'RE HEROES.
IT'S ABOUT TIME WE STARTED ACTING THAT WAY.
SOUNDS LIKE A PLAN.
TITANS TOGETHER?

"TITANS TOGETHER!"

CALCULATOR'S LAIR...

"FEARSOME" FIVE, *INDEED.* I'LL RECOMMEND YOU TO MY *FRIENDS.*

LET ME GO! PLEASE!

WHAT DID YOU *DO* TO MY *FRIENDS?!?* WHAT DO YOU *WANT?!?*

WHY, *MARVIN--* I JUST WANT WHAT ANY *FATHER* WANTS...

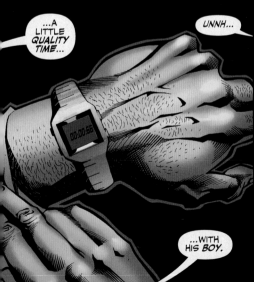

...A LITTLE *QUALITY* TIME...

UNNH...

...WITH HIS *BOY.*

PUH... PLEASE...

DON'T WORRY...

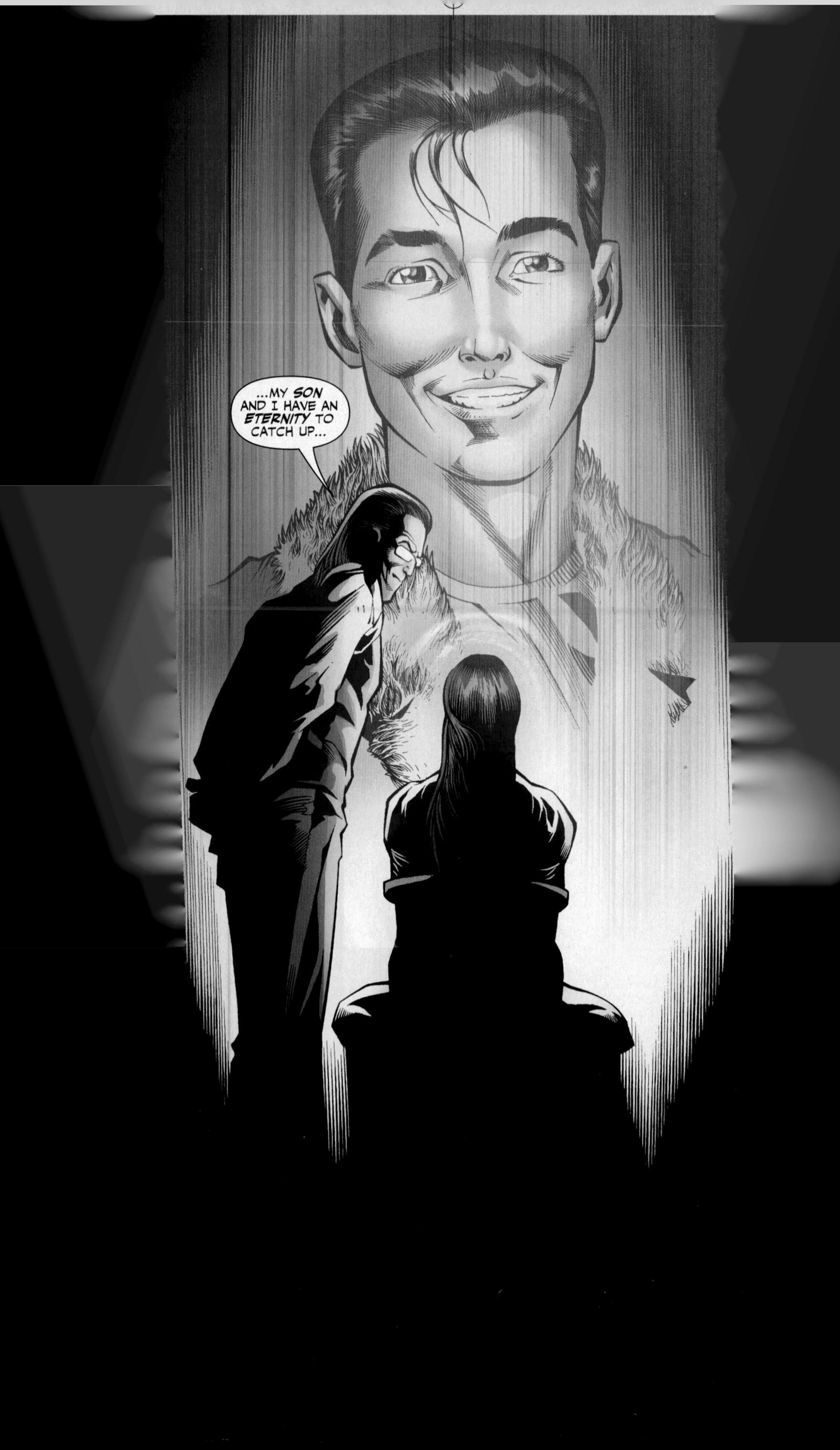
...MY SON AND I HAVE AN ETERNITY TO CATCH UP...

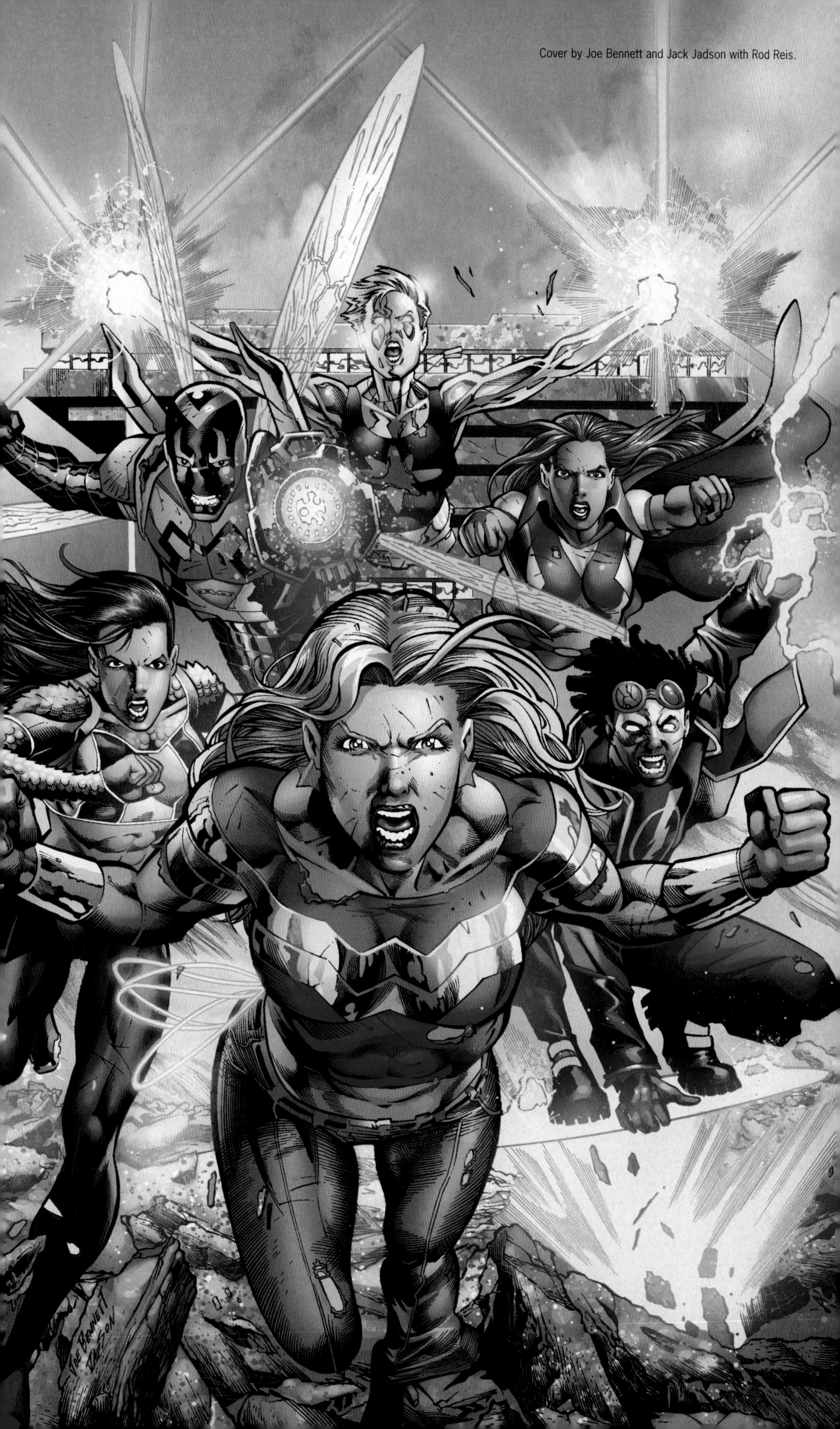

Cover by Joe Bennett and Jack Jadson with Rod Reis.

WYLD THING PART 1

Felicia D. Henderson
Writer

Joe Bennett
Pencils

Jack Jadson
Inks

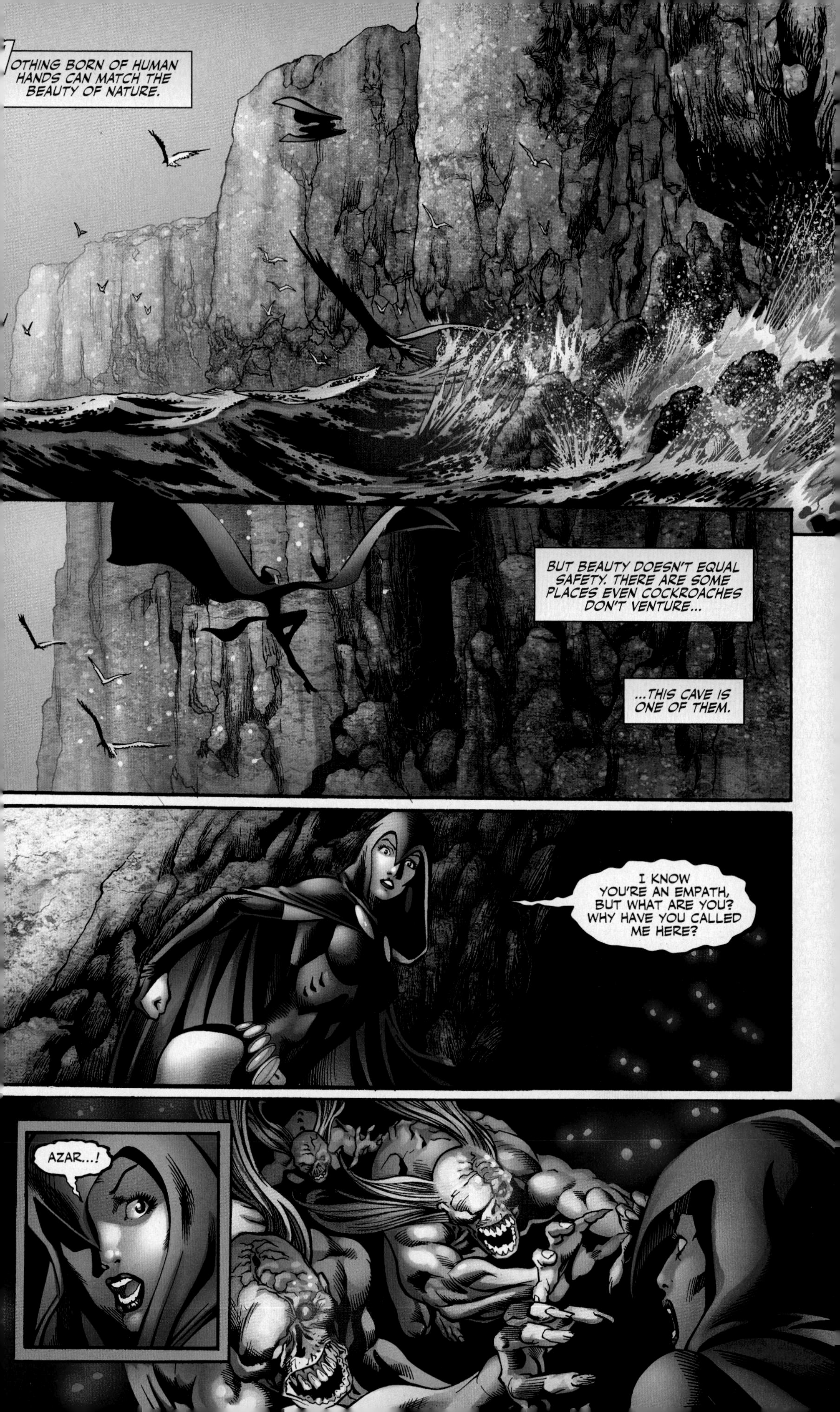
NOTHING BORN OF HUMAN HANDS CAN MATCH THE BEAUTY OF NATURE.
BUT BEAUTY DOESN'T EQUAL SAFETY. THERE ARE SOME PLACES EVEN COCKROACHES DON'T VENTURE...
...THIS CAVE IS ONE OF THEM.
I KNOW YOU'RE AN EMPATH, BUT WHAT ARE YOU? WHY HAVE YOU CALLED ME HERE?
AZAR...!

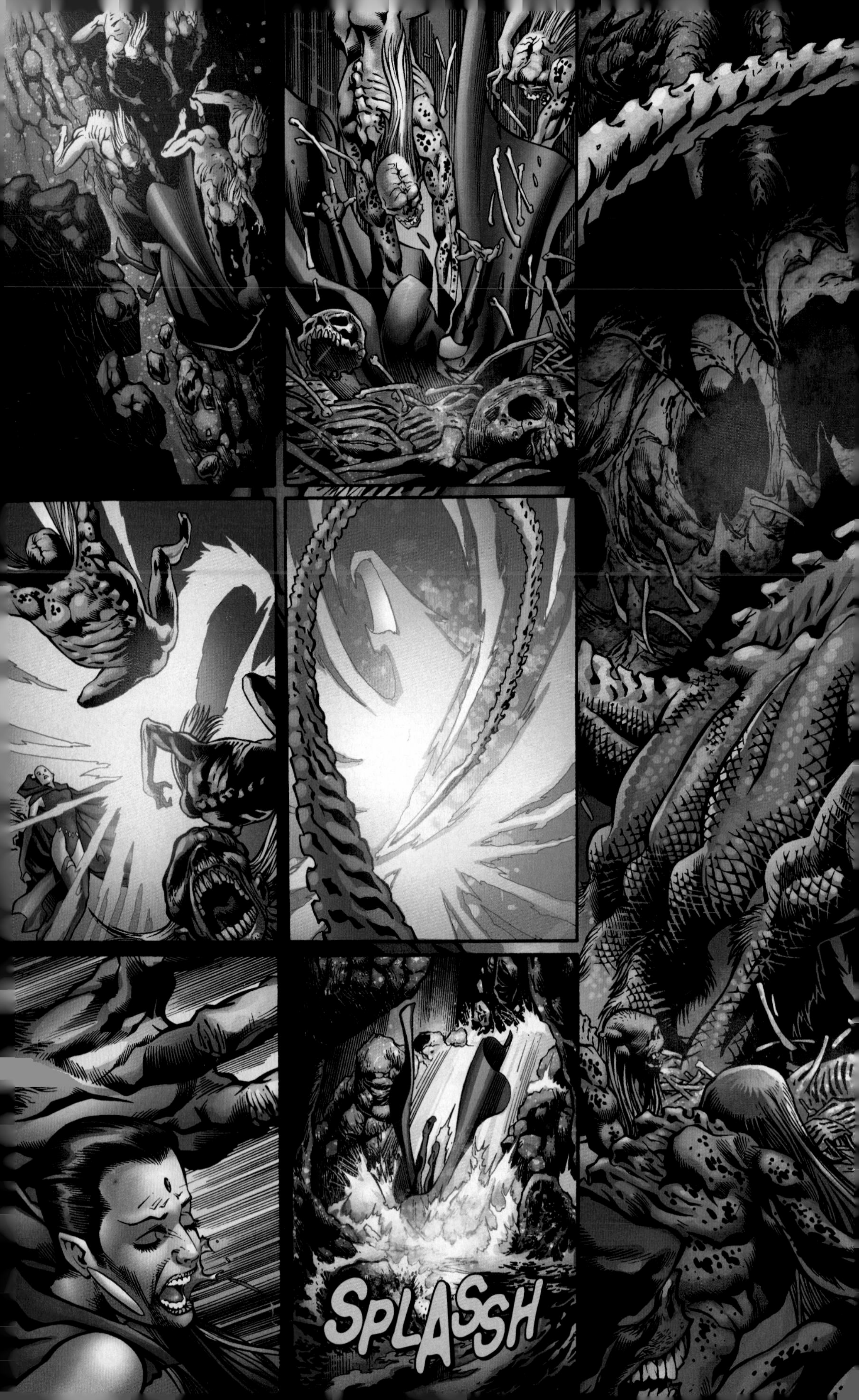
SPLASSH

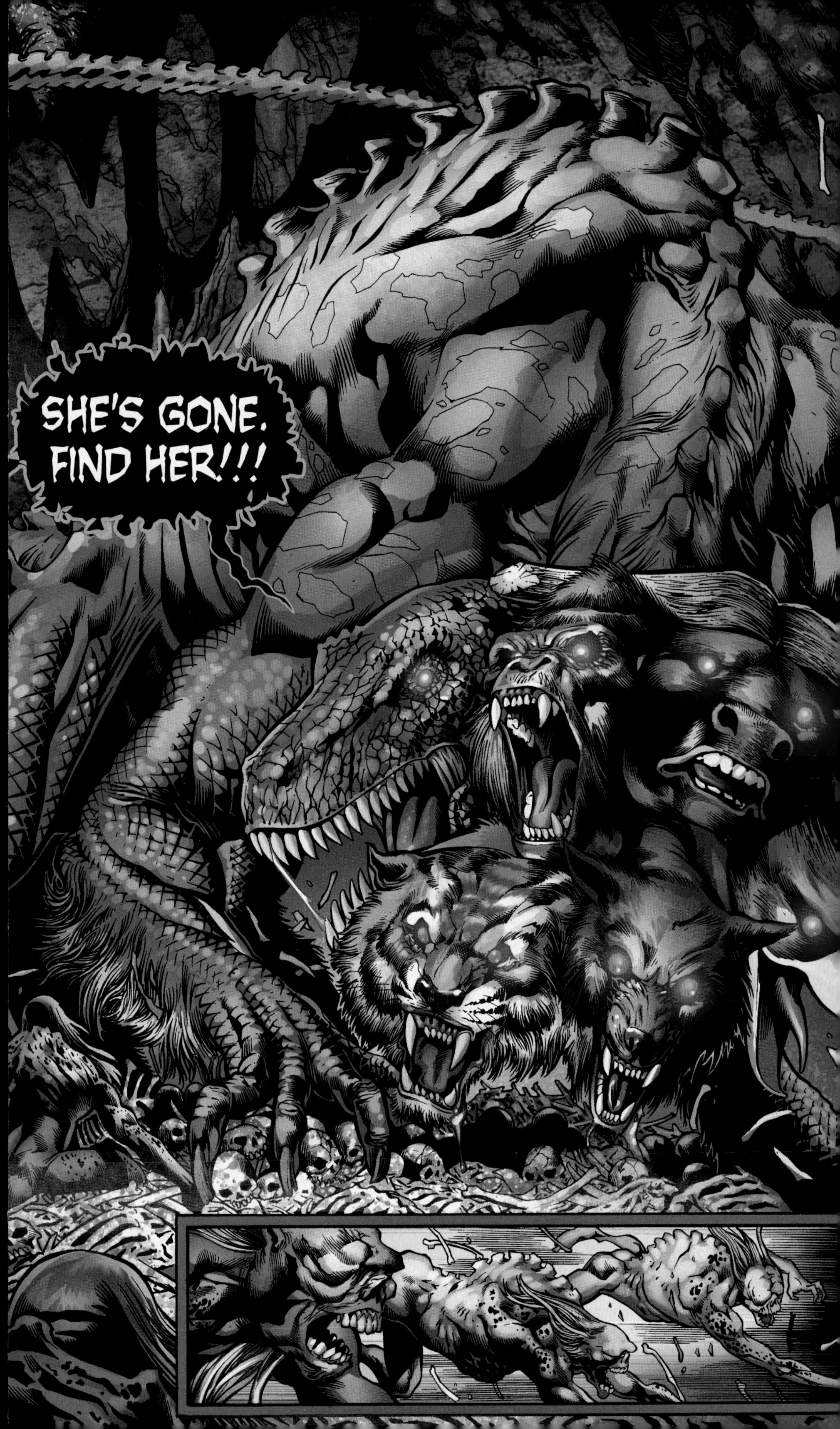
SHE'S GONE.
FIND HER!!!

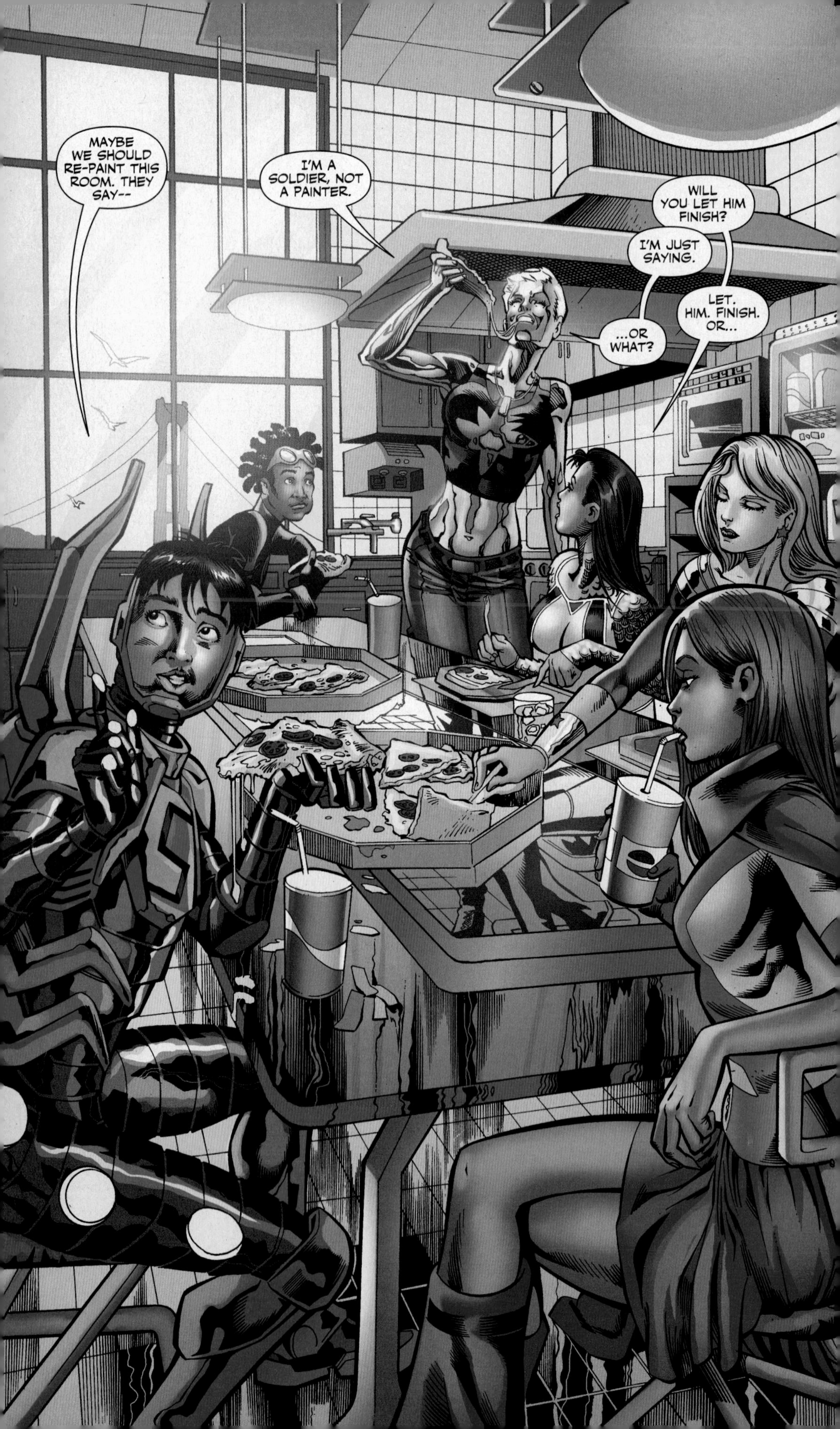
MAYBE WE SHOULD RE-PAINT THIS ROOM. THEY SAY--
I'M A SOLDIER, NOT A PAINTER.
WILL YOU LET HIM FINISH?
I'M JUST SAYING.
LET. HIM. FINISH. OR...
...OR WHAT?

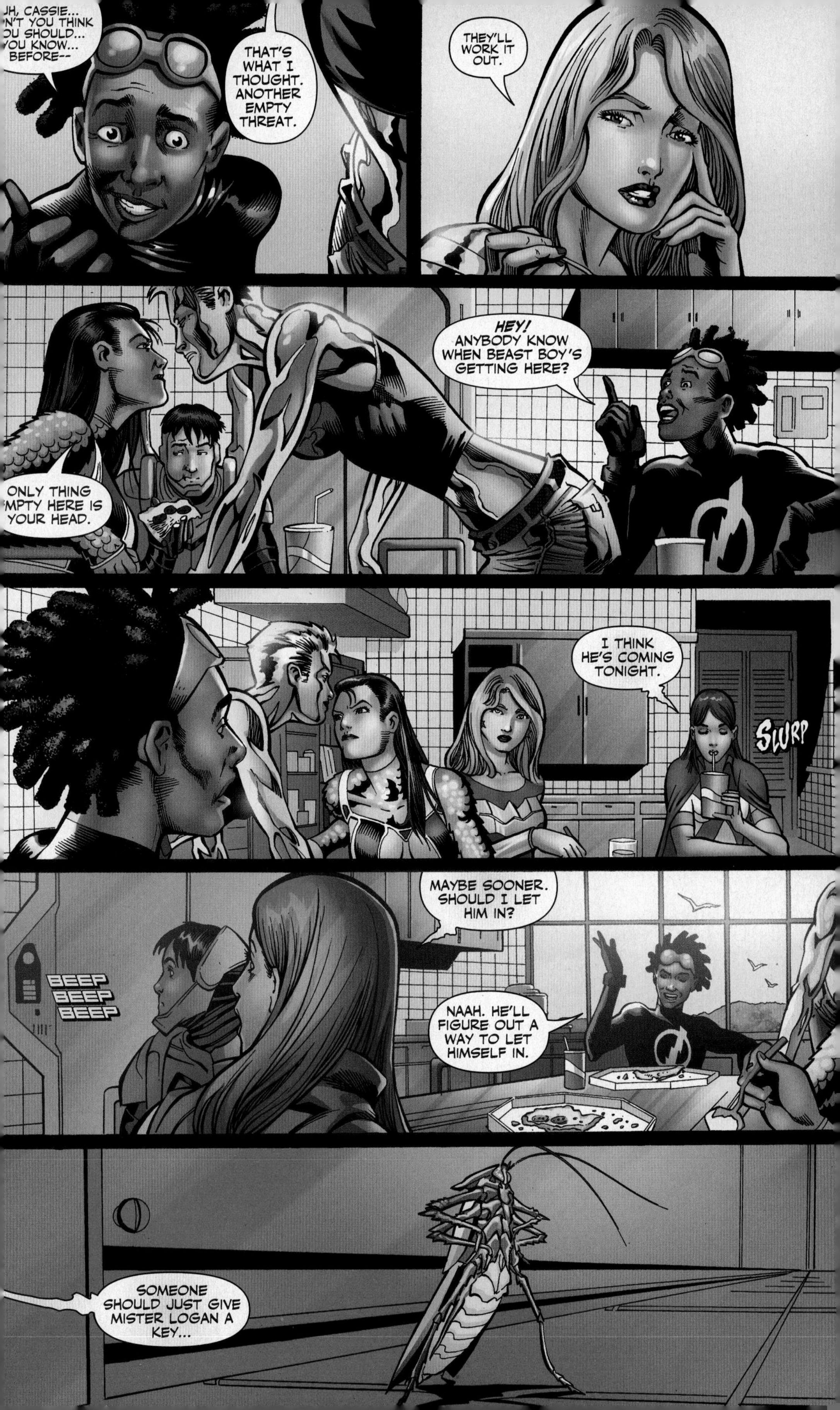

UH, CASSIE... N'T YOU THINK OU SHOULD... YOU KNOW... BEFORE--
THAT'S WHAT I THOUGHT. ANOTHER EMPTY THREAT.
THEY'LL WORK IT OUT.
HEY! ANYBODY KNOW WHEN BEAST BOY'S GETTING HERE?
ONLY THING MPTY HERE IS YOUR HEAD.
I THINK HE'S COMING TONIGHT.
SLURP
MAYBE SOONER. SHOULD I LET HIM IN?
BEEP BEEP BEEP
NAAH. HE'LL FIGURE OUT A WAY TO LET HIMSELF IN.
SOMEONE SHOULD JUST GIVE MISTER LOGAN A KEY...

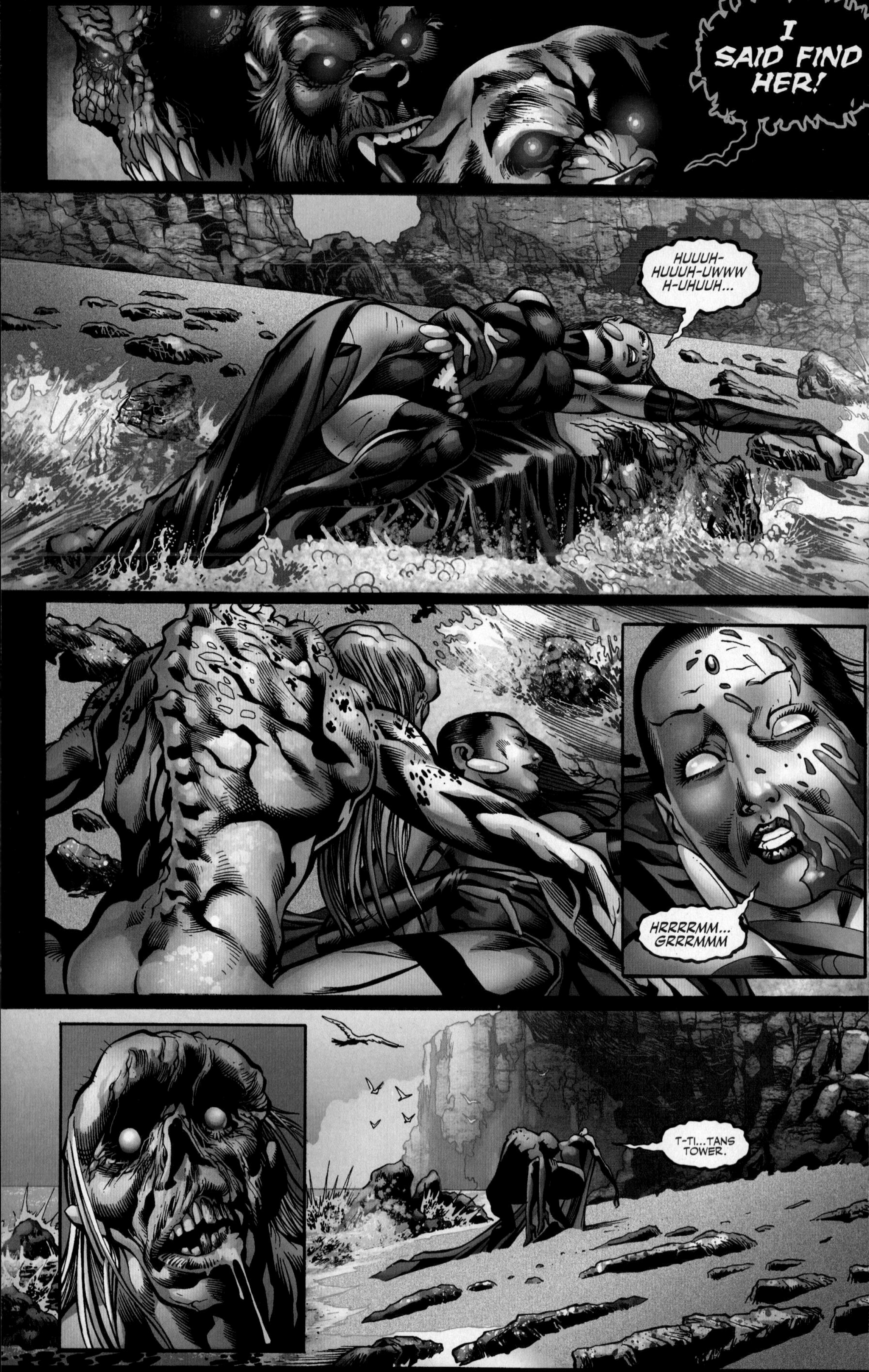
I SAID FIND HER!
HUUUH-HUUUH-UWWW H-UHUUH...
HRRRRMM... GRRRMMM
T-TI...TANS TOWER.

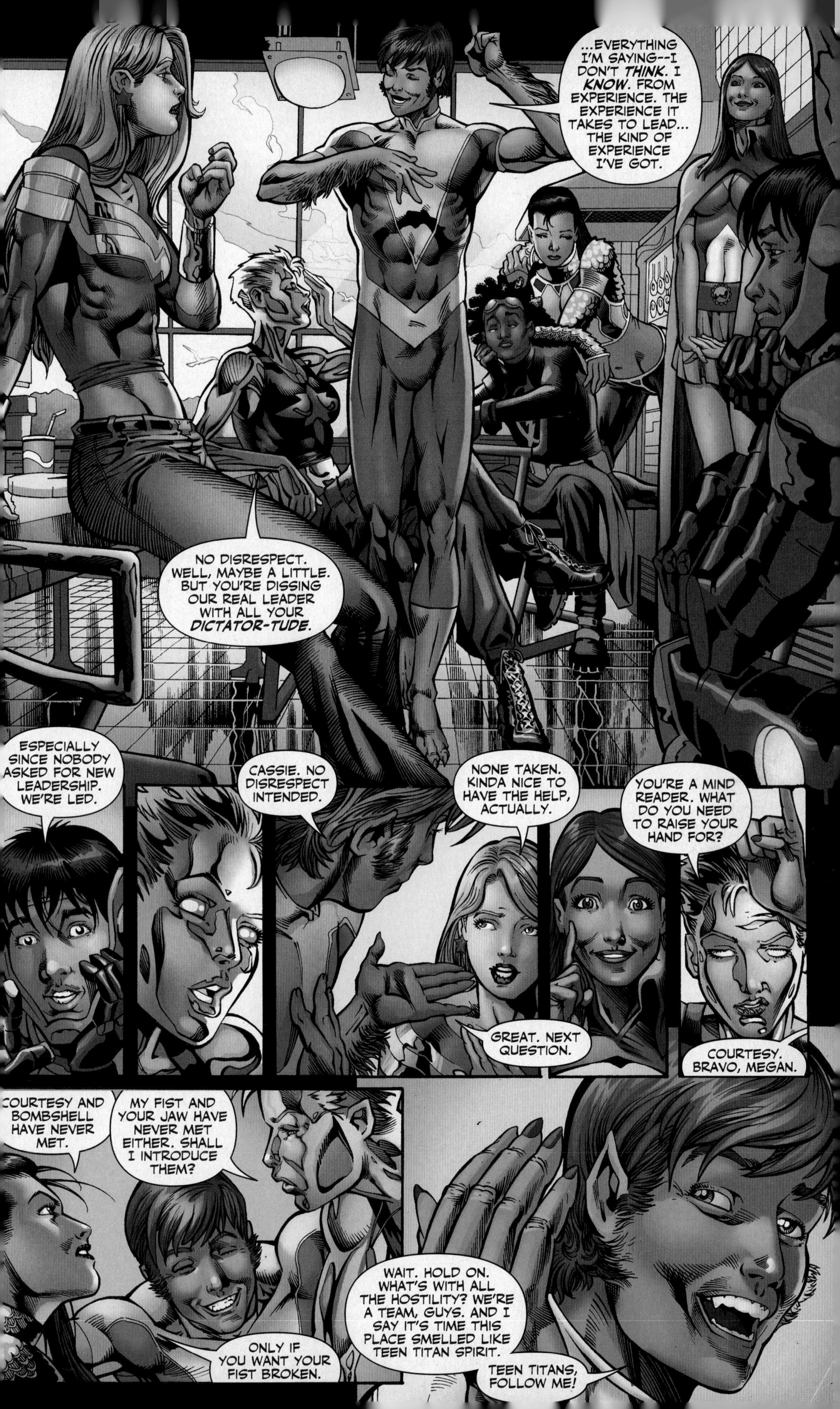
...EVERYTHING I'M SAYING--I DON'T *THINK*. I *KNOW*. FROM EXPERIENCE. THE EXPERIENCE IT TAKES TO LEAD... THE KIND OF EXPERIENCE I'VE GOT.
NO DISRESPECT. WELL, MAYBE A LITTLE. BUT YOU'RE DISSING OUR REAL LEADER WITH ALL YOUR *DICTATOR-TUDE*.
ESPECIALLY SINCE NOBODY ASKED FOR NEW LEADERSHIP. WE'RE LED.
CASSIE. NO DISRESPECT INTENDED.
NONE TAKEN. KINDA NICE TO HAVE THE HELP, ACTUALLY.
GREAT. NEXT QUESTION.
YOU'RE A MIND READER. WHAT DO YOU NEED TO RAISE YOUR HAND FOR?
COURTESY. BRAVO, MEGAN.
COURTESY AND BOMBSHELL HAVE NEVER MET.
MY FIST AND YOUR JAW HAVE NEVER MET EITHER. SHALL I INTRODUCE THEM?
ONLY IF YOU WANT YOUR FIST BROKEN.
WAIT. HOLD ON. WHAT'S WITH ALL THE HOSTILITY? WE'RE A TEAM, GUYS. AND I SAY IT'S TIME THIS PLACE SMELLED LIKE TEEN TITAN SPIRIT.
TEEN TITANS, FOLLOW ME!

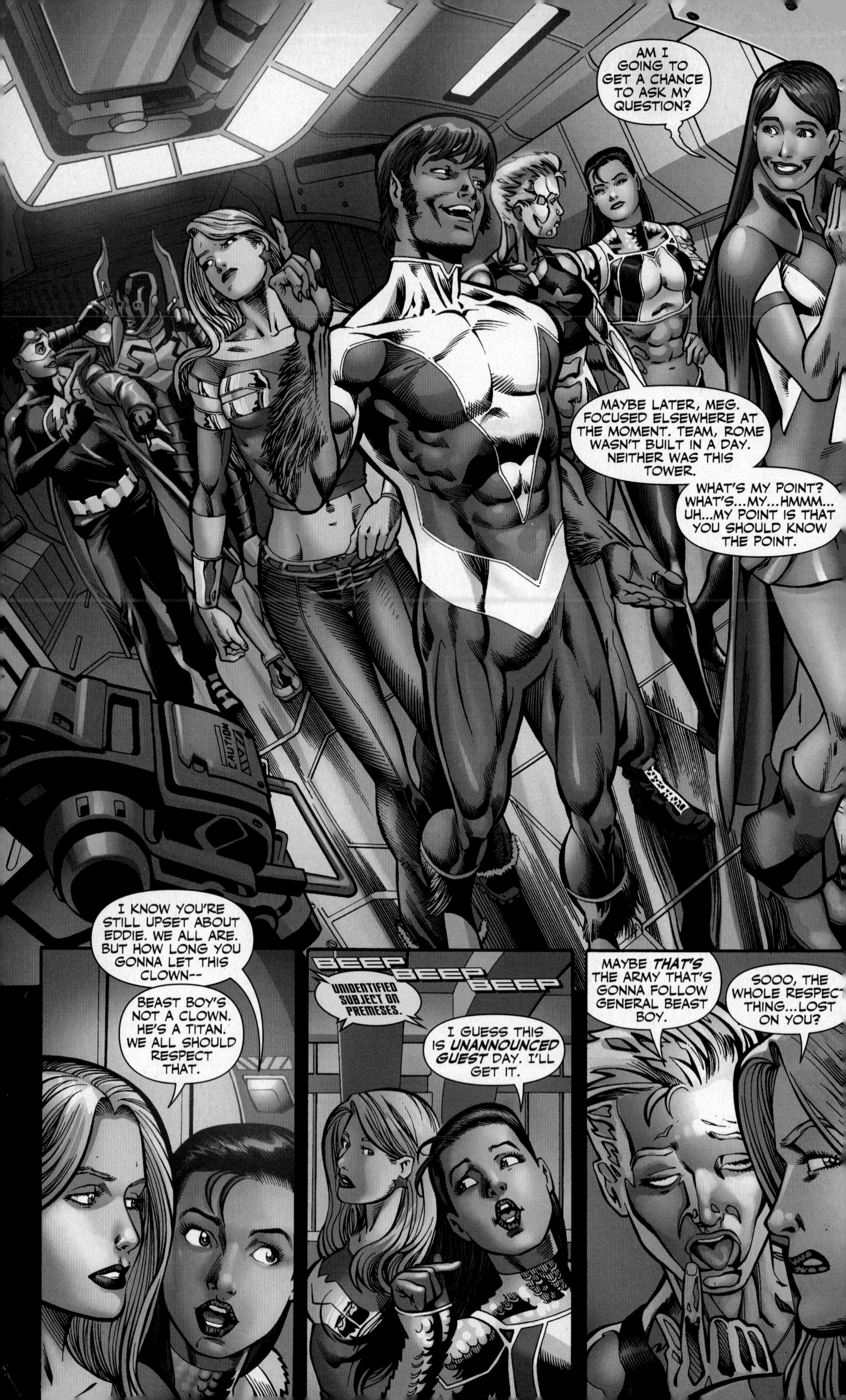
AM I GOING TO GET A CHANCE TO ASK MY QUESTION?
MAYBE LATER, MEG. FOCUSED ELSEWHERE AT THE MOMENT. TEAM, ROME WASN'T BUILT IN A DAY. NEITHER WAS THIS TOWER.
WHAT'S MY POINT? WHAT'S...MY...HMMM... UH...MY POINT IS THAT YOU SHOULD KNOW THE POINT.
CAUTION
I KNOW YOU'RE STILL UPSET ABOUT EDDIE. WE ALL ARE. BUT HOW LONG YOU GONNA LET THIS CLOWN--
BEAST BOY'S NOT A CLOWN. HE'S A TITAN. WE ALL SHOULD RESPECT THAT.
BEEP BEEP BEEP
UNIDENTIFIED SUBJECT ON PREMESES.
I GUESS THIS IS *UNANNOUNCED GUEST* DAY. I'LL GET IT.
MAYBE *THAT'S* THE ARMY THAT'S GONNA FOLLOW GENERAL BEAST BOY.
SOOO, THE WHOLE RESPECT THING...LOST ON YOU?

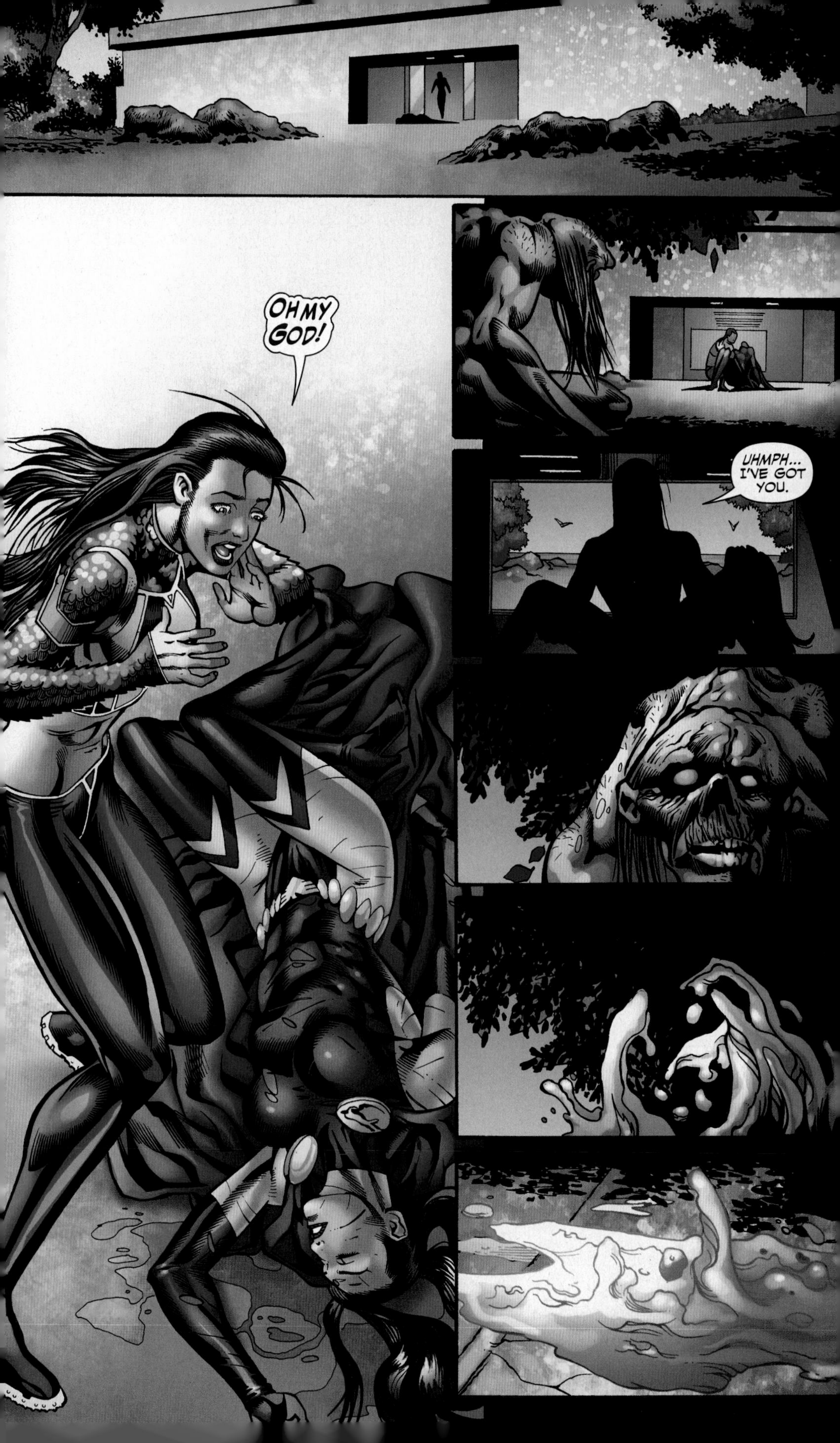
OH MY GOD!
UHMPH... I'VE GOT YOU.

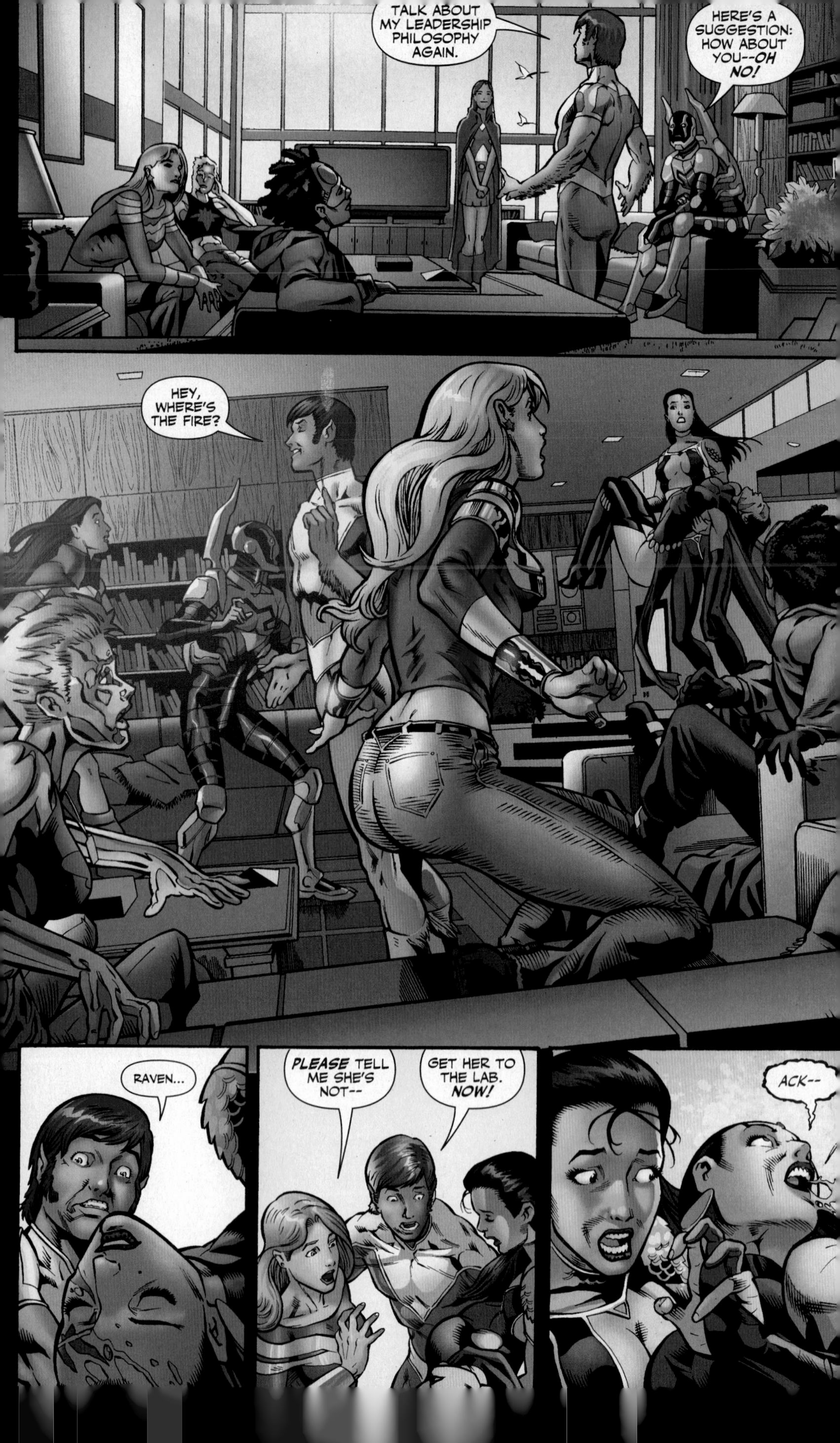
TALK ABOUT MY LEADERSHIP PHILOSOPHY AGAIN.
HERE'S A SUGGESTION: HOW ABOUT YOU--OH NO!
HEY, WHERE'S THE FIRE?
RAVEN...
PLEASE TELL ME SHE'S NOT--
GET HER TO THE LAB. NOW!
ACK--

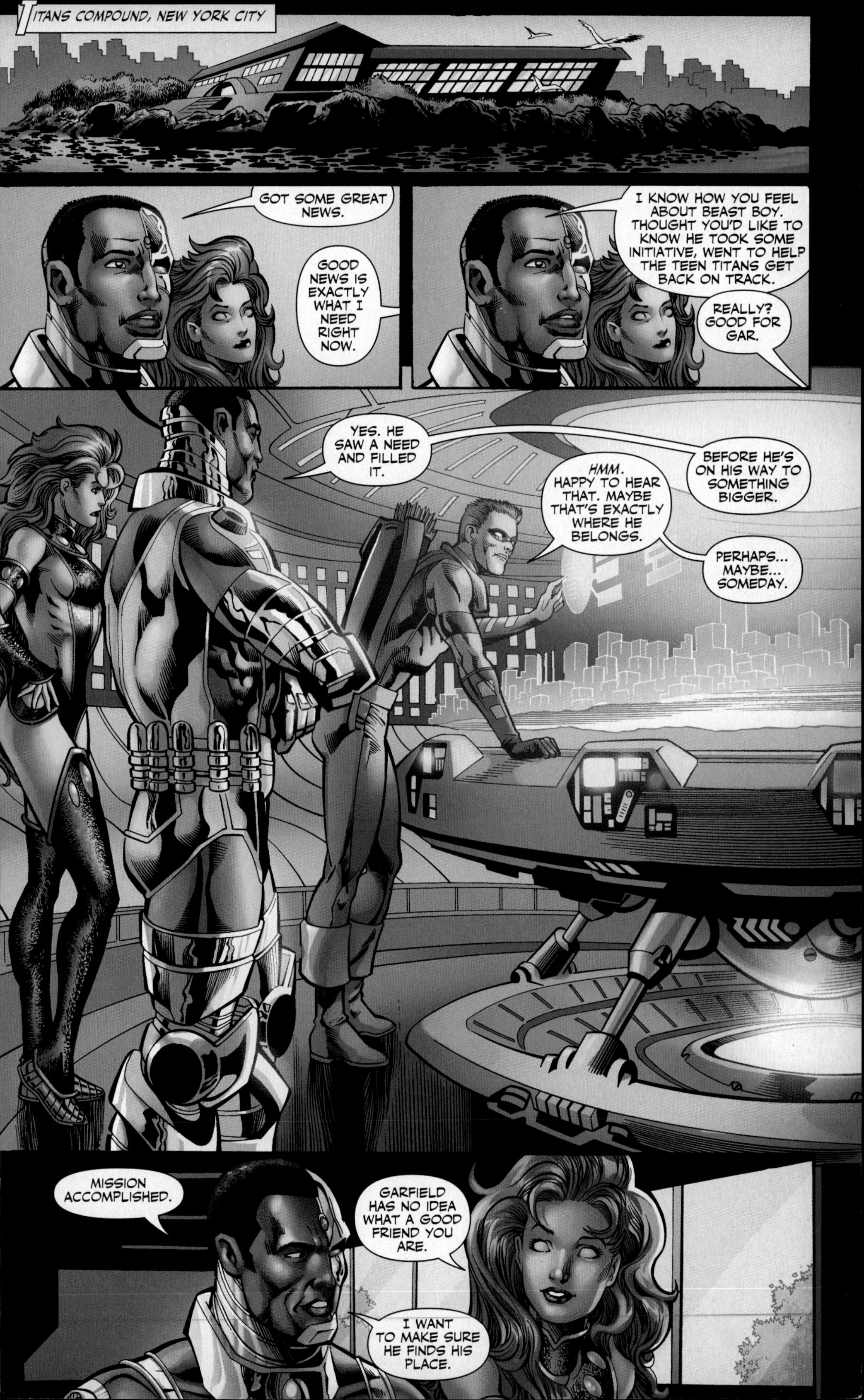
TITANS COMPOUND, NEW YORK CITY
GOT SOME GREAT NEWS.
GOOD NEWS IS EXACTLY WHAT I NEED RIGHT NOW.
I KNOW HOW YOU FEEL ABOUT BEAST BOY. THOUGHT YOU'D LIKE TO KNOW HE TOOK SOME INITIATIVE, WENT TO HELP THE TEEN TITANS GET BACK ON TRACK.
REALLY? GOOD FOR GAR.
YES. HE SAW A NEED AND FILLED IT.
BEFORE HE'S ON HIS WAY TO SOMETHING BIGGER.
HMM. HAPPY TO HEAR THAT. MAYBE THAT'S EXACTLY WHERE HE BELONGS.
PERHAPS... MAYBE... SOMEDAY.
MISSION ACCOMPLISHED.
GARFIELD HAS NO IDEA WHAT A GOOD FRIEND YOU ARE.
I WANT TO MAKE SURE HE FINDS HIS PLACE.

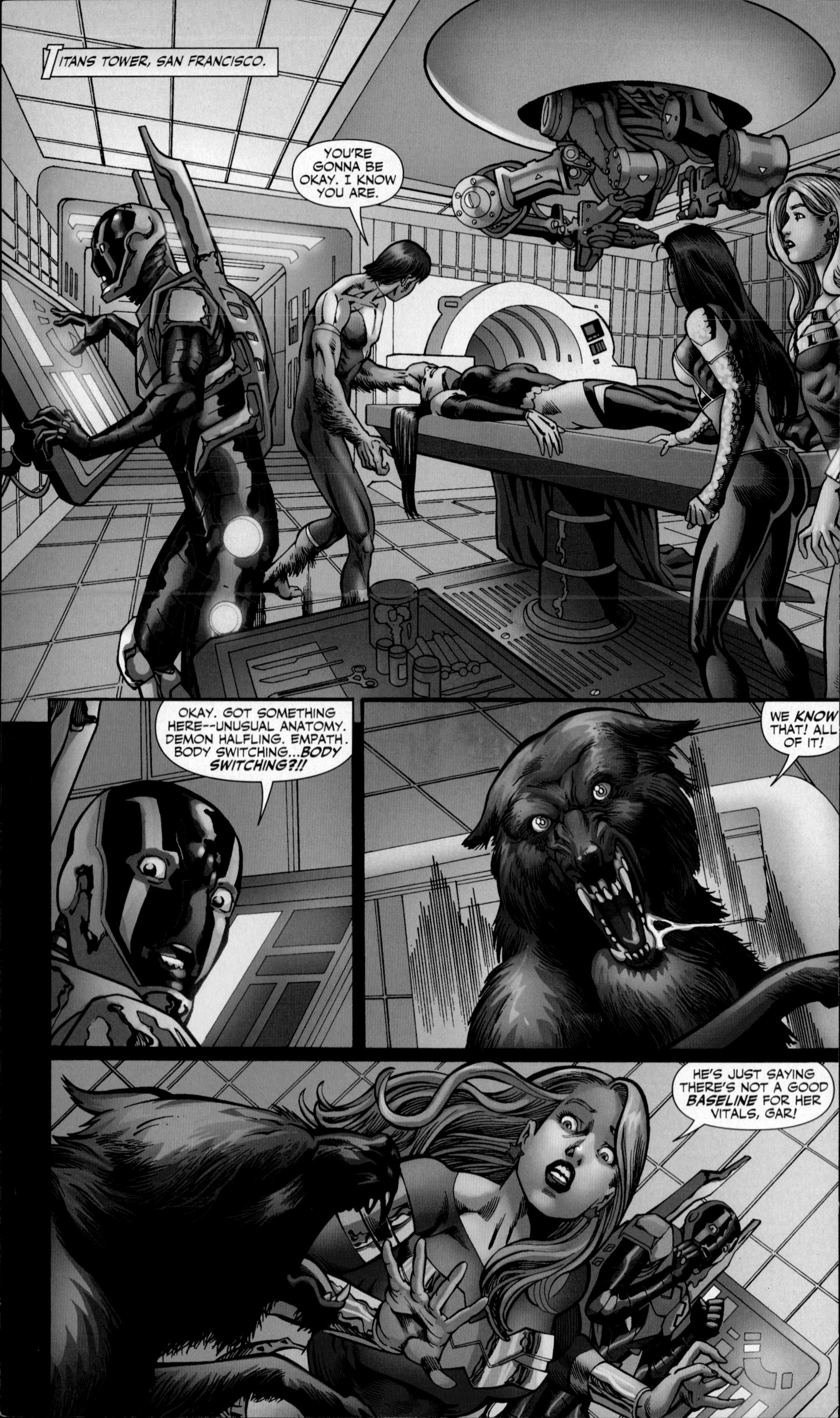
TITANS TOWER, SAN FRANCISCO.
YOU'RE GONNA BE OKAY. I KNOW YOU ARE.
OKAY. GOT SOMETHING HERE--UNUSUAL ANATOMY. DEMON HALFLING. EMPATH. BODY SWITCHING...BODY SWITCHING?!!
WE KNOW THAT! ALL OF IT!
HE'S JUST SAYING THERE'S NOT A GOOD BASELINE FOR HER VITALS, GAR!

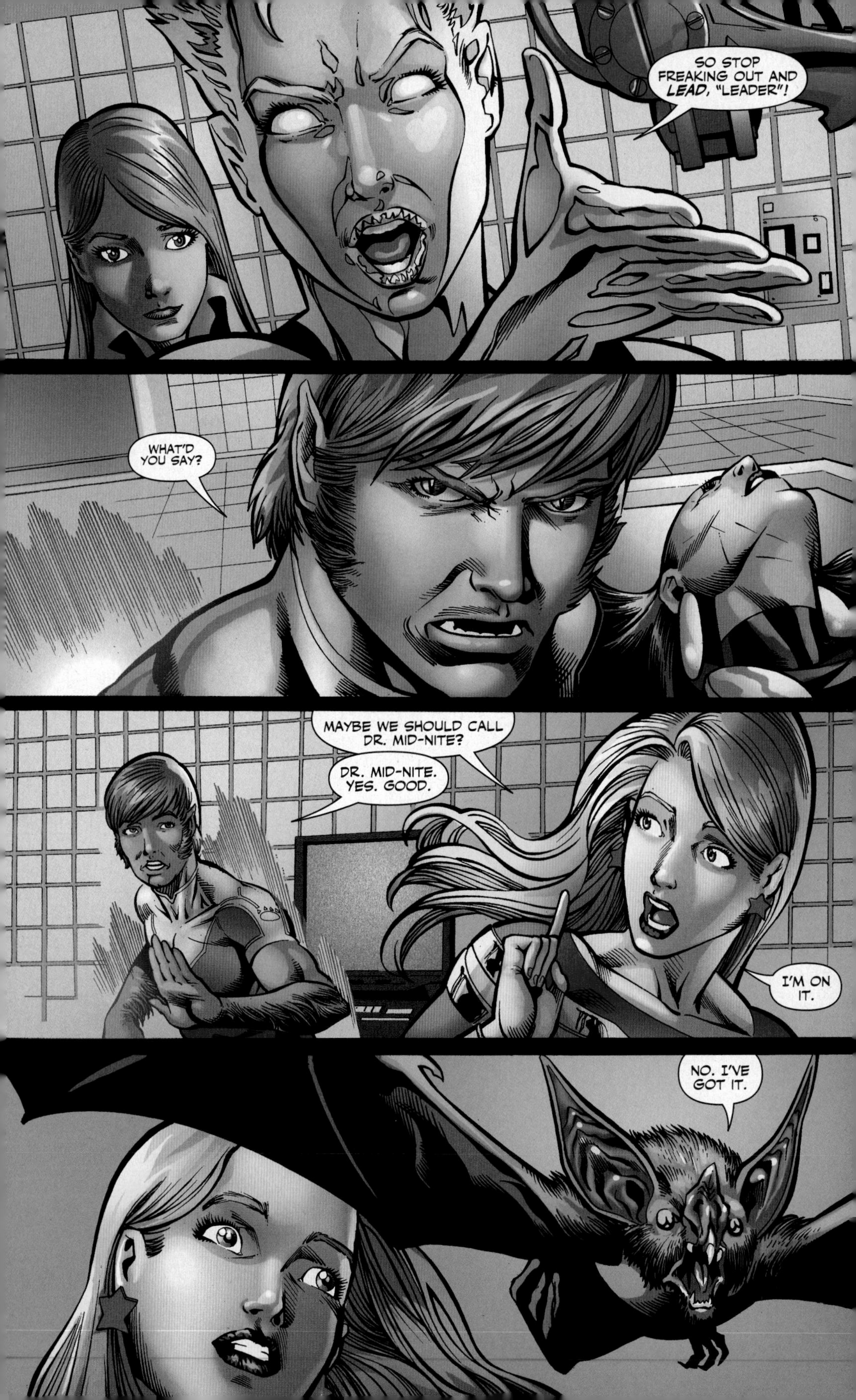
SO STOP FREAKING OUT AND *LEAD*, "LEADER"!
WHAT'D YOU SAY?
MAYBE WE SHOULD CALL DR. MID-NITE?
DR. MID-NITE. YES. GOOD.
I'M ON IT.
NO. I'VE GOT IT.

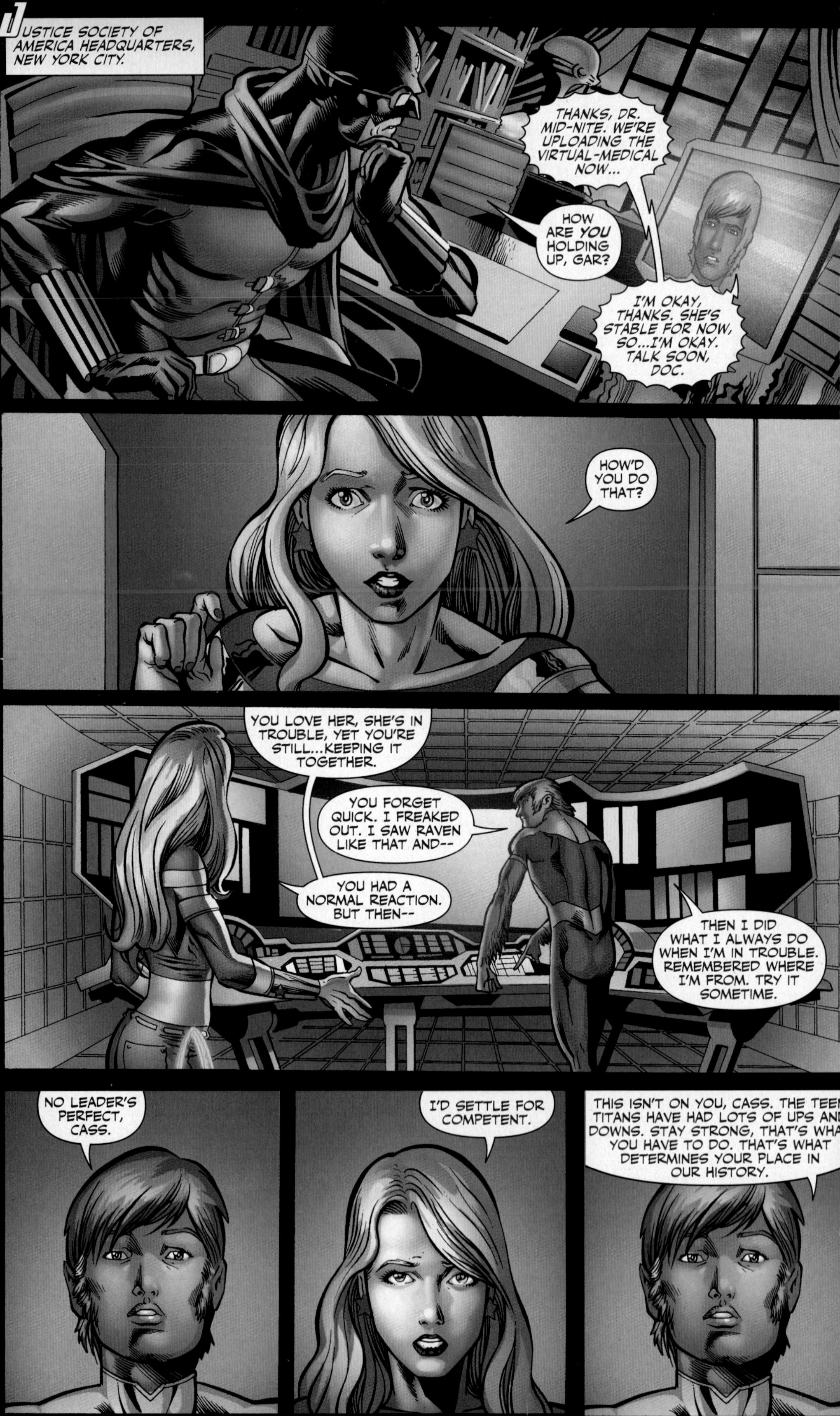
JUSTICE SOCIETY OF AMERICA HEADQUARTERS, NEW YORK CITY.
THANKS, DR. MID-NITE. WE'RE UPLOADING THE VIRTUAL-MEDICAL NOW...
HOW ARE YOU HOLDING UP, GAR?
I'M OKAY, THANKS. SHE'S STABLE FOR NOW, SO...I'M OKAY. TALK SOON, DOC.
HOW'D YOU DO THAT?
YOU LOVE HER, SHE'S IN TROUBLE, YET YOU'RE STILL...KEEPING IT TOGETHER.
YOU FORGET QUICK. I FREAKED OUT. I SAW RAVEN LIKE THAT AND--
YOU HAD A NORMAL REACTION. BUT THEN--
THEN I DID WHAT I ALWAYS DO WHEN I'M IN TROUBLE. REMEMBERED WHERE I'M FROM. TRY IT SOMETIME.
NO LEADER'S PERFECT, CASS.
I'D SETTLE FOR COMPETENT.
THIS ISN'T ON YOU, CASS. THE TEEN TITANS HAVE HAD LOTS OF UPS AND DOWNS. STAY STRONG, THAT'S WHAT YOU HAVE TO DO. THAT'S WHAT DETERMINES YOUR PLACE IN OUR HISTORY.

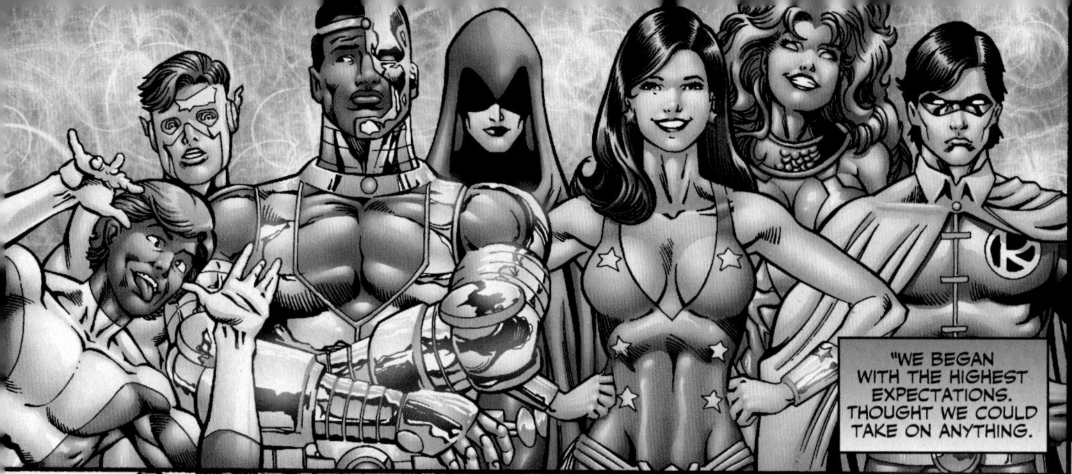
"WE BEGAN WITH THE HIGHEST EXPECTATIONS. THOUGHT WE COULD TAKE ON ANYTHING.

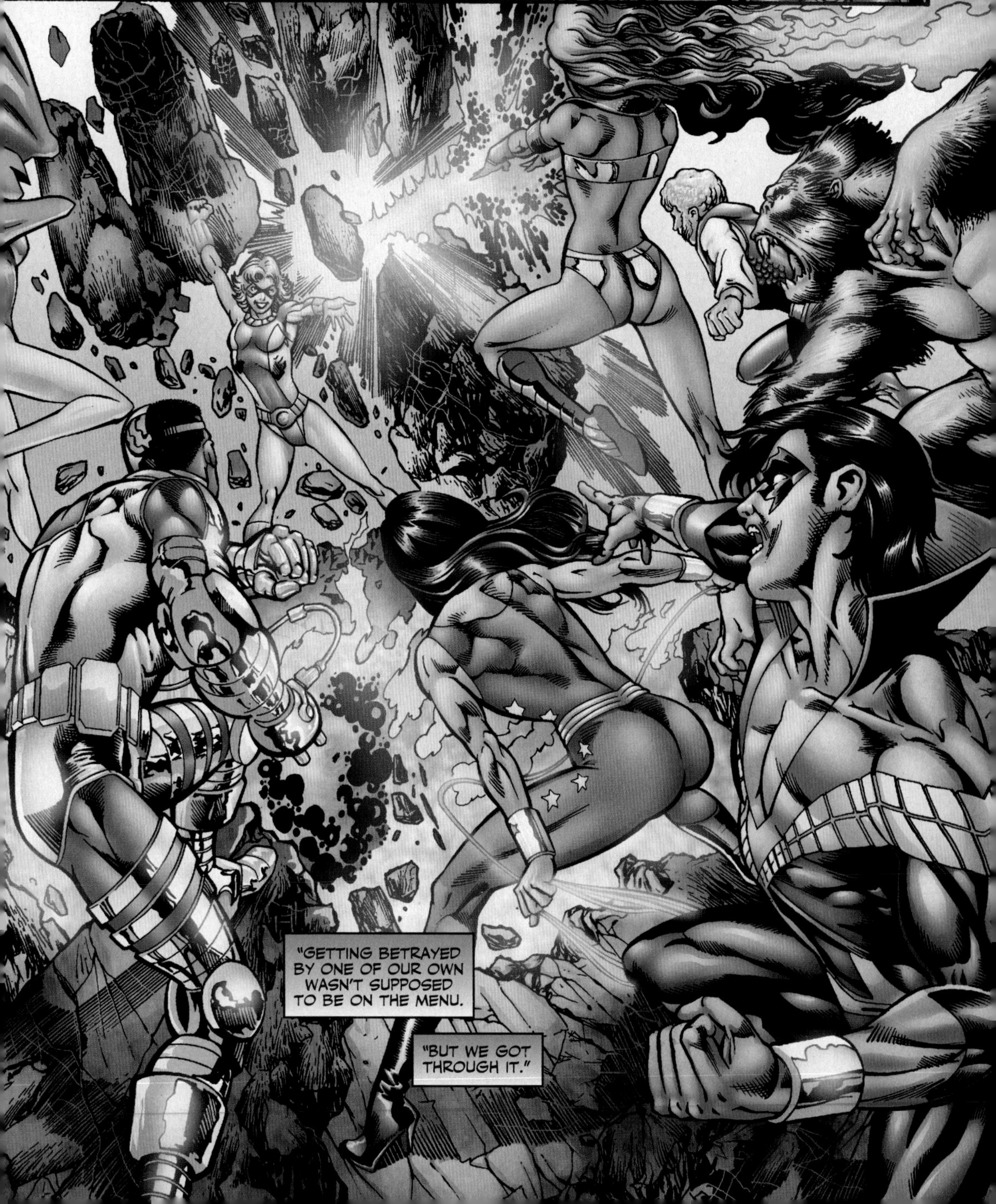
"GETTING BETRAYED BY ONE OF OUR OWN WASN'T SUPPOSED TO BE ON THE MENU.
"BUT WE GOT THROUGH IT."

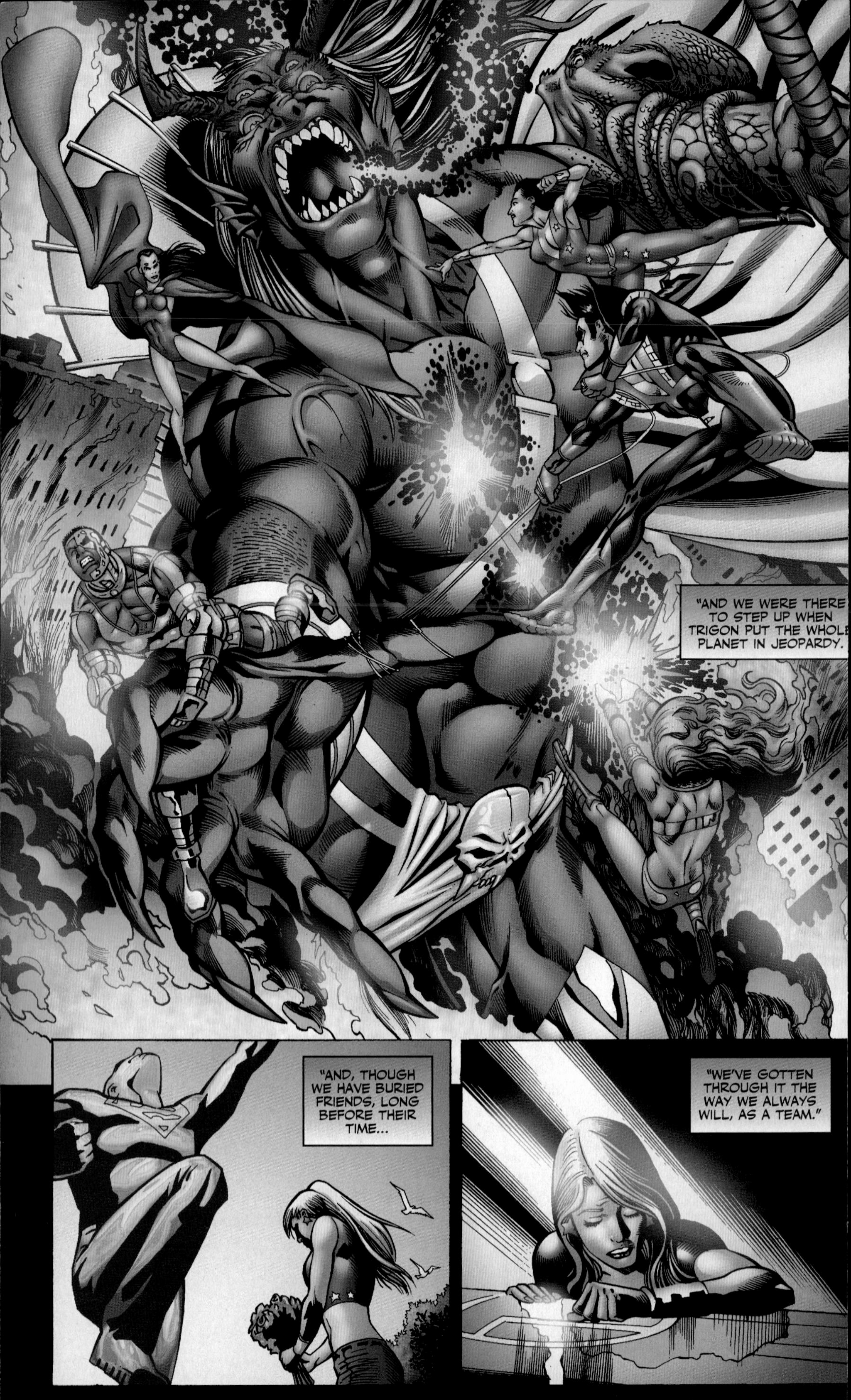
"AND WE WERE THERE TO STEP UP WHEN TRIGON PUT THE WHOLE PLANET IN JEOPARDY.
"AND, THOUGH WE HAVE BURIED FRIENDS, LONG BEFORE THEIR TIME...
"WE'VE GOTTEN THROUGH IT THE WAY WE ALWAYS WILL, AS A TEAM."

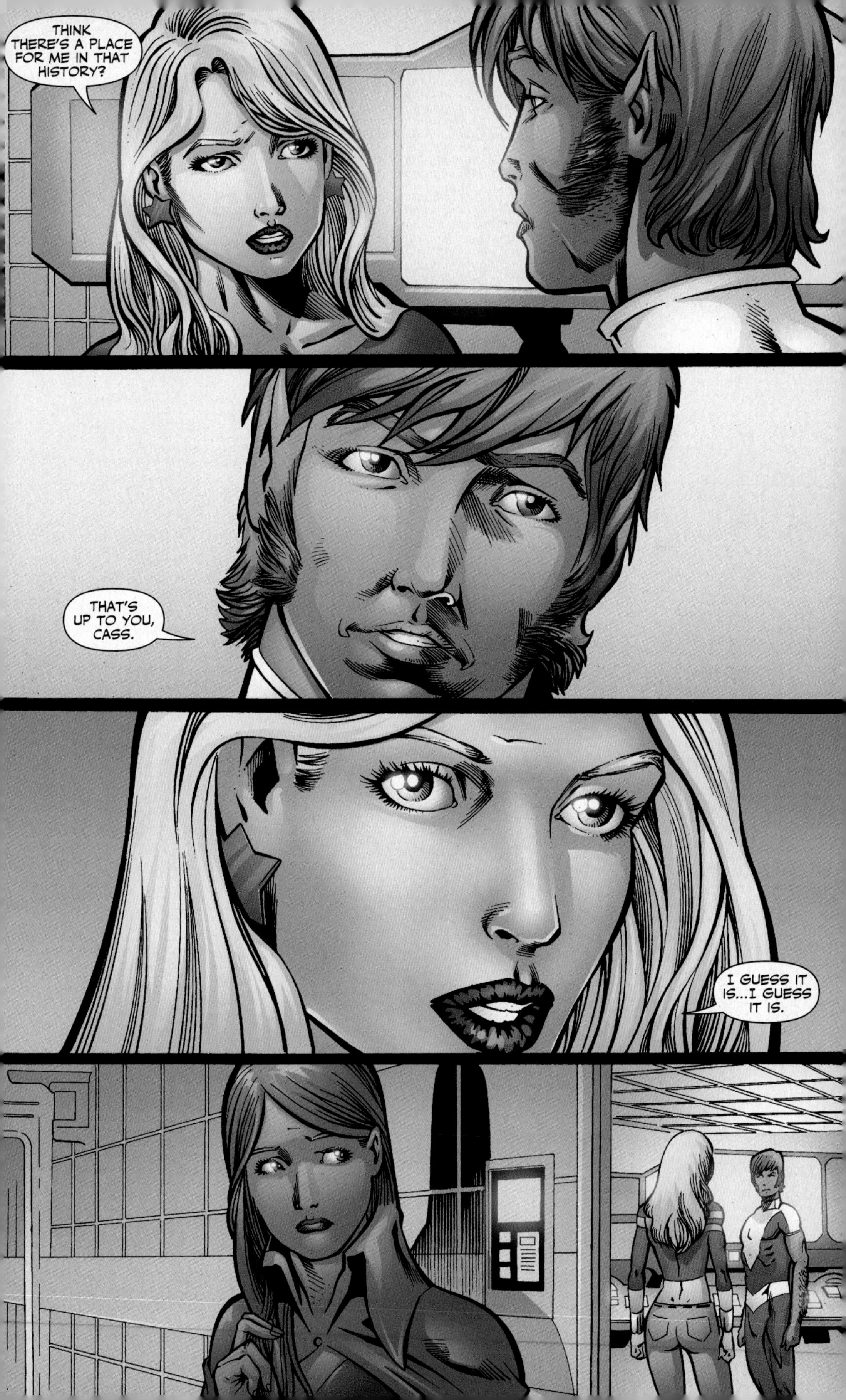
THINK THERE'S A PLACE FOR ME IN THAT HISTORY?
THAT'S UP TO YOU, CASS.
I GUESS IT IS...I GUESS IT IS.

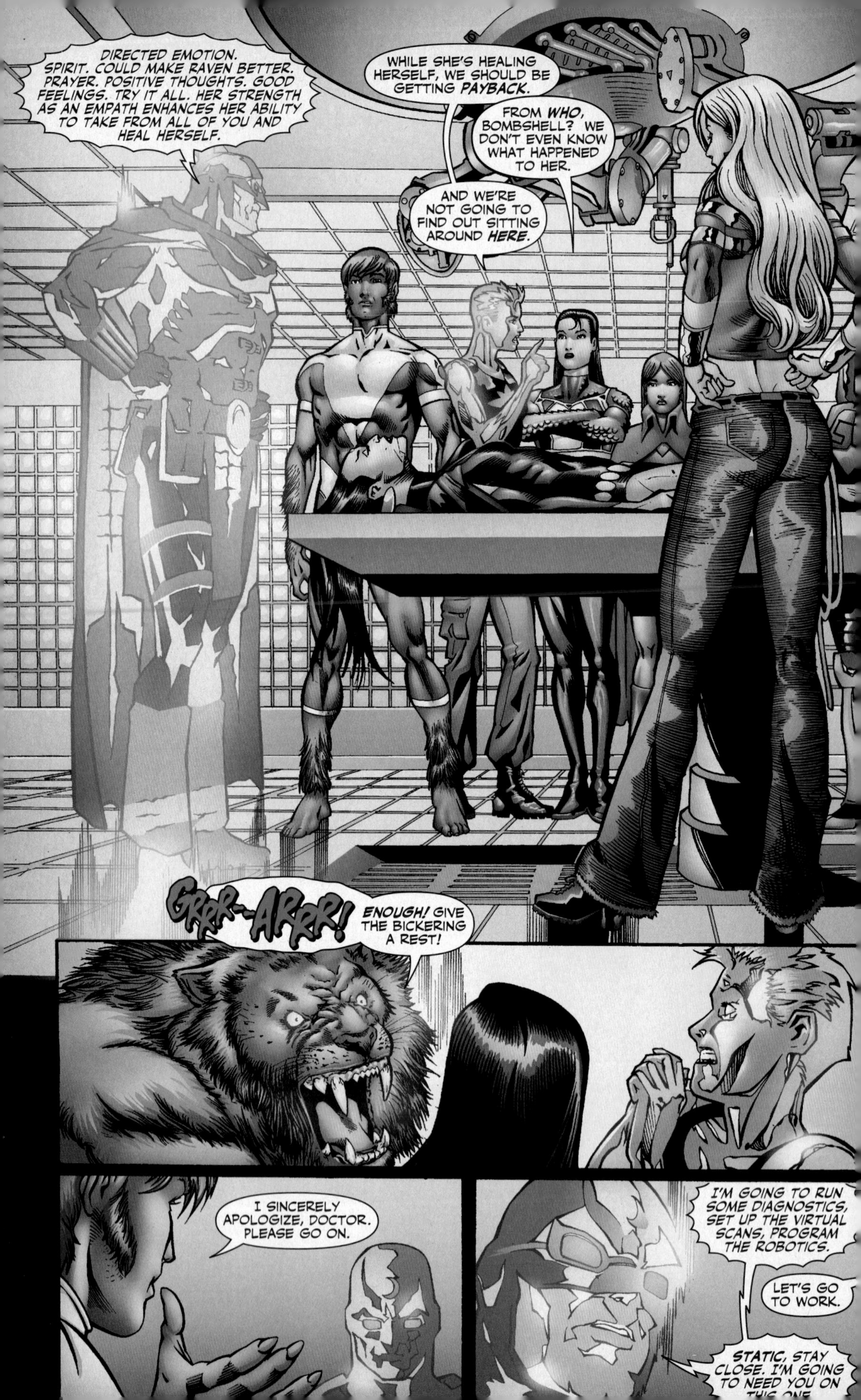
DIRECTED EMOTION. SPIRIT. COULD MAKE RAVEN BETTER. PRAYER. POSITIVE THOUGHTS. GOOD FEELINGS. TRY IT ALL. HER STRENGTH AS AN EMPATH ENHANCES HER ABILITY TO TAKE FROM ALL OF YOU AND HEAL HERSELF.
WHILE SHE'S HEALING HERSELF, WE SHOULD BE GETTING PAYBACK.
FROM WHO, BOMBSHELL? WE DON'T EVEN KNOW WHAT HAPPENED TO HER.
AND WE'RE NOT GOING TO FIND OUT SITTING AROUND HERE.
GRRR--ARRR!
ENOUGH! GIVE THE BICKERING A REST!
I SINCERELY APOLOGIZE, DOCTOR. PLEASE GO ON.
I'M GOING TO RUN SOME DIAGNOSTICS, SET UP THE VIRTUAL SCANS, PROGRAM THE ROBOTICS.
LET'S GO TO WORK.
STATIC, STAY CLOSE. I'M GOING TO NEED YOU ON

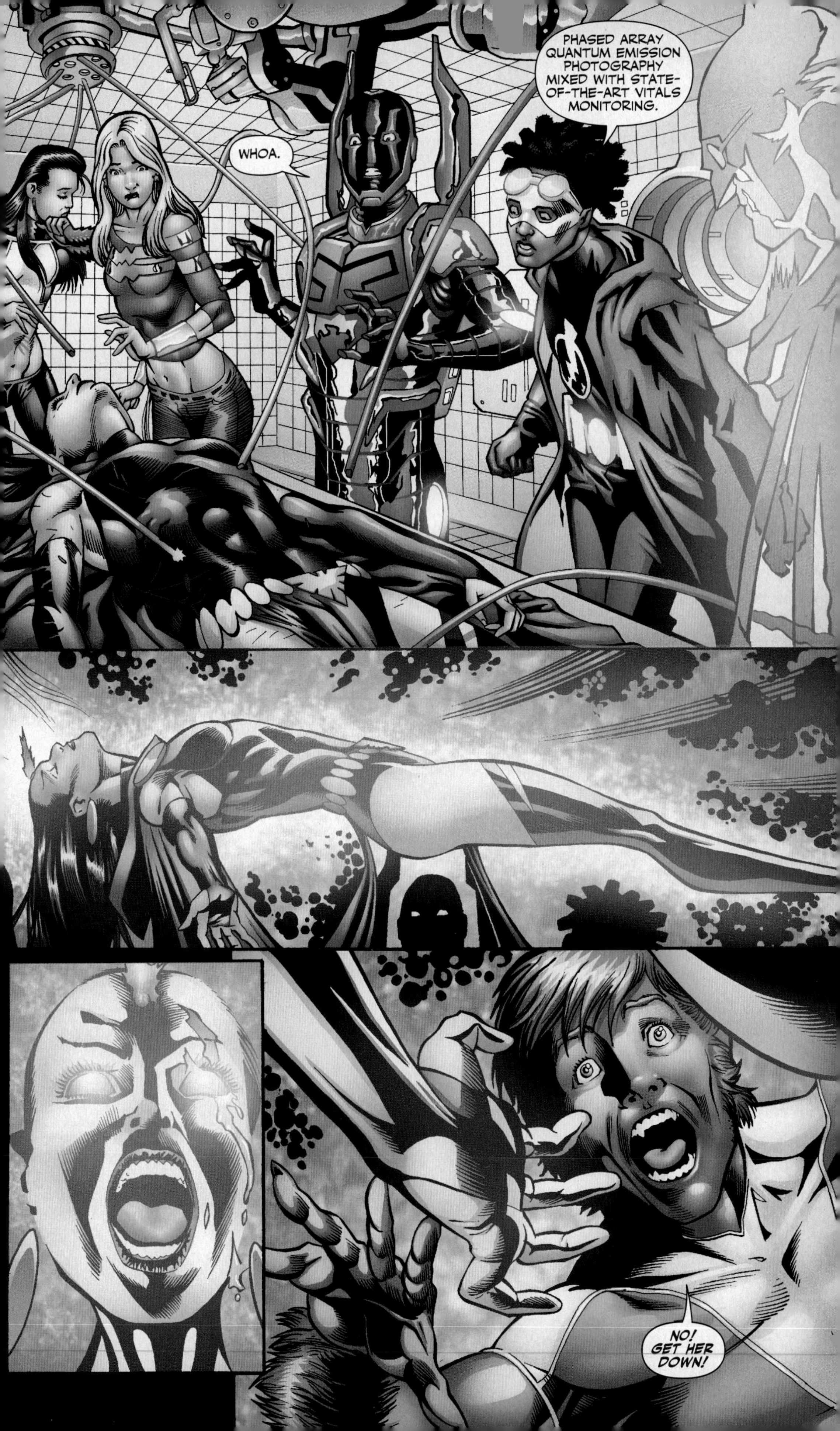
PHASED ARRAY QUANTUM EMISSION PHOTOGRAPHY MIXED WITH STATE-OF-THE-ART VITALS MONITORING.
WHOA.
NO! GET HER DOWN!

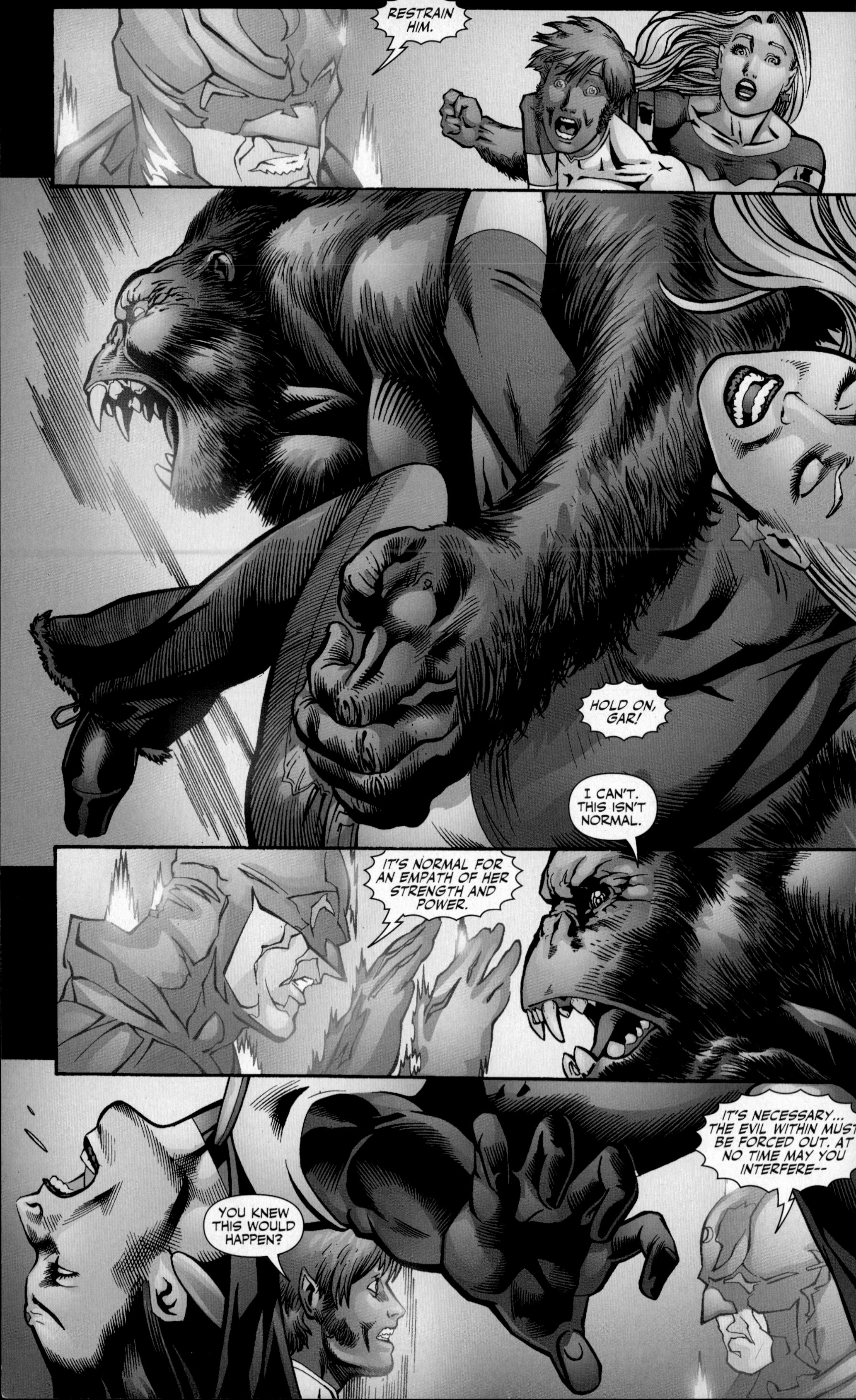
RESTRAIN HIM.
HOLD ON, GAR!
I CAN'T. THIS ISN'T NORMAL.
IT'S NORMAL FOR AN EMPATH OF HER STRENGTH AND POWER.
IT'S NECESSARY... THE EVIL WITHIN MUST BE FORCED OUT. AT NO TIME MAY YOU INTERFERE--
YOU KNEW THIS WOULD HAPPEN?

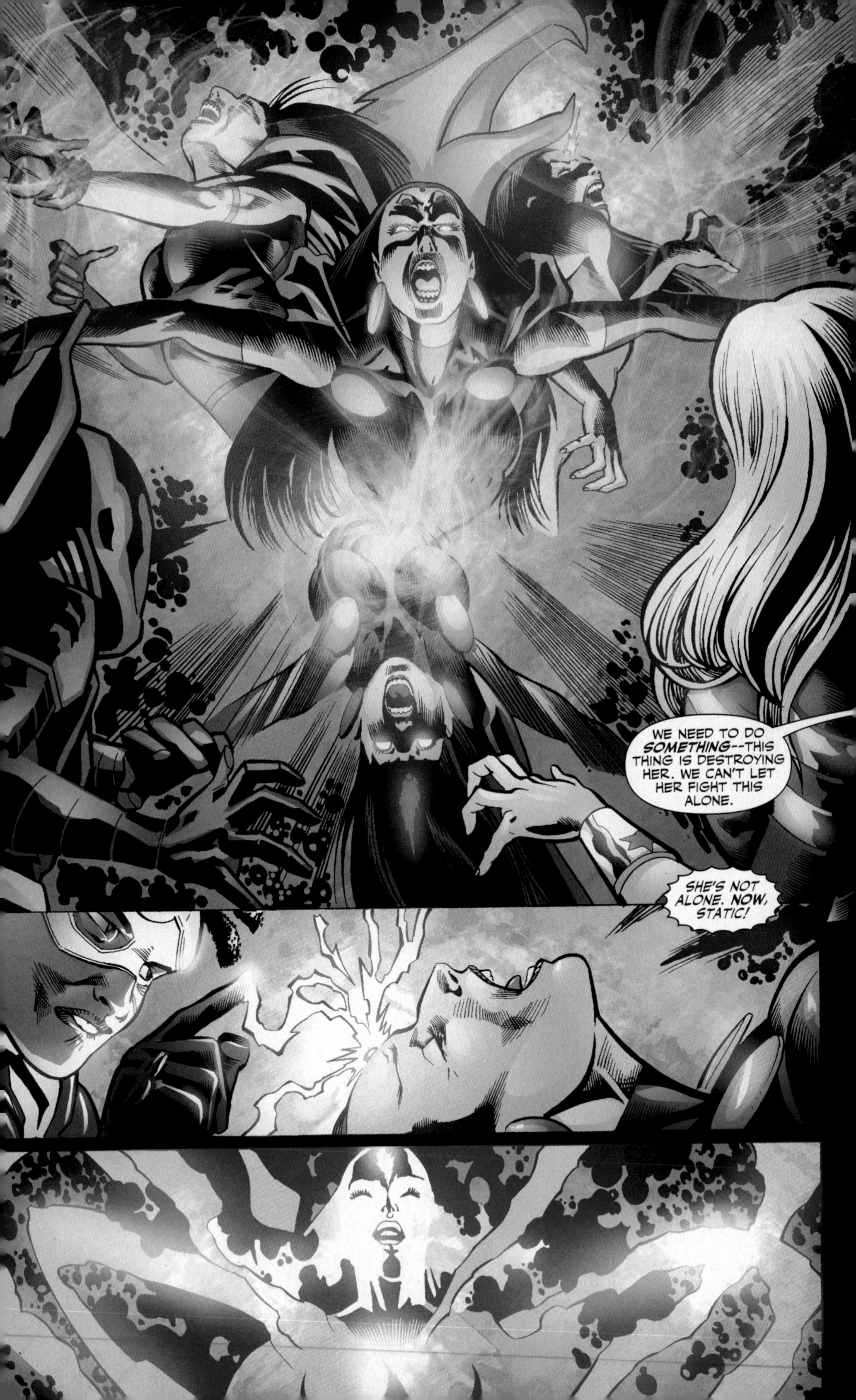
WE NEED TO DO SOMETHING--THIS THING IS DESTROYING HER. WE CAN'T LET HER FIGHT THIS ALONE.
SHE'S NOT ALONE. NOW, STATIC!

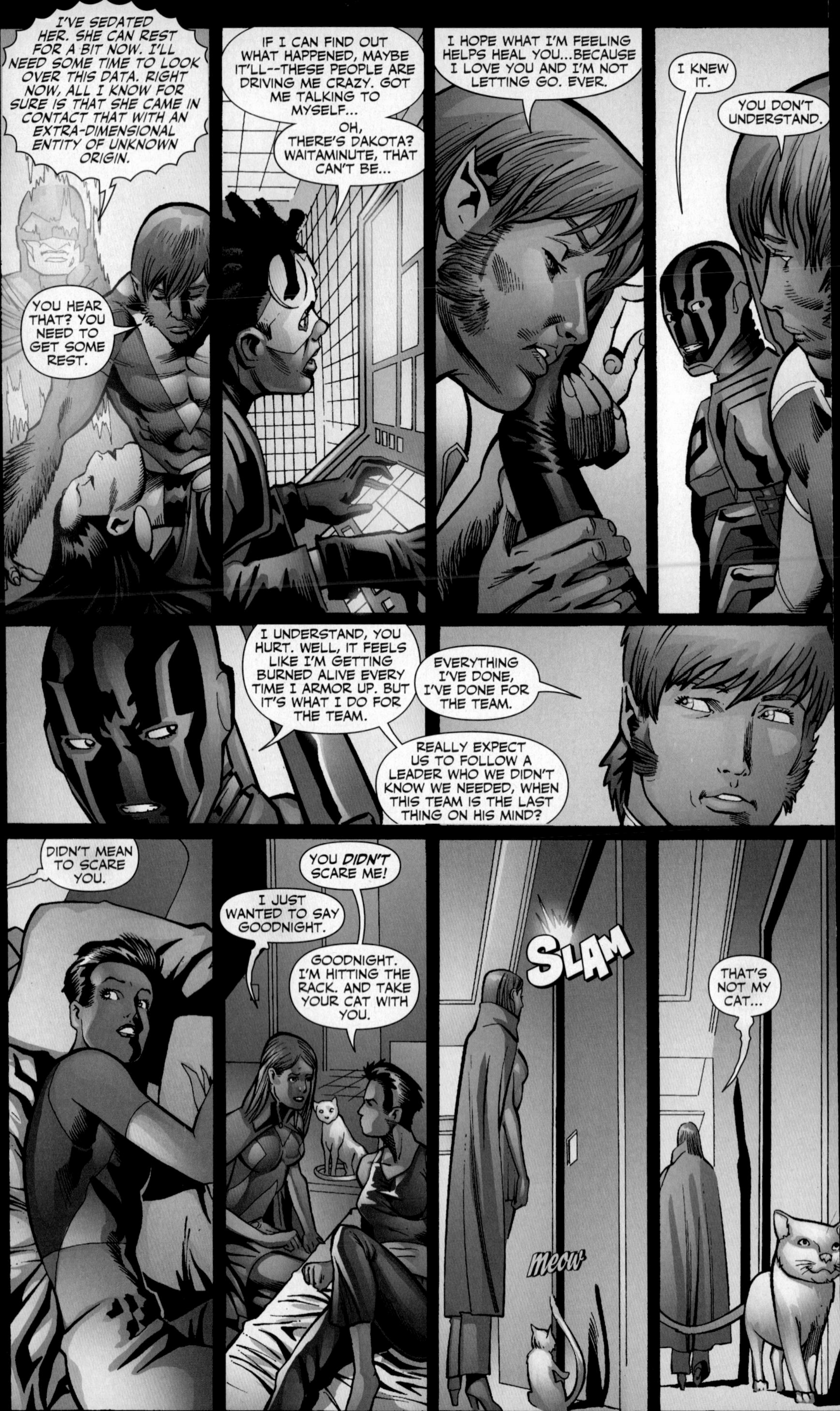
I'VE SEDATED HER. SHE CAN REST FOR A BIT NOW. I'LL NEED SOME TIME TO LOOK OVER THIS DATA. RIGHT NOW, ALL I KNOW FOR SURE IS THAT SHE CAME IN CONTACT THAT WITH AN EXTRA-DIMENSIONAL ENTITY OF UNKNOWN ORIGIN.
YOU HEAR THAT? YOU NEED TO GET SOME REST.
IF I CAN FIND OUT WHAT HAPPENED, MAYBE IT'LL--THESE PEOPLE ARE DRIVING ME CRAZY. GOT ME TALKING TO MYSELF...
OH, THERE'S DAKOTA? WAITAMINUTE, THAT CAN'T BE...
I HOPE WHAT I'M FEELING HELPS HEAL YOU...BECAUSE I LOVE YOU AND I'M NOT LETTING GO. EVER.
I KNEW IT.
YOU DON'T UNDERSTAND.
I UNDERSTAND, YOU HURT. WELL, IT FEELS LIKE I'M GETTING BURNED ALIVE EVERY TIME I ARMOR UP. BUT IT'S WHAT I DO FOR THE TEAM.
EVERYTHING I'VE DONE, I'VE DONE FOR THE TEAM.
REALLY EXPECT US TO FOLLOW A LEADER WHO WE DIDN'T KNOW WE NEEDED, WHEN THIS TEAM IS THE LAST THING ON HIS MIND?
DIDN'T MEAN TO SCARE YOU.
YOU *DIDN'T* SCARE ME!
I JUST WANTED TO SAY GOODNIGHT.
GOODNIGHT. I'M HITTING THE RACK. AND TAKE YOUR CAT WITH YOU.
SLAM
meow
THAT'S NOT MY CAT...

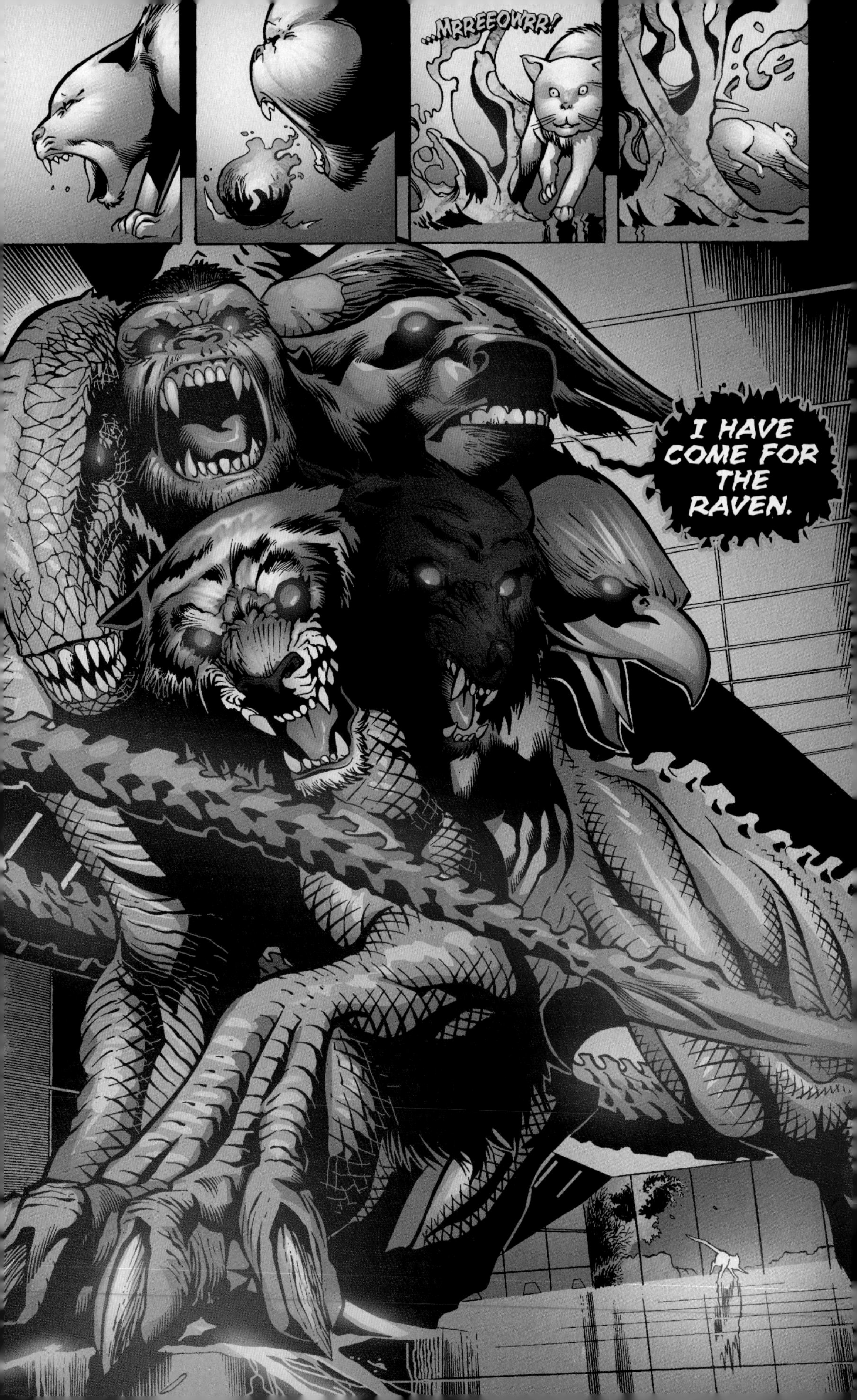
...MRREEOWRR!
I HAVE COME FOR THE RAVEN.

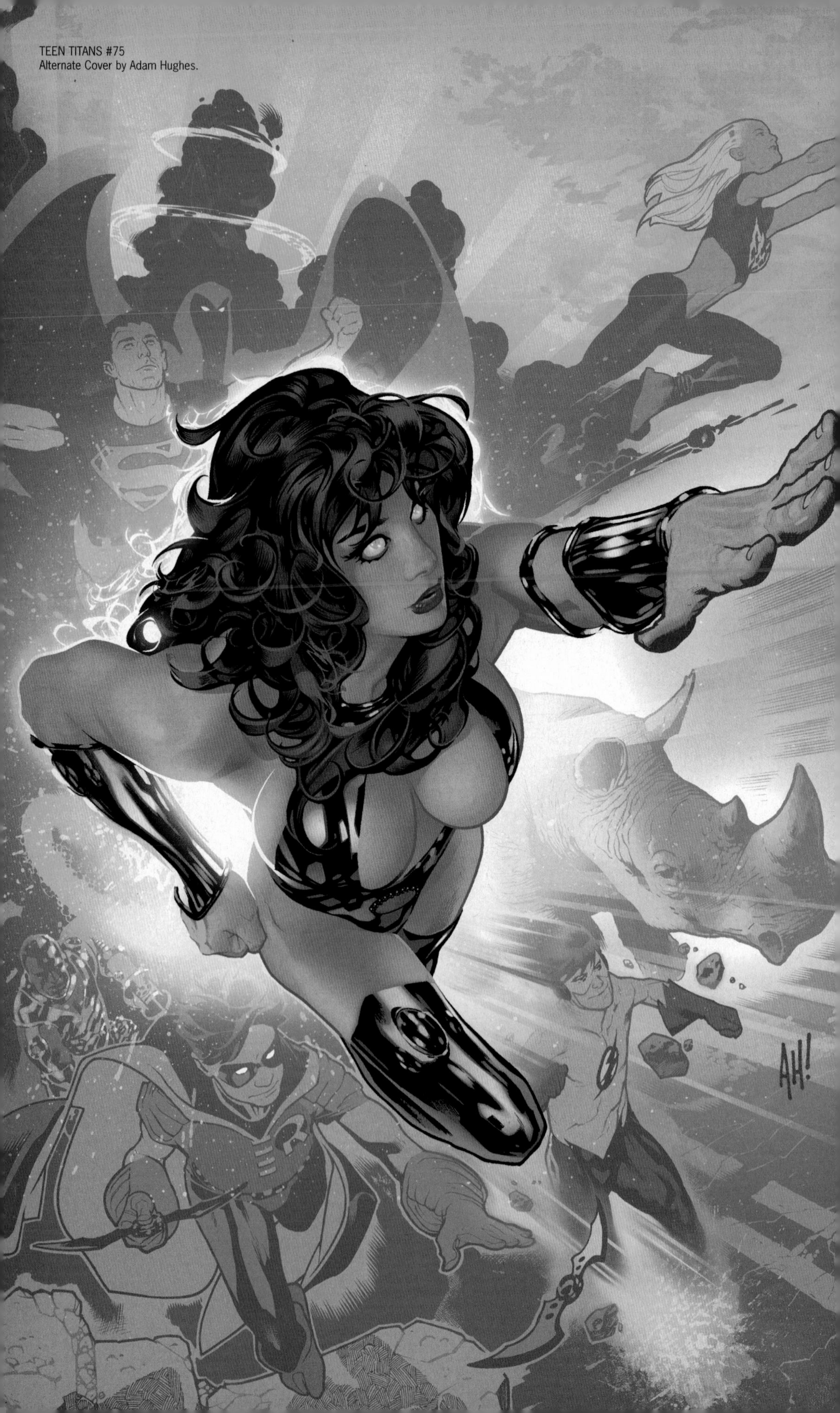
AH!

TEEN TITANS #75
Alternate Cover by Adam Hughes.

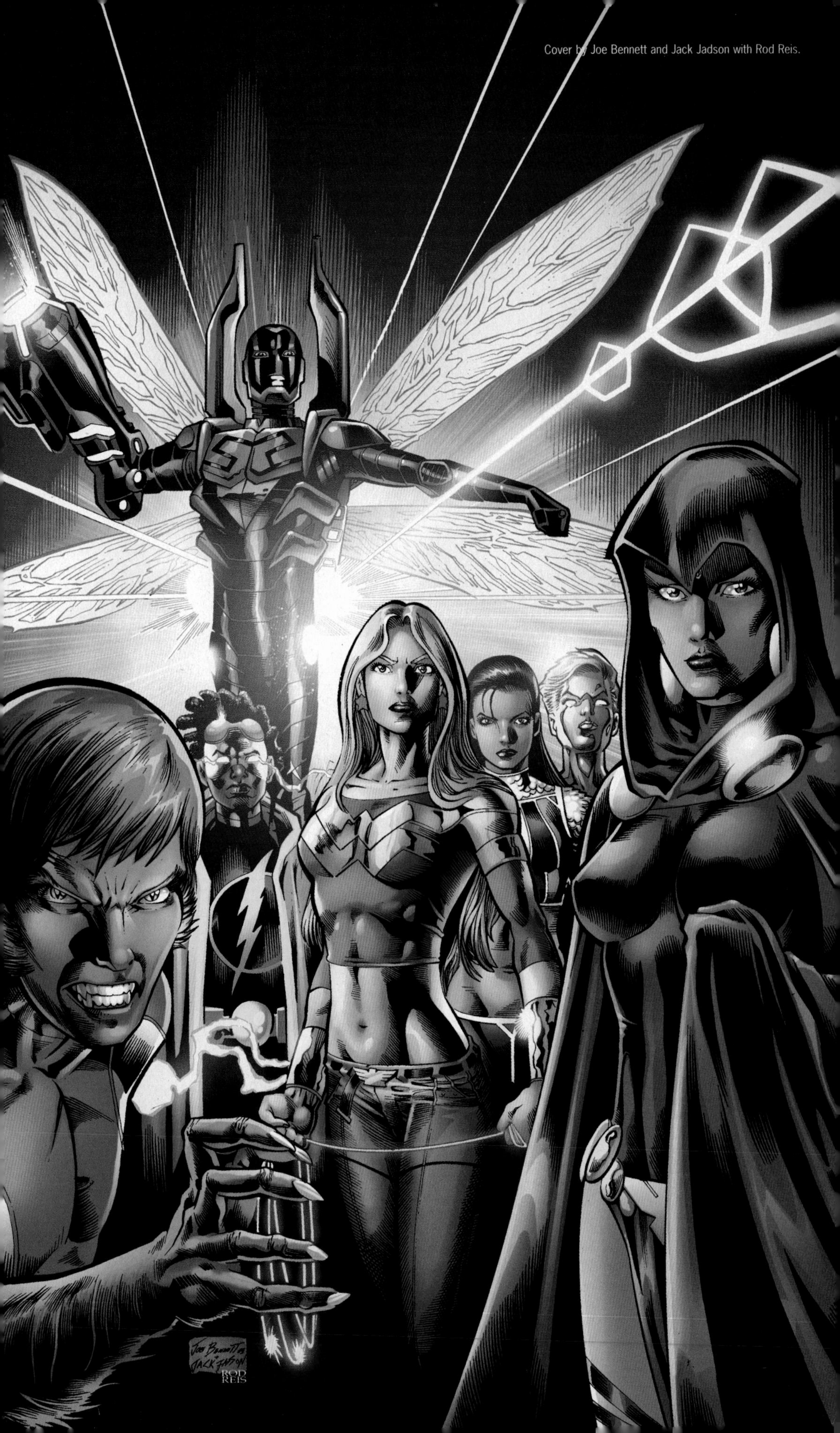
Cover by Joe Bennett and Jack Jadson with Rod Reis.

WYLD THING PART 2

Felicia D. Henderson
Writer

Yildiray Cinar
Pencils

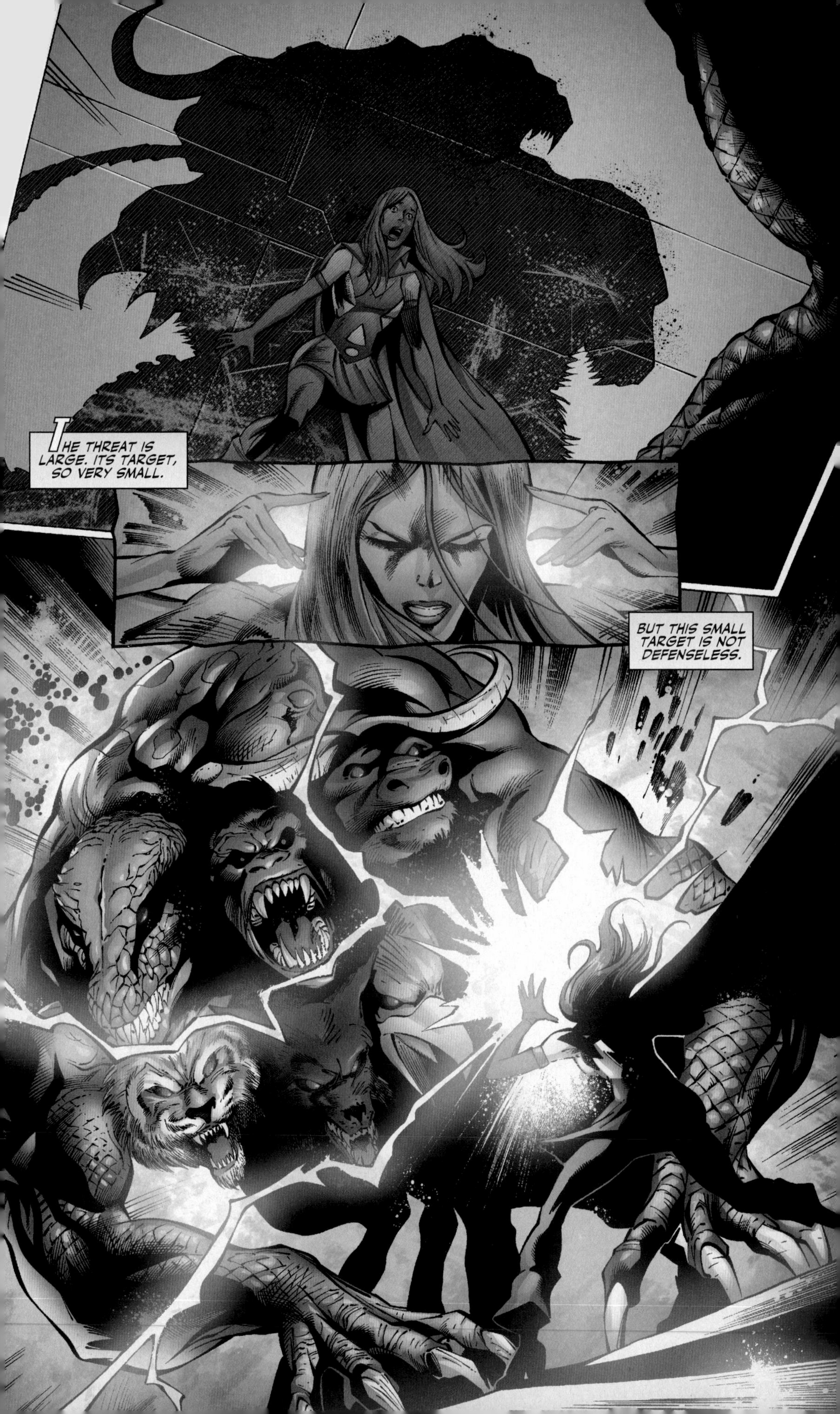
THE THREAT IS LARGE. ITS TARGET, SO VERY SMALL.
BUT THIS SMALL TARGET IS NOT DEFENSELESS.

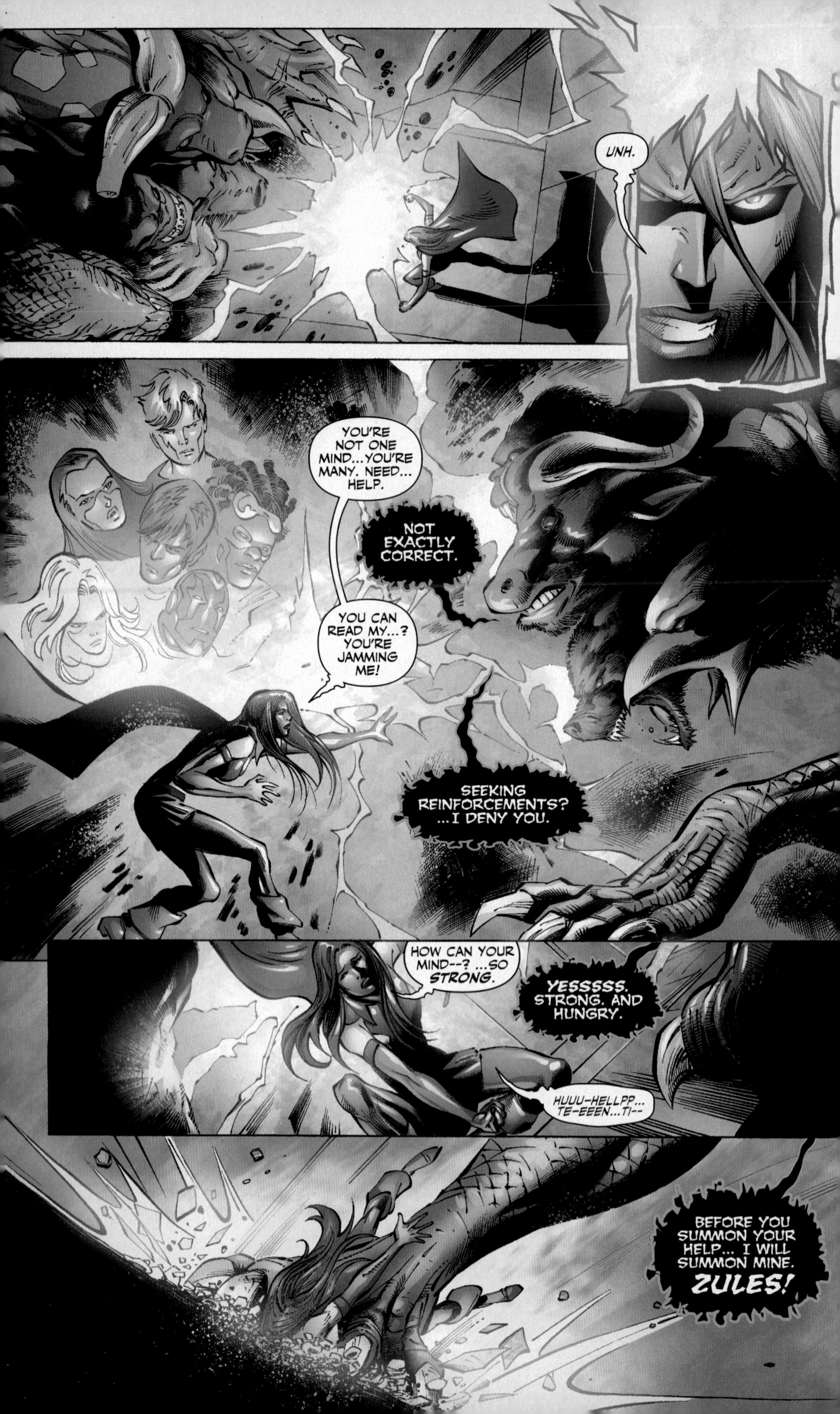
UNH.
YOU'RE NOT ONE MIND...YOU'RE MANY. NEED... HELP.
NOT EXACTLY CORRECT.
YOU CAN READ MY...? YOU'RE JAMMING ME!
SEEKING REINFORCEMENTS? ...I DENY YOU.
HOW CAN YOUR MIND--? ...SO STRONG.
YESSSSS. STRONG. AND HUNGRY.
HUUU-HELLPP... TE-EEEN...TI--
BEFORE YOU SUMMON YOUR HELP... I WILL SUMMON MINE. ZULES!

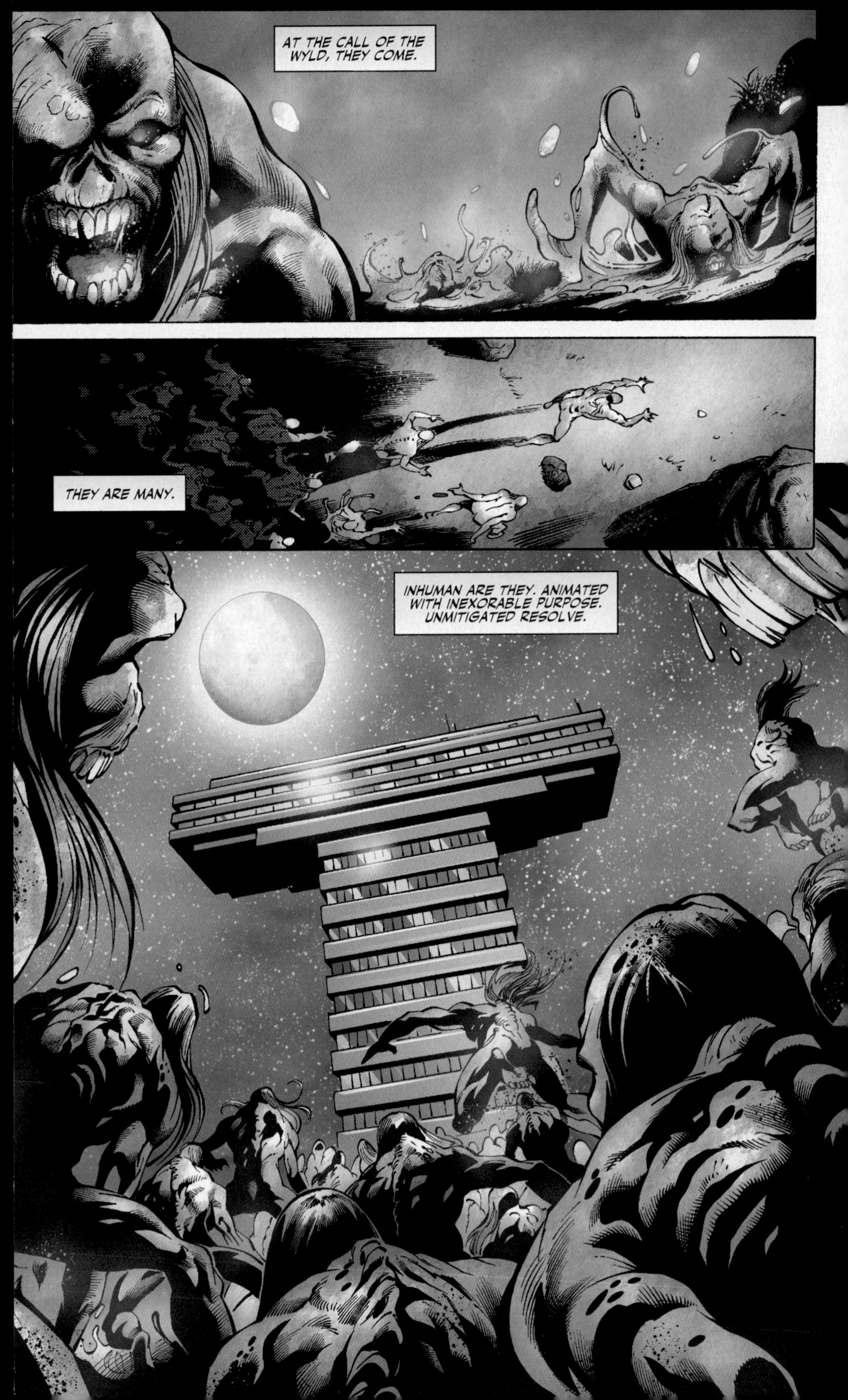
AT THE CALL OF THE WYLD, THEY COME.
THEY ARE MANY.
INHUMAN ARE THEY. ANIMATED WITH INEXORABLE PURPOSE. UNMITIGATED RESOLVE.

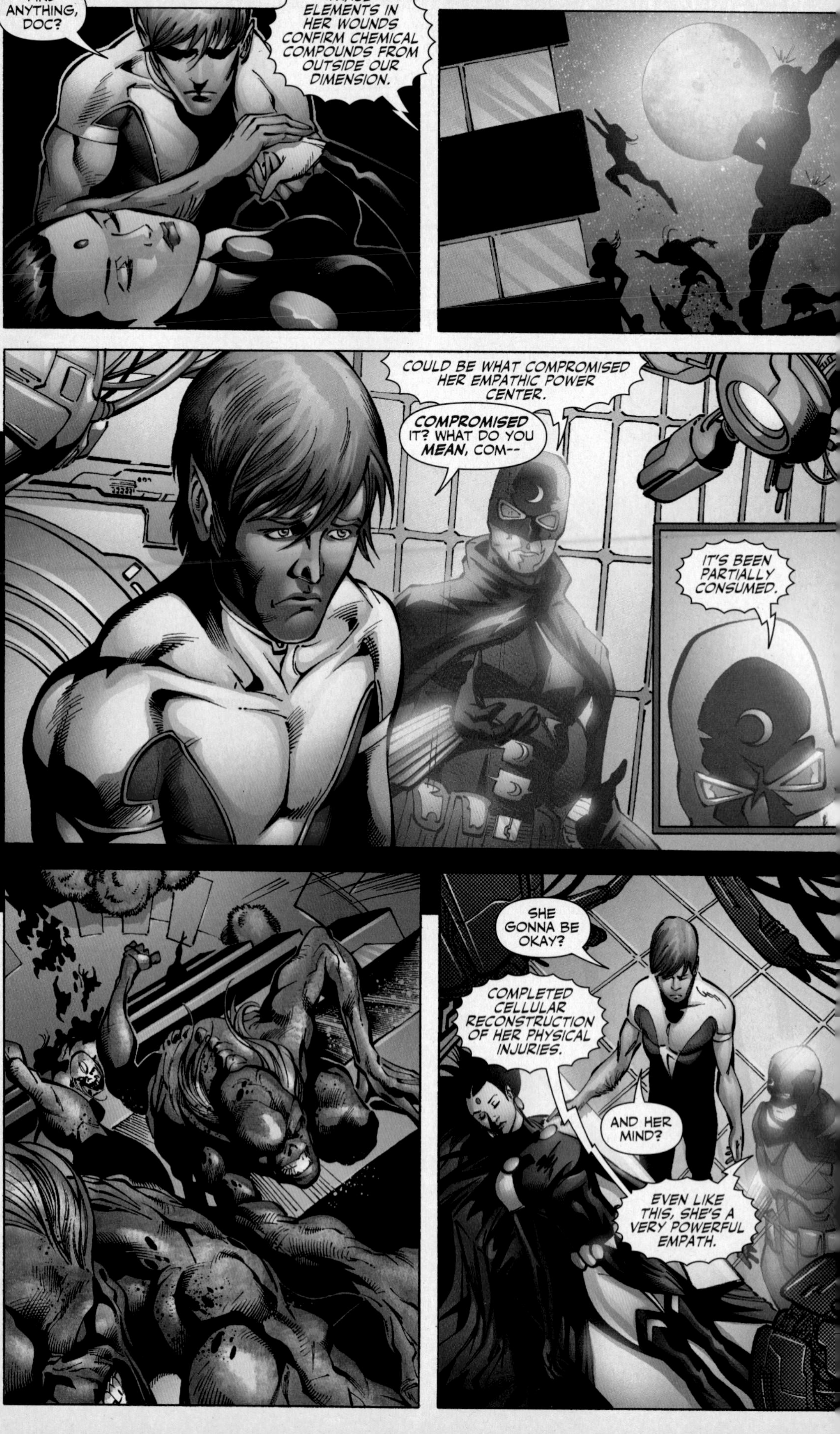
FIND ANYTHING, DOC?
TRACE ELEMENTS IN HER WOUNDS CONFIRM CHEMICAL COMPOUNDS FROM OUTSIDE OUR DIMENSION.
COULD BE WHAT COMPROMISED HER EMPATHIC POWER CENTER.
COMPROMISED IT? WHAT DO YOU MEAN, COM--
IT'S BEEN PARTIALLY CONSUMED.
SHE GONNA BE OKAY?
COMPLETED CELLULAR RECONSTRUCTION OF HER PHYSICAL INJURIES.
AND HER MIND?
EVEN LIKE THIS, SHE'S A VERY POWERFUL EMPATH.

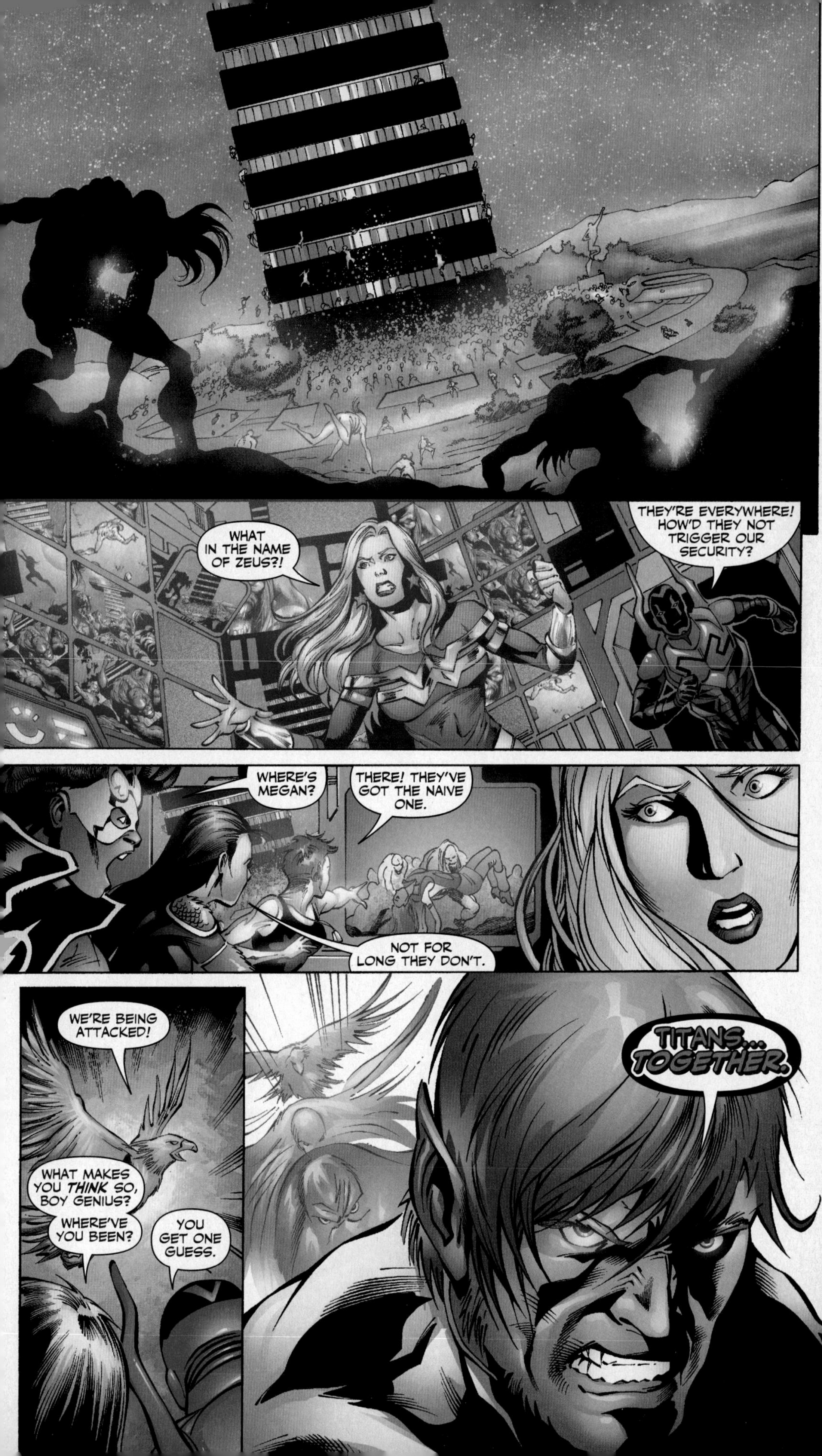
WHAT IN THE NAME OF ZEUS?!
THEY'RE EVERYWHERE! HOW'D THEY NOT TRIGGER OUR SECURITY?
WHERE'S MEGAN?
THERE! THEY'VE GOT THE NAIVE ONE.
NOT FOR LONG THEY DON'T.
WE'RE BEING ATTACKED!
WHAT MAKES YOU *THINK* SO, BOY GENIUS?
WHERE'VE YOU BEEN?
YOU GET ONE GUESS.
TITANS... TOGETHER.

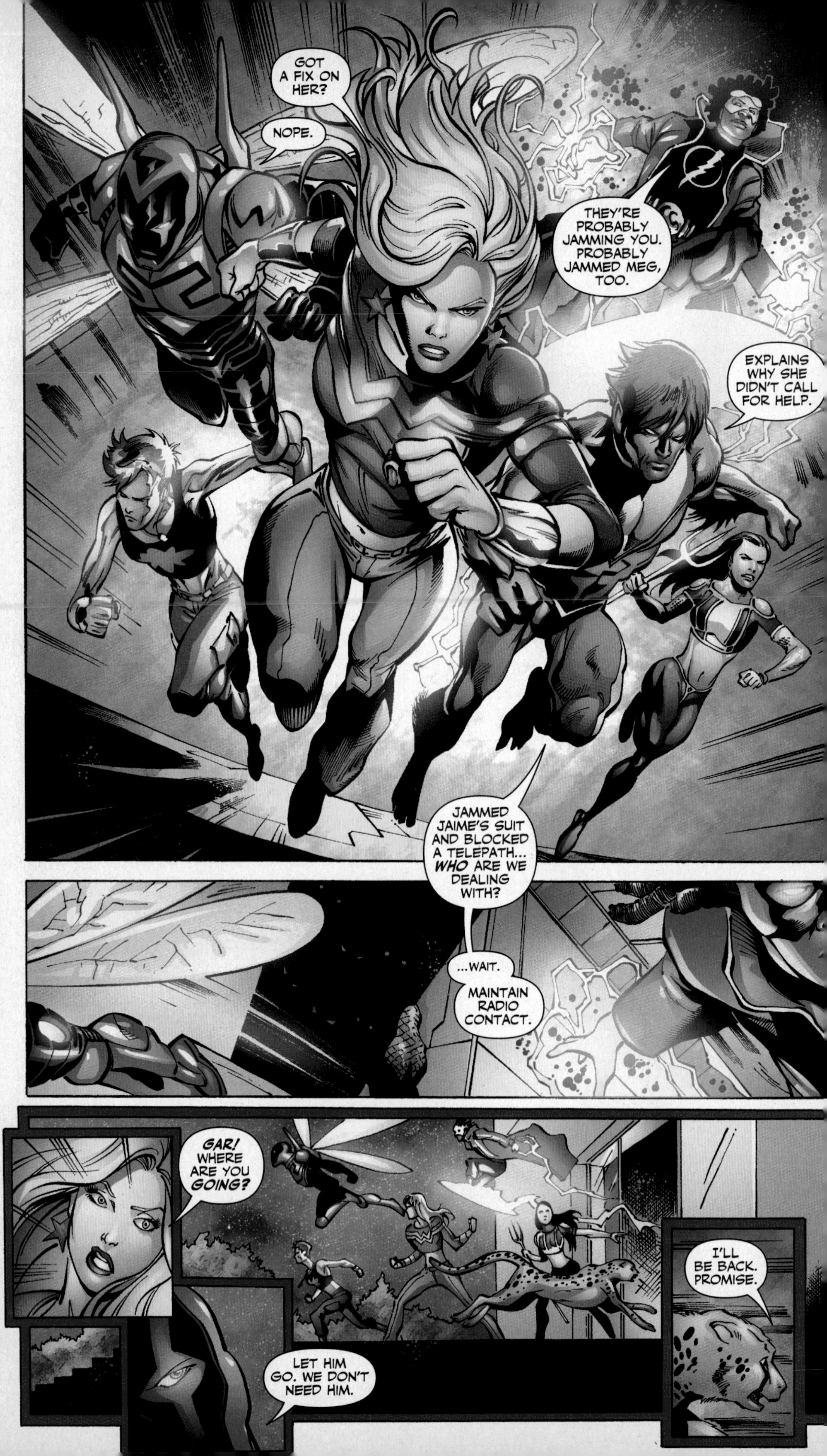
GOT A FIX ON HER?
NOPE.
THEY'RE PROBABLY JAMMING YOU. PROBABLY JAMMED MEG, TOO.
EXPLAINS WHY SHE DIDN'T CALL FOR HELP.
JAMMED JAIME'S SUIT AND BLOCKED A TELEPATH... *WHO* ARE WE DEALING WITH?
...WAIT.
MAINTAIN RADIO CONTACT.
GAR! WHERE ARE YOU *GOING?*
I'LL BE BACK. PROMISE.
LET HIM GO. WE DON'T NEED HIM.

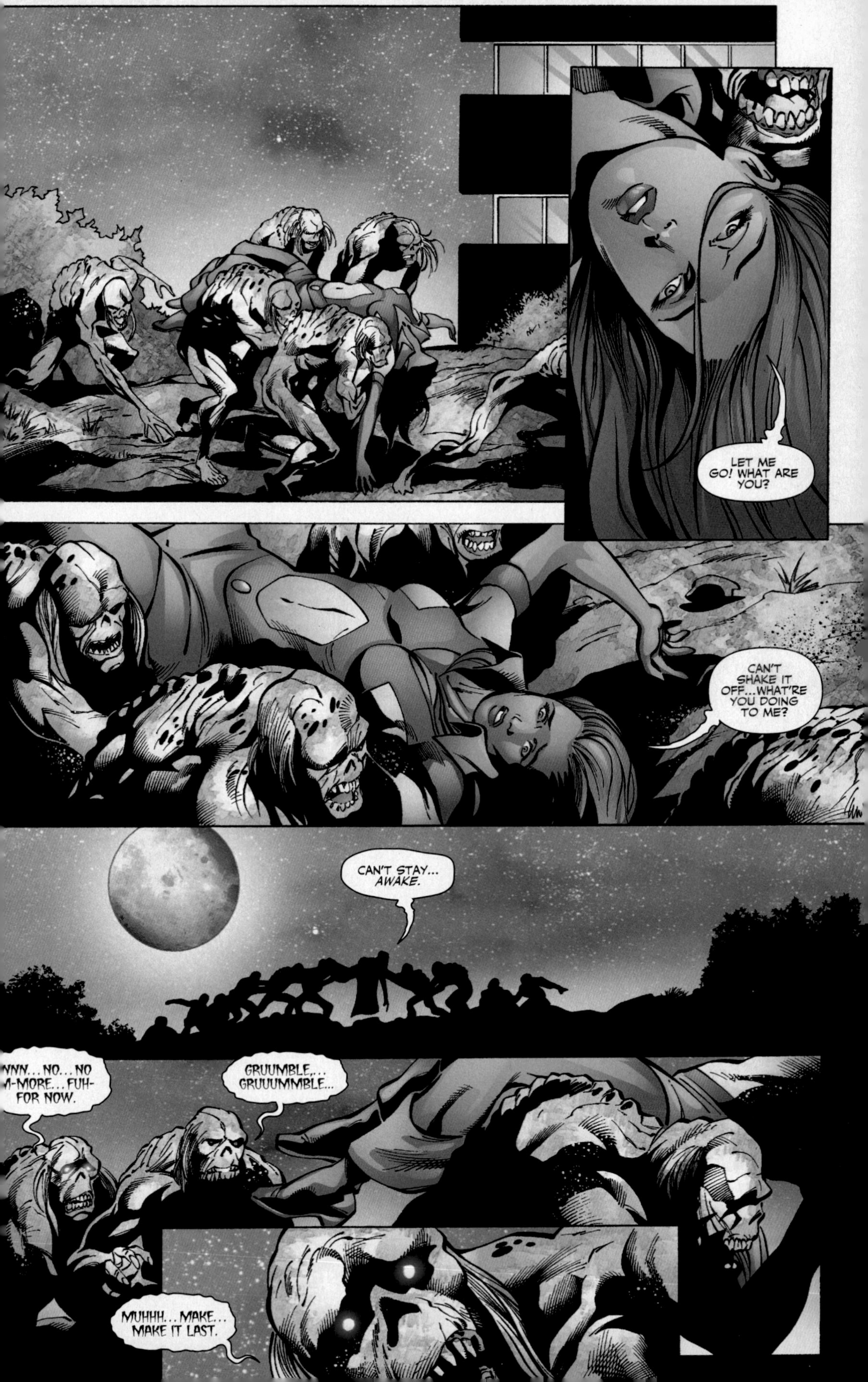
LET ME GO! WHAT ARE YOU?
CAN'T SHAKE IT OFF...WHAT'RE YOU DOING TO ME?
CAN'T STAY... AWAKE.
NNN... NO... NO M-MORE... FUH-FOR NOW.
GRUUMBLE... GRUUUMMBLE...
MUHHH... MAKE... MAKE IT LAST.

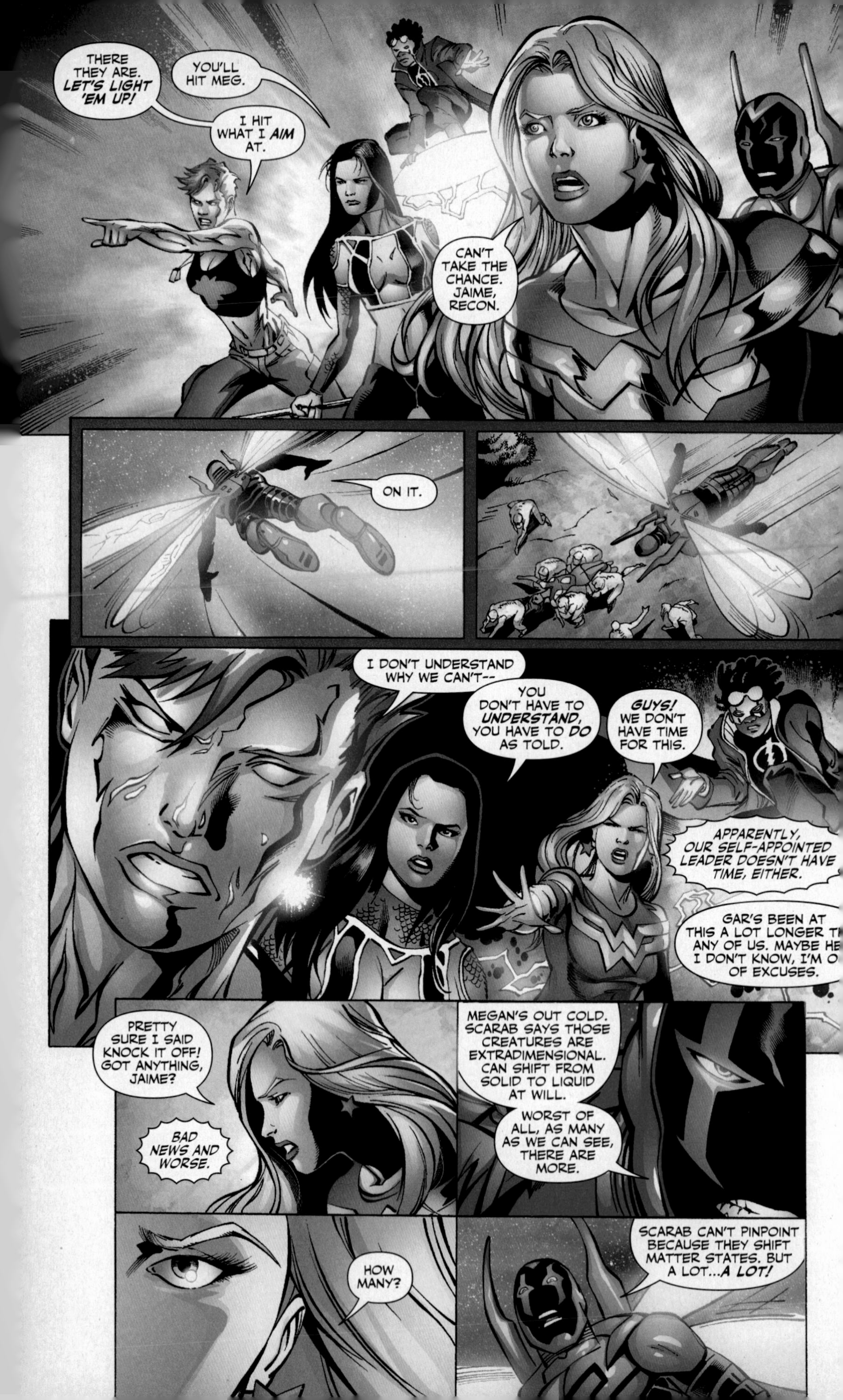
THERE THEY ARE. LET'S LIGHT 'EM UP!
YOU'LL HIT MEG.
I HIT WHAT I AIM AT.
CAN'T TAKE THE CHANCE. JAIME, RECON.
ON IT.
I DON'T UNDERSTAND WHY WE CAN'T--
YOU DON'T HAVE TO UNDERSTAND, YOU HAVE TO DO AS TOLD.
GUYS! WE DON'T HAVE TIME FOR THIS.
APPARENTLY, OUR SELF-APPOINTED LEADER DOESN'T HAVE TIME, EITHER.
GAR'S BEEN AT THIS A LOT LONGER T
ANY OF US. MAYBE HE
I DON'T KNOW, I'M O
OF EXCUSES.
PRETTY SURE I SAID KNOCK IT OFF! GOT ANYTHING, JAIME?
BAD NEWS AND WORSE.
MEGAN'S OUT COLD. SCARAB SAYS THOSE CREATURES ARE EXTRADIMENSIONAL. CAN SHIFT FROM SOLID TO LIQUID AT WILL.
WORST OF ALL, AS MANY AS WE CAN SEE, THERE ARE MORE.
HOW MANY?
SCARAB CAN'T PINPOINT BECAUSE THEY SHIFT MATTER STATES. BUT A LOT...A LOT!

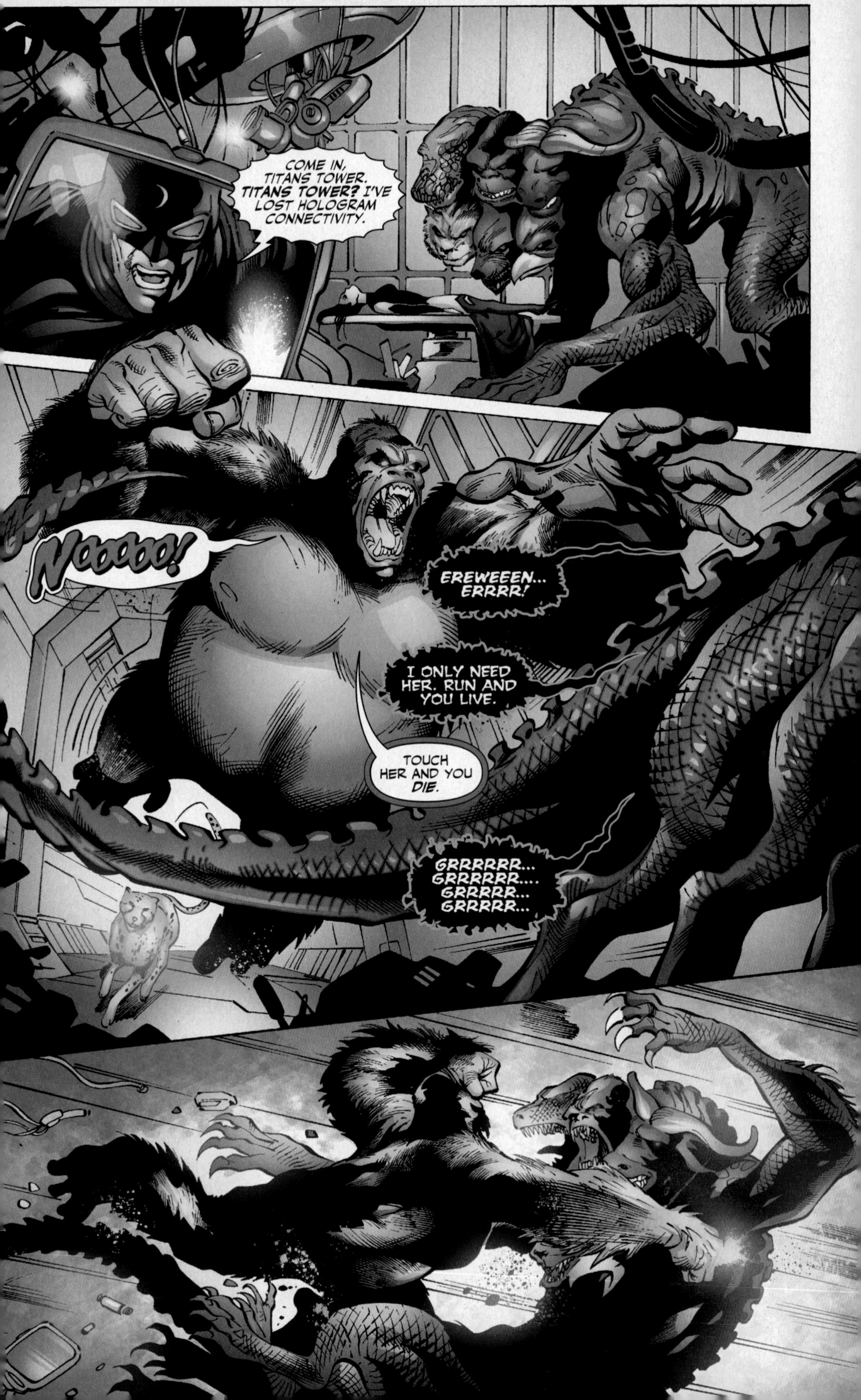
COME IN, TITANS TOWER. TITANS TOWER? I'VE LOST HOLOGRAM CONNECTIVITY.
NOOOOO!
EREWEEEN... ERRRR!
I ONLY NEED HER. RUN AND YOU LIVE.
TOUCH HER AND YOU DIE.
GRRRRRR... GRRRRRR.... GRRRRR... GRRRRR...

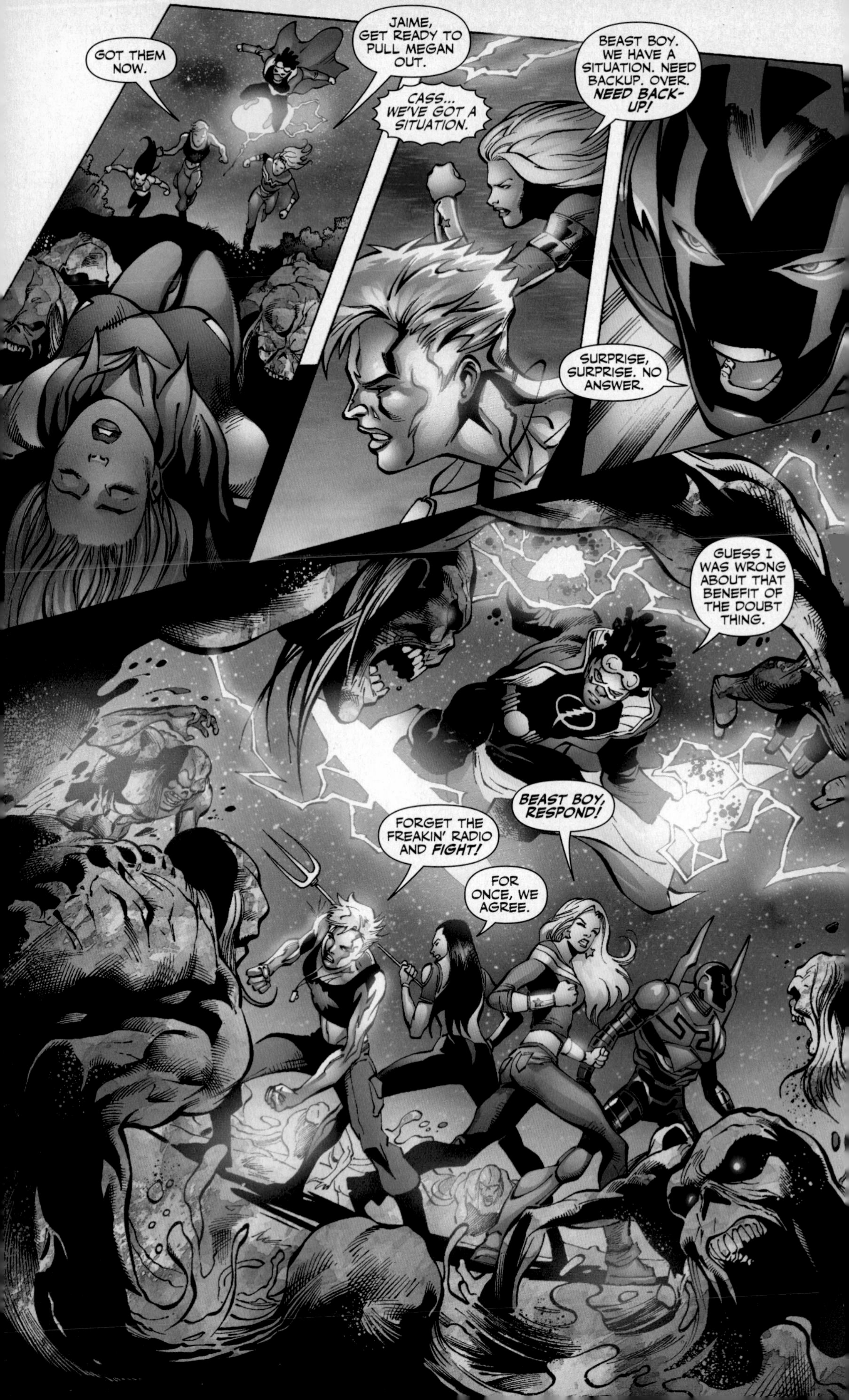
GOT THEM NOW.
JAIME, GET READY TO PULL MEGAN OUT.
CASS... WE'VE GOT A SITUATION.
BEAST BOY. WE HAVE A SITUATION. NEED BACKUP. OVER. NEED BACK-UP!
SURPRISE, SURPRISE. NO ANSWER.
GUESS I WAS WRONG ABOUT THAT BENEFIT OF THE DOUBT THING.
BEAST BOY, RESPOND!
FORGET THE FREAKIN' RADIO AND FIGHT!
FOR ONCE, WE AGREE.

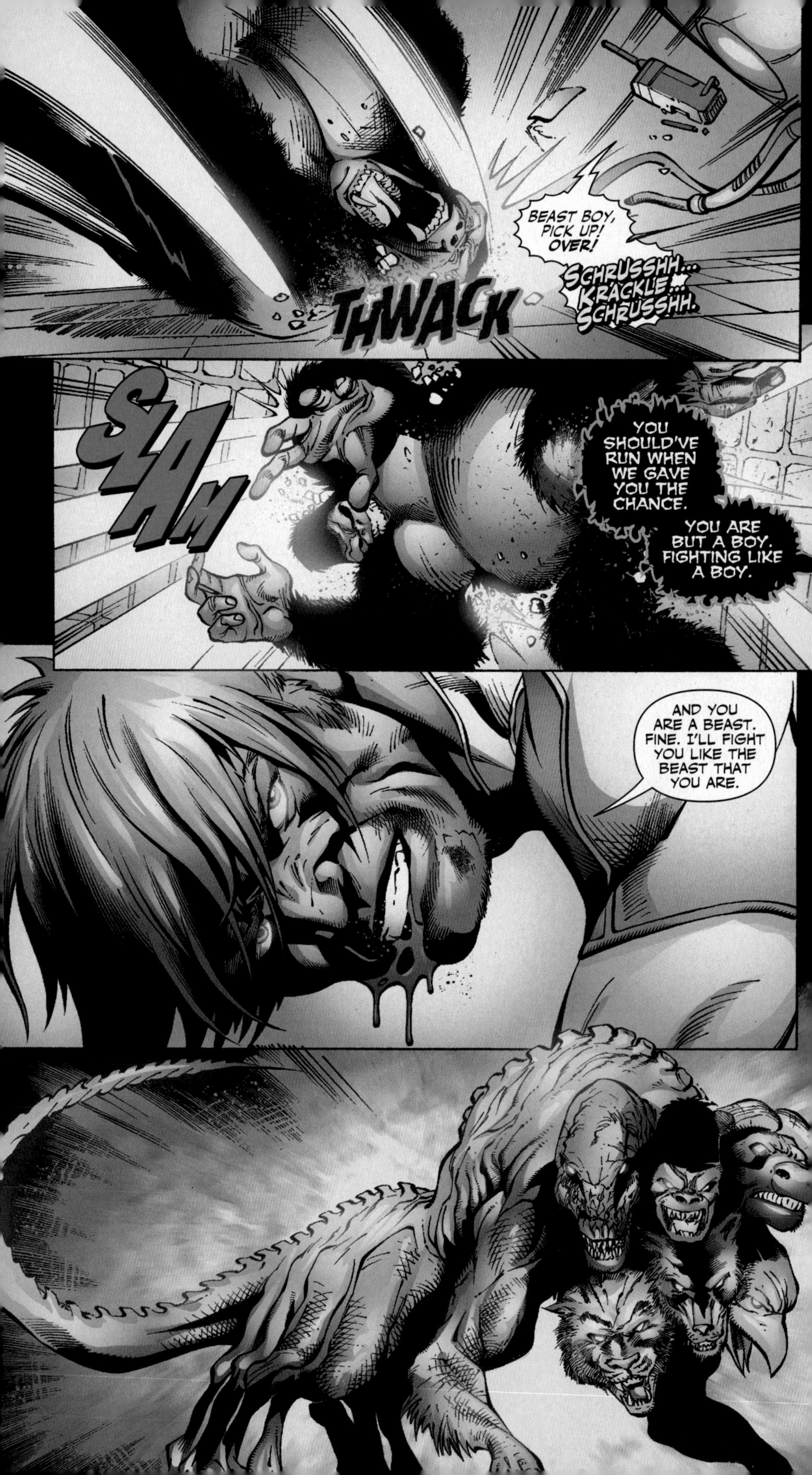
BEAST BOY, PICK UP! OVER!
SCHRUSSHH... KRACKLE... SCHRUSSHH.
THWACK
SLAM
YOU SHOULD'VE RUN WHEN WE GAVE YOU THE CHANCE.
YOU ARE BUT A BOY. FIGHTING LIKE A BOY.
AND YOU ARE A BEAST. FINE. I'LL FIGHT YOU LIKE THE BEAST THAT YOU ARE.

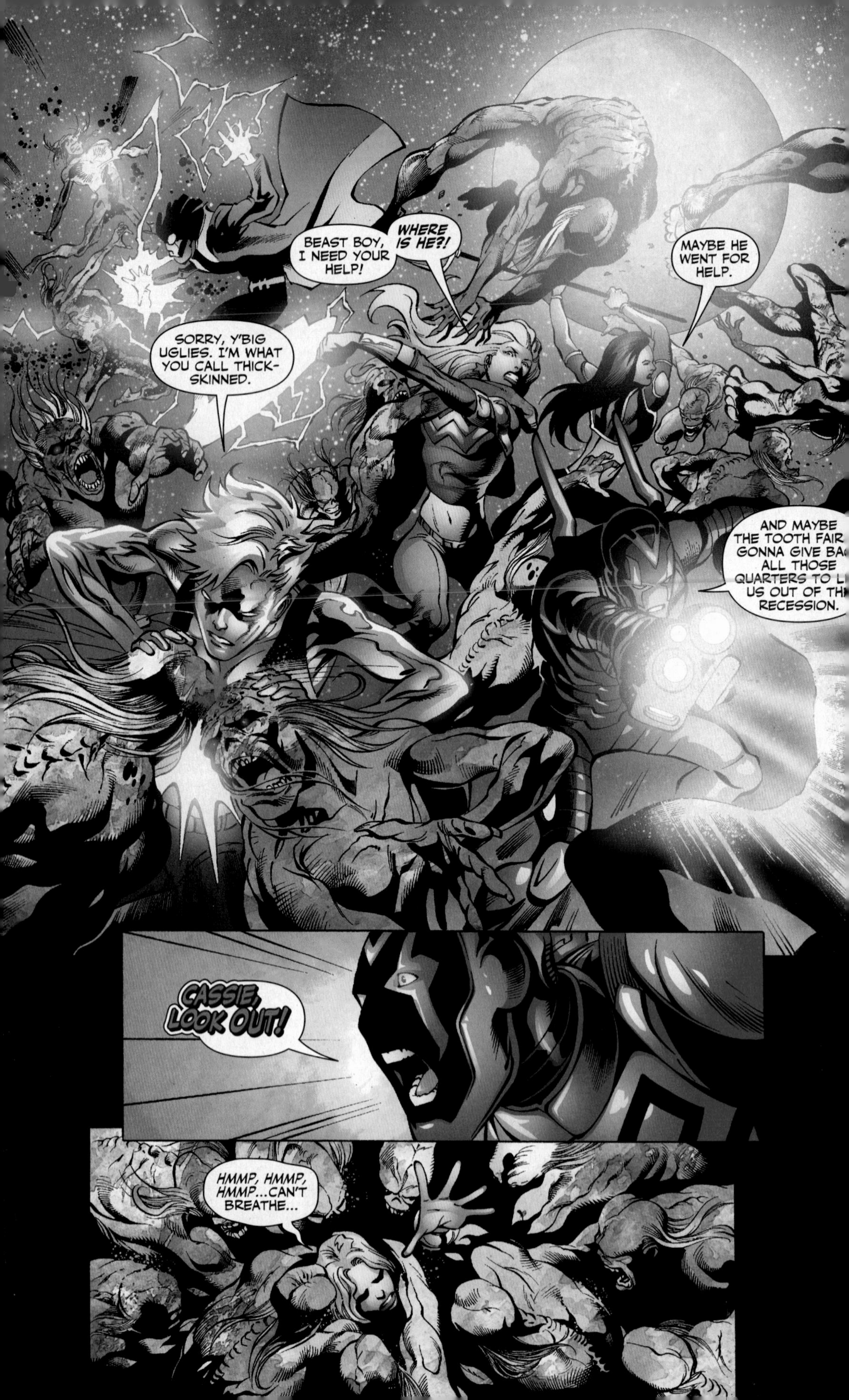
BEAST BOY, I NEED YOUR HELP!
WHERE IS HE?!
MAYBE HE WENT FOR HELP.
SORRY, Y'BIG UGLIES. I'M WHAT YOU CALL THICK-SKINNED.
AND MAYBE THE TOOTH FAIR GONNA GIVE BA ALL THOSE QUARTERS TO L US OUT OF TH RECESSION.
CASSIE, LOOK OUT!
HMMP, HMMP, HMMP...CAN'T BREATHE...

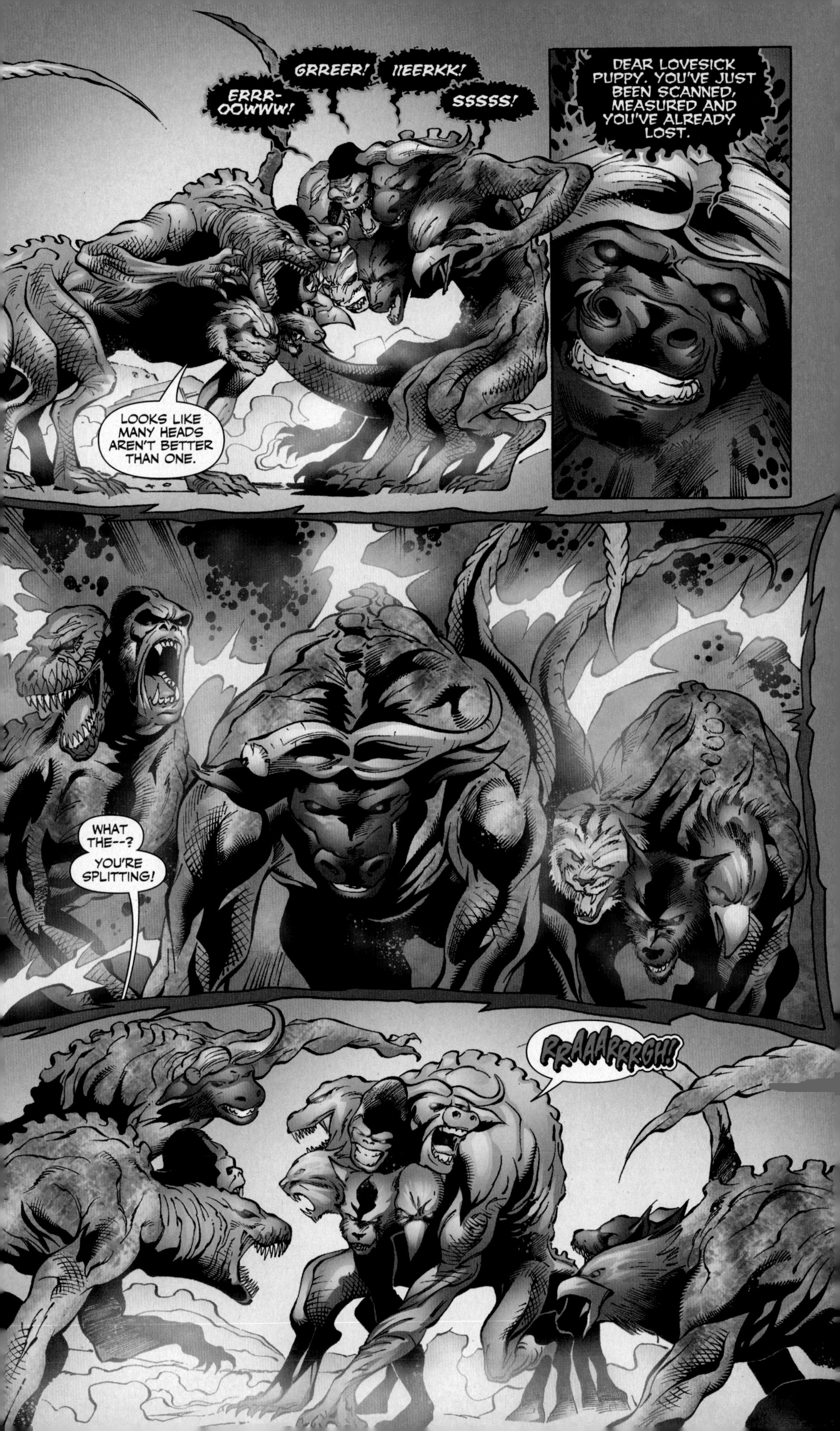

ERRR-OOWWW!
GRREER!
!!EERKK!
SSSSS!
DEAR LOVESICK PUPPY. YOU'VE JUST BEEN SCANNED, MEASURED AND YOU'VE ALREADY LOST.
LOOKS LIKE MANY HEADS AREN'T BETTER THAN ONE.
WHAT THE--? YOU'RE SPLITTING!
RRAAARRRGH!!

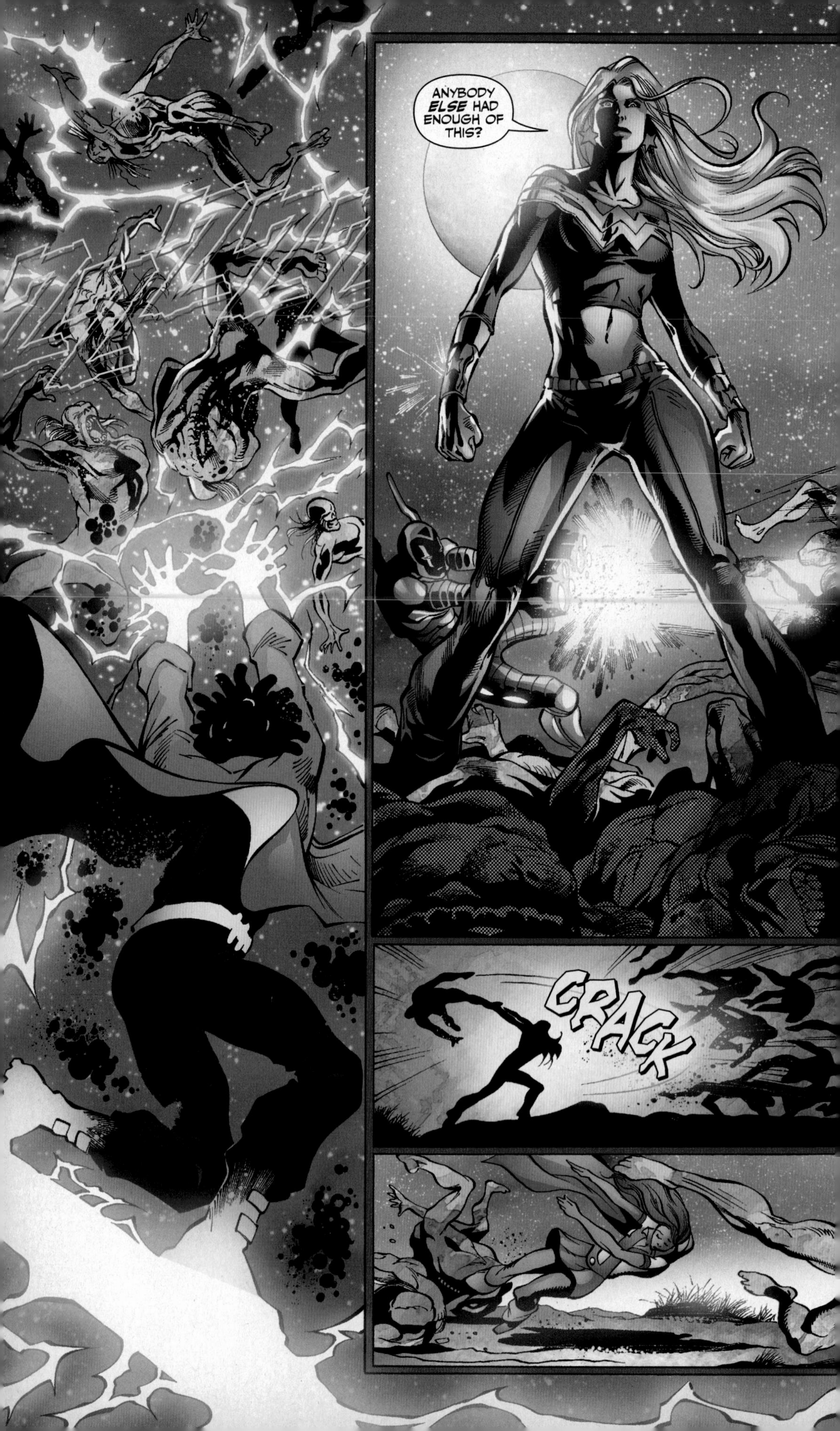
ANYBODY ELSE HAD ENOUGH OF THIS?
CRACK

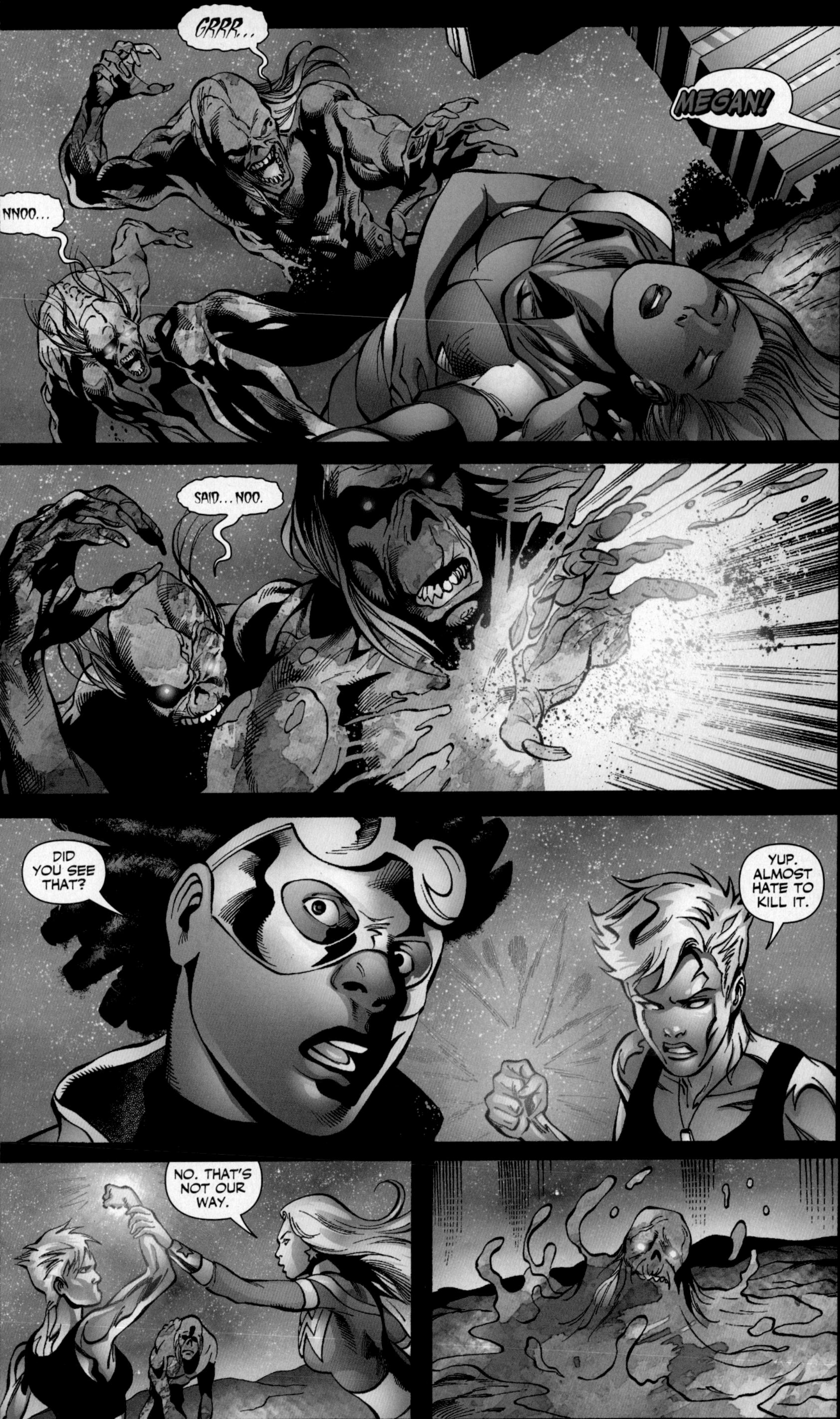
GRRR...
MEGAN!
NNOO...
SAID... NOO.
DID YOU SEE THAT?
YUP. ALMOST HATE TO KILL IT.
NO. THAT'S NOT OUR WAY.

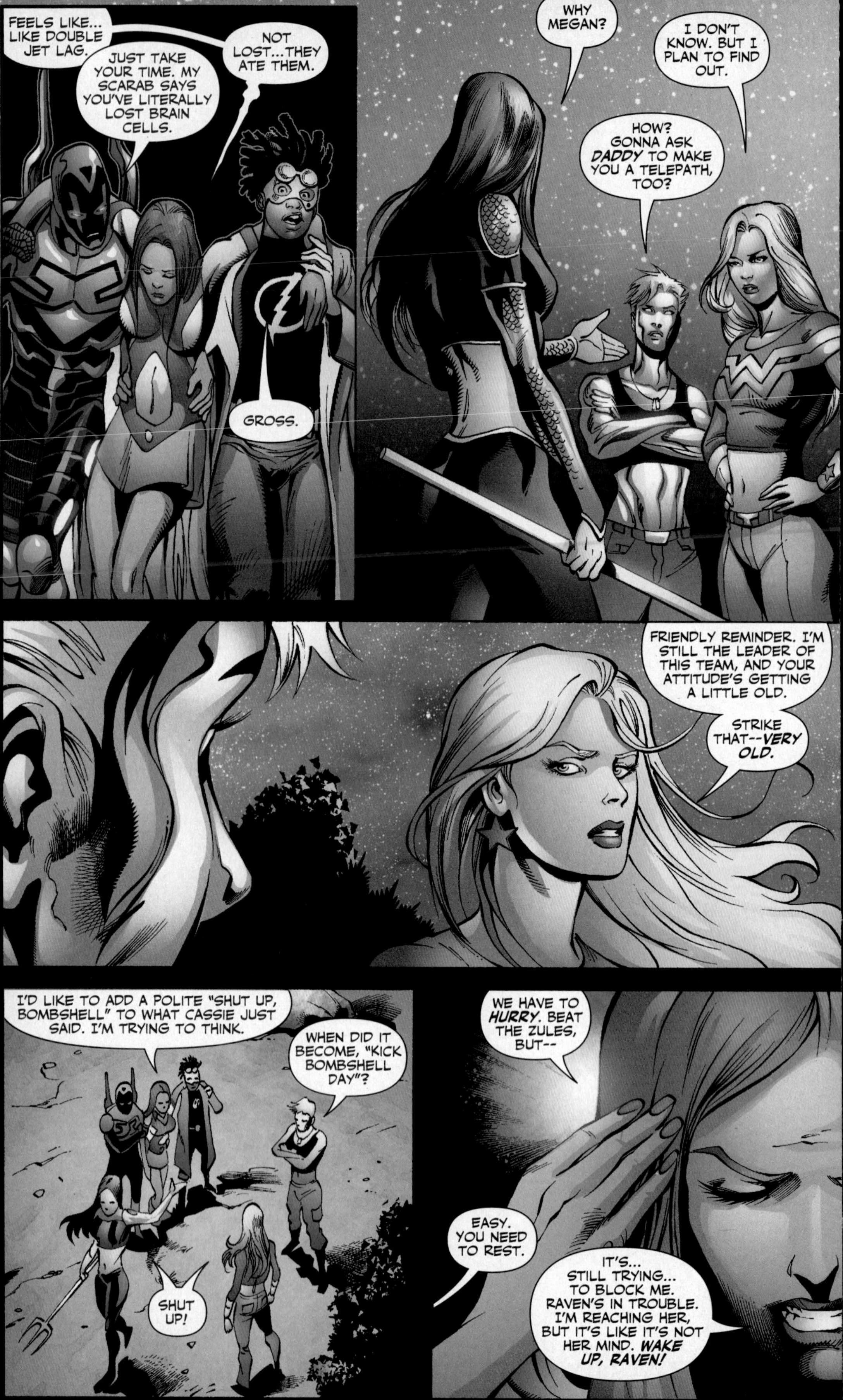
FEELS LIKE... LIKE DOUBLE JET LAG.
JUST TAKE YOUR TIME. MY SCARAB SAYS YOU'VE LITERALLY LOST BRAIN CELLS.
NOT LOST...THEY ATE THEM.
GROSS.
WHY MEGAN?
I DON'T KNOW. BUT I PLAN TO FIND OUT.
HOW? GONNA ASK *DADDY* TO MAKE YOU A TELEPATH, TOO?
FRIENDLY REMINDER. I'M STILL THE LEADER OF THIS TEAM, AND YOUR ATTITUDE'S GETTING A LITTLE OLD.
STRIKE THAT--*VERY OLD.*
I'D LIKE TO ADD A POLITE "SHUT UP, BOMBSHELL" TO WHAT CASSIE JUST SAID. I'M TRYING TO THINK.
WHEN DID IT BECOME, "KICK BOMBSHELL DAY"?
SHUT UP!
WE HAVE TO *HURRY*. BEAT THE ZULES, BUT--
EASY. YOU NEED TO REST.
IT'S... STILL TRYING... TO BLOCK ME. RAVEN'S IN TROUBLE. I'M REACHING HER, BUT IT'S LIKE IT'S NOT HER MIND. *WAKE UP, RAVEN!*

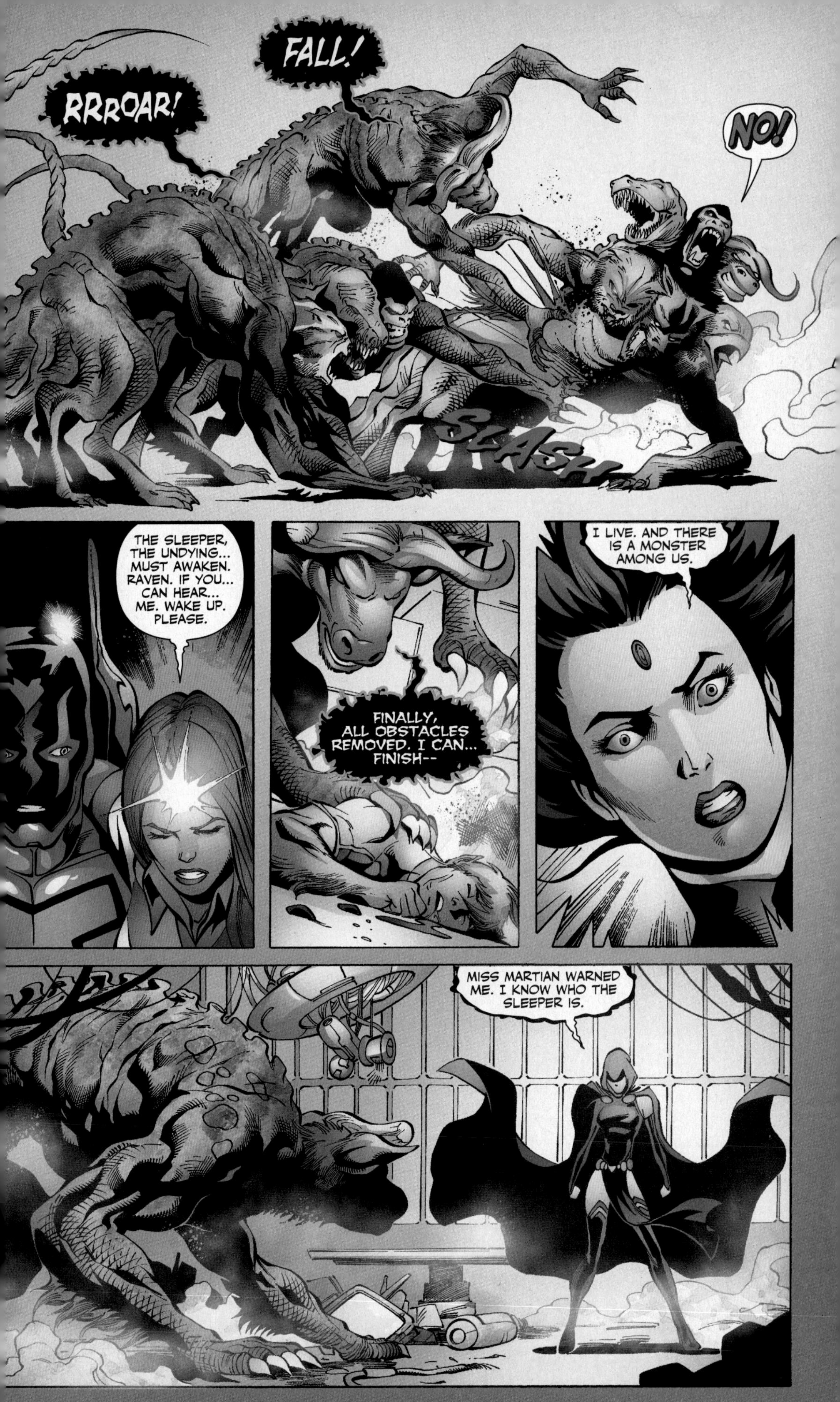
RRROAR!
FALL!
NO!
SLASH
THE SLEEPER, THE UNDYING... MUST AWAKEN. RAVEN. IF YOU... CAN HEAR... ME. WAKE UP. PLEASE.
FINALLY, ALL OBSTACLES REMOVED. I CAN... FINISH--
I LIVE. AND THERE IS A MONSTER AMONG US.
MISS MARTIAN WARNED ME. I KNOW WHO THE SLEEPER IS.

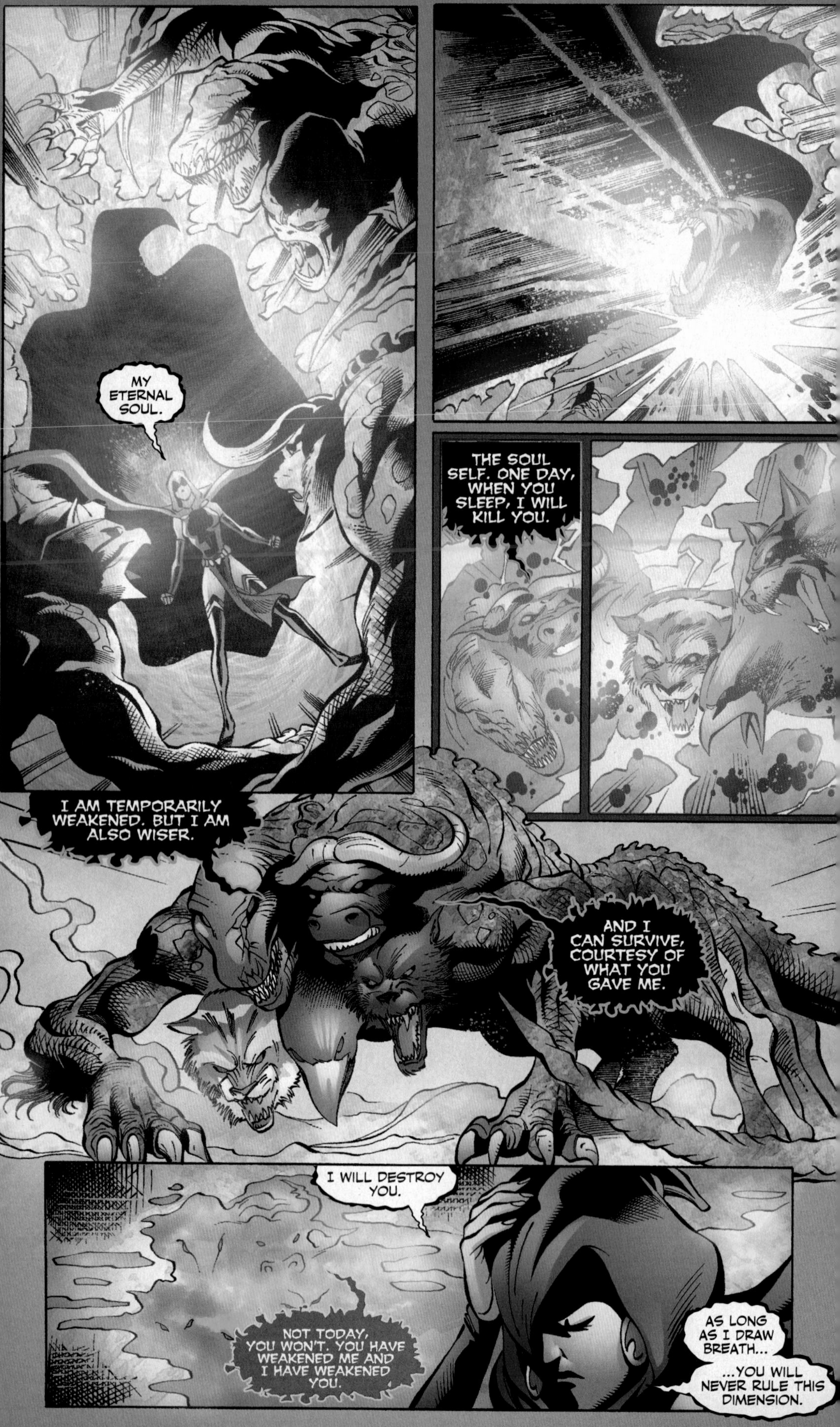
MY ETERNAL SOUL.
THE SOUL SELF. ONE DAY, WHEN YOU SLEEP, I WILL KILL YOU.
I AM TEMPORARILY WEAKENED. BUT I AM ALSO WISER.
AND I CAN SURVIVE, COURTESY OF WHAT YOU GAVE ME.
I WILL DESTROY YOU.
NOT TODAY, YOU WON'T. YOU HAVE WEAKENED ME AND I HAVE WEAKENED YOU.
AS LONG AS I DRAW BREATH...
...YOU WILL NEVER RULE THIS DIMENSION.

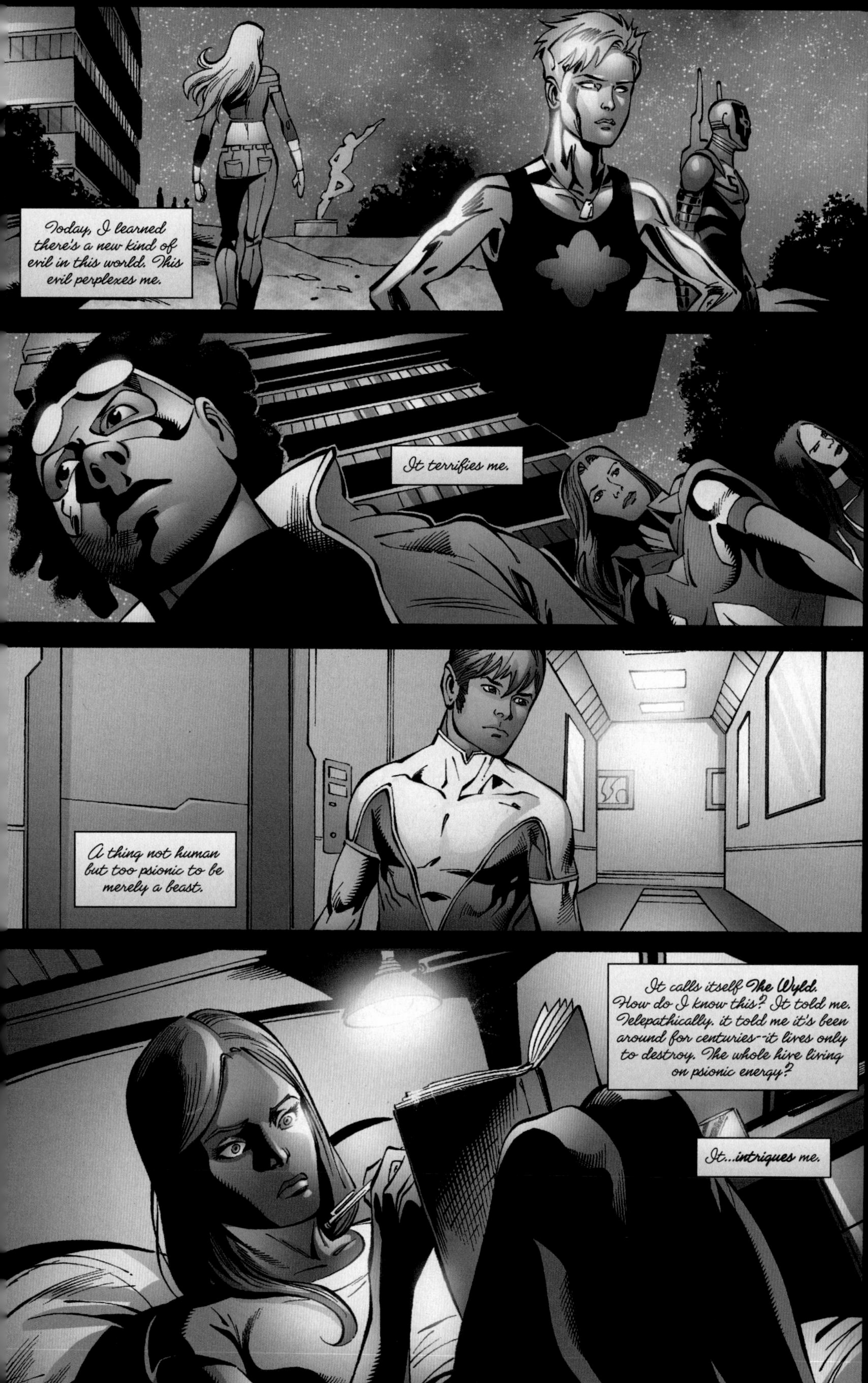
Today, I learned there's a new kind of evil in this world. This evil perplexes me.
It terrifies me.
A thing not human but too psionic to be merely a beast.
It calls itself The Wyld. How do I know this? It told me. Telepathically, it told me it's been around for centuries--it lives only to destroy. The whole hive living on psionic energy?
It...intriques me.

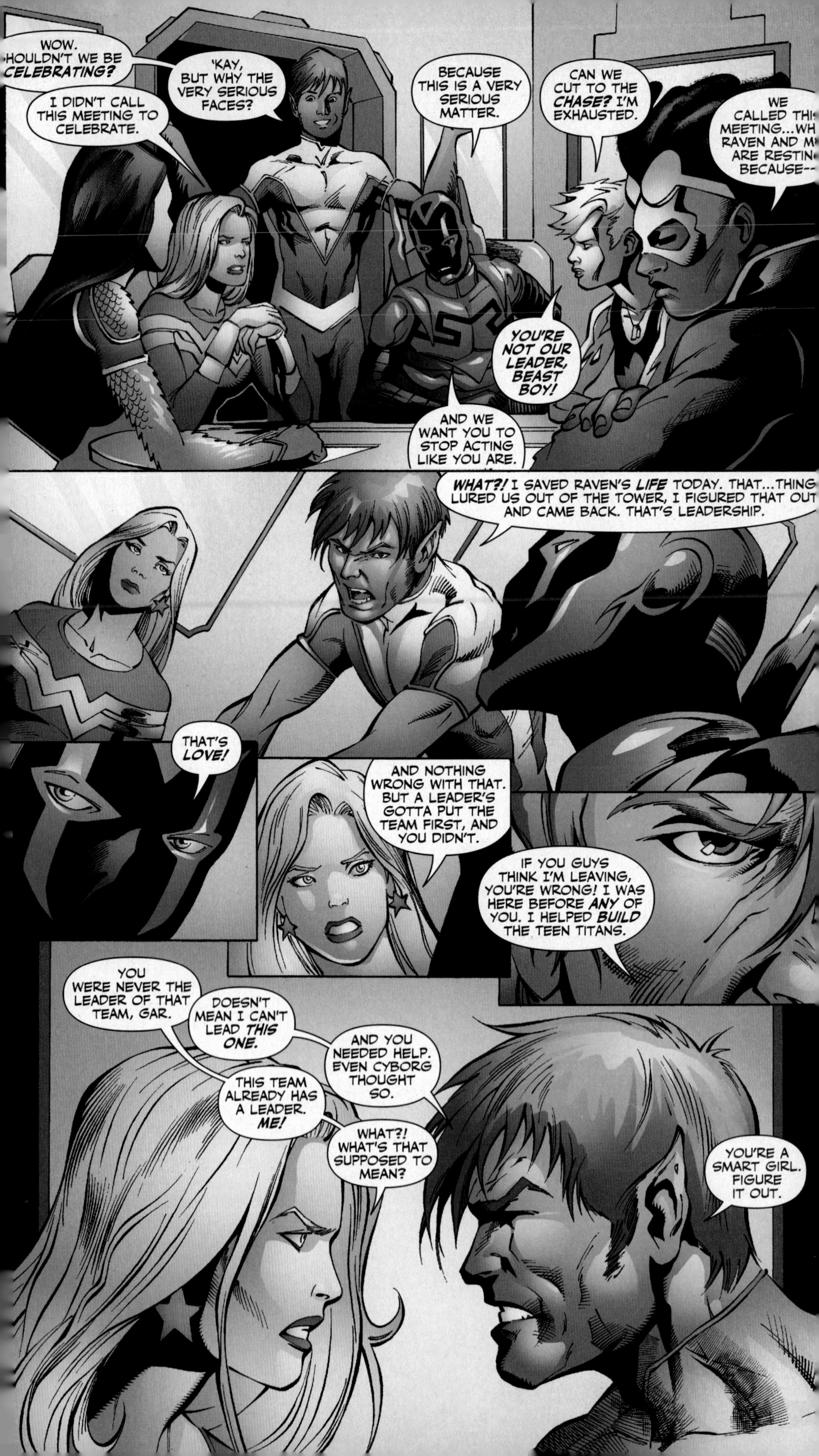
WOW. HOULDN'T WE BE CELEBRATING?
'KAY, BUT WHY THE VERY SERIOUS FACES?
I DIDN'T CALL THIS MEETING TO CELEBRATE.
BECAUSE THIS IS A VERY SERIOUS MATTER.
CAN WE CUT TO THE CHASE? I'M EXHAUSTED.
WE CALLED THI MEETING...WH RAVEN AND M ARE RESTIN BECAUSE--
YOU'RE NOT OUR LEADER, BEAST BOY!
AND WE WANT YOU TO STOP ACTING LIKE YOU ARE.
WHAT?! I SAVED RAVEN'S LIFE TODAY. THAT...THING LURED US OUT OF THE TOWER, I FIGURED THAT OUT AND CAME BACK. THAT'S LEADERSHIP.
THAT'S LOVE!
AND NOTHING WRONG WITH THAT. BUT A LEADER'S GOTTA PUT THE TEAM FIRST, AND YOU DIDN'T.
IF YOU GUYS THINK I'M LEAVING, YOU'RE WRONG! I WAS HERE BEFORE ANY OF YOU. I HELPED BUILD THE TEEN TITANS.
YOU WERE NEVER THE LEADER OF THAT TEAM, GAR.
DOESN'T MEAN I CAN'T LEAD THIS ONE.
AND YOU NEEDED HELP. EVEN CYBORG THOUGHT SO.
THIS TEAM ALREADY HAS A LEADER. ME!
WHAT?! WHAT'S THAT SUPPOSED TO MEAN?
YOU'RE A SMART GIRL. FIGURE IT OUT.

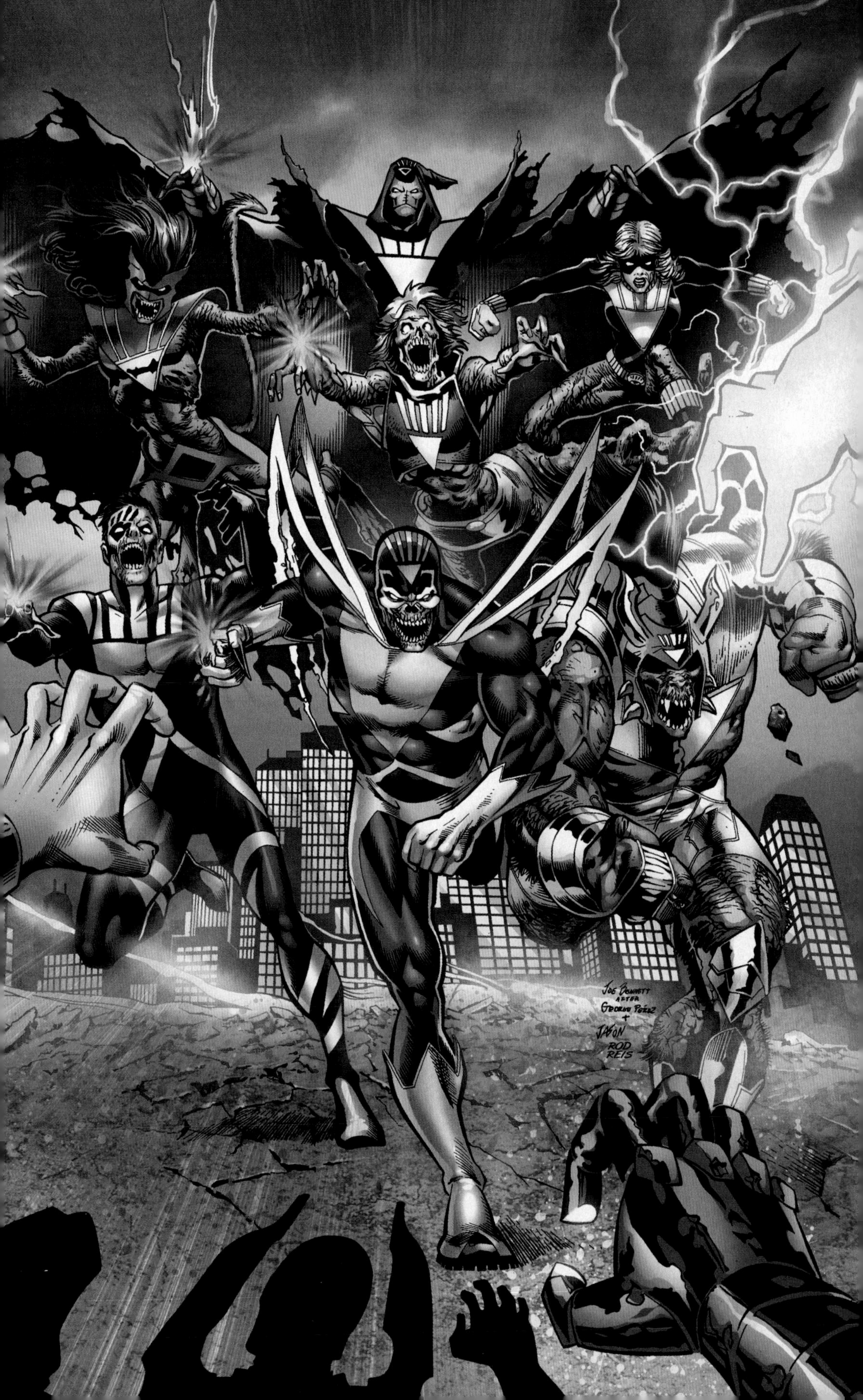
AFTER
+
ROD
REIS
Cover by Joe Bennett and Jack Jadson with Rod Reis after George Pérez.

A FAMILY AFFAIR

J.T. Krul
Writer

Joe Bennett
Pencils

Jack Jadson and Ruy José
Inks

TARGET LOCKED.

ROGERS

WILSON

SLADE WILSON. ALAS--I KNEW HIM WELL. WELL BEFORE HE BECAME *DEATHSTROKE THE TERMINATOR.*

SLADE WAS THE BEST SOLDIER I HAD EVER KNOWN. AND WHEN HE RISKED EVERYTHING TO SAVE MY LIFE, I VOWED TO STAY AT HIS SIDE--NO MATTER WHAT.

[I] WOULD NOT [CA]LL US FRIENDS. [SL]ADE HAD NO [TIME] FOR FRIENDS. [FO]R HIM, EVERY [M]OMENT WAS [PRE]PARATION FOR [THE] NEXT BATTLE.

[EVEN] HIS DECISION [TO] GET MARRIED WAS [TIE]D TO THAT DRIVE. *ADELINE KANE* WAS [HIS] SPECIAL FORCES [TR]AINER. ONE OF THE [FEW] PEOPLE HE [RES]PECTED ON THE [B]ATTLEFIELD.

I WAS AT HIS SIDE WHEN SLADE UNDERWENT A MILITARY EXPERIMENT THAT TURNED HIM INTO A SUPER SOLDIER.

AND THUS *DEATHSTROKE* WAS BORN--A SOLDIER OF FORTUNE. A *MERCENARY* FOR HIRE. AN *ASSASSIN* WHO REFUSED TO FAIL.

I NEVER FOUND TIME FOR A LIFE OF MY OWN WHILE I WAS IN SLADE'S SERVICE AS HIS *FACILITATOR.* HE WAS THE ONE WITH THE FAMILY--ADELINE AND THEIR TWO SONS, *GRANT* AND *JOSEPH.*

THE DAFT FOOL THOUGHT HE COULD HAVE IT ALL.

THE JACKAL FOUND SLADE'S FAMILY AND TRIED TO USE THEM AGAINST HIM. SLADE'S *PRIDE* WAS ALWAYS HIS GREATEST WEAKNESS.

ON THAT DAY, IT COST *JOSEPH* HIS ABILITY TO SPEAK.

ADELINE NEVER FORGAVE HIM. BEFORE SHE DIED, ADELINE TOOK HER OWN FORM OF REVENGE ON SLADE--HIS *EYE*.

GRANT UNKNOWINGLY FOLLOWED IN HIS FATHER'S FOOTSTEPS-- VOLUNTEERING FOR HIS OWN EXPERIMENT WITH THE TERRORIST ORGANIZATION KNOWN AS THE H.I.V.E.

AS *RAVAGER*, HIS FIRST ASSASSINATION CONTRACT WAS TO KILL THE *TEEN TITANS*.

WHEN GRANT DIED FROM THE EXPERIMENT'S FATAL SIDE EFFECTS, SLADE TOOK IT UPON HIMSELF TO COMPLETE THE CONTRACT.

IT MAY HAVE BEEN H
ONLY PROFESSIONA
FAILURE. BUT IT WAS
FOR LACK OF TRYIN

WITH ONE SON MAIMED AND THE OTHER SIX FEET UNDER, SLADE DISCOVERED HE HAD MORE FAMILY--A FORMER LOVER, *LILLIAN WORTH*, AND THEIR DAUGHTER, *ROSE*.

IT DIDN'T TAKE LONG FOR SLADE'S TRAGIC KARMA TO TERRORIZE ITS NEXT VICTIMS.

A NEW *RAVAGER*, SLADE'S JADED HALF-BROTHER, *WADE DEFARGE*, HUNTED DOWN LILLIAN AND ROSE TO FEED HIS OWN AGENDA AGAINST SLADE.

WHEN ROSE WAS LEFT ALONE, SLADE DID HIS BEST TO DISTANCE HIMSELF FROM HER--THINKING THAT IT WOULD BE THE ONLY WAY TO KEEP HER SAFE.

LILLIAN WORTH

IN HINDSIGHT, PERHAPS I SHOULD HAVE KEPT MY DISTANCE AS WELL.

SHNNT

SHNNT

BUT IT WOULD NOT HAVE MATTERED.

SHNNT

I SUPPOSE IT WAS ONLY A MATTER OF TIME. HIS NAME SAID IT ALL.

EVERYONE AROUND HIM-- REGARDLESS OF THEIR INVOLVEMENT...

EVERYONE AROUND HIM *DIES*.

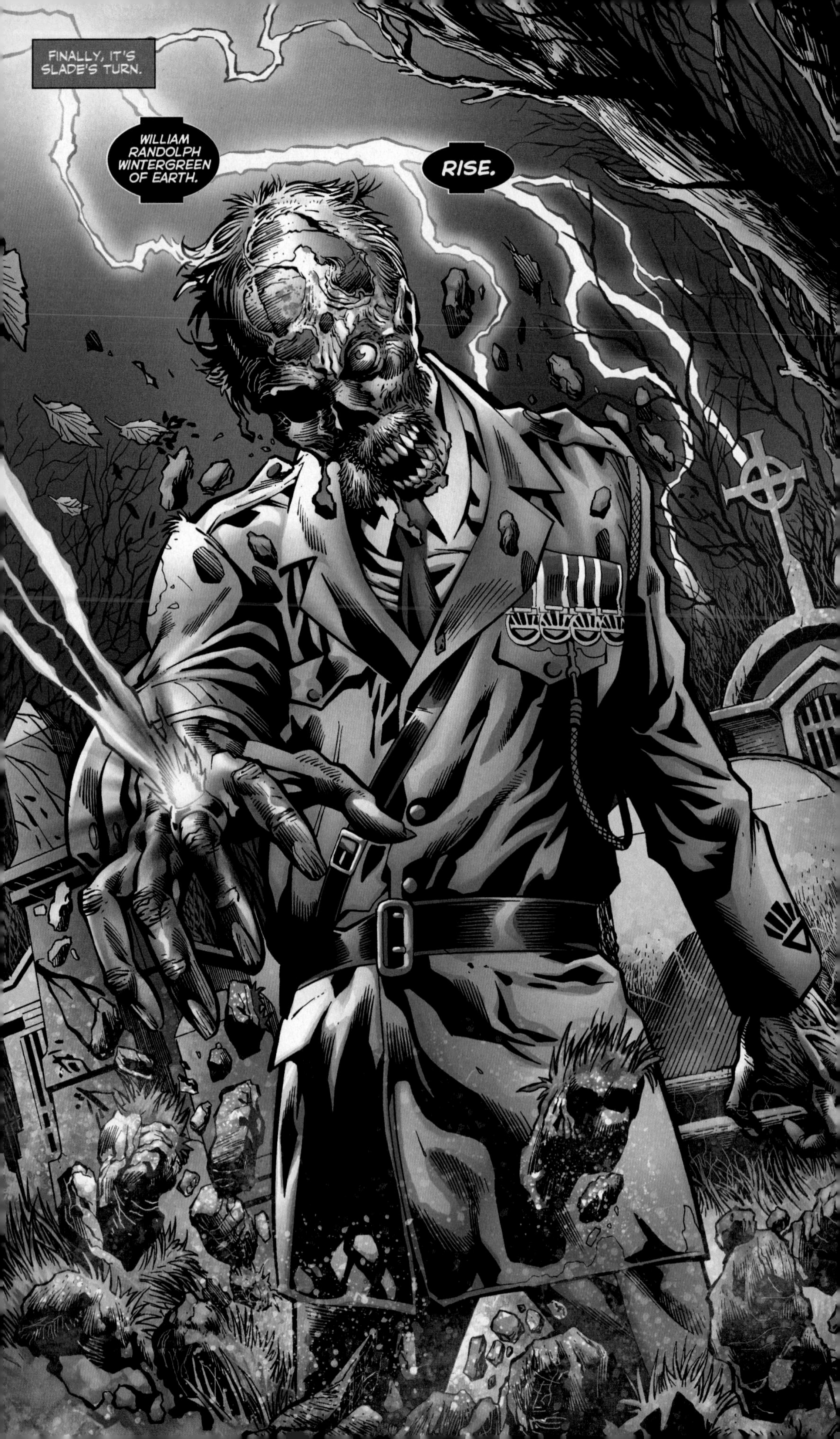
FINALLY, IT'S SLADE'S TURN.
WILLIAM RANDOLPH WINTERGREEN OF EARTH.
RISE.

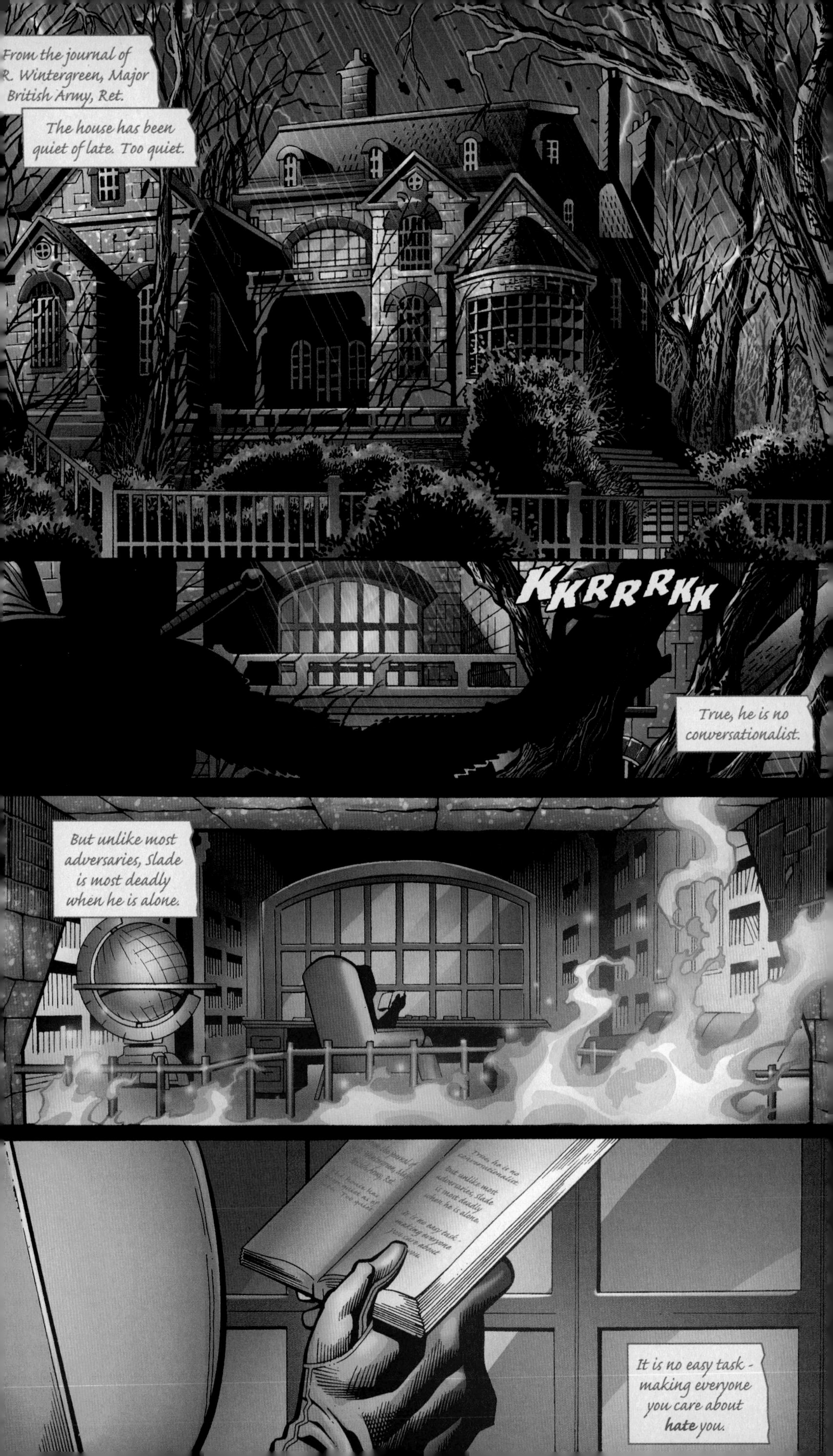
From the journal of R. Wintergreen, Major British Army, Ret.
The house has been quiet of late. Too quiet.
KKRRRRKK
True, he is no conversationalist.
But unlike most adversaries, Slade is most deadly when he is alone.
It is no easy task - making everyone you care about **hate** you.

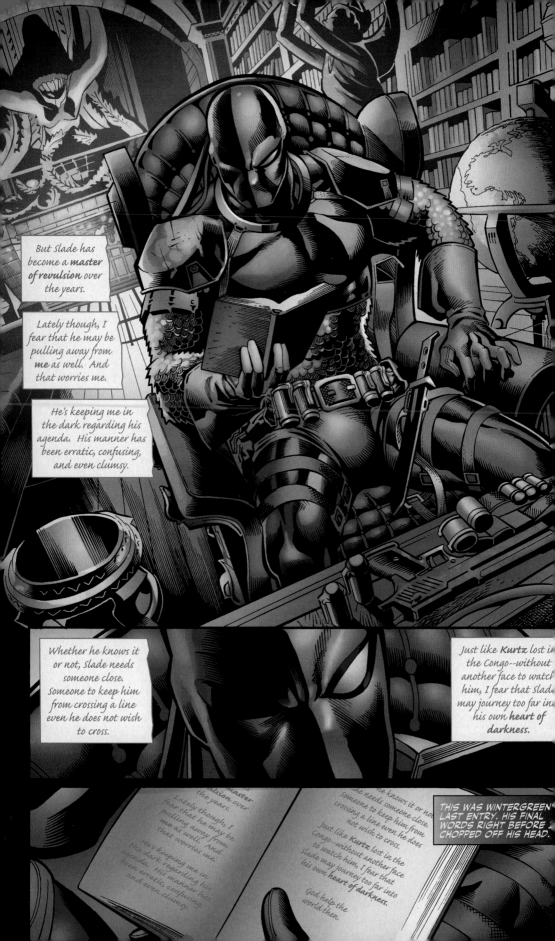

But Slade has become a **master of revulsion** over the years.

Lately though, I fear that he may be pulling away from **me** as well. And that worries me.

He's keeping me in the dark regarding his agenda. His manner has been erratic, confusing, and even clumsy.

Whether he knows it or not, Slade needs someone close. Someone to keep him from crossing a line even he does not wish to cross.

Just like **Kurtz** lost in the Congo--without another face to watch him, I fear that Slade may journey too far into his own **heart of darkness**.

THIS WAS WINTERGREEN'S LAST ENTRY. HIS FINAL WORDS RIGHT BEFORE I CHOPPED OFF HIS HEAD.

IT WASN'T REALLY ME. AT THE TIME I WAS POSSESSED BY THE MIND OF MY SON, JOSEPH, WHO HAD GONE MAD.

SOUNDS LIKE AN EXCUSE, BUT IT'S NOT.

Slade has ...e a **master** ...**lsion** over ...years.

...ugh, I ...may be ... from ...nd ...e.

...in ...his ...has

Whether he knows ... Slade needs someon... someone to keep him ... crossing a line even he ... not wish to cross.

Just like **Kurtz** lost in ... Congo--without anothe... to watch him, I fear tha... Slade may journey too far in... his own **heart of darkness.**

God help th... world the...

I DON'T MAKE EXCUSES.

LNNNNN
NNNNN

IT DOESN'T MATTER HOW IT HAPPENED. HIS **DEATH** IS ON ME.

IT'S ALL ON ME.

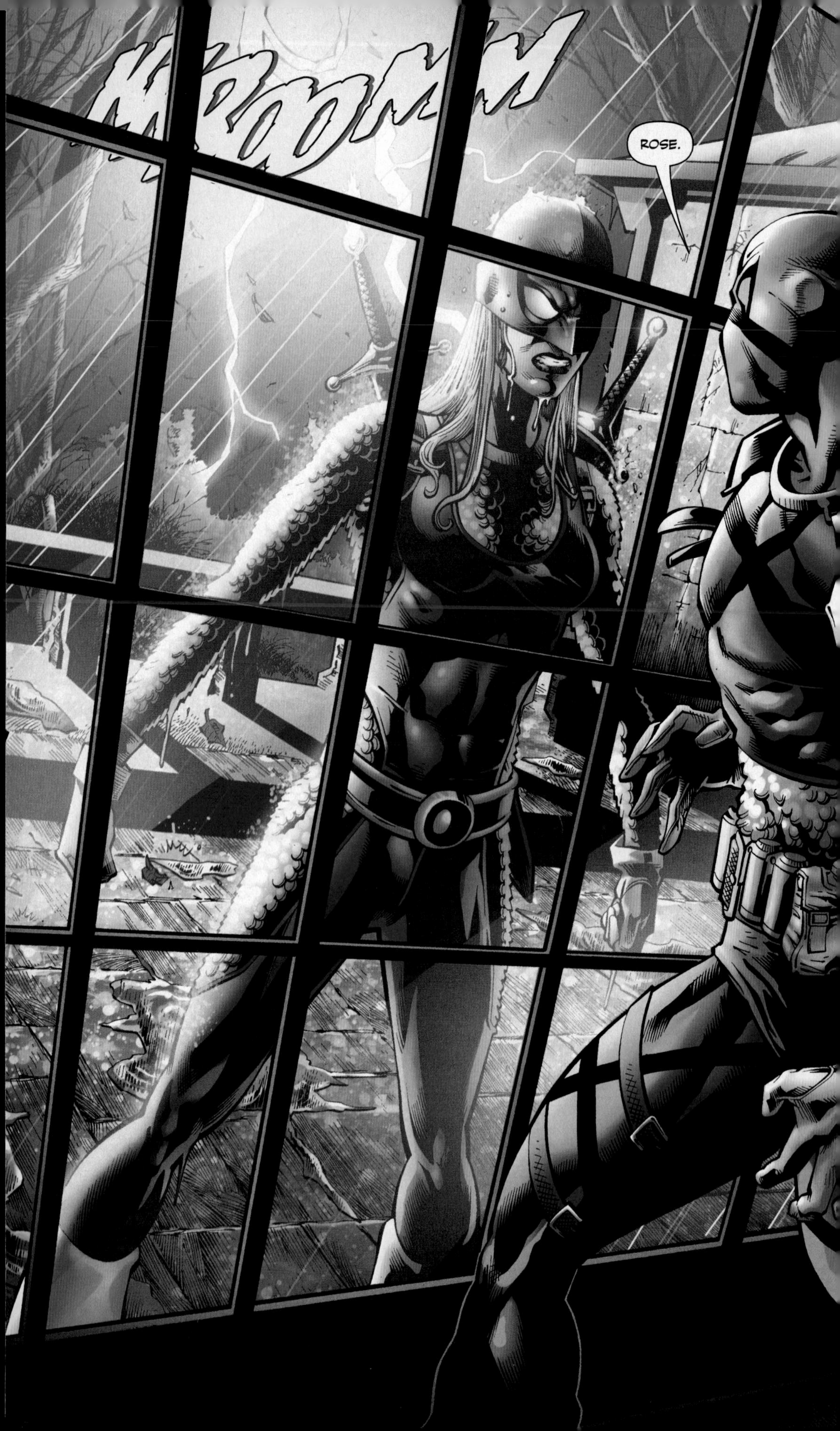
ROSE.

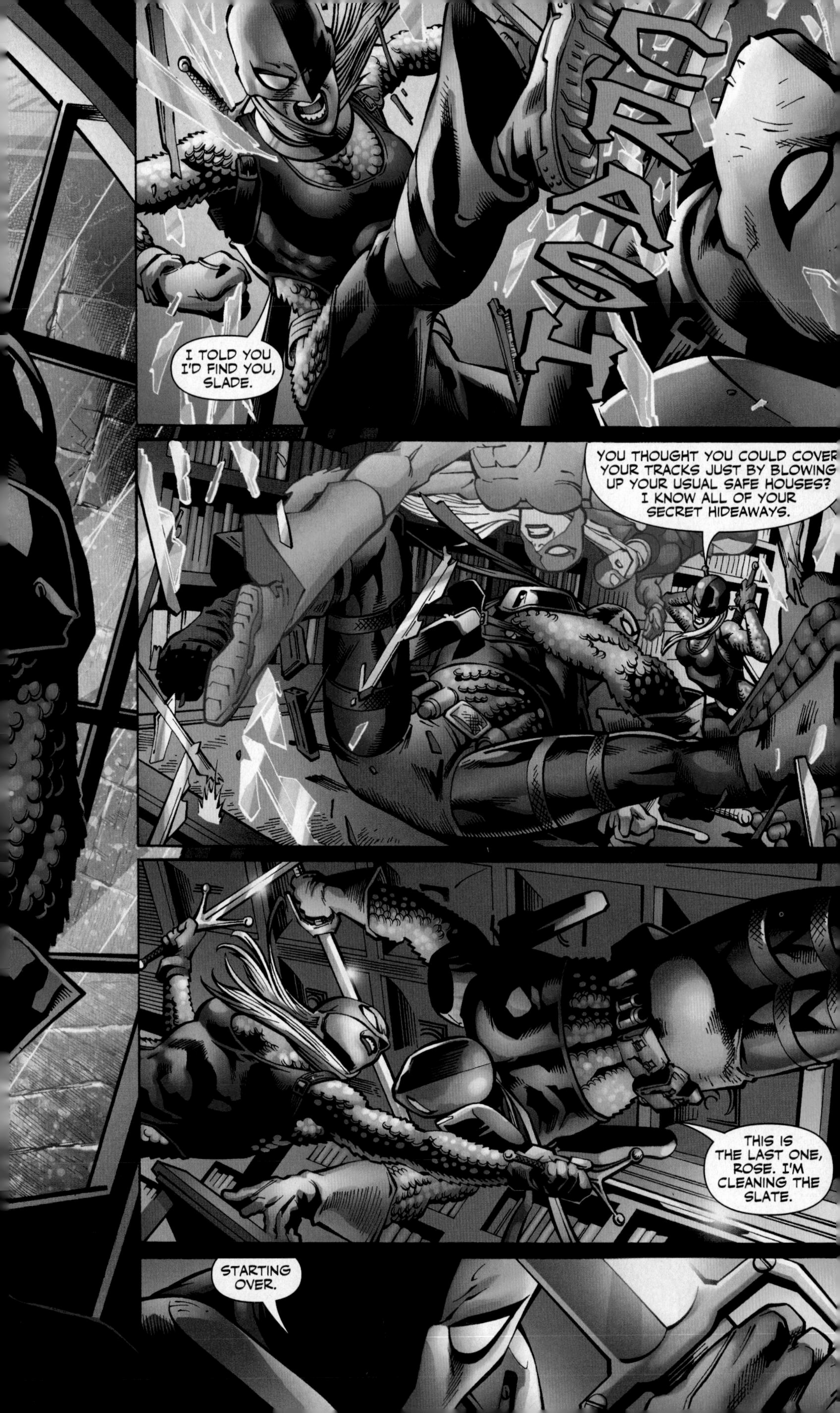
CRASH
I TOLD YOU I'D FIND YOU, SLADE.
YOU THOUGHT YOU COULD COVER YOUR TRACKS JUST BY BLOWING UP YOUR USUAL SAFE HOUSES? I KNOW ALL OF YOUR SECRET HIDEAWAYS.
THIS IS THE LAST ONE, ROSE. I'M CLEANING THE SLATE.
STARTING OVER.

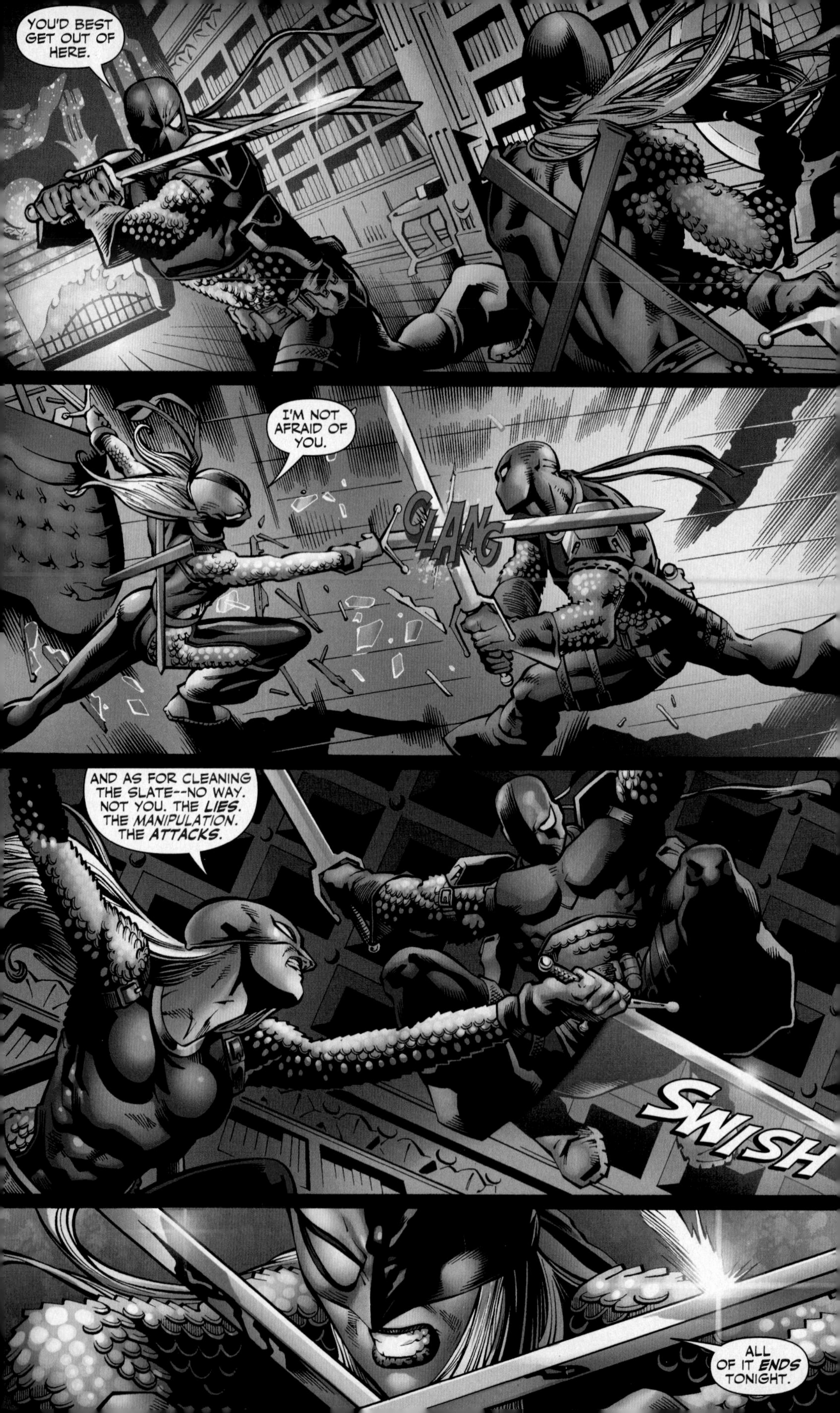
YOU'D BEST GET OUT OF HERE.
I'M NOT AFRAID OF YOU.
CLANG
AND AS FOR CLEANING THE SLATE--NO WAY. NOT YOU. THE LIES. THE MANIPULATION. THE ATTACKS.
SWISH
ALL OF IT ENDS TONIGHT.

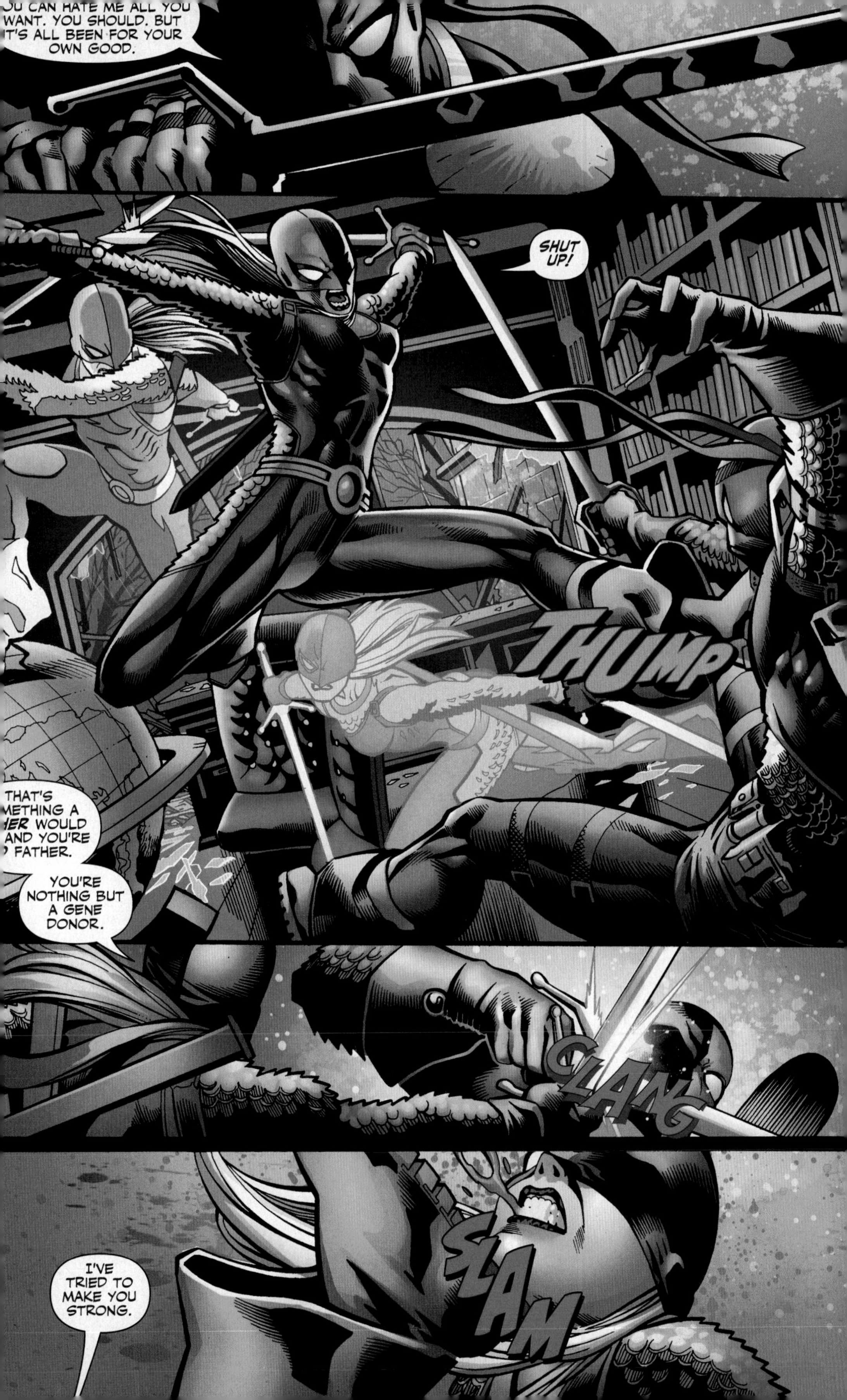
OU CAN HATE ME ALL YOU WANT. YOU SHOULD. BUT IT'S ALL BEEN FOR YOUR OWN GOOD.
SHUT UP!
THUMP
THAT'S METHING A HER WOULD AND YOU'RE FATHER.
YOU'RE NOTHING BUT A GENE DONOR.
CLANG
I'VE TRIED TO MAKE YOU STRONG.
SLAM

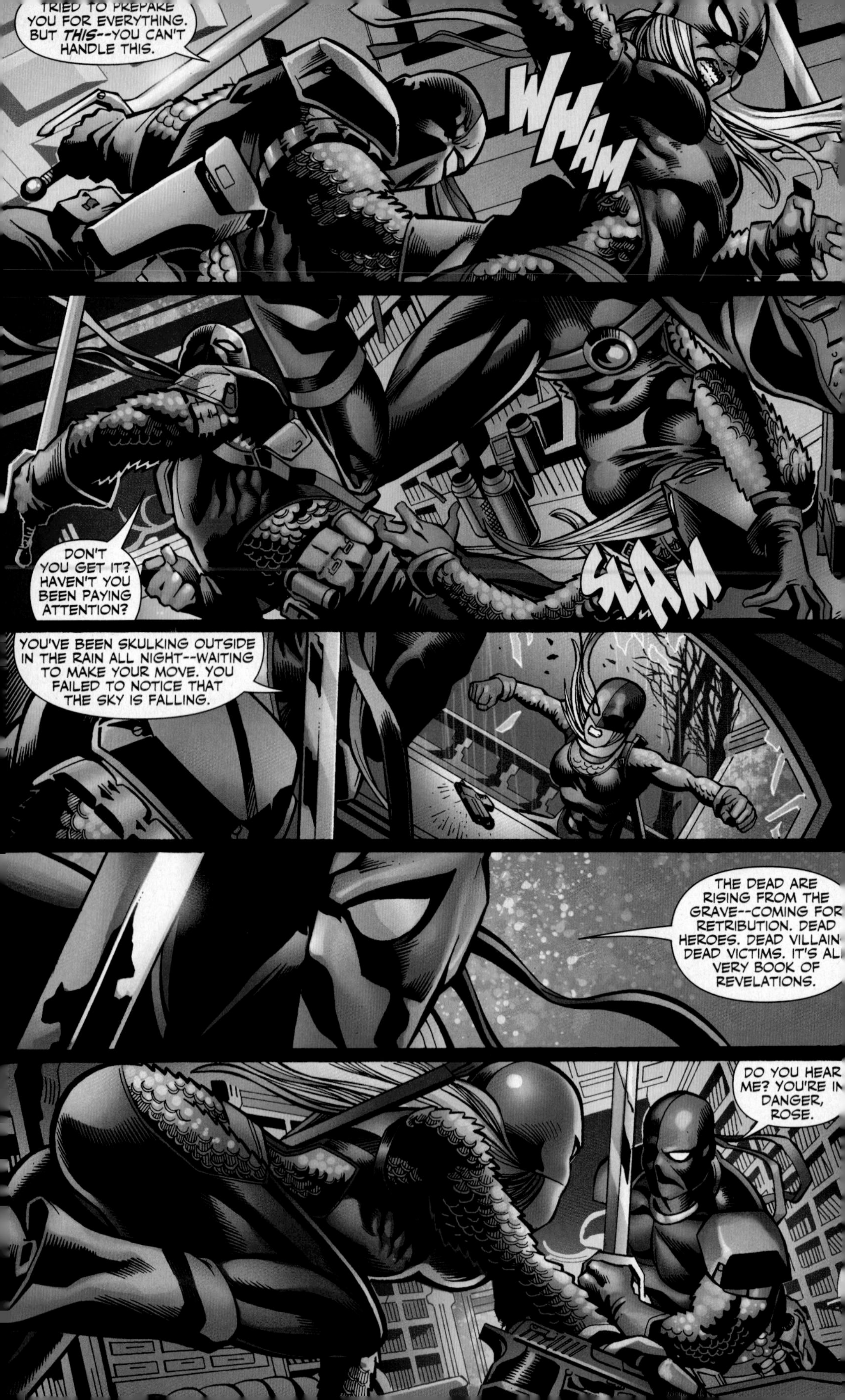
TRIED TO PREPARE YOU FOR EVERYTHING. BUT THIS--YOU CAN'T HANDLE THIS.
WHAM
DON'T YOU GET IT? HAVEN'T YOU BEEN PAYING ATTENTION?
SLAM
YOU'VE BEEN SKULKING OUTSIDE IN THE RAIN ALL NIGHT--WAITING TO MAKE YOUR MOVE. YOU FAILED TO NOTICE THAT THE SKY IS FALLING.
THE DEAD ARE RISING FROM THE GRAVE--COMING FOR RETRIBUTION. DEAD HEROES. DEAD VILLAIN DEAD VICTIMS. IT'S AL VERY BOOK OF REVELATIONS.
DO YOU HEAR ME? YOU'RE IN DANGER, ROSE.

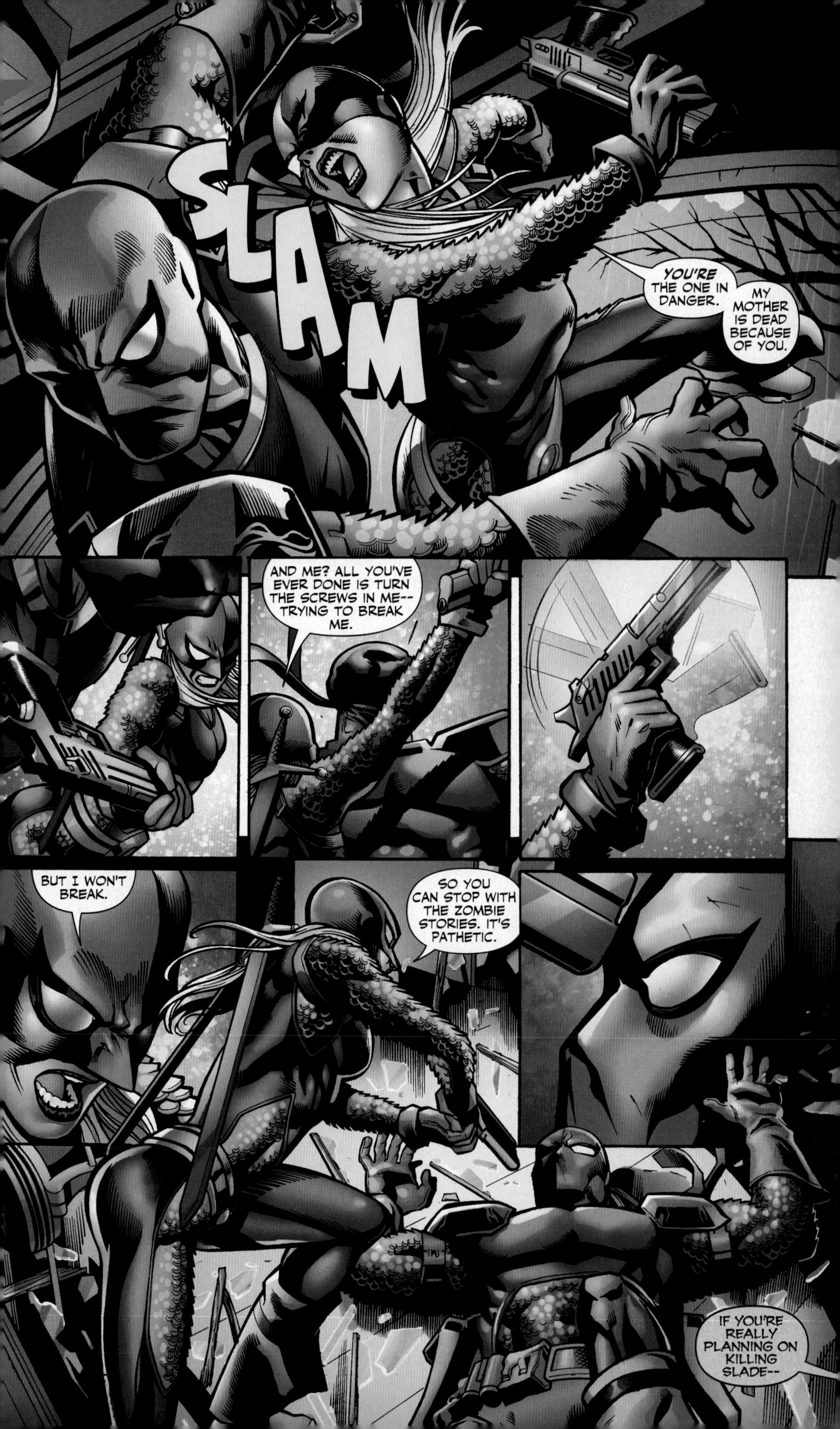
SLAM
YOU'RE THE ONE IN DANGER.
MY MOTHER IS DEAD BECAUSE OF YOU.
AND ME? ALL YOU'VE EVER DONE IS TURN THE SCREWS IN ME-- TRYING TO BREAK ME.
BUT I WON'T BREAK.
SO YOU CAN STOP WITH THE ZOMBIE STORIES. IT'S PATHETIC.
IF YOU'RE REALLY PLANNING ON KILLING SLADE--

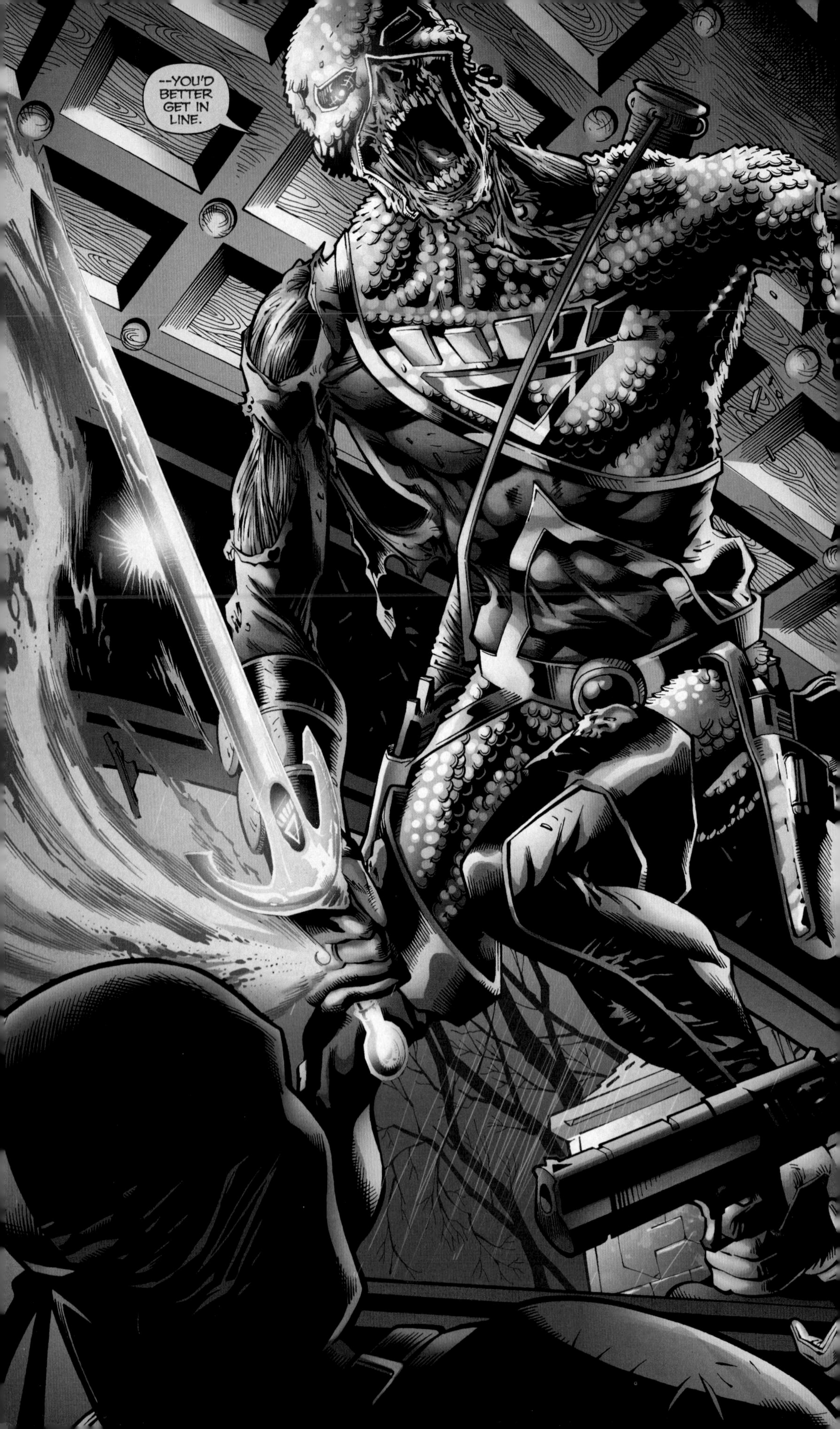
--YOU'D BETTER GET IN LINE.

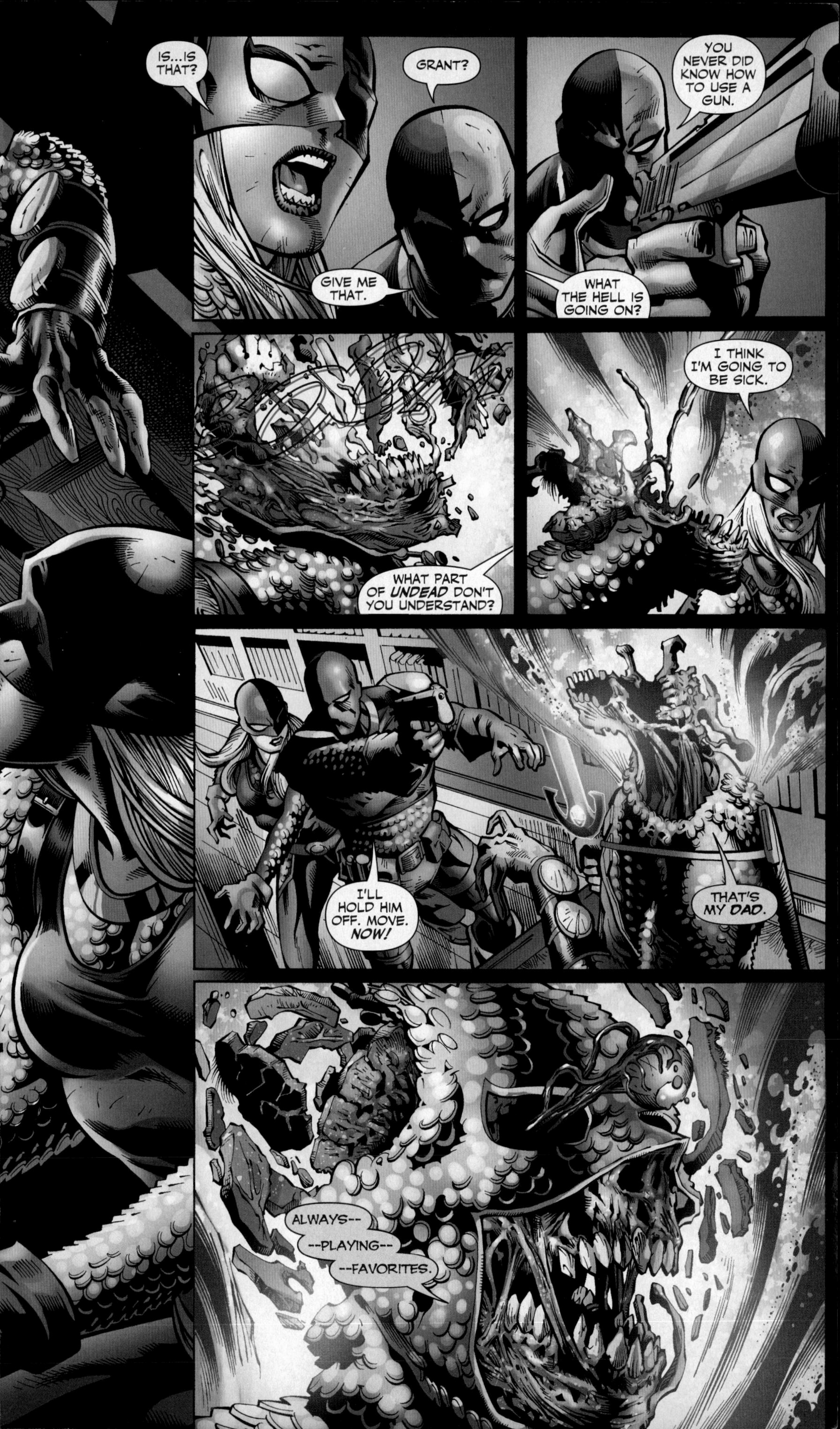
IS...IS THAT?
GRANT?
GIVE ME THAT.
YOU NEVER DID KNOW HOW TO USE A GUN.
WHAT THE HELL IS GOING ON?
WHAT PART OF UNDEAD DON'T YOU UNDERSTAND?
I THINK I'M GOING TO BE SICK.
I'LL HOLD HIM OFF. MOVE. NOW!
THAT'S MY DAD.
ALWAYS--
--PLAYING--
--FAVORITES.

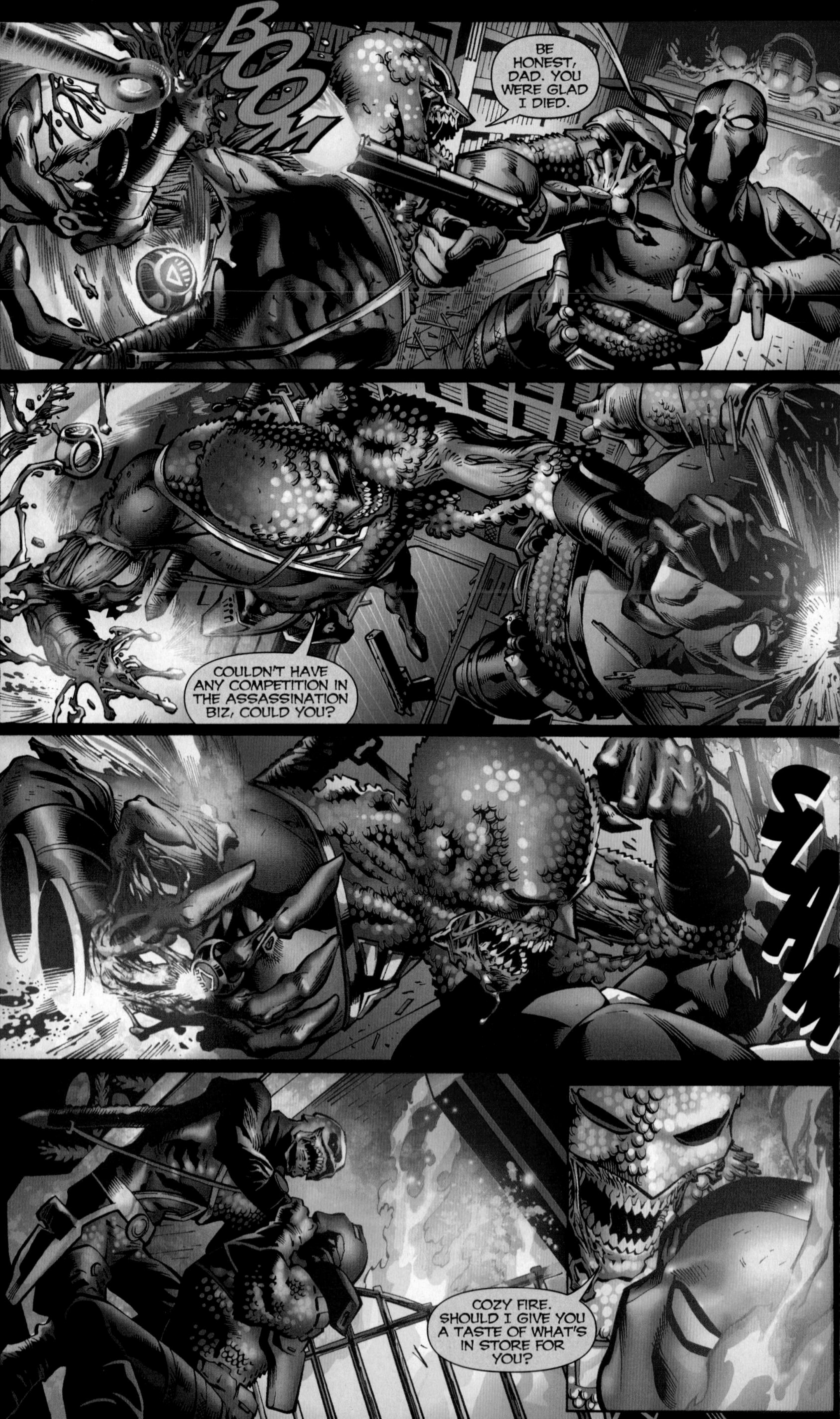
BOOM
BE HONEST, DAD. YOU WERE GLAD I DIED.
COULDN'T HAVE ANY COMPETITION IN THE ASSASSINATION BIZ, COULD YOU?
COZY FIRE. SHOULD I GIVE YOU A TASTE OF WHAT'S IN STORE FOR YOU?

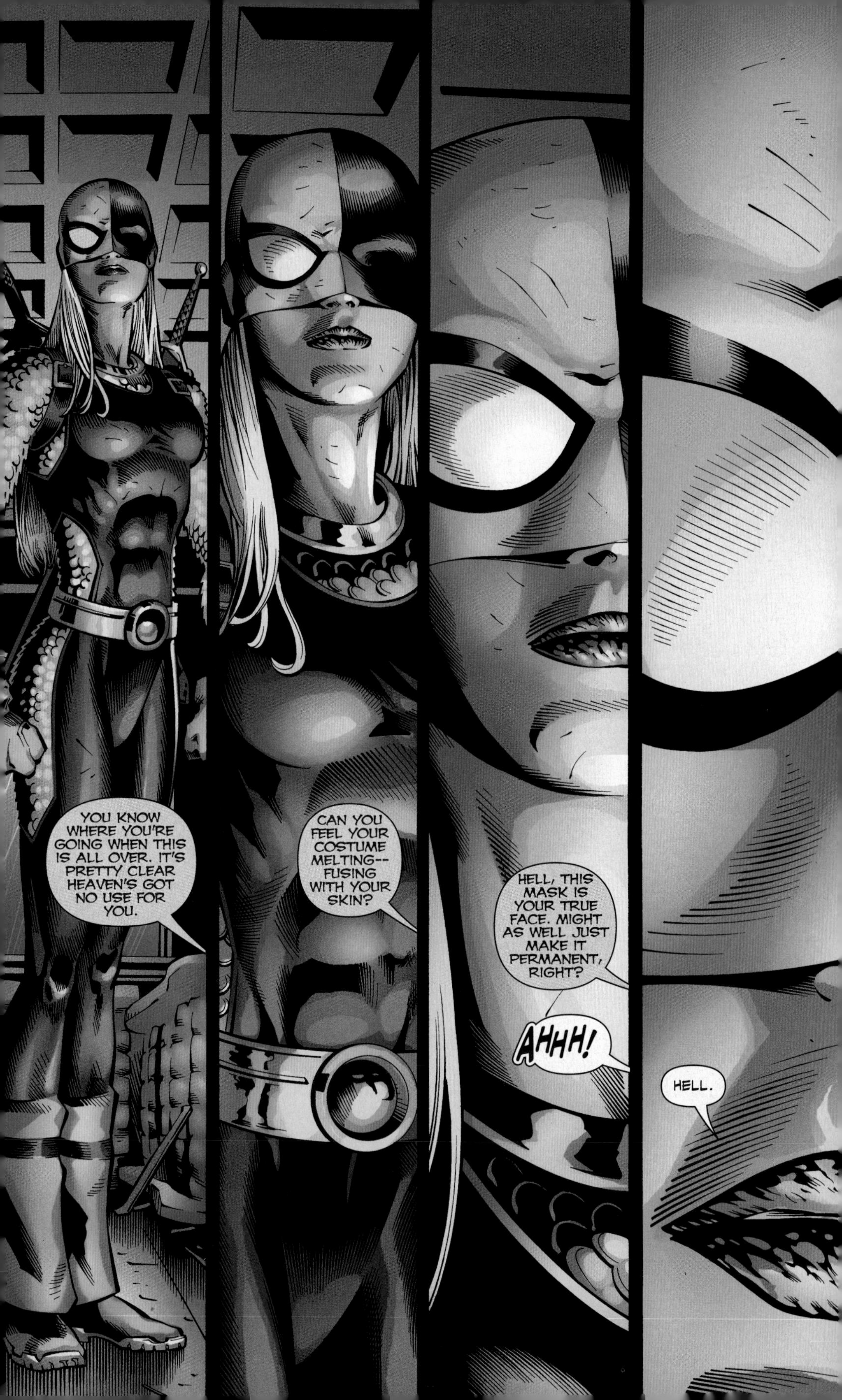
YOU KNOW WHERE YOU'RE GOING WHEN THIS IS ALL OVER. IT'S PRETTY CLEAR HEAVEN'S GOT NO USE FOR YOU.
CAN YOU FEEL YOUR COSTUME MELTING-- FUSING WITH YOUR SKIN?
HELL, THIS MASK IS YOUR TRUE FACE. MIGHT AS WELL JUST MAKE IT PERMANENT, RIGHT?
AHHH!
HELL.

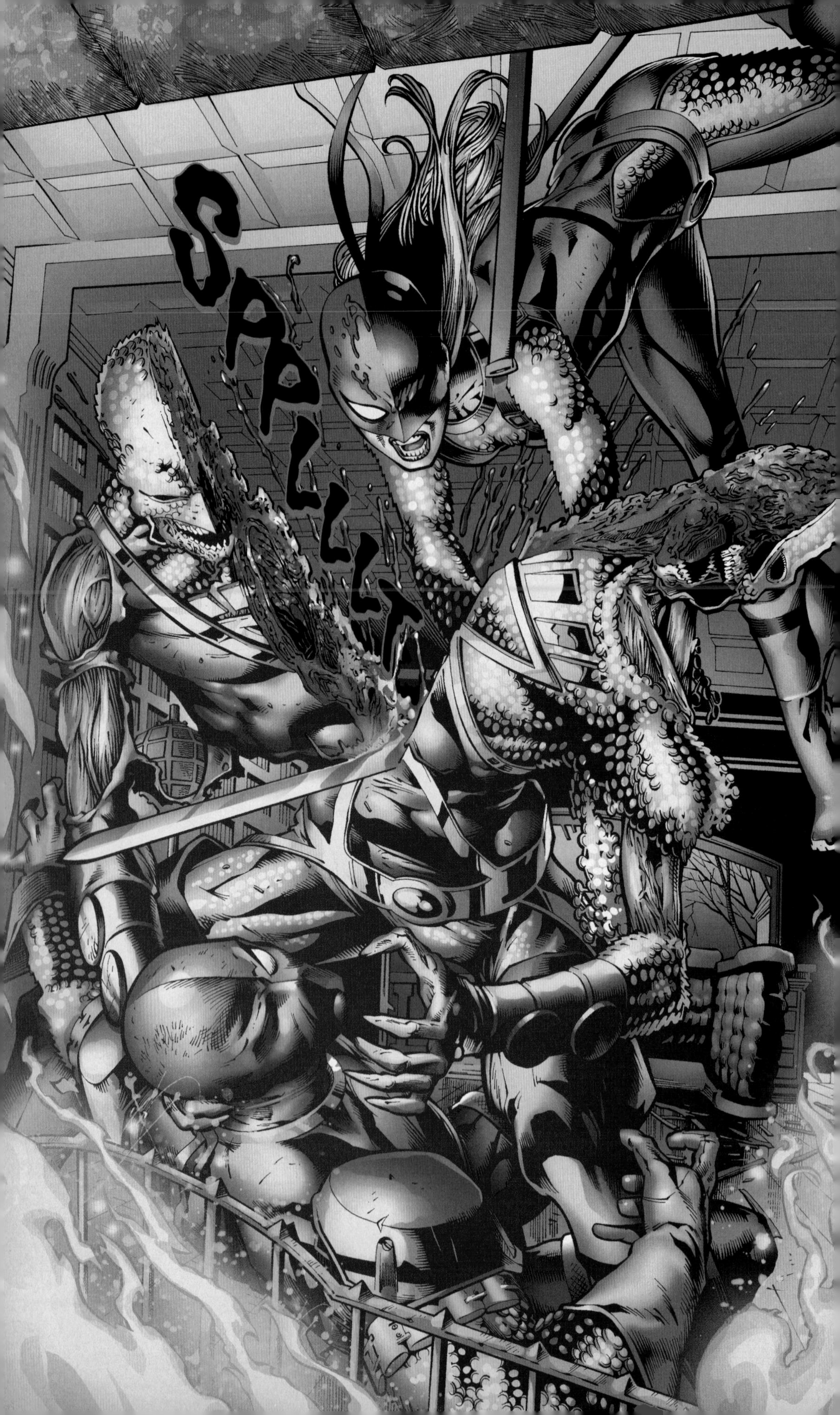
SPPLLLT

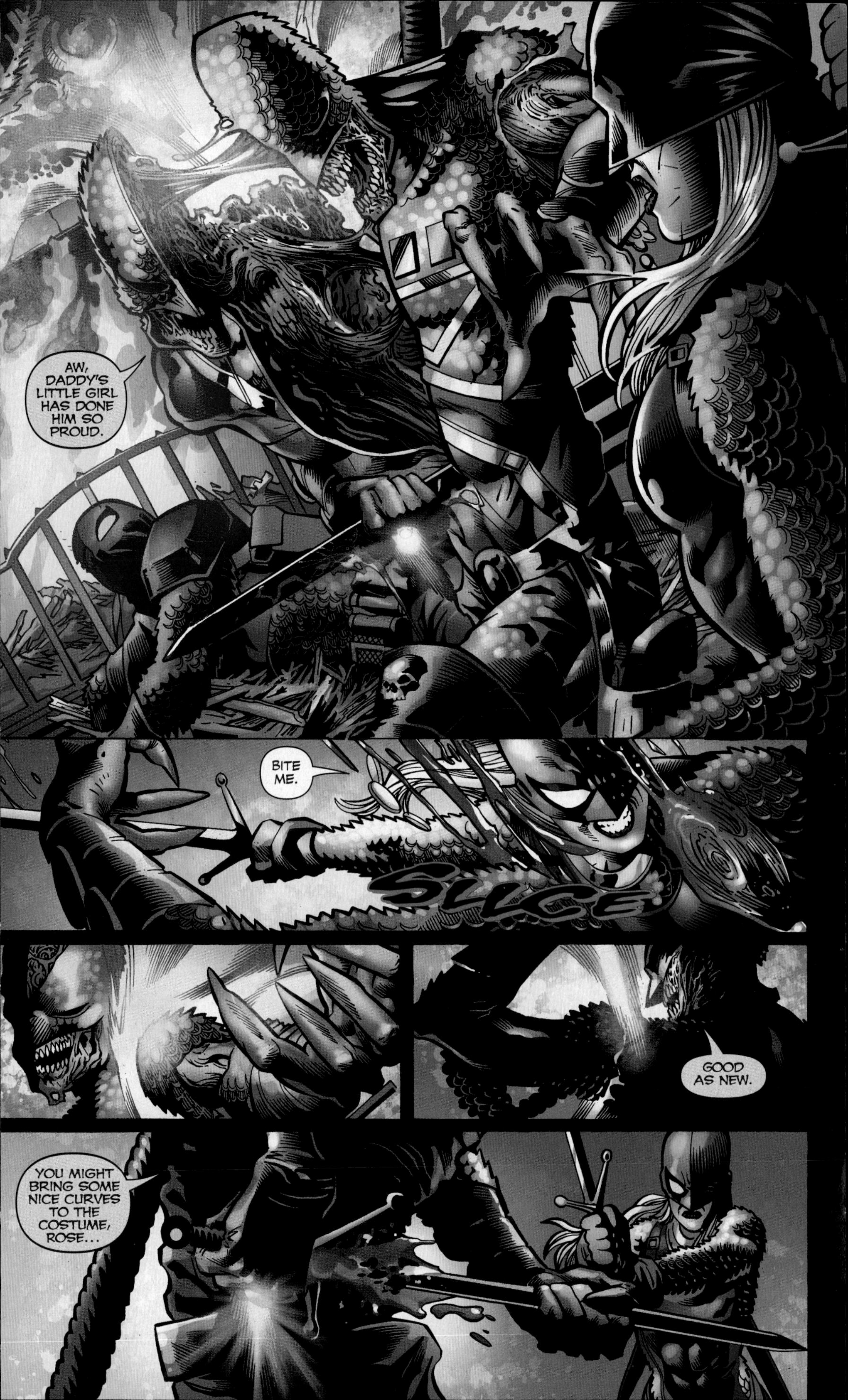
AW, DADDY'S LITTLE GIRL HAS DONE HIM SO PROUD.
BITE ME.
SLICE
GOOD AS NEW.
YOU MIGHT BRING SOME NICE CURVES TO THE COSTUME, ROSE...

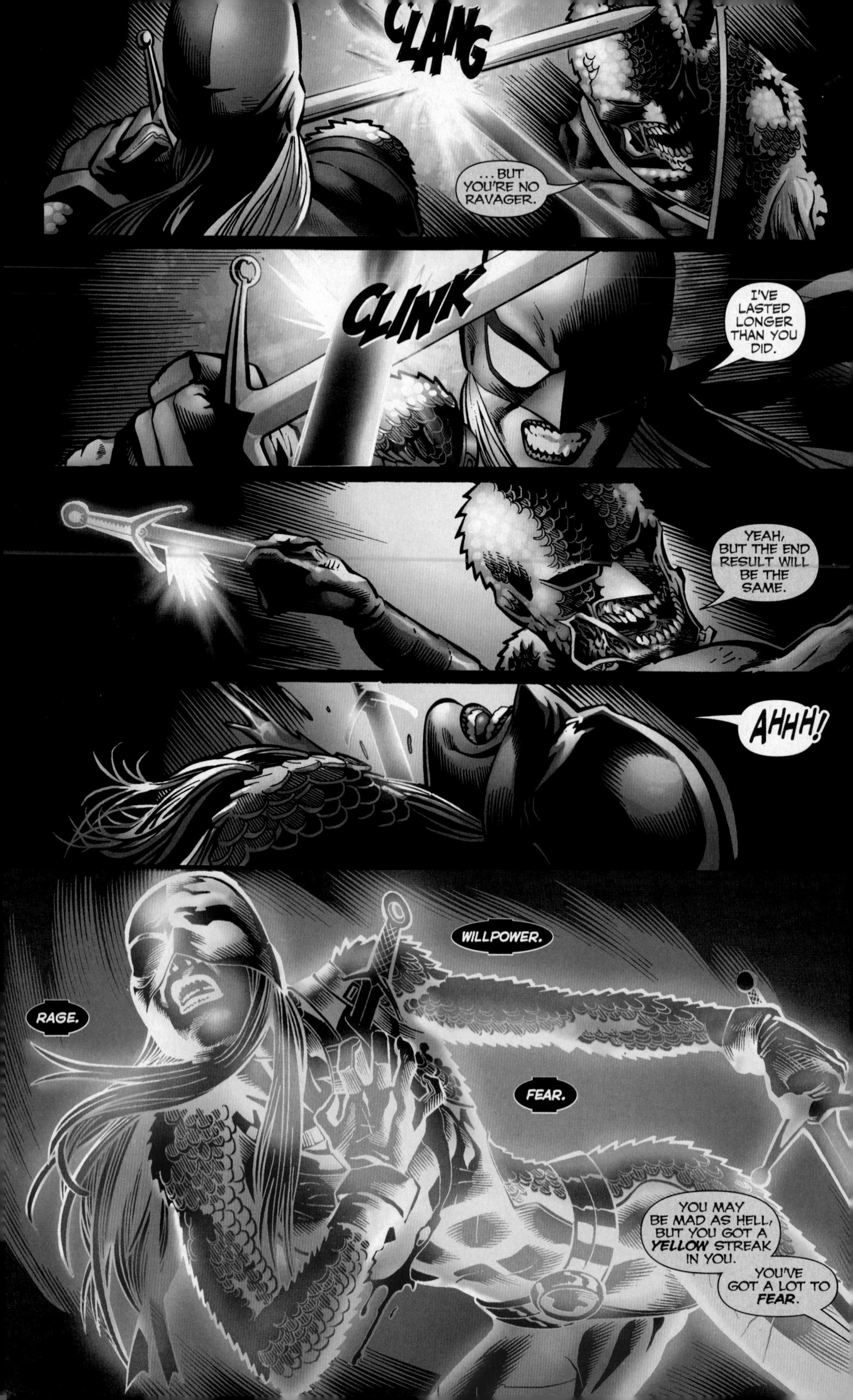
CLANG
...BUT YOU'RE NO RAVAGER.
CLINK
I'VE LASTED LONGER THAN YOU DID.
YEAH, BUT THE END RESULT WILL BE THE SAME.
AHHH!
WILLPOWER.
RAGE.
FEAR.
YOU MAY BE MAD AS HELL, BUT YOU GOT A YELLOW STREAK IN YOU.
YOU'VE GOT A LOT TO FEAR.

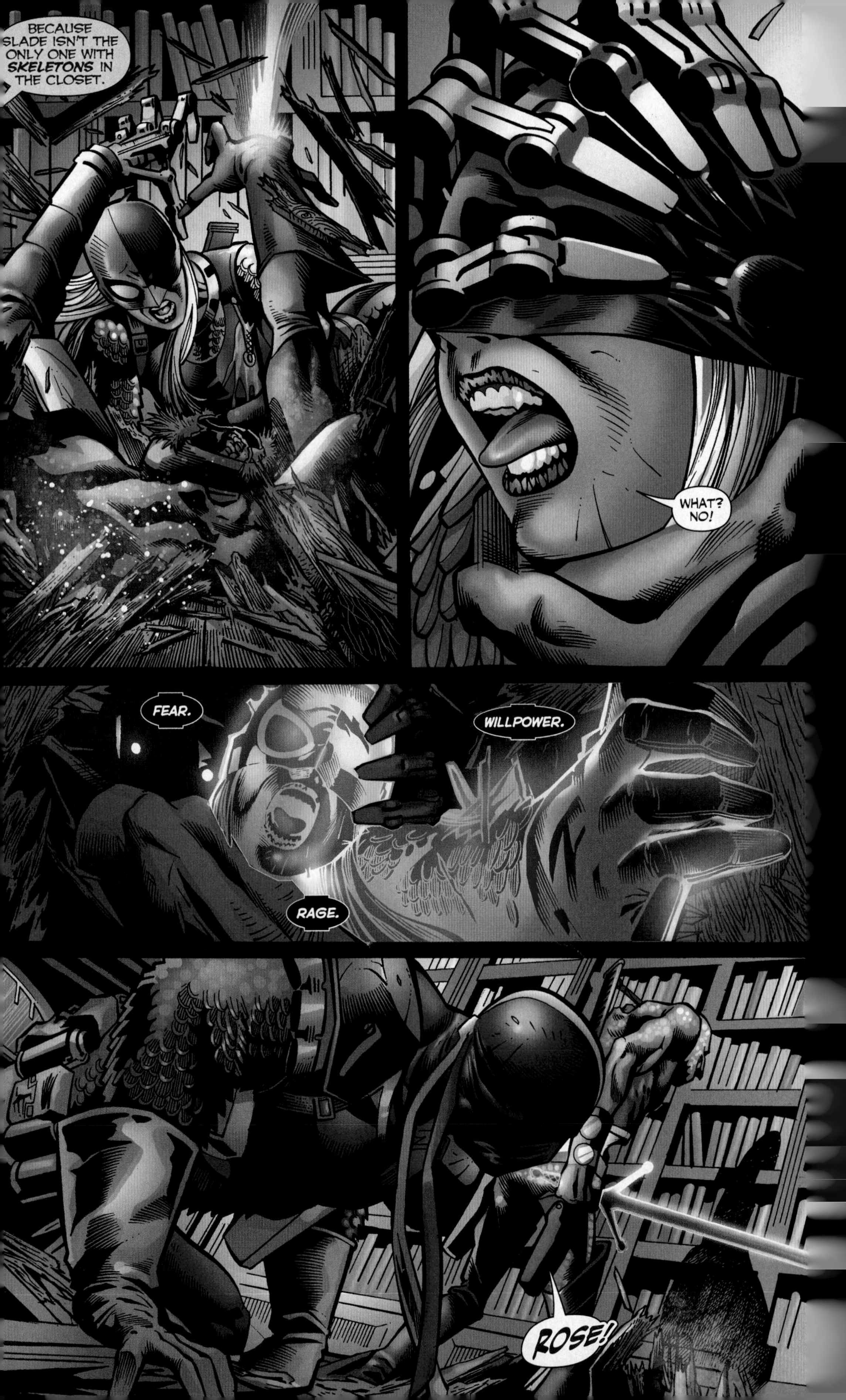
BECAUSE SLADE ISN'T THE ONLY ONE WITH SKELETONS IN THE CLOSET.
WHAT? NO!
FEAR.
WILLPOWER.
RAGE.
ROSE!

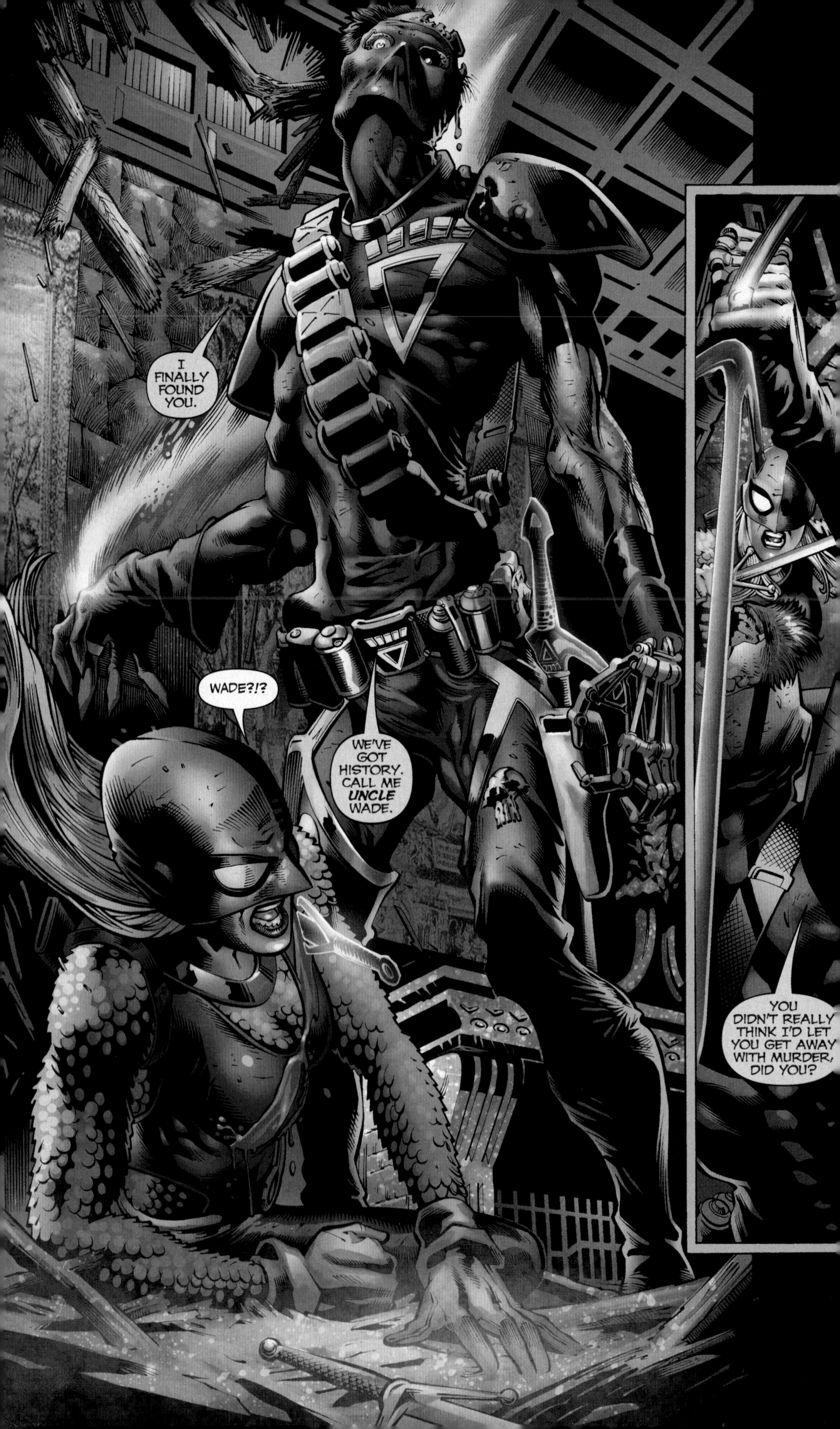
I FINALLY FOUND YOU.
WADE?!?
WE'VE GOT HISTORY. CALL ME *UNCLE* WADE.
YOU DIDN'T REALLY THINK I'D LET YOU GET AWAY WITH MURDER, DID YOU?

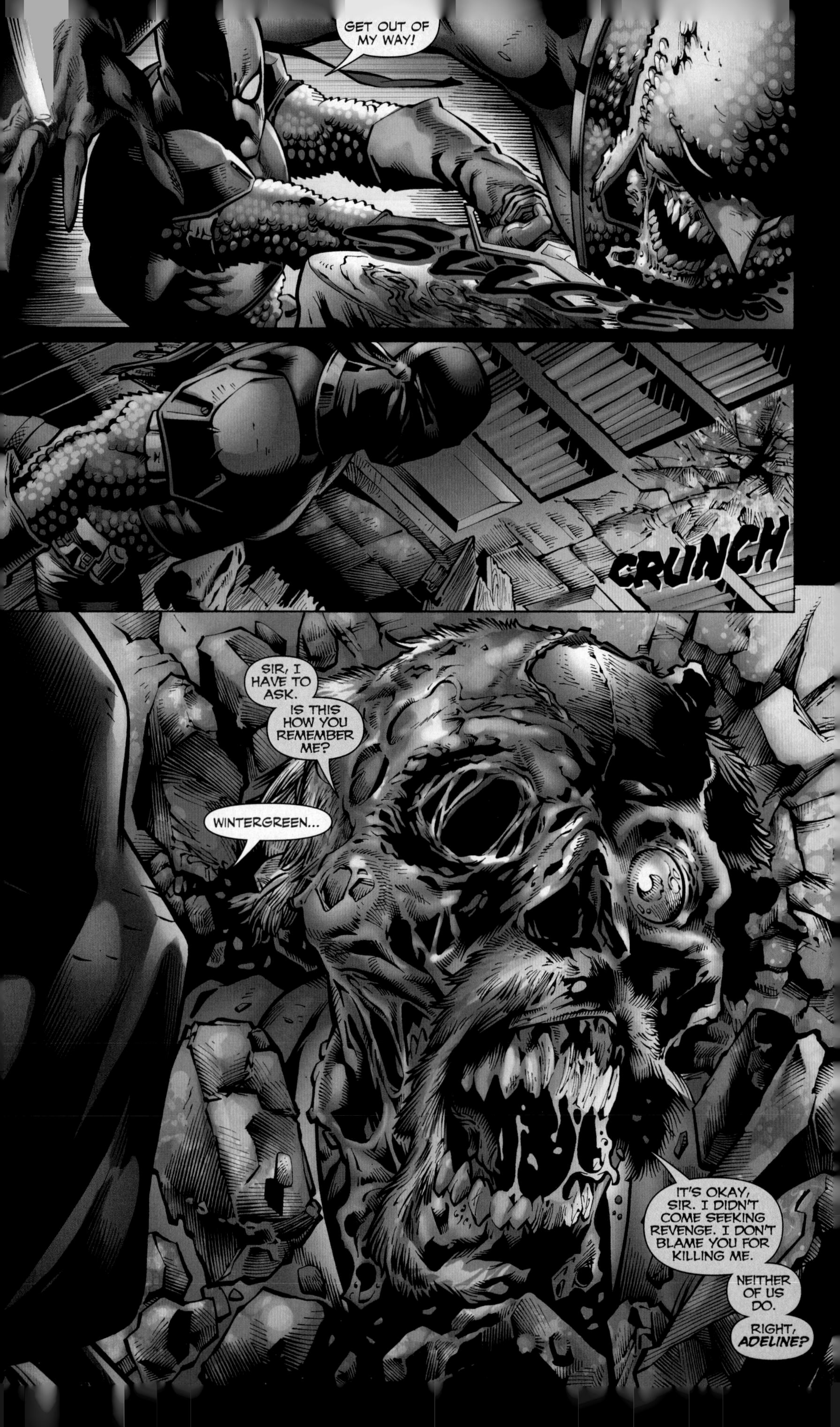

GET OUT OF MY WAY!
SHLUCK
CRUNCH
SIR, I HAVE TO ASK.
IS THIS HOW YOU REMEMBER ME?
WINTERGREEN...
IT'S OKAY, SIR. I DIDN'T COME SEEKING REVENGE. I DON'T BLAME YOU FOR KILLING ME.
NEITHER OF US DO.
RIGHT, *ADELINE*?

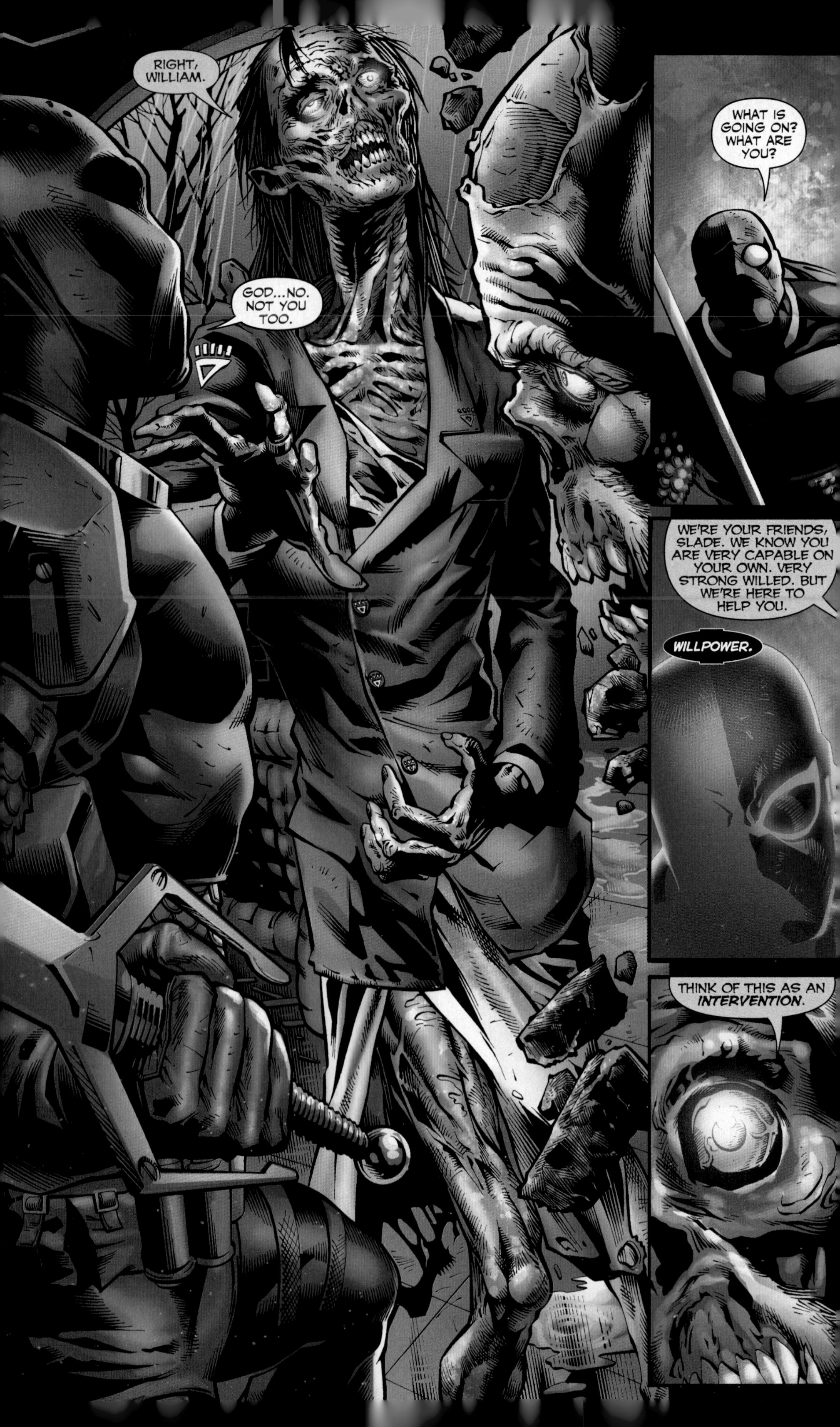
RIGHT, WILLIAM.
GOD...NO. NOT YOU TOO.
WHAT IS GOING ON? WHAT ARE YOU?
WE'RE YOUR FRIENDS, SLADE. WE KNOW YOU ARE VERY CAPABLE ON YOUR OWN. VERY STRONG WILLED. BUT WE'RE HERE TO HELP YOU.
WILLPOWER.
THINK OF THIS AS AN *INTERVENTION*.

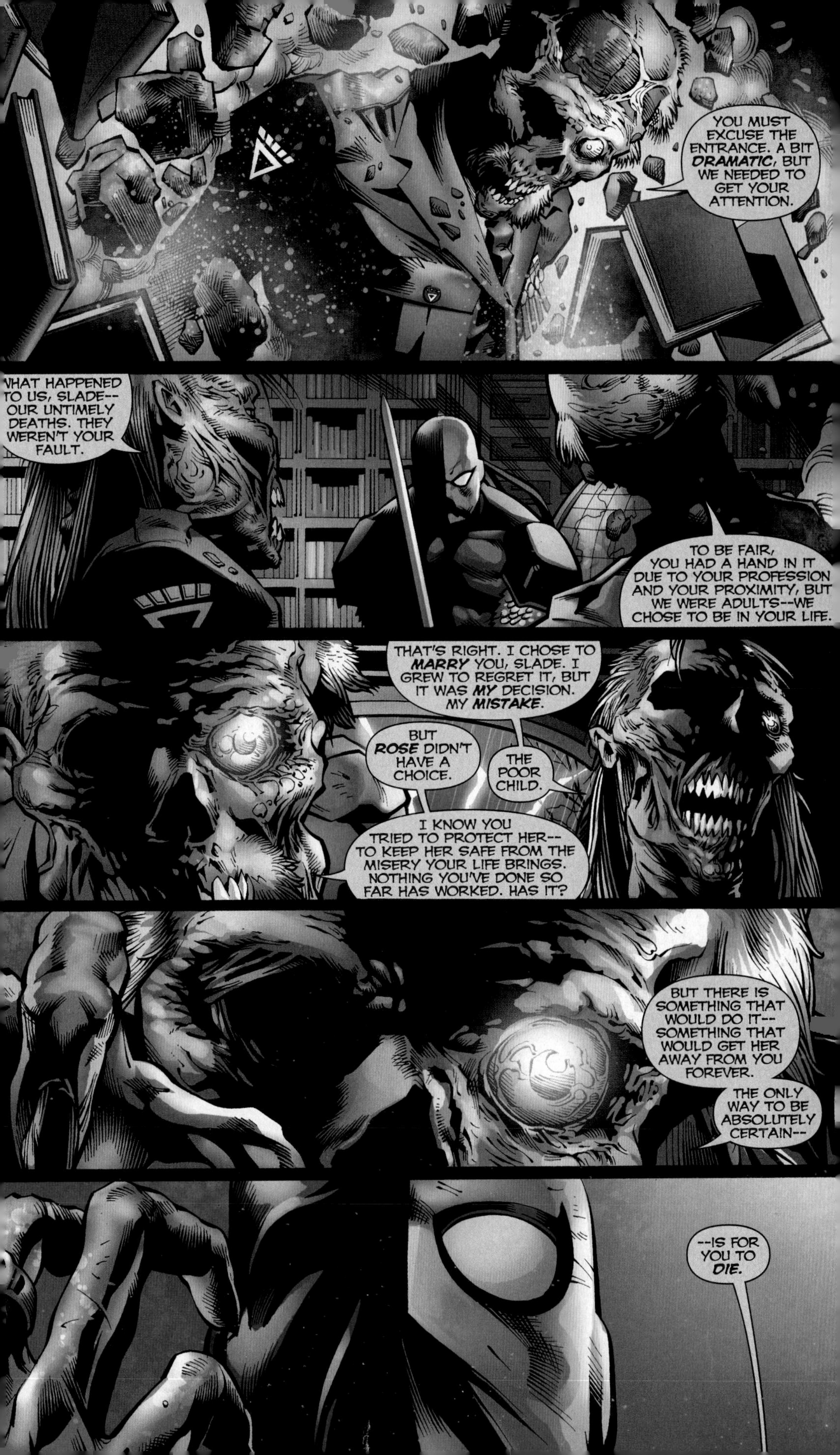
YOU MUST EXCUSE THE ENTRANCE. A BIT DRAMATIC, BUT WE NEEDED TO GET YOUR ATTENTION.
WHAT HAPPENED TO US, SLADE-- OUR UNTIMELY DEATHS. THEY WEREN'T YOUR FAULT.
TO BE FAIR, YOU HAD A HAND IN IT DUE TO YOUR PROFESSION AND YOUR PROXIMITY, BUT WE WERE ADULTS--WE CHOSE TO BE IN YOUR LIFE.
THAT'S RIGHT. I CHOSE TO MARRY YOU, SLADE. I GREW TO REGRET IT, BUT IT WAS MY DECISION. MY MISTAKE.
BUT ROSE DIDN'T HAVE A CHOICE.
THE POOR CHILD.
I KNOW YOU TRIED TO PROTECT HER-- TO KEEP HER SAFE FROM THE MISERY YOUR LIFE BRINGS. NOTHING YOU'VE DONE SO FAR HAS WORKED. HAS IT?
BUT THERE IS SOMETHING THAT WOULD DO IT-- SOMETHING THAT WOULD GET HER AWAY FROM YOU FOREVER.
THE ONLY WAY TO BE ABSOLUTELY CERTAIN--
--IS FOR YOU TO DIE.

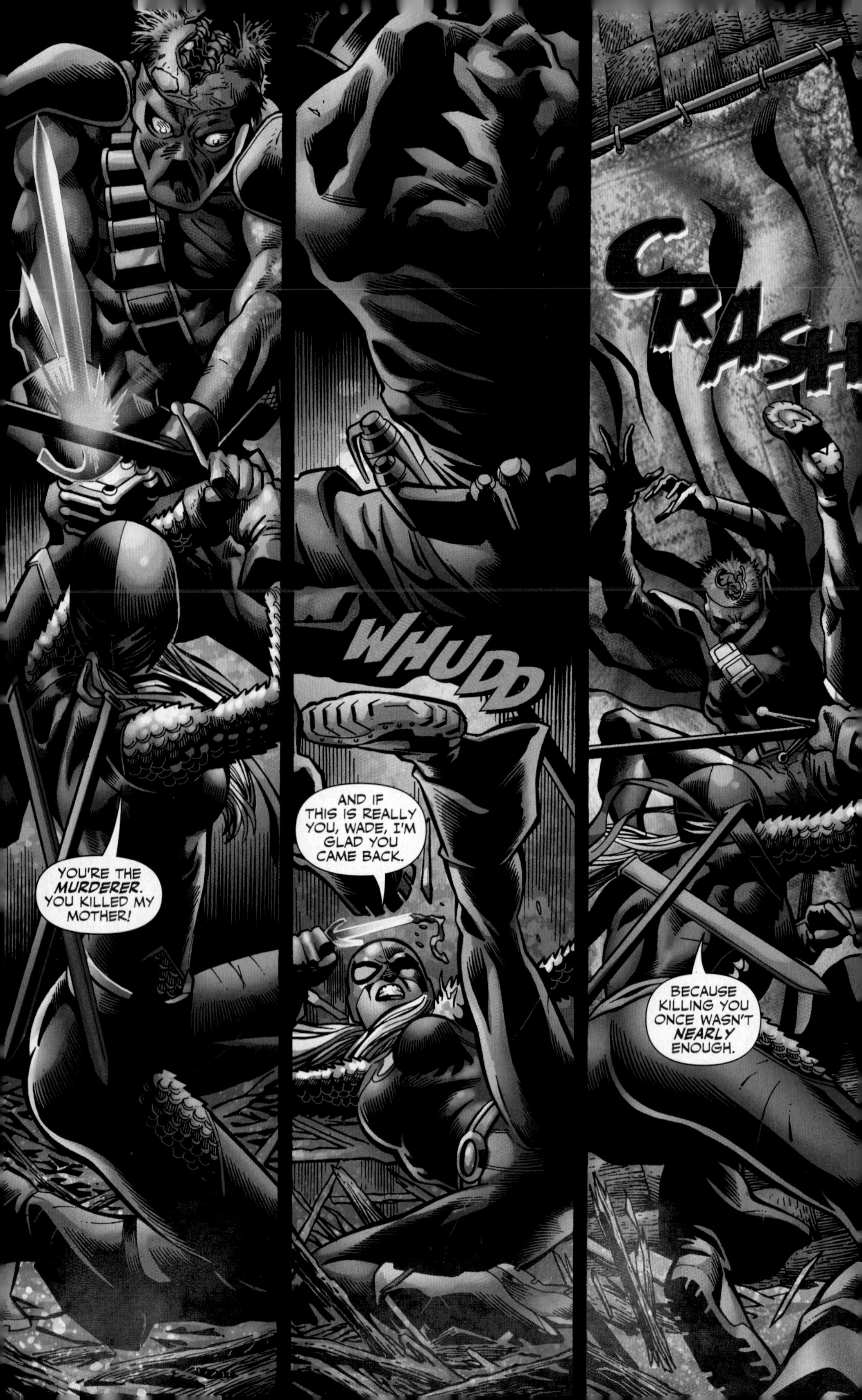
YOU'RE THE MURDERER. YOU KILLED MY MOTHER!
WHUDD
AND IF THIS IS REALLY YOU, WADE, I'M GLAD YOU CAME BACK.
CRASH
BECAUSE KILLING YOU ONCE WASN'T NEARLY ENOUGH.

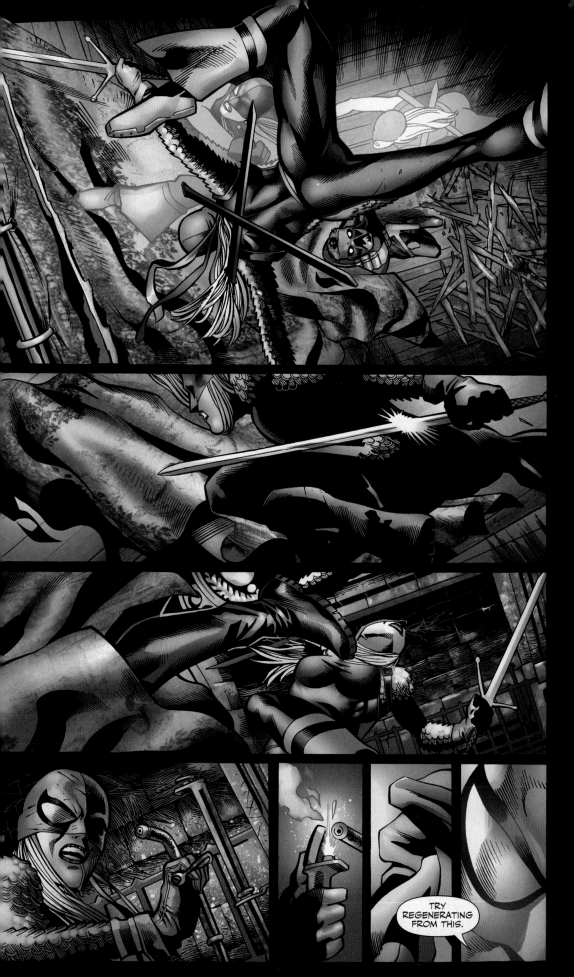

TRY REGENERATING FROM THIS.

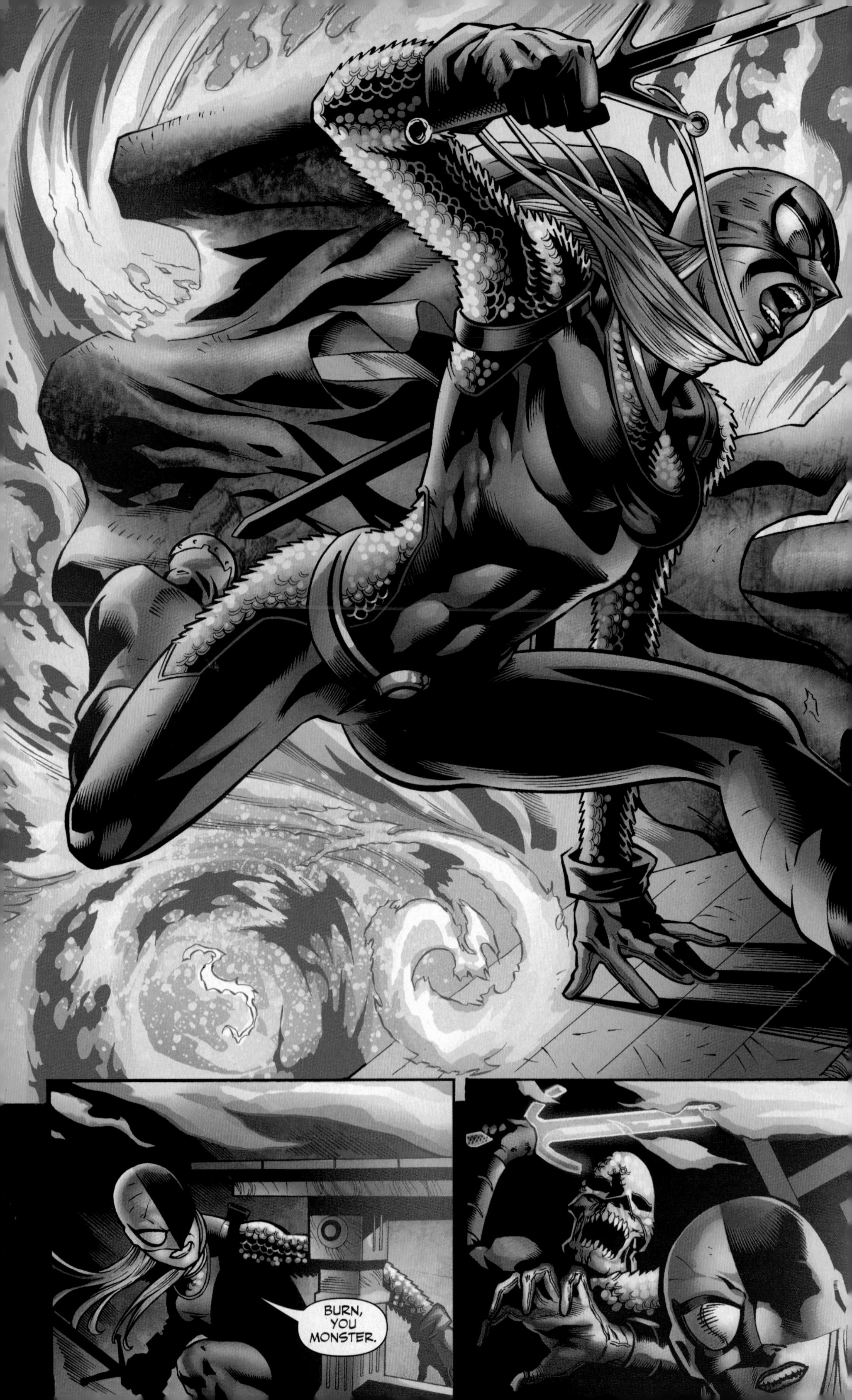
BURN, YOU MONSTER.

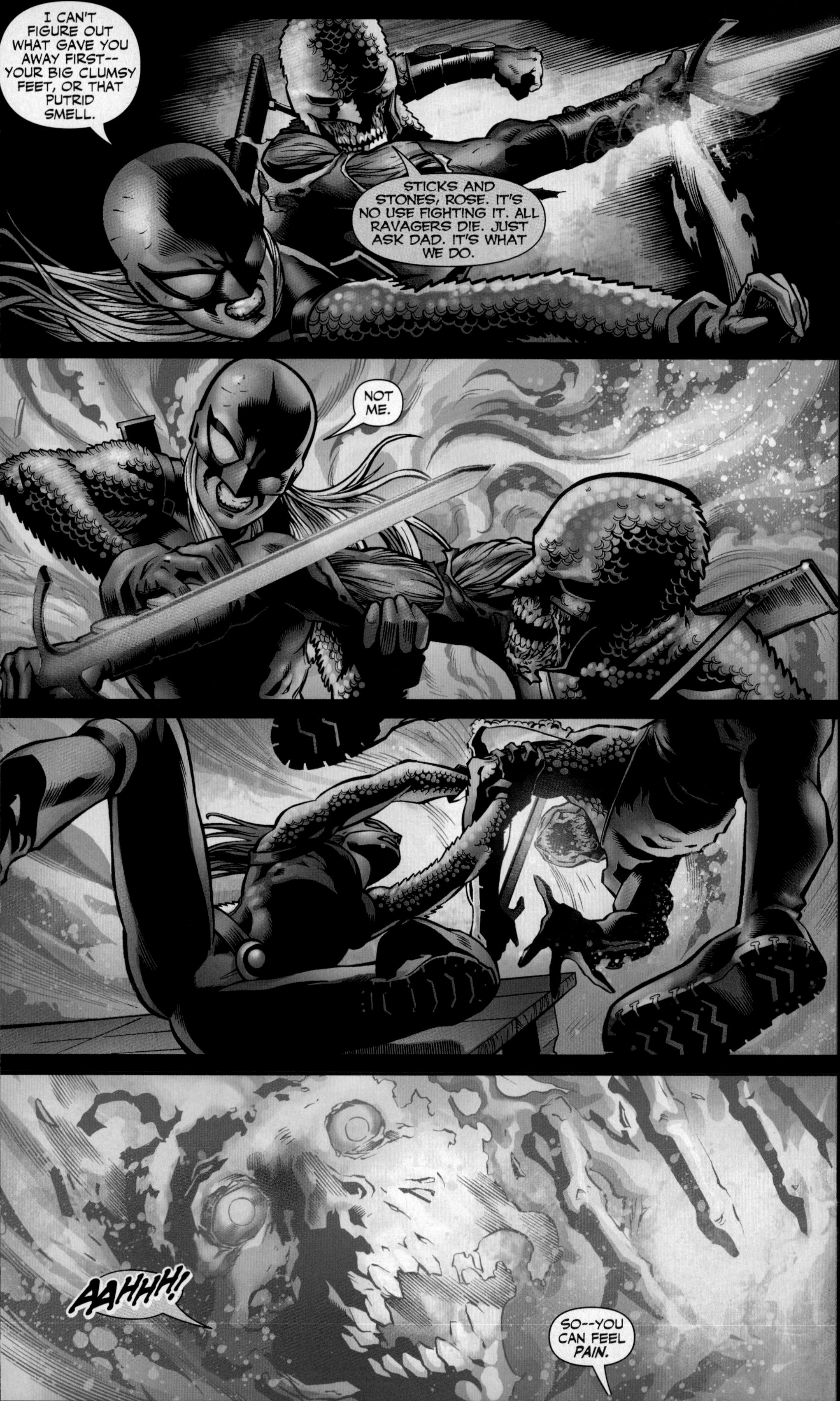

I CAN'T FIGURE OUT WHAT GAVE YOU AWAY FIRST-- YOUR BIG CLUMSY FEET, OR THAT PUTRID SMELL.
STICKS AND STONES, ROSE. IT'S NO USE FIGHTING IT. ALL RAVAGERS DIE. JUST ASK DAD. IT'S WHAT WE DO.
NOT ME.
AAHHH!
SO--YOU CAN FEEL PAIN.

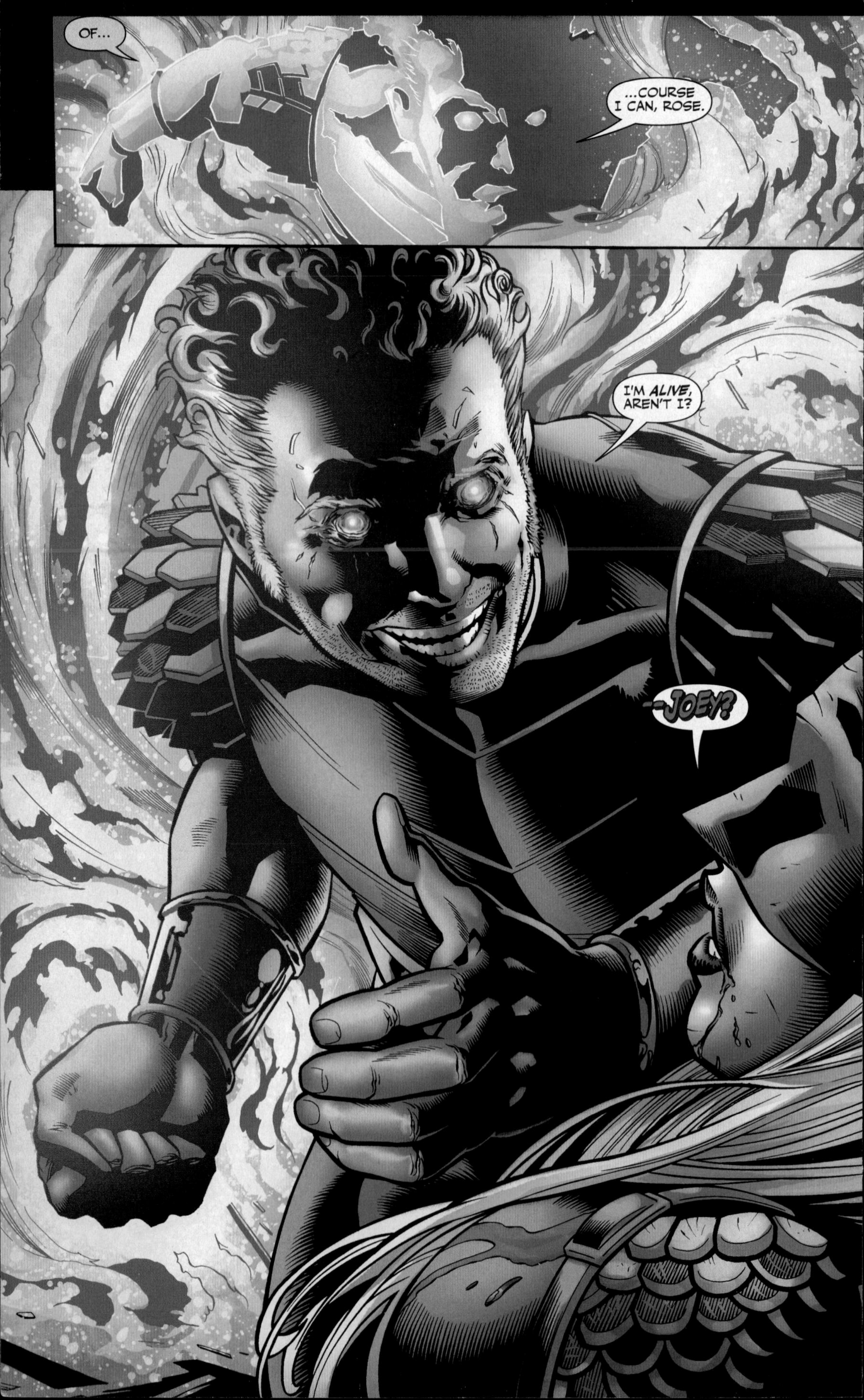
OF...
...COURSE I CAN, ROSE.
I'M ALIVE, AREN'T I?
--JOEY?

Cover by Joe Bennett and Jack Jadson with Rod Reis.

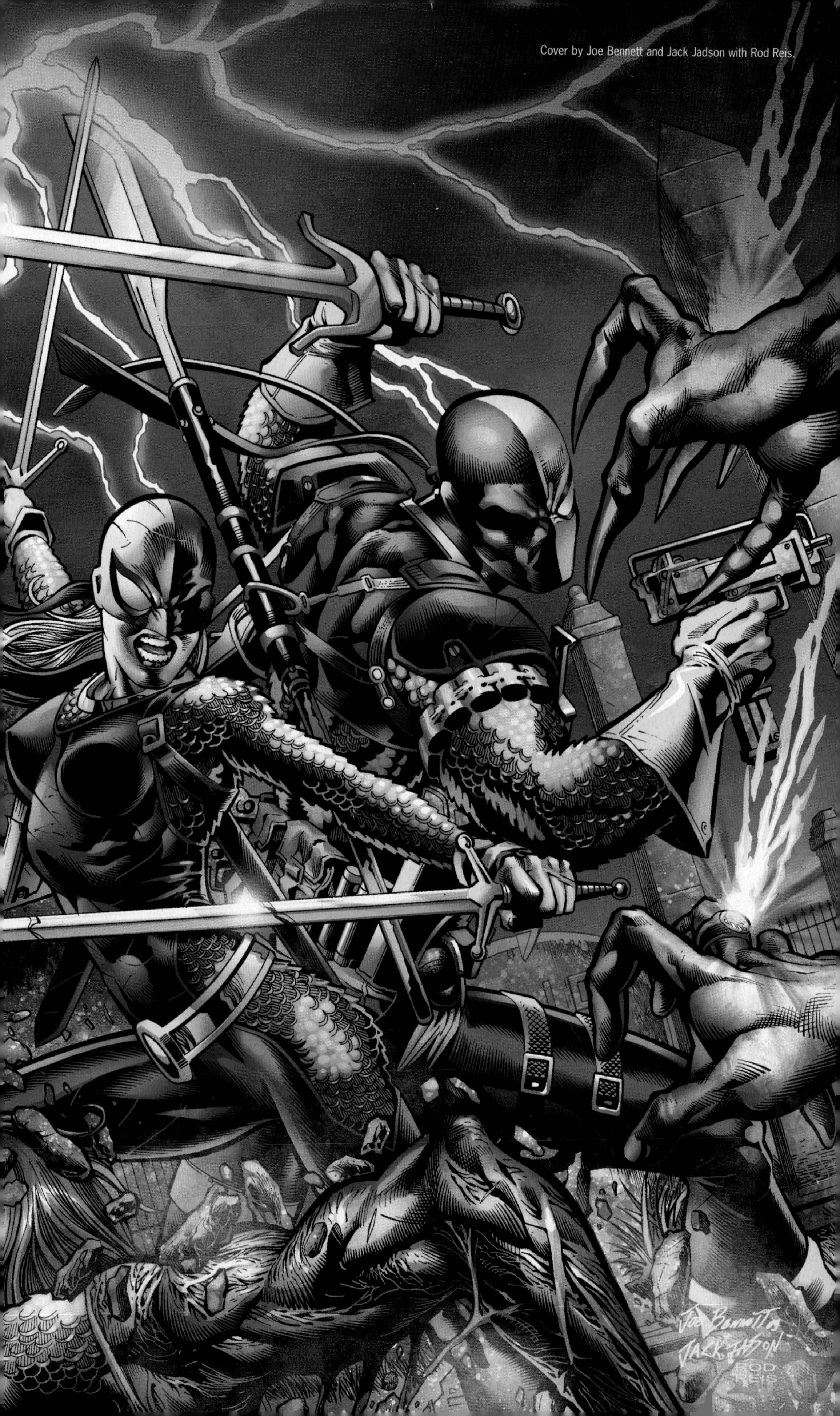

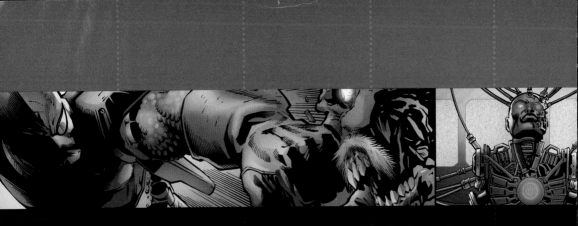

TORTURED SOULS

J.T. Krul
Writer

Joe Bennett
Pencils

Jack Jadson and Ruy José
Inks

JOSEPH WILSON, SON OF SLADE AND ADELINE WILSON. I REMEMBER--I REMEMBER HOW MY MOTHER WAS ALWAYS THERE FOR ME--ALWAYS WATCHING OVER ME.

...NOT SO MUCH.

HE WAS TOO BUSY MAKING A NAME FOR HIMSELF--*DEATHSTROKE.*

THE ONLY TIME HE GAVE ME ANY ATTENTION WAS WHEN I WAS *BAIT.* HE MAY HAVE SAVED MY LIFE, BUT THE ASSASSIN'S BLADE CUT MY *THROAT* AND TOOK MY *VOICE.*

AFTER THAT, MY MEEK EXISTENCE CONTINUED UNTIL I DISCOVERED MY OWN SPECIAL TALENT--THE ABILITY TO POSSESS AND CONTROL ANY PERSON SIMPLY BY GAZING INTO THEIR EYES.

AND WHEN I JOINED THE TITANS, *JERICHO* WAS BORN.

BUT THE EFFECT OF POSSESSING OTHER PEOPLE'S MINDS QUICKLY BEGAN TO TAX MY OWN PSYCHE--SLOWLY DRIVING ME MAD.

WHICH MADE ME AN EASY *VICTIM* ONCE MORE--THIS TIME FOR A *DEMONIC* POWER THAT WAS MUCH BETTER AT *POSSESSION* THAN I WOULD EVER WISH TO BE.

COMPLETELY OUT OF CONTROL AND IN DANGER OF KILLING EVERYONE I CARED ABOUT, MY FATHER WAS THE ONLY ONE *STRONG* ENOUGH TO DO WHAT HAD TO BE DONE.

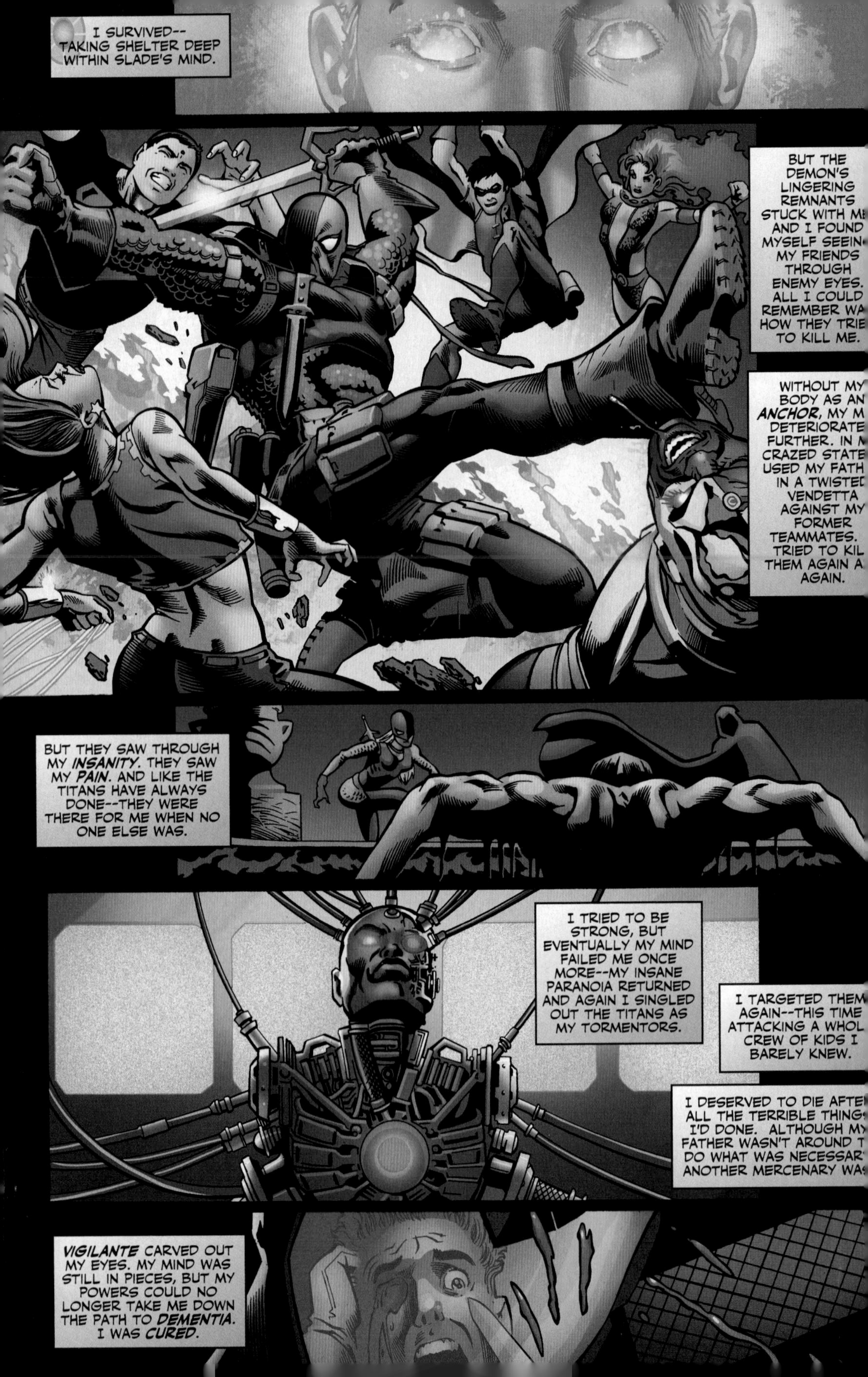
I SURVIVED--
TAKING SHELTER DEEP
WITHIN SLADE'S MIND.
BUT THE DEMON'S LINGERING REMNANTS STUCK WITH M AND I FOUND MYSELF SEEIN MY FRIENDS THROUGH ENEMY EYES. ALL I COULD REMEMBER WA HOW THEY TRIE TO KILL ME.
WITHOUT MY BODY AS AN *ANCHOR*, MY M DETERIORATE FURTHER. IN M CRAZED STATE USED MY FATH IN A TWISTED VENDETTA AGAINST MY FORMER TEAMMATES. TRIED TO KIL THEM AGAIN A AGAIN.
BUT THEY SAW THROUGH MY *INSANITY*. THEY SAW MY *PAIN*. AND LIKE THE TITANS HAVE ALWAYS DONE--THEY WERE THERE FOR ME WHEN NO ONE ELSE WAS.
I TRIED TO BE STRONG, BUT EVENTUALLY MY MIND FAILED ME ONCE MORE--MY INSANE PARANOIA RETURNED AND AGAIN I SINGLED OUT THE TITANS AS MY TORMENTORS.
I TARGETED THEM AGAIN--THIS TIME ATTACKING A WHOL CREW OF KIDS I BARELY KNEW.
I DESERVED TO DIE AFTE ALL THE TERRIBLE THING I'D DONE. ALTHOUGH MY FATHER WASN'T AROUND T DO WHAT WAS NECESSAR ANOTHER MERCENARY WA
VIGILANTE CARVED OUT MY EYES. MY MIND WAS STILL IN PIECES, BUT MY POWERS COULD NO LONGER TAKE ME DOWN THE PATH TO *DEMENTIA*. I WAS *CURED*.

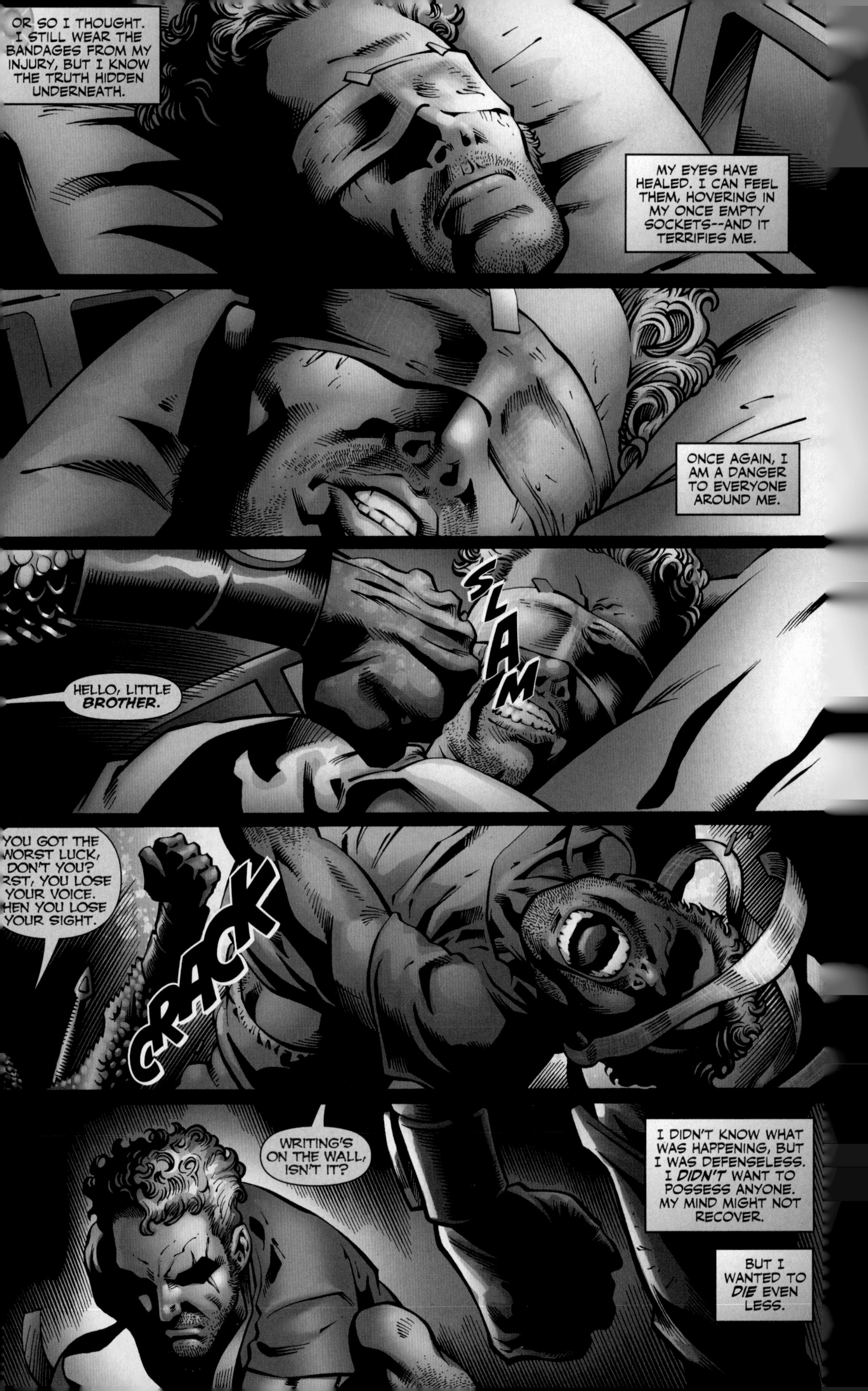
OR SO I THOUGHT. I STILL WEAR THE BANDAGES FROM MY INJURY, BUT I KNOW THE TRUTH HIDDEN UNDERNEATH.
MY EYES HAVE HEALED. I CAN FEEL THEM, HOVERING IN MY ONCE EMPTY SOCKETS--AND IT TERRIFIES ME.
ONCE AGAIN, I AM A DANGER TO EVERYONE AROUND ME.
SLAM
HELLO, LITTLE BROTHER.
YOU GOT THE WORST LUCK, DON'T YOU? RST, YOU LOSE YOUR VOICE. HEN YOU LOSE YOUR SIGHT.
CRACK
WRITING'S ON THE WALL, ISN'T IT?
I DIDN'T KNOW WHAT WAS HAPPENING, BUT I WAS DEFENSELESS. I DIDN'T WANT TO POSSESS ANYONE. MY MIND MIGHT NOT RECOVER.
BUT I WANTED TO DIE EVEN LESS.

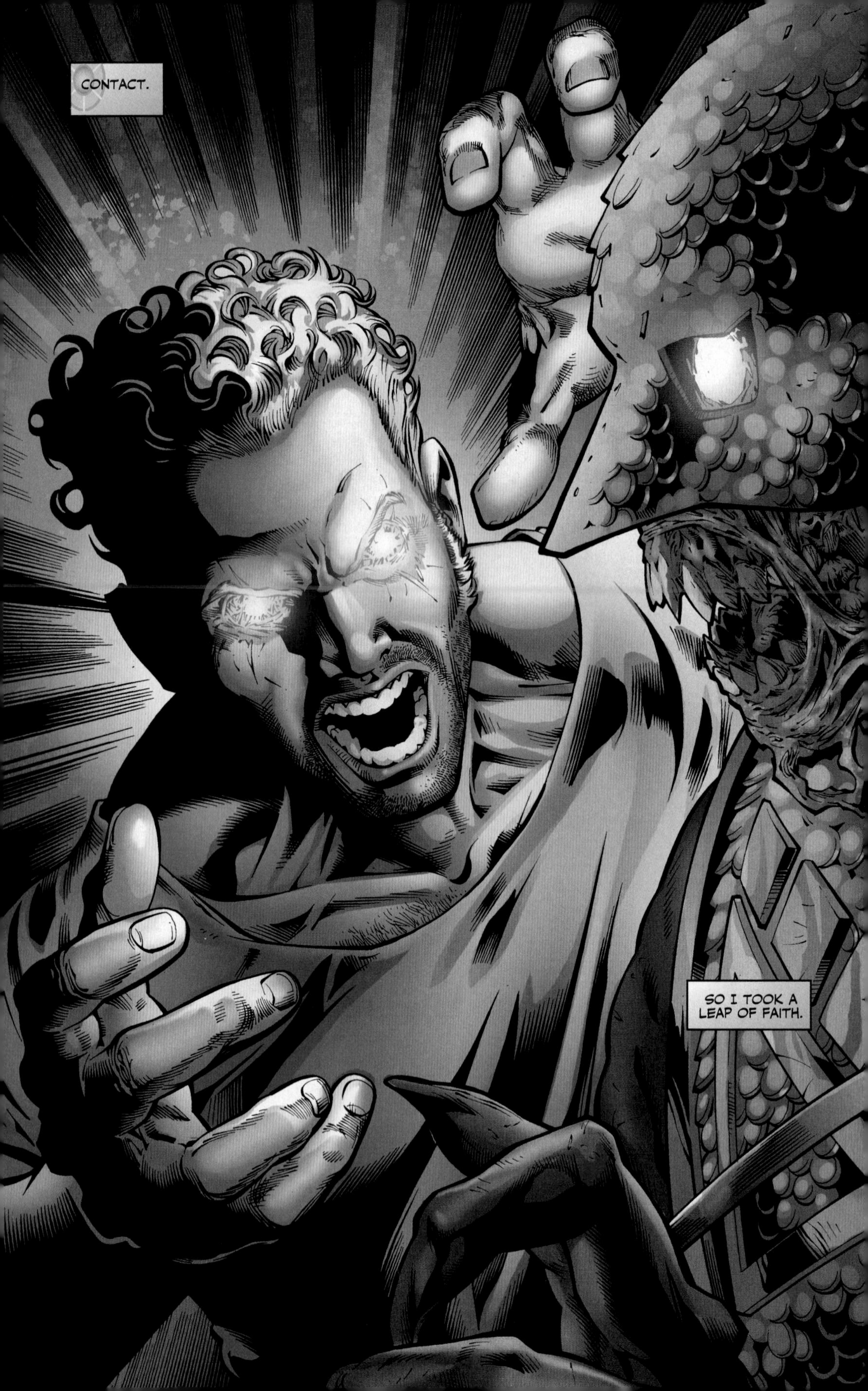
CONTACT.
SO I TOOK A
LEAP OF FAITH.

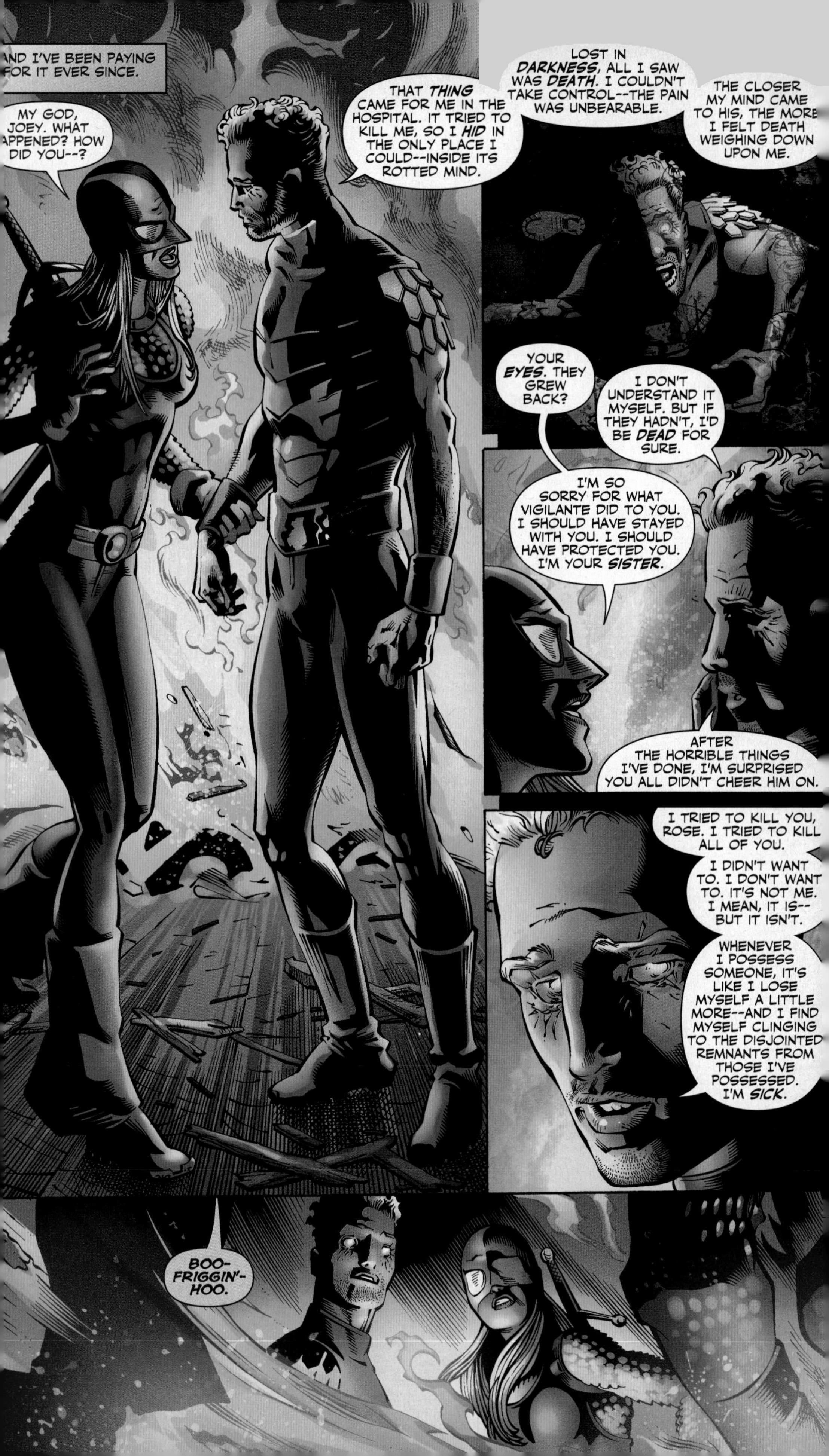
AND I'VE BEEN PAYING FOR IT EVER SINCE.
MY GOD, JOEY. WHAT APPENED? HOW DID YOU--?
THAT THING CAME FOR ME IN THE HOSPITAL. IT TRIED TO KILL ME, SO I HID IN THE ONLY PLACE I COULD--INSIDE ITS ROTTED MIND.
LOST IN DARKNESS, ALL I SAW WAS DEATH. I COULDN'T TAKE CONTROL--THE PAIN WAS UNBEARABLE.
THE CLOSER MY MIND CAME TO HIS, THE MORE I FELT DEATH WEIGHING DOWN UPON ME.
YOUR EYES. THEY GREW BACK?
I DON'T UNDERSTAND IT MYSELF. BUT IF THEY HADN'T, I'D BE DEAD FOR SURE.
I'M SO SORRY FOR WHAT VIGILANTE DID TO YOU. I SHOULD HAVE STAYED WITH YOU. I SHOULD HAVE PROTECTED YOU. I'M YOUR SISTER.
AFTER THE HORRIBLE THINGS I'VE DONE, I'M SURPRISED YOU ALL DIDN'T CHEER HIM ON.
I TRIED TO KILL YOU, ROSE. I TRIED TO KILL ALL OF YOU.
I DIDN'T WANT TO. I DON'T WANT TO. IT'S NOT ME. I MEAN, IT IS--BUT IT ISN'T.
WHENEVER I POSSESS SOMEONE, IT'S LIKE I LOSE MYSELF A LITTLE MORE--AND I FIND MYSELF CLINGING TO THE DISJOINTED REMNANTS FROM THOSE I'VE POSSESSED. I'M SICK.
BOO-FRIGGIN'-HOO.

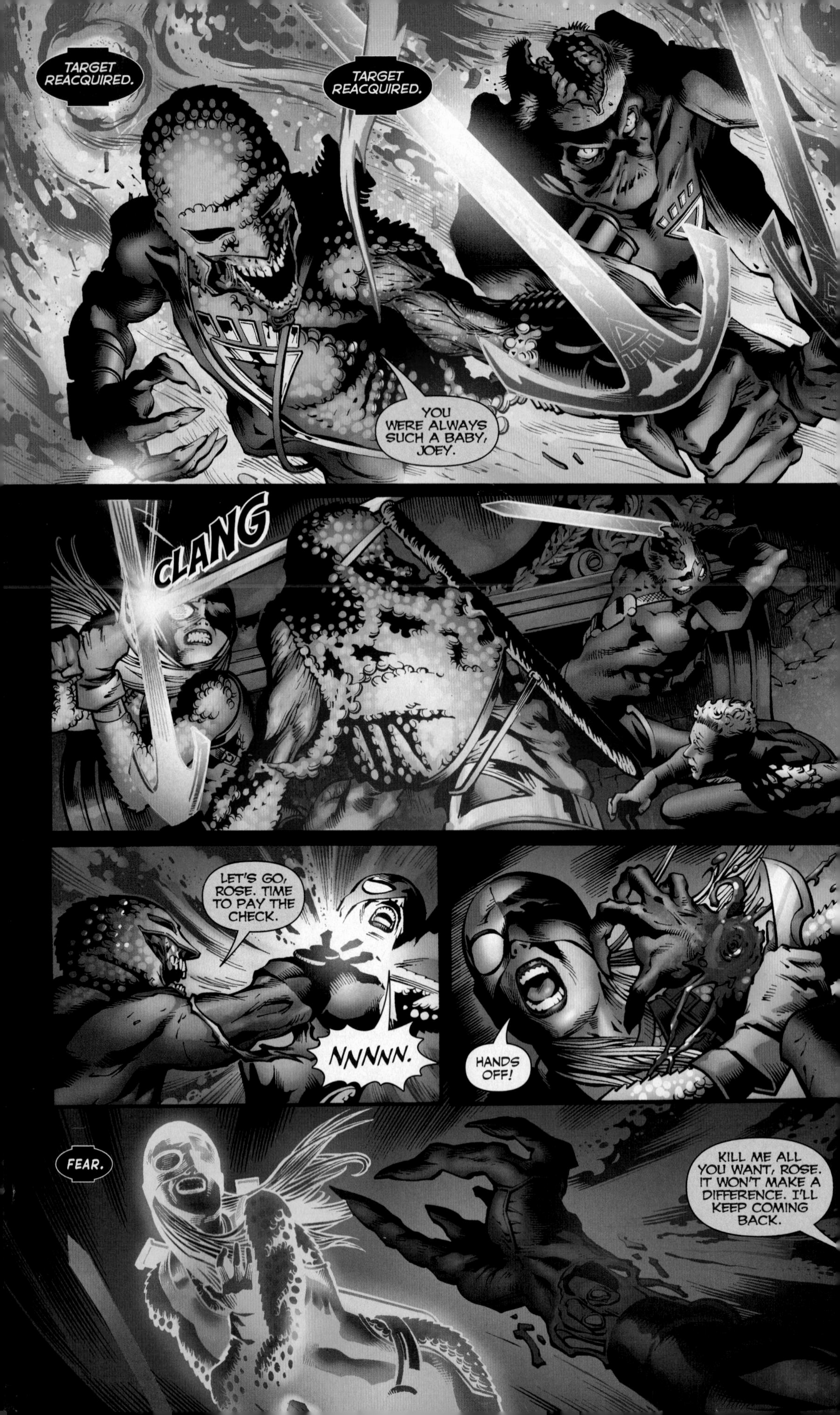
TARGET REACQUIRED.
TARGET REACQUIRED.
YOU WERE ALWAYS SUCH A BABY, JOEY.
CLANG
LET'S GO, ROSE. TIME TO PAY THE CHECK.
NNNNN.
HANDS OFF!
FEAR.
KILL ME ALL YOU WANT, ROSE. IT WON'T MAKE A DIFFERENCE. I'LL KEEP COMING BACK.

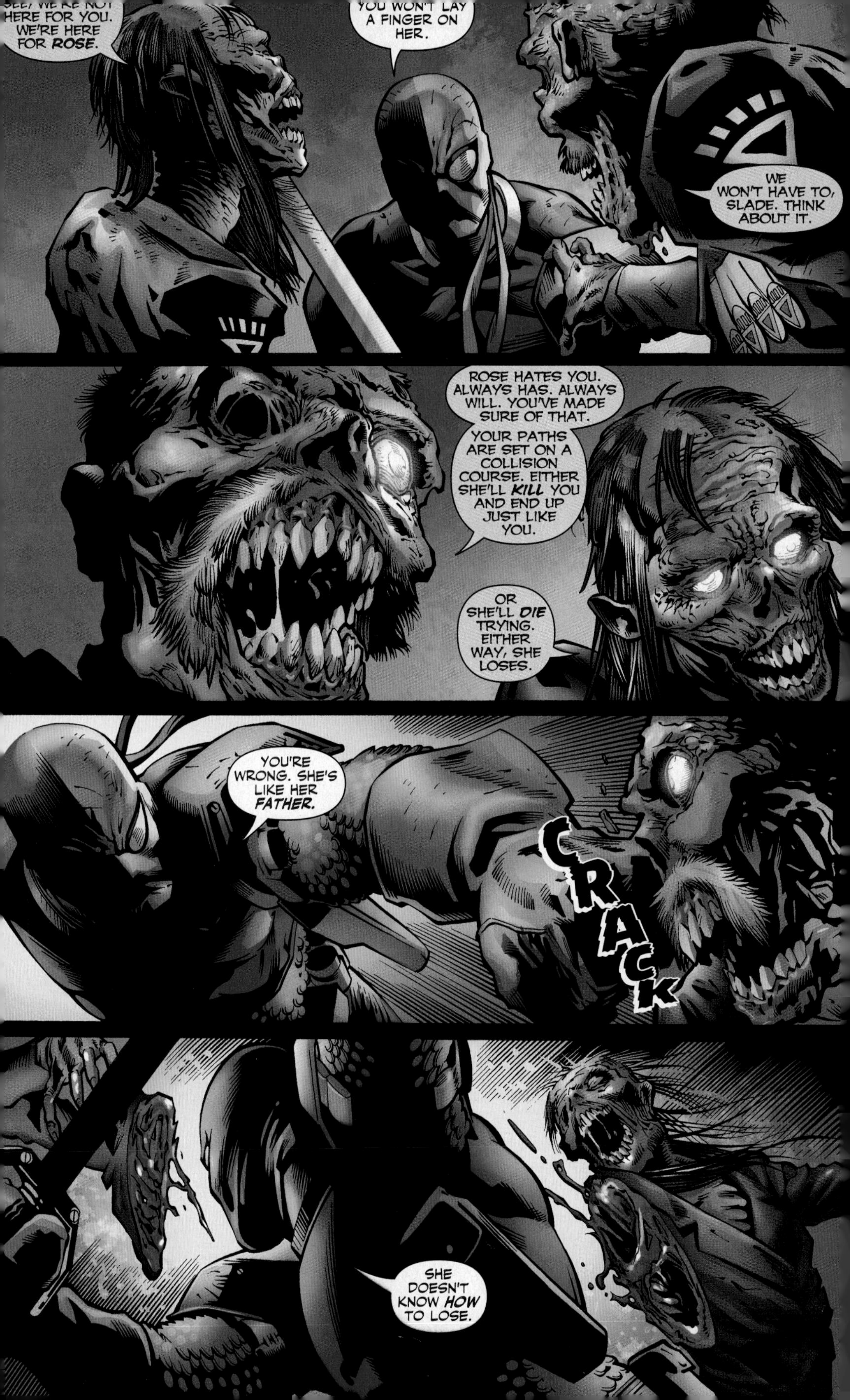
HERE FOR YOU. WE'RE HERE FOR ROSE.
YOU WON'T LAY A FINGER ON HER.
WE WON'T HAVE TO, SLADE. THINK ABOUT IT.
ROSE HATES YOU. ALWAYS HAS. ALWAYS WILL. YOU'VE MADE SURE OF THAT.
YOUR PATHS ARE SET ON A COLLISION COURSE. EITHER SHE'LL KILL YOU AND END UP JUST LIKE YOU.
OR SHE'LL DIE TRYING. EITHER WAY, SHE LOSES.
YOU'RE WRONG. SHE'S LIKE HER FATHER.
CRACK
SHE DOESN'T KNOW HOW TO LOSE.

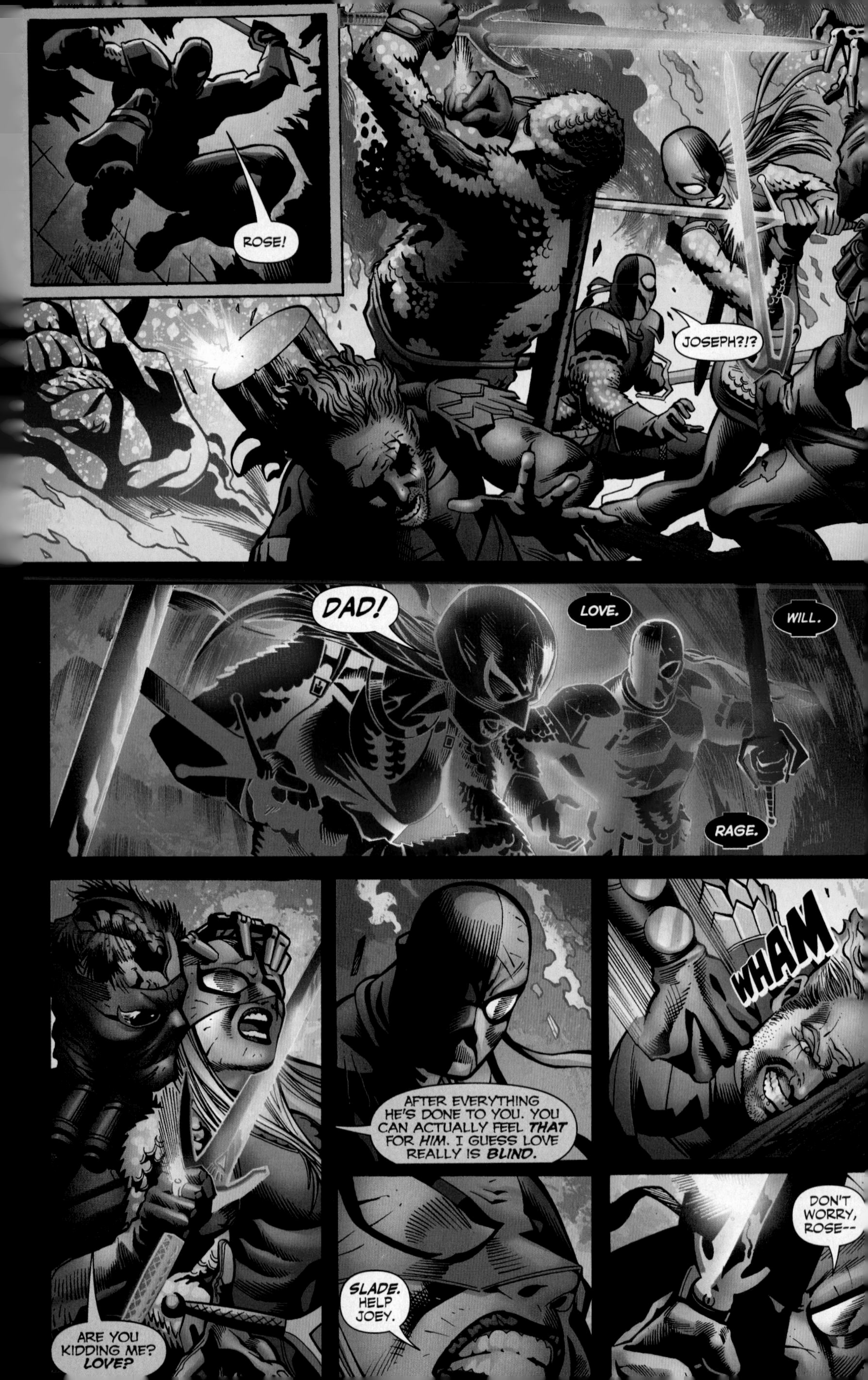

ROSE!
JOSEPH?!?
DAD!
LOVE.
WILL.
RAGE.
ARE YOU KIDDING ME? LOVE?
AFTER EVERYTHING HE'S DONE TO YOU. YOU CAN ACTUALLY FEEL THAT FOR HIM. I GUESS LOVE REALLY IS BLIND.
SLADE. HELP JOEY.
WHAM
DON'T WORRY, ROSE--

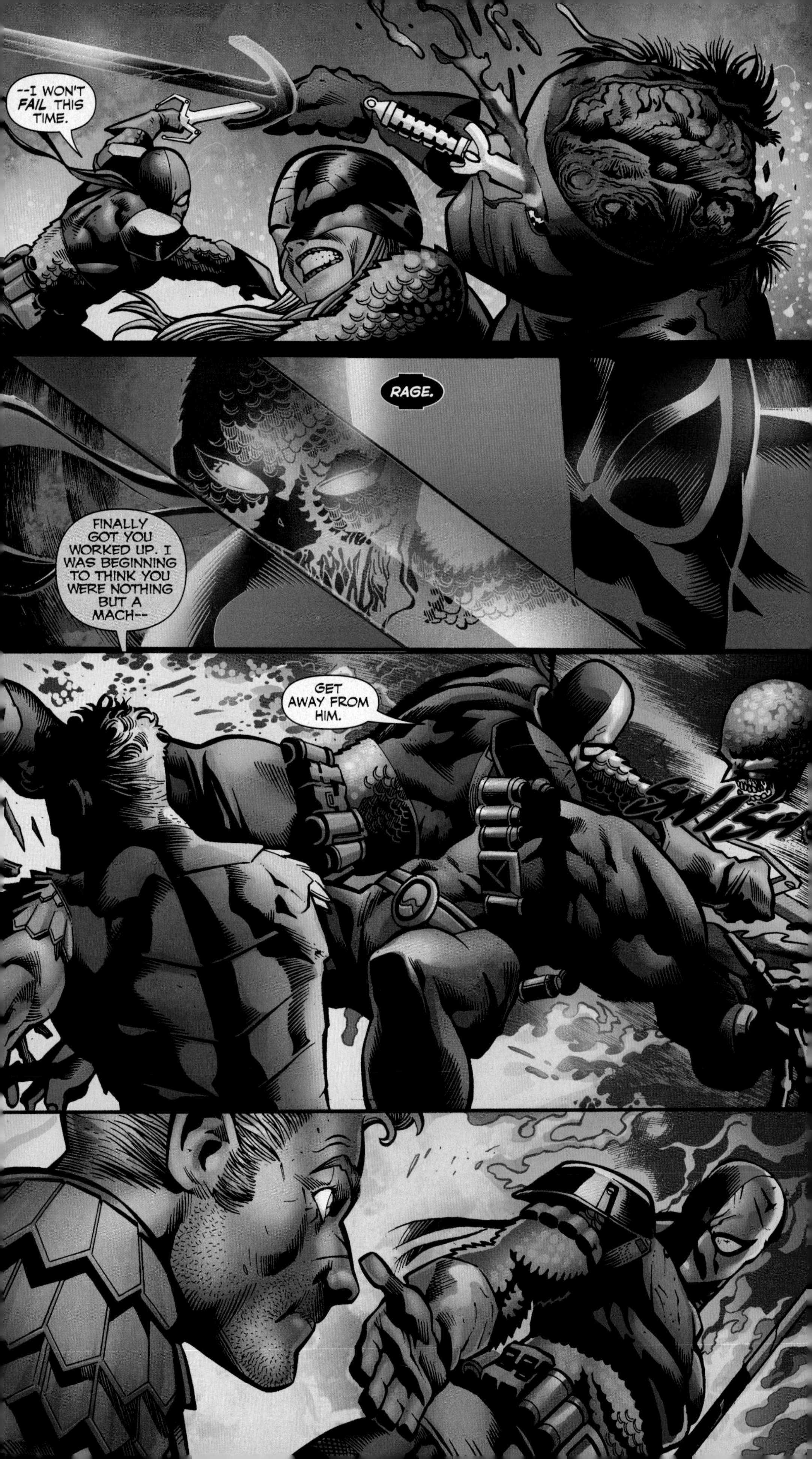
--I WON'T FAIL THIS TIME.
RAGE.
FINALLY GOT YOU WORKED UP. I WAS BEGINNING TO THINK YOU WERE NOTHING BUT A MACH--
GET AWAY FROM HIM.
SHNK

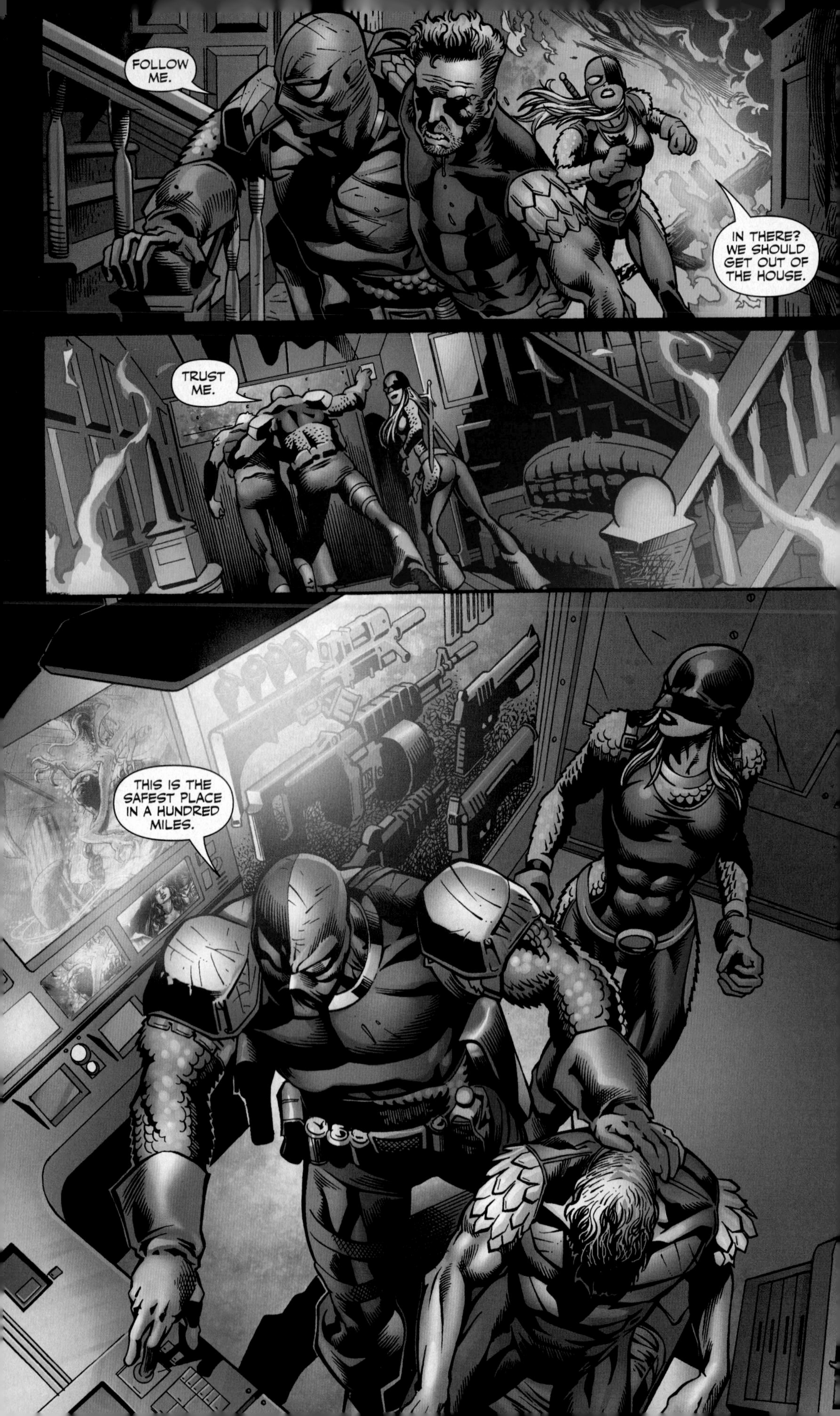
FOLLOW ME.
IN THERE? WE SHOULD GET OUT OF THE HOUSE.
TRUST ME.
THIS IS THE SAFEST PLACE IN A HUNDRED MILES.

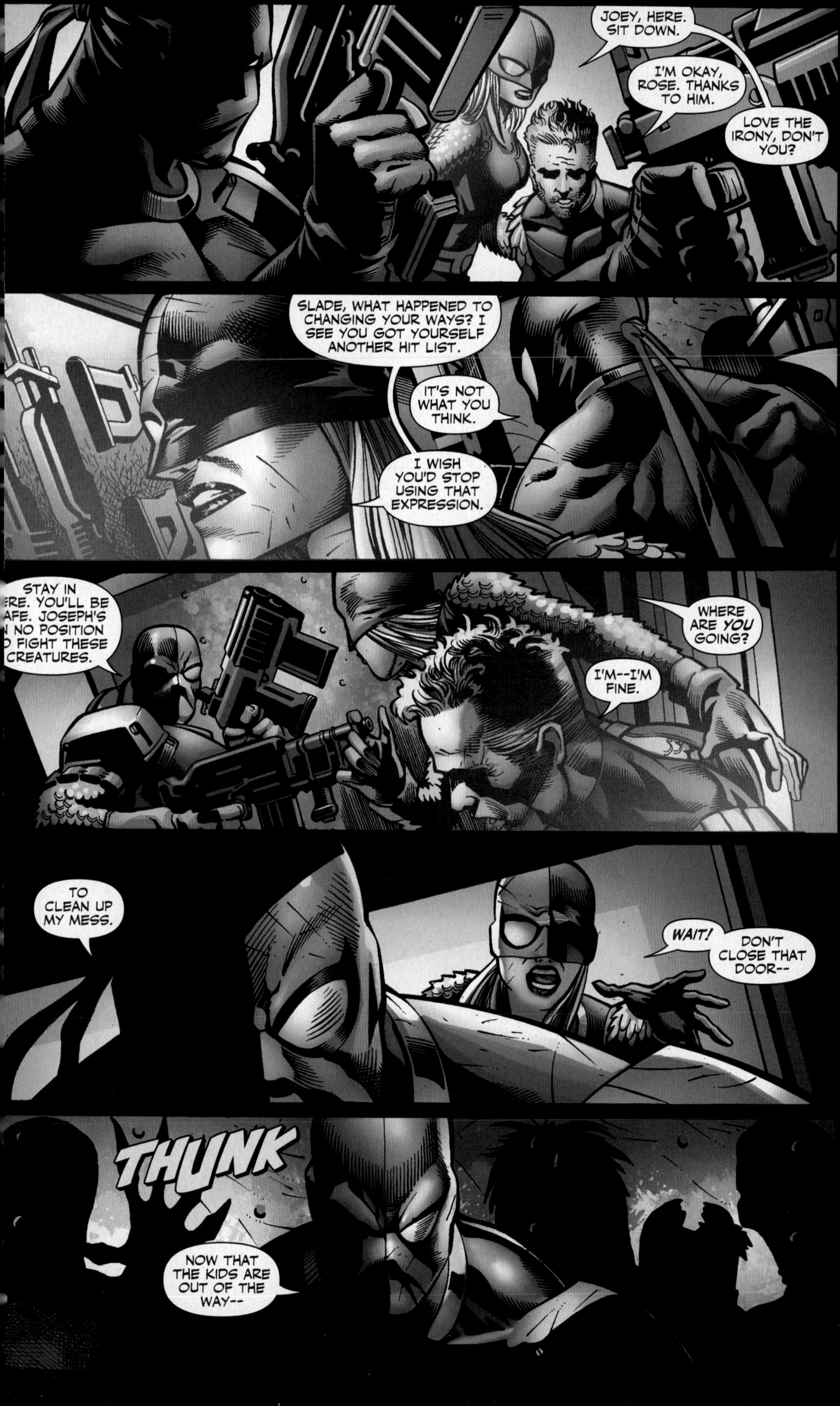
JOEY, HERE. SIT DOWN.
I'M OKAY, ROSE. THANKS TO HIM.
LOVE THE IRONY, DON'T YOU?
SLADE, WHAT HAPPENED TO CHANGING YOUR WAYS? I SEE YOU GOT YOURSELF ANOTHER HIT LIST.
IT'S NOT WHAT YOU THINK.
I WISH YOU'D STOP USING THAT EXPRESSION.
STAY IN ERE. YOU'LL BE AFE. JOSEPH'S NO POSITION D FIGHT THESE CREATURES.
WHERE ARE *YOU* GOING?
I'M--I'M FINE.
TO CLEAN UP MY MESS.
WAIT!
DON'T CLOSE THAT DOOR--
THUNK
NOW THAT THE KIDS ARE OUT OF THE WAY--

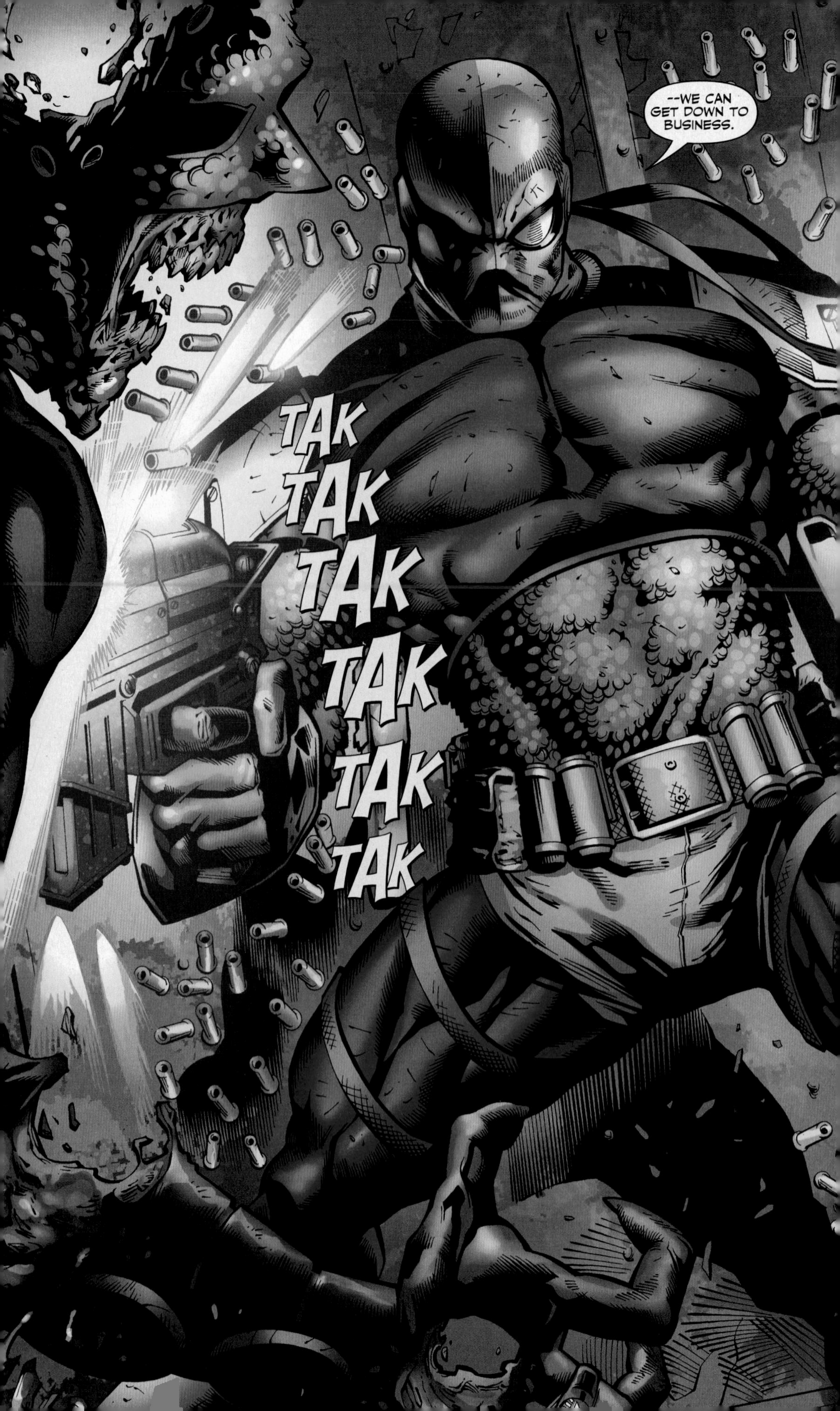
--WE CAN GET DOWN TO BUSINESS.
TAK TAK TAK TAK TAK TAK

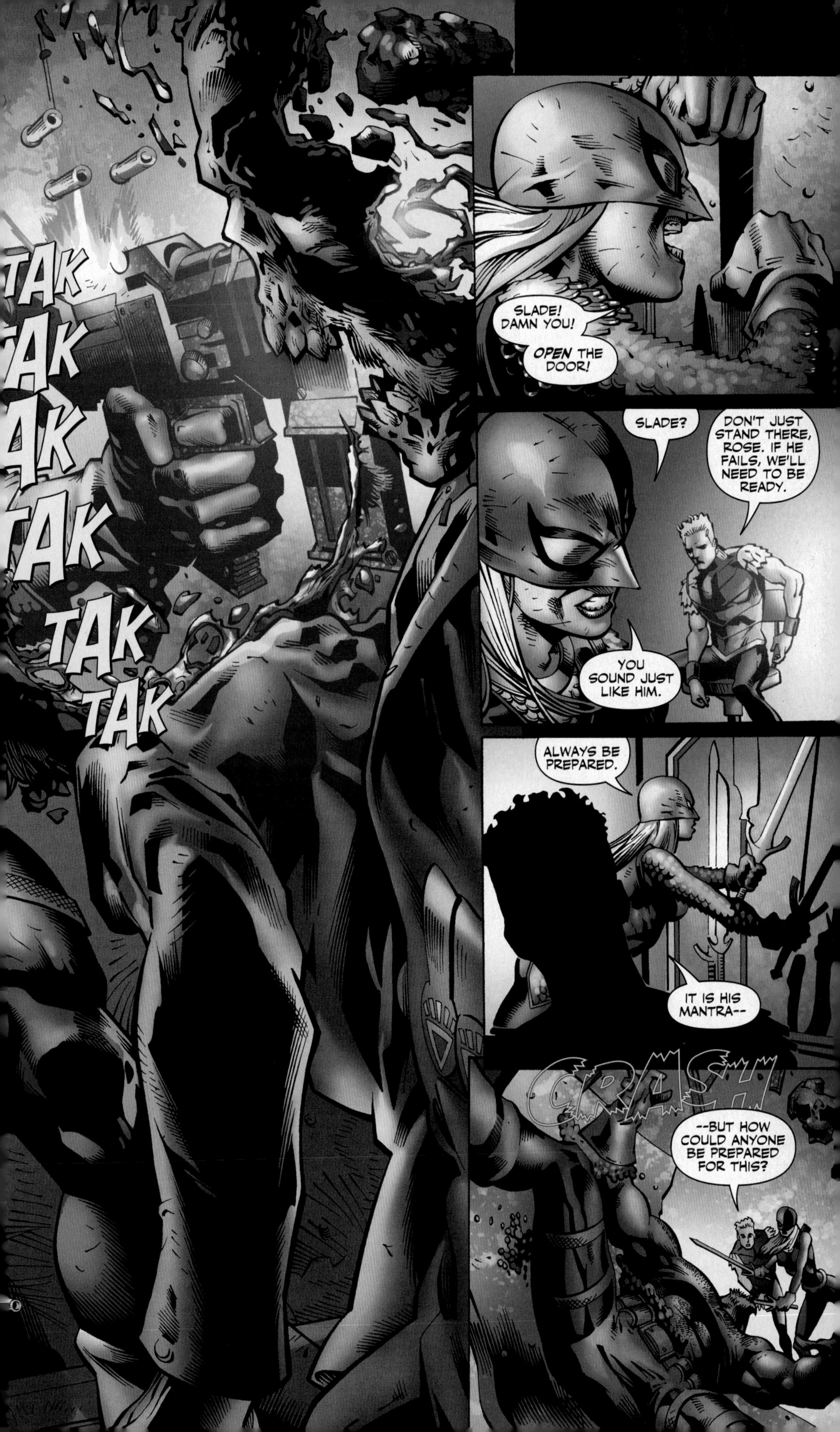
TAK
TAK
TAK
TAK
TAK
TAK
SLADE! DAMN YOU!
OPEN THE DOOR!
SLADE?
DON'T JUST STAND THERE, ROSE. IF HE FAILS, WE'LL NEED TO BE READY.
YOU SOUND JUST LIKE HIM.
ALWAYS BE PREPARED.
IT IS HIS MANTRA--
CRASH
--BUT HOW COULD ANYONE BE PREPARED FOR THIS?

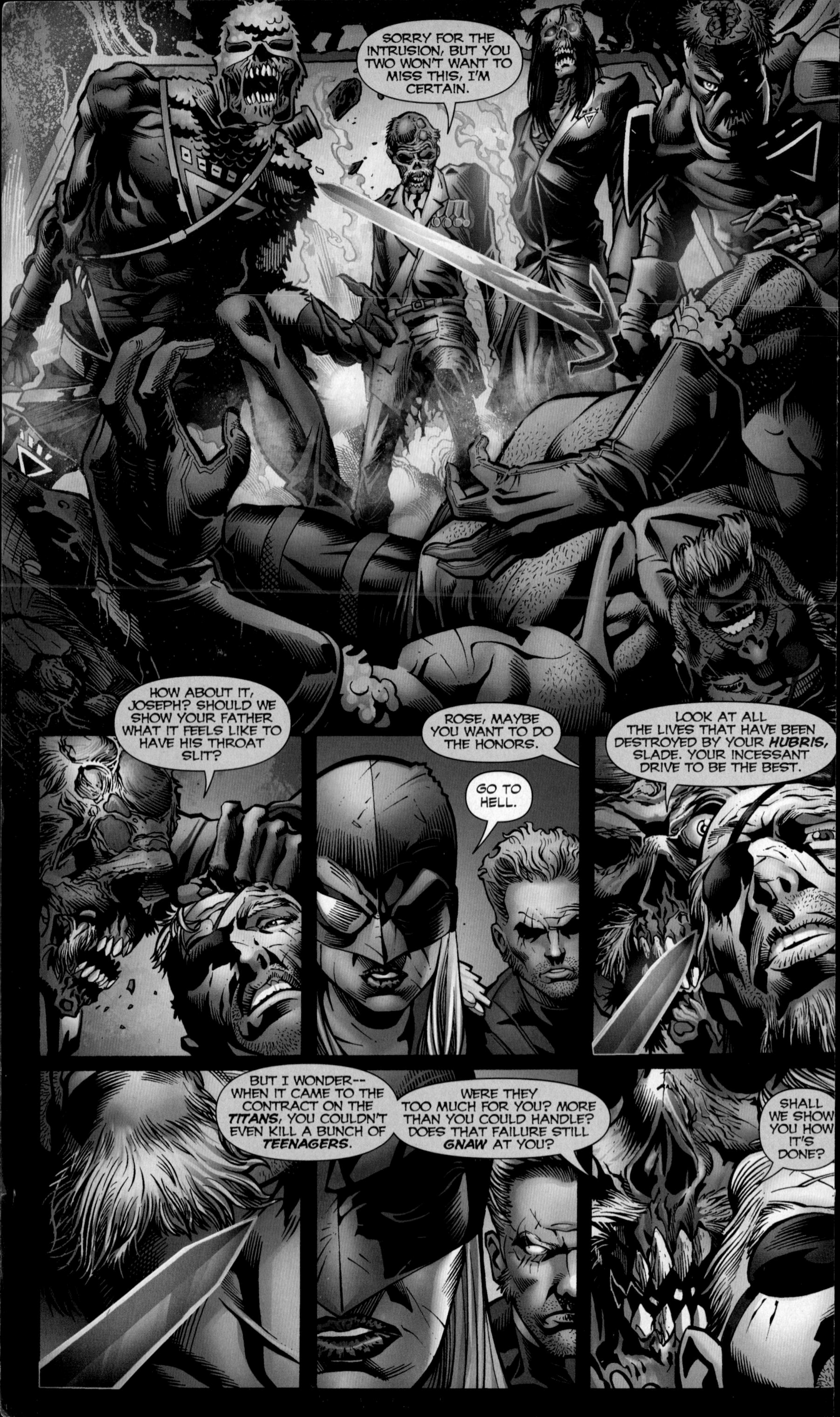
SORRY FOR THE INTRUSION, BUT YOU TWO WON'T WANT TO MISS THIS, I'M CERTAIN.
HOW ABOUT IT, JOSEPH? SHOULD WE SHOW YOUR FATHER WHAT IT FEELS LIKE TO HAVE HIS THROAT SLIT?
ROSE, MAYBE YOU WANT TO DO THE HONORS.
GO TO HELL.
LOOK AT ALL THE LIVES THAT HAVE BEEN DESTROYED BY YOUR HUBRIS, SLADE. YOUR INCESSANT DRIVE TO BE THE BEST.
BUT I WONDER-- WHEN IT CAME TO THE CONTRACT ON THE TITANS, YOU COULDN'T EVEN KILL A BUNCH OF TEENAGERS.
WERE THEY TOO MUCH FOR YOU? MORE THAN YOU COULD HANDLE? DOES THAT FAILURE STILL GNAW AT YOU?
SHALL WE SHOW YOU HOW IT'S DONE?

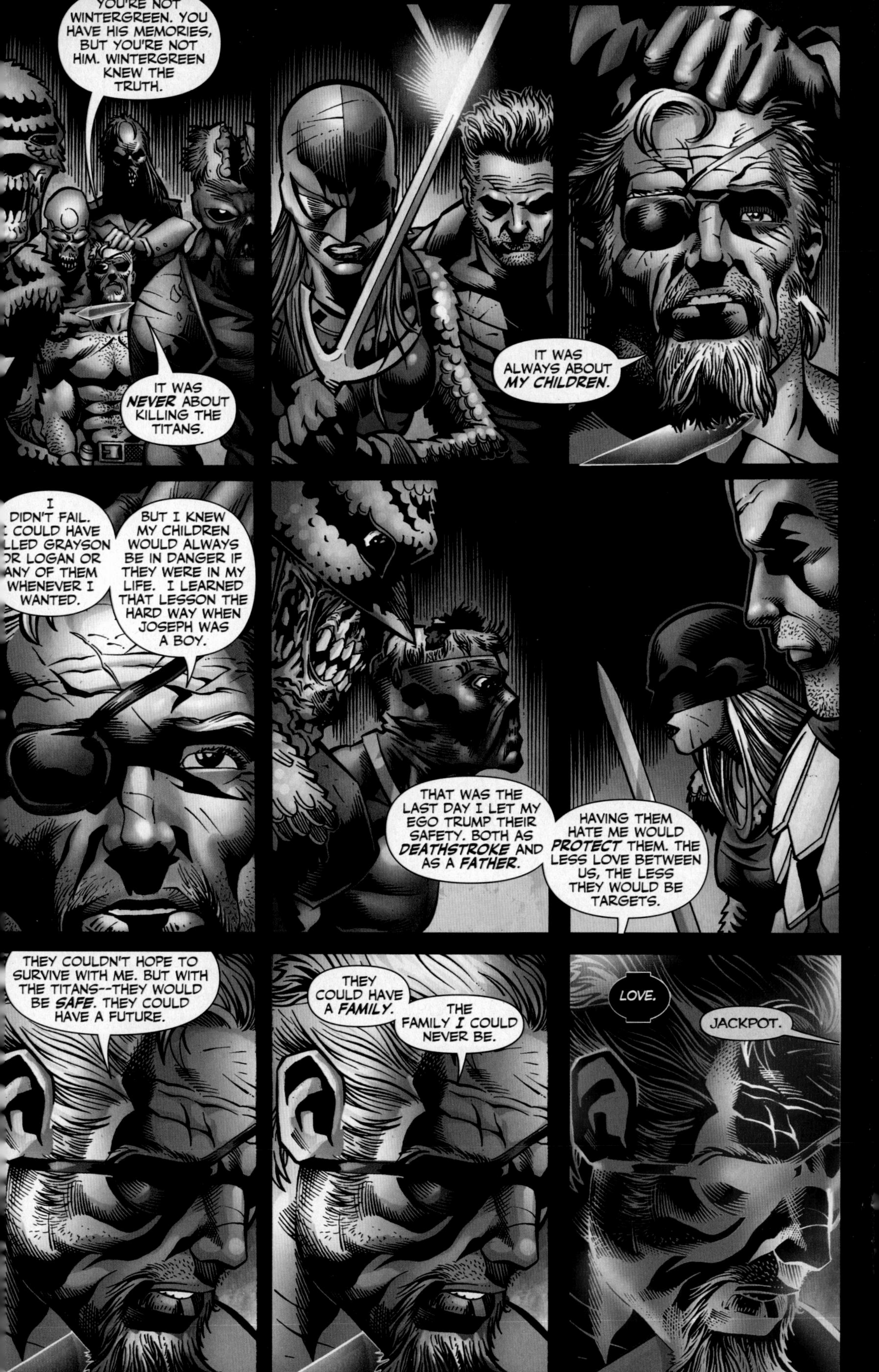

YOU'RE NOT WINTERGREEN. YOU HAVE HIS MEMORIES, BUT YOU'RE NOT HIM. WINTERGREEN KNEW THE TRUTH.
IT WAS NEVER ABOUT KILLING THE TITANS.
IT WAS ALWAYS ABOUT MY CHILDREN.
I DIDN'T FAIL. I COULD HAVE KILLED GRAYSON OR LOGAN OR ANY OF THEM WHENEVER I WANTED.
BUT I KNEW MY CHILDREN WOULD ALWAYS BE IN DANGER IF THEY WERE IN MY LIFE. I LEARNED THAT LESSON THE HARD WAY WHEN JOSEPH WAS A BOY.
THAT WAS THE LAST DAY I LET MY EGO TRUMP THEIR SAFETY. BOTH AS DEATHSTROKE AND AS A FATHER.
HAVING THEM HATE ME WOULD PROTECT THEM. THE LESS LOVE BETWEEN US, THE LESS THEY WOULD BE TARGETS.
THEY COULDN'T HOPE TO SURVIVE WITH ME. BUT WITH THE TITANS--THEY WOULD BE SAFE. THEY COULD HAVE A FUTURE.
THEY COULD HAVE A FAMILY.
THE FAMILY I COULD NEVER BE.
LOVE.
JACKPOT.

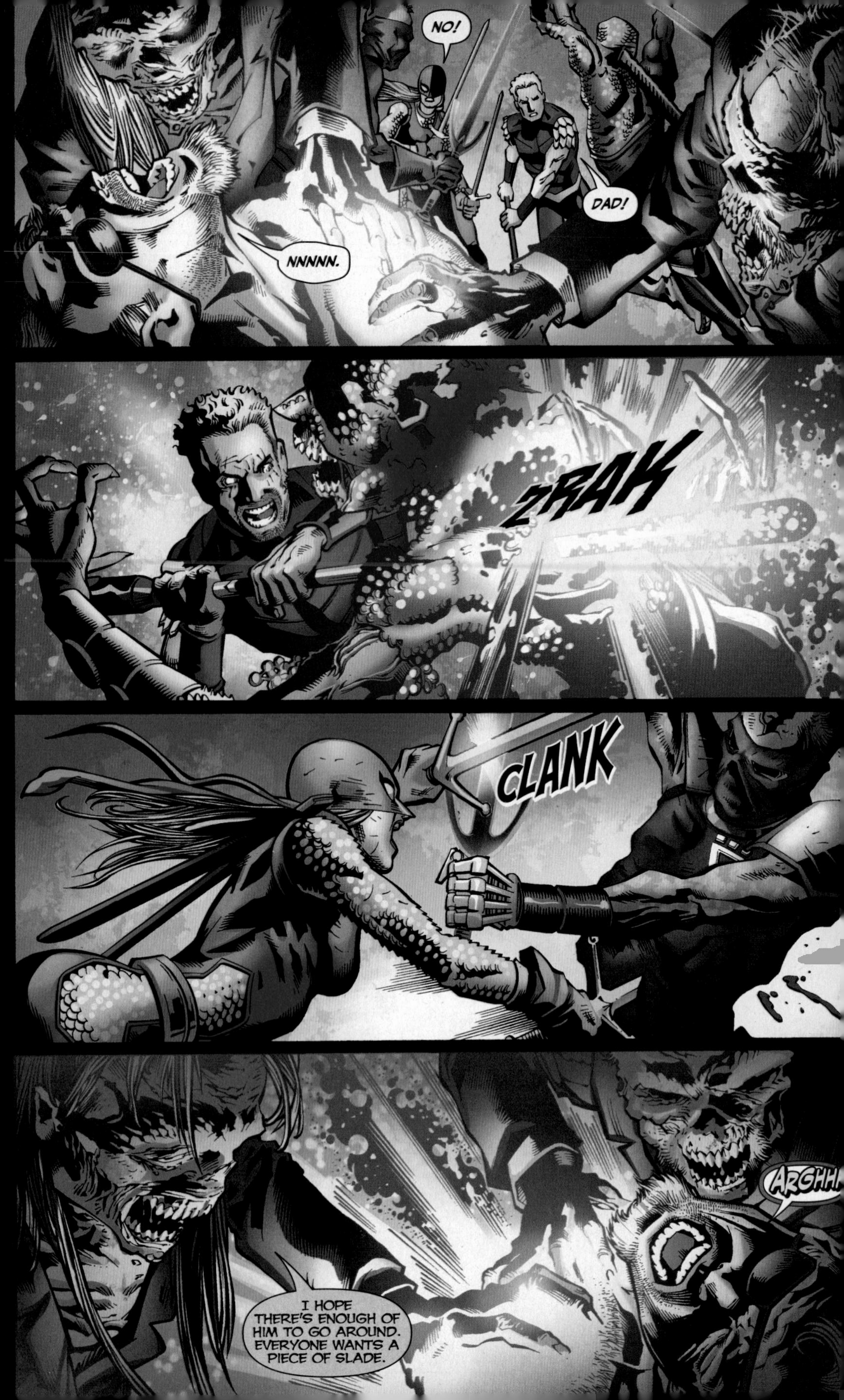
NO!
DAD!
NNNNN.
ZRAK
CLANK
ARGHH
I HOPE THERE'S ENOUGH OF HIM TO GO AROUND. EVERYONE WANTS A PIECE OF SLADE.

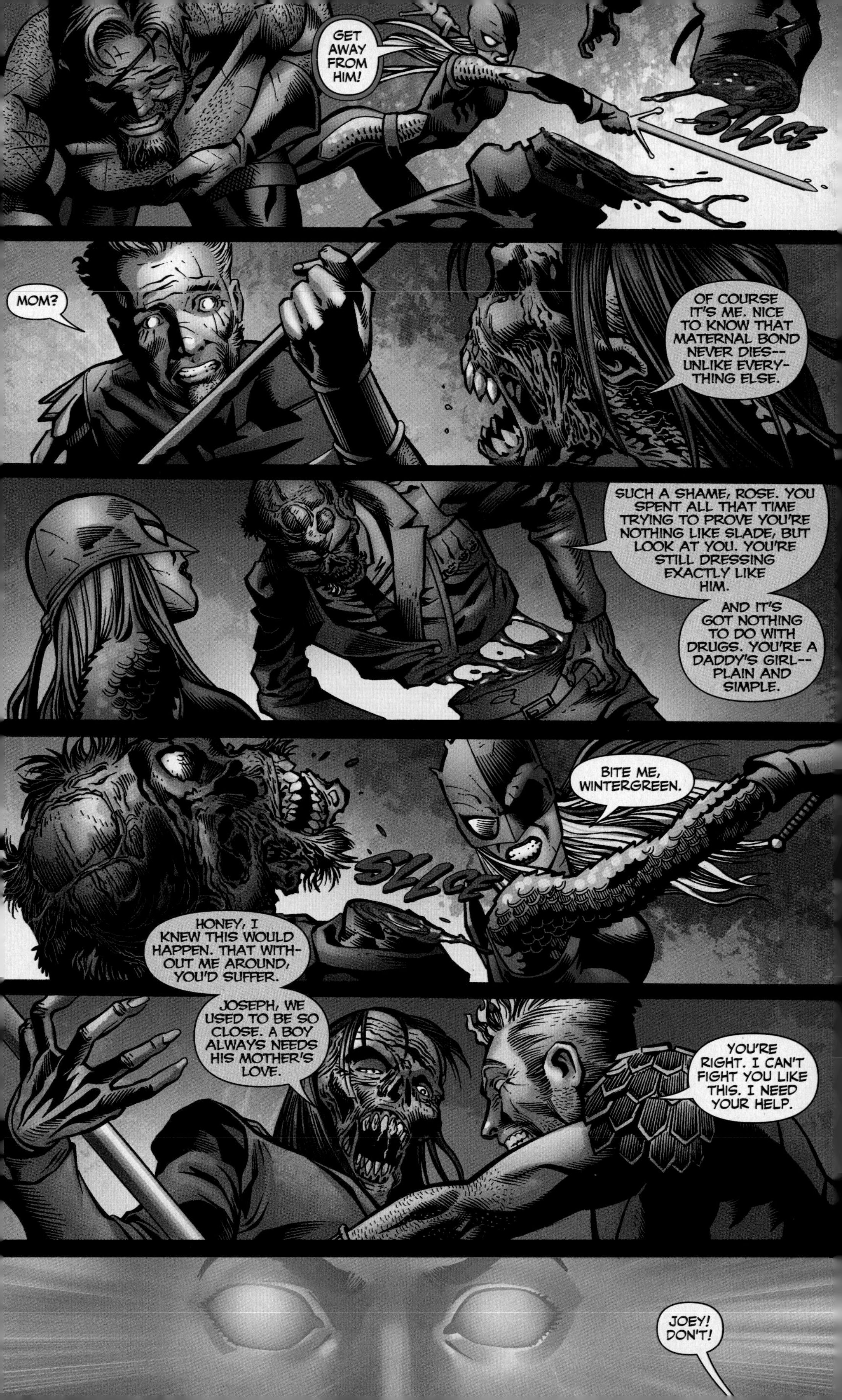
GET AWAY FROM HIM!
SLICE
MOM?
OF COURSE IT'S ME. NICE TO KNOW THAT MATERNAL BOND NEVER DIES-- UNLIKE EVERY-THING ELSE.
SUCH A SHAME, ROSE. YOU SPENT ALL THAT TIME TRYING TO PROVE YOU'RE NOTHING LIKE SLADE, BUT LOOK AT YOU. YOU'RE STILL DRESSING EXACTLY LIKE HIM.
AND IT'S GOT NOTHING TO DO WITH DRUGS. YOU'RE A DADDY'S GIRL-- PLAIN AND SIMPLE.
BITE ME, WINTERGREEN.
SLICE
HONEY, I KNEW THIS WOULD HAPPEN. THAT WITH-OUT ME AROUND, YOU'D SUFFER.
JOSEPH, WE USED TO BE SO CLOSE. A BOY ALWAYS NEEDS HIS MOTHER'S LOVE.
YOU'RE RIGHT. I CAN'T FIGHT YOU LIKE THIS. I NEED YOUR HELP.
JOEY! DON'T!

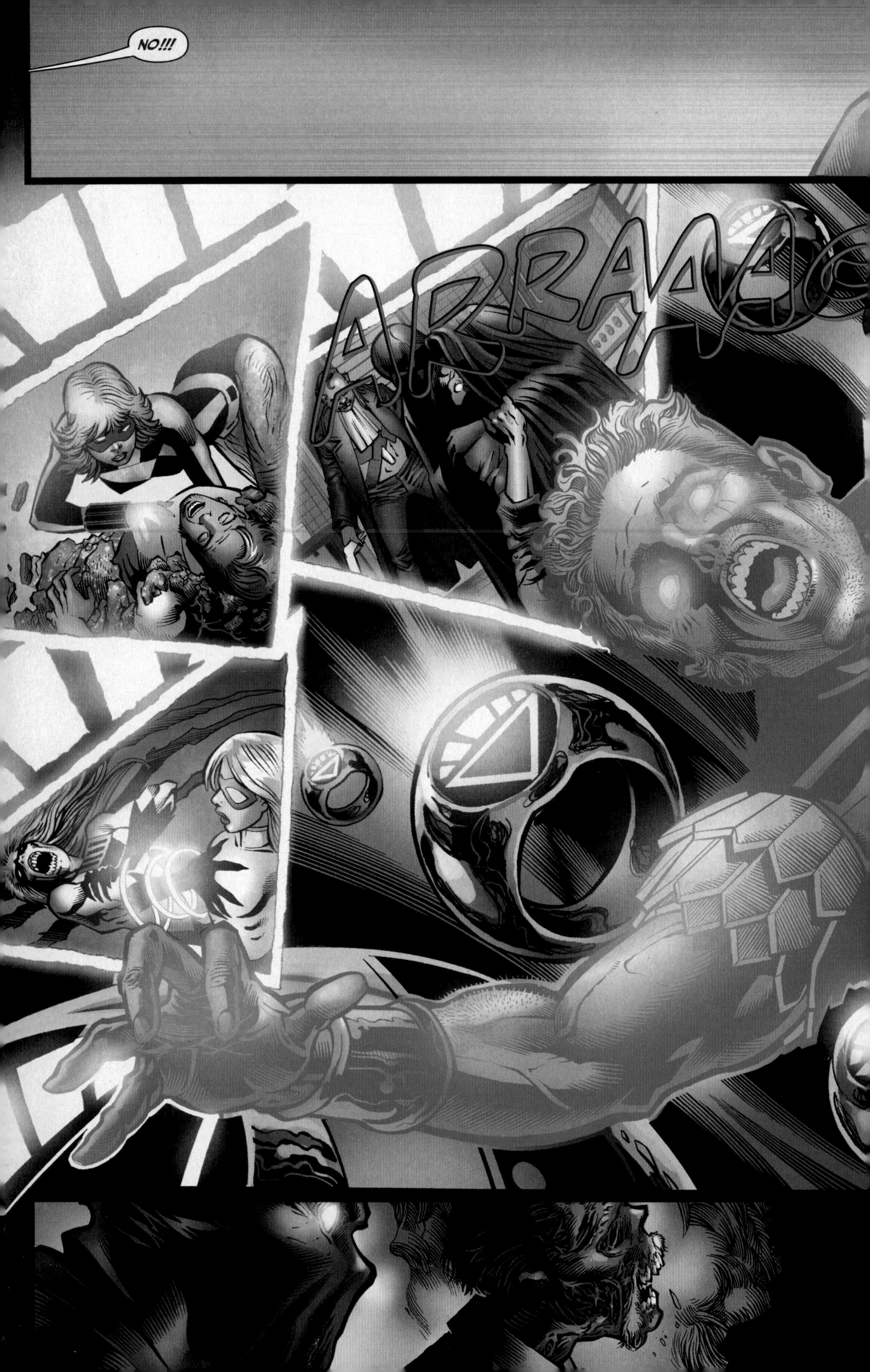
NO!!!
ARRAAAG

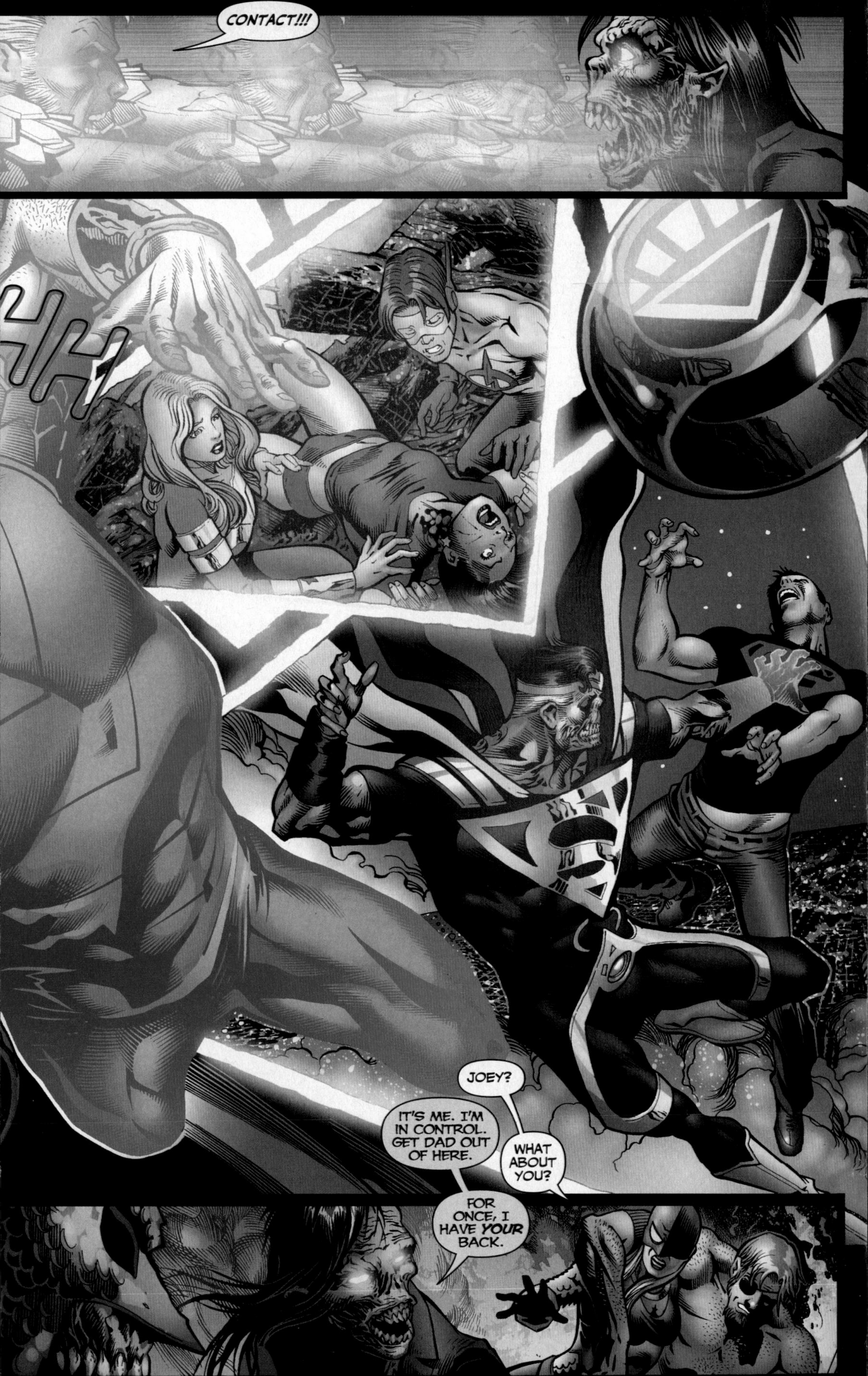
CONTACT!!!
JOEY?
IT'S ME. I'M IN CONTROL. GET DAD OUT OF HERE.
WHAT ABOUT YOU?
FOR ONCE, I HAVE YOUR BACK.

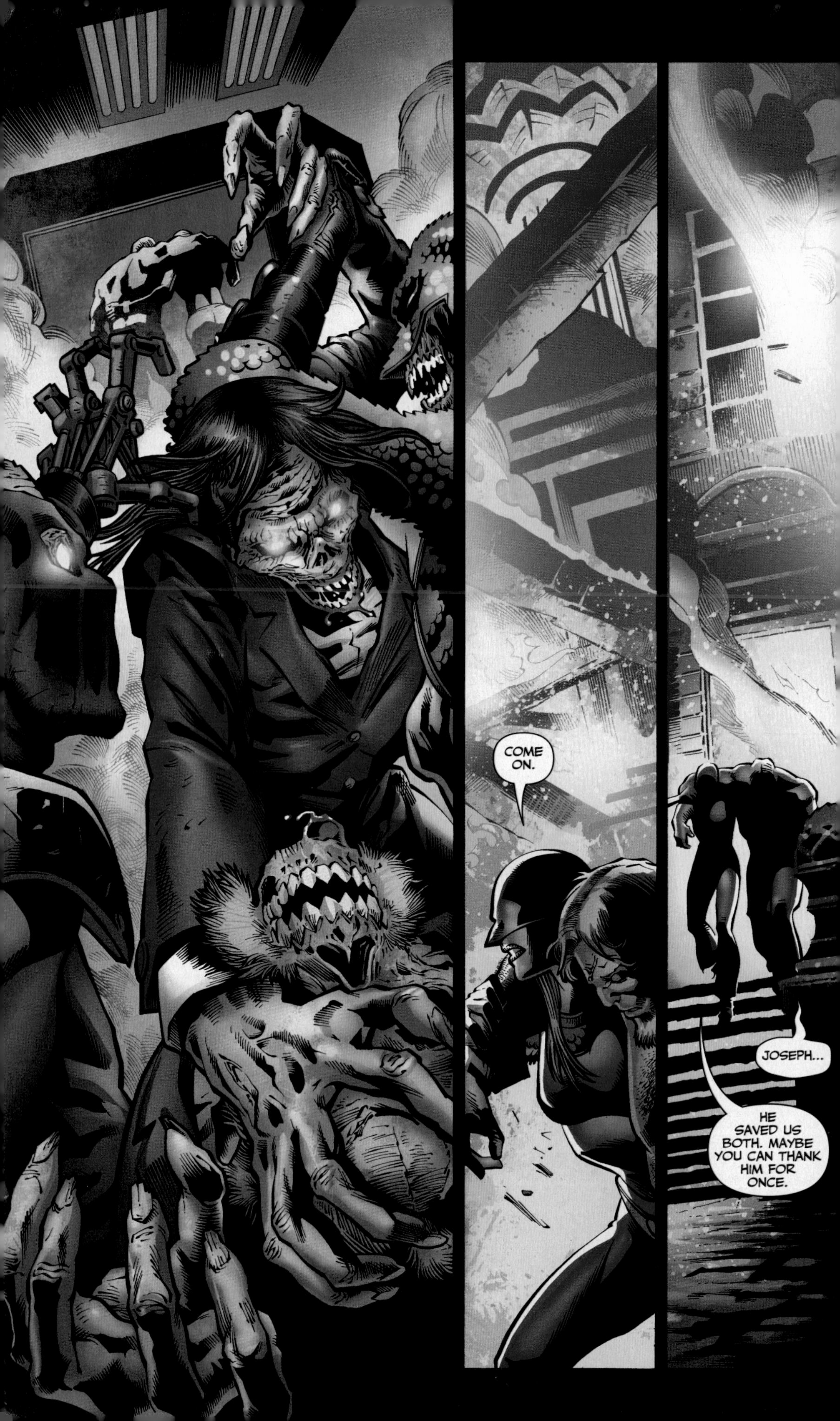
COME ON.
JOSEPH...
HE SAVED US BOTH. MAYBE YOU CAN THANK HIM FOR ONCE.

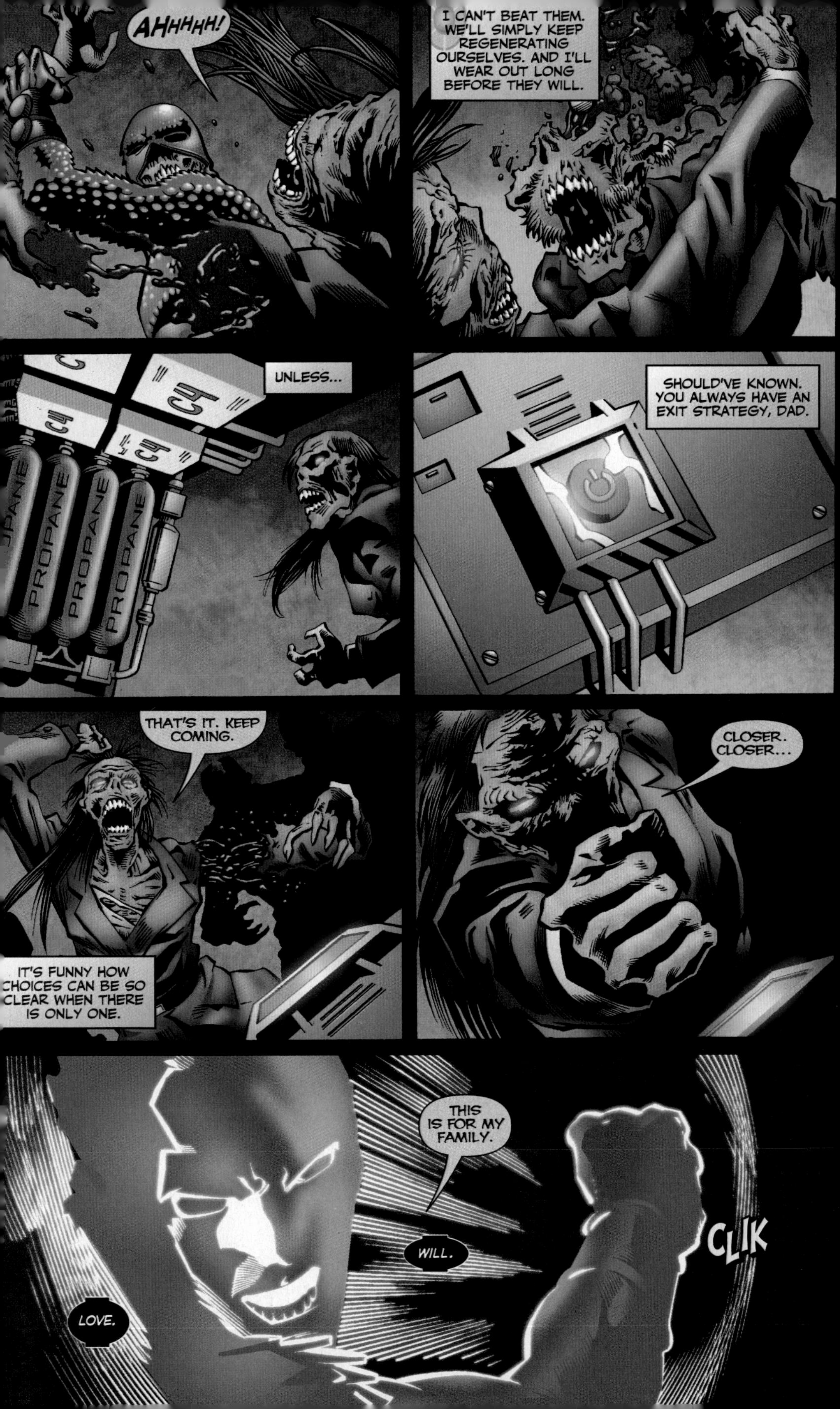
AHHHHH!
I CAN'T BEAT THEM. WE'LL SIMPLY KEEP REGENERATING OURSELVES. AND I'LL WEAR OUT LONG BEFORE THEY WILL.
UNLESS...
C4
C4
C4
C4
PROPANE
PROPANE
PROPANE
SHOULD'VE KNOWN. YOU ALWAYS HAVE AN EXIT STRATEGY, DAD.
THAT'S IT. KEEP COMING.
IT'S FUNNY HOW CHOICES CAN BE SO CLEAR WHEN THERE IS ONLY ONE.
CLOSER. CLOSER...
THIS IS FOR MY FAMILY.
WILL.
LOVE.
CLIK

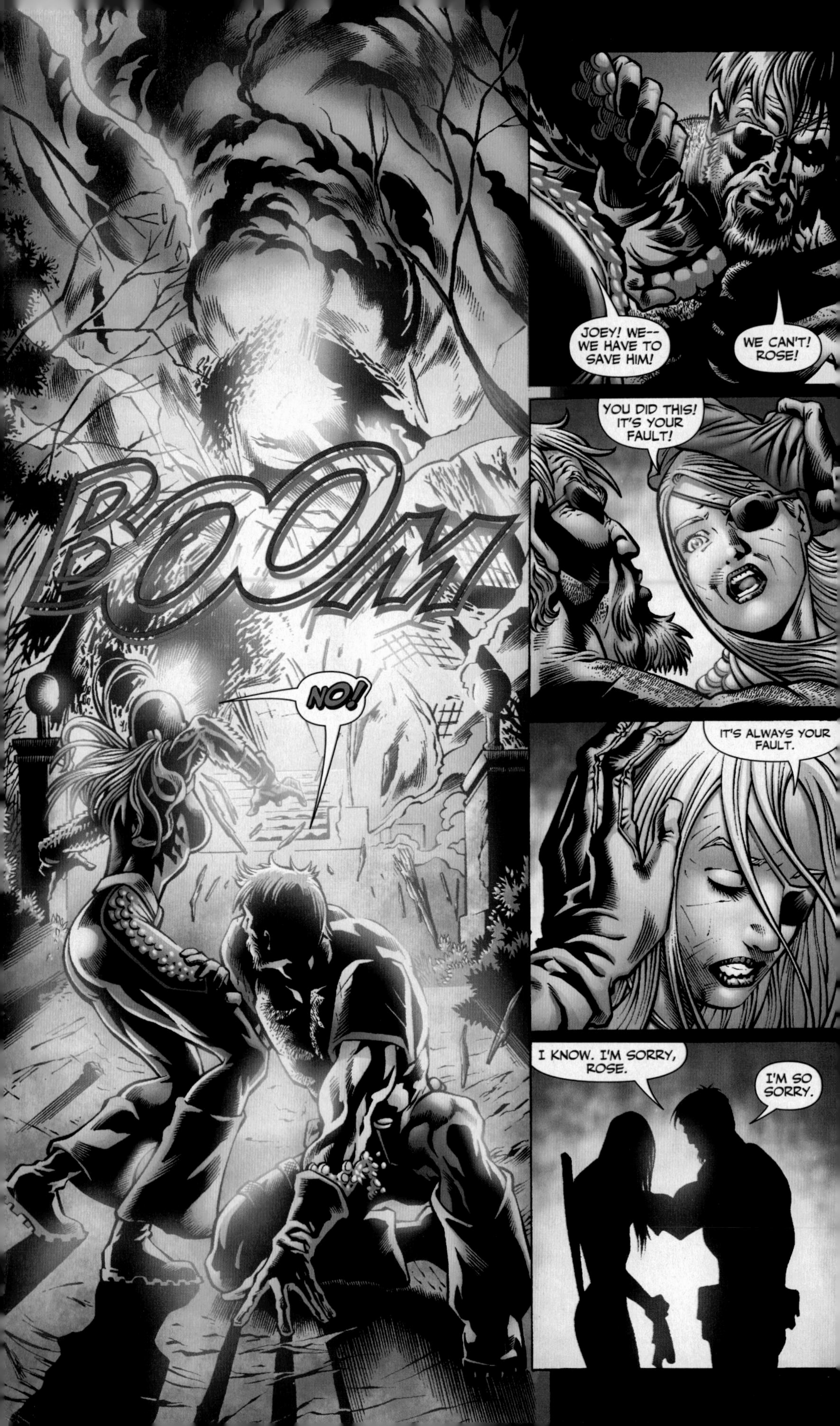
BOOM
NO!
JOEY! WE-- WE HAVE TO SAVE HIM!
WE CAN'T! ROSE!
YOU DID THIS! IT'S YOUR FAULT!
IT'S ALWAYS YOUR FAULT.
I KNOW. I'M SORRY, ROSE.
I'M SO SORRY.

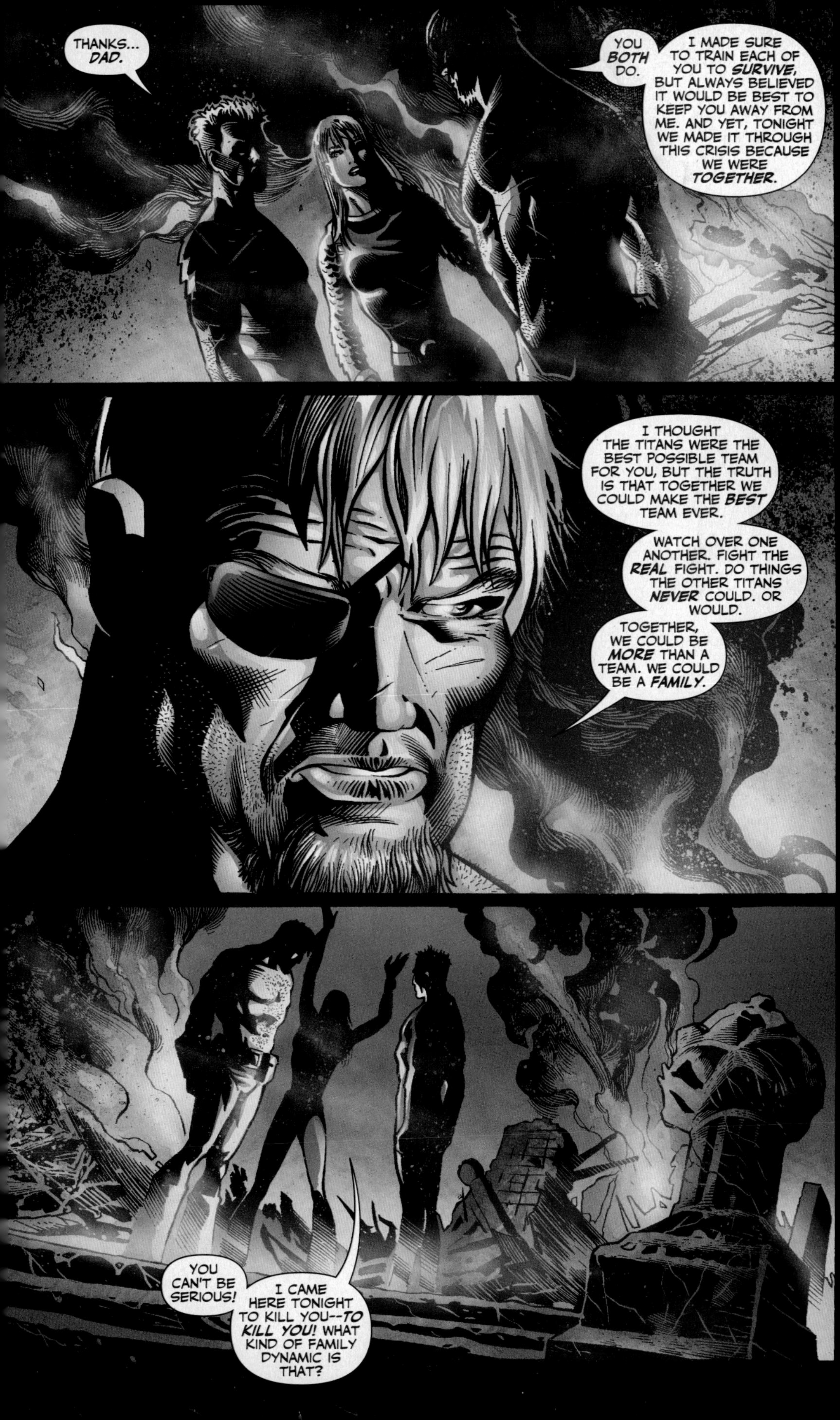
THANKS... DAD.
YOU BOTH DO.
I MADE SURE TO TRAIN EACH OF YOU TO SURVIVE, BUT ALWAYS BELIEVED IT WOULD BE BEST TO KEEP YOU AWAY FROM ME. AND YET, TONIGHT WE MADE IT THROUGH THIS CRISIS BECAUSE WE WERE TOGETHER.
I THOUGHT THE TITANS WERE THE BEST POSSIBLE TEAM FOR YOU, BUT THE TRUTH IS THAT TOGETHER WE COULD MAKE THE BEST TEAM EVER.
WATCH OVER ONE ANOTHER. FIGHT THE REAL FIGHT. DO THINGS THE OTHER TITANS NEVER COULD. OR WOULD.
TOGETHER, WE COULD BE MORE THAN A TEAM. WE COULD BE A FAMILY.
YOU CAN'T BE SERIOUS!
I CAME HERE TONIGHT TO KILL YOU--TO KILL YOU! WHAT KIND OF FAMILY DYNAMIC IS THAT?

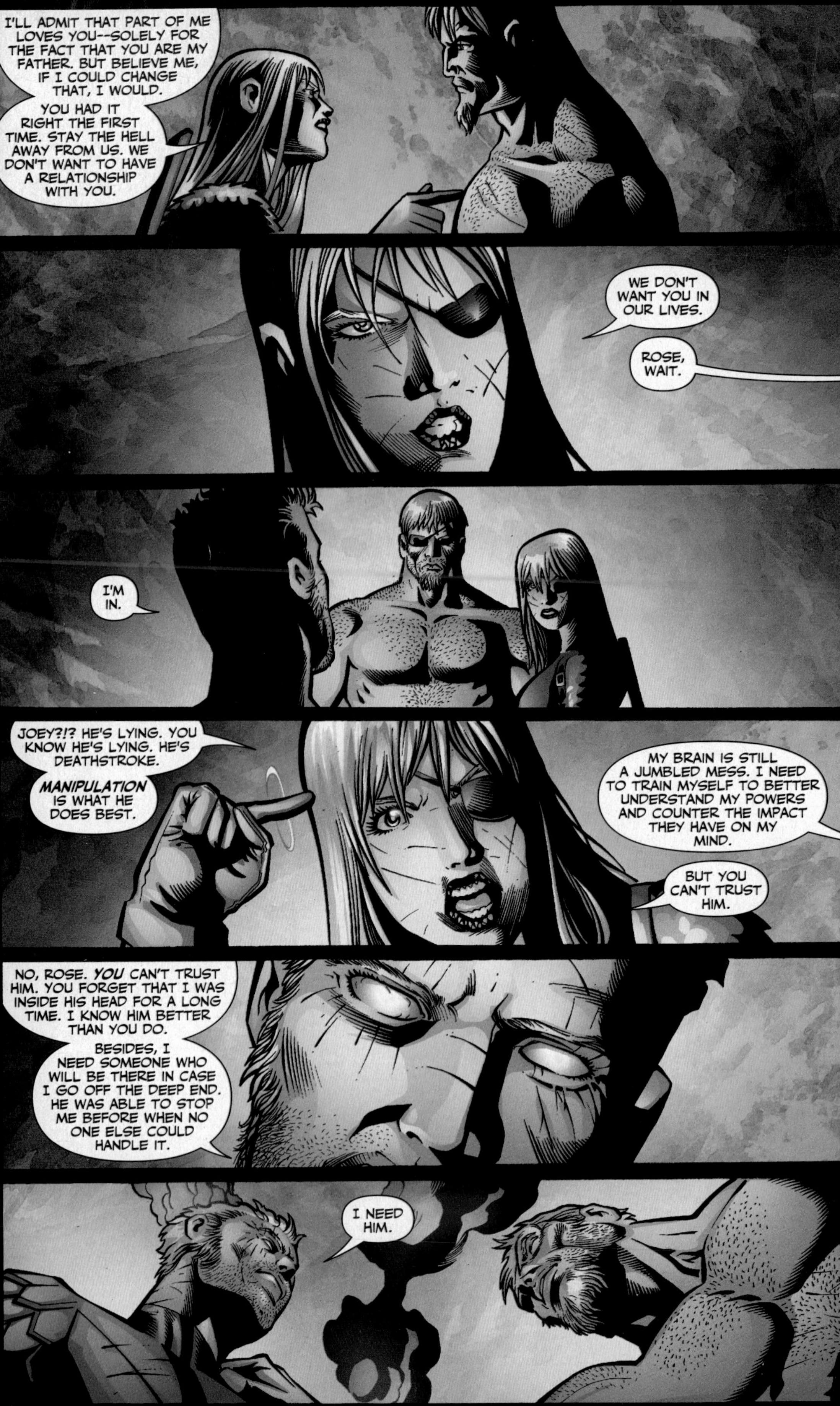
I'LL ADMIT THAT PART OF ME LOVES YOU--SOLELY FOR THE FACT THAT YOU ARE MY FATHER. BUT BELIEVE ME, IF I COULD CHANGE THAT, I WOULD.
YOU HAD IT RIGHT THE FIRST TIME. STAY THE HELL AWAY FROM US. WE DON'T WANT TO HAVE A RELATIONSHIP WITH YOU.
WE DON'T WANT YOU IN OUR LIVES.
ROSE, WAIT.
I'M IN.
JOEY?!? HE'S LYING. YOU KNOW HE'S LYING. HE'S DEATHSTROKE.
MANIPULATION IS WHAT HE DOES BEST.
MY BRAIN IS STILL A JUMBLED MESS. I NEED TO TRAIN MYSELF TO BETTER UNDERSTAND MY POWERS AND COUNTER THE IMPACT THEY HAVE ON MY MIND.
BUT YOU CAN'T TRUST HIM.
NO, ROSE. YOU CAN'T TRUST HIM. YOU FORGET THAT I WAS INSIDE HIS HEAD FOR A LONG TIME. I KNOW HIM BETTER THAN YOU DO.
BESIDES, I NEED SOMEONE WHO WILL BE THERE IN CASE I GO OFF THE DEEP END. HE WAS ABLE TO STOP ME BEFORE WHEN NO ONE ELSE COULD HANDLE IT.
I NEED HIM.

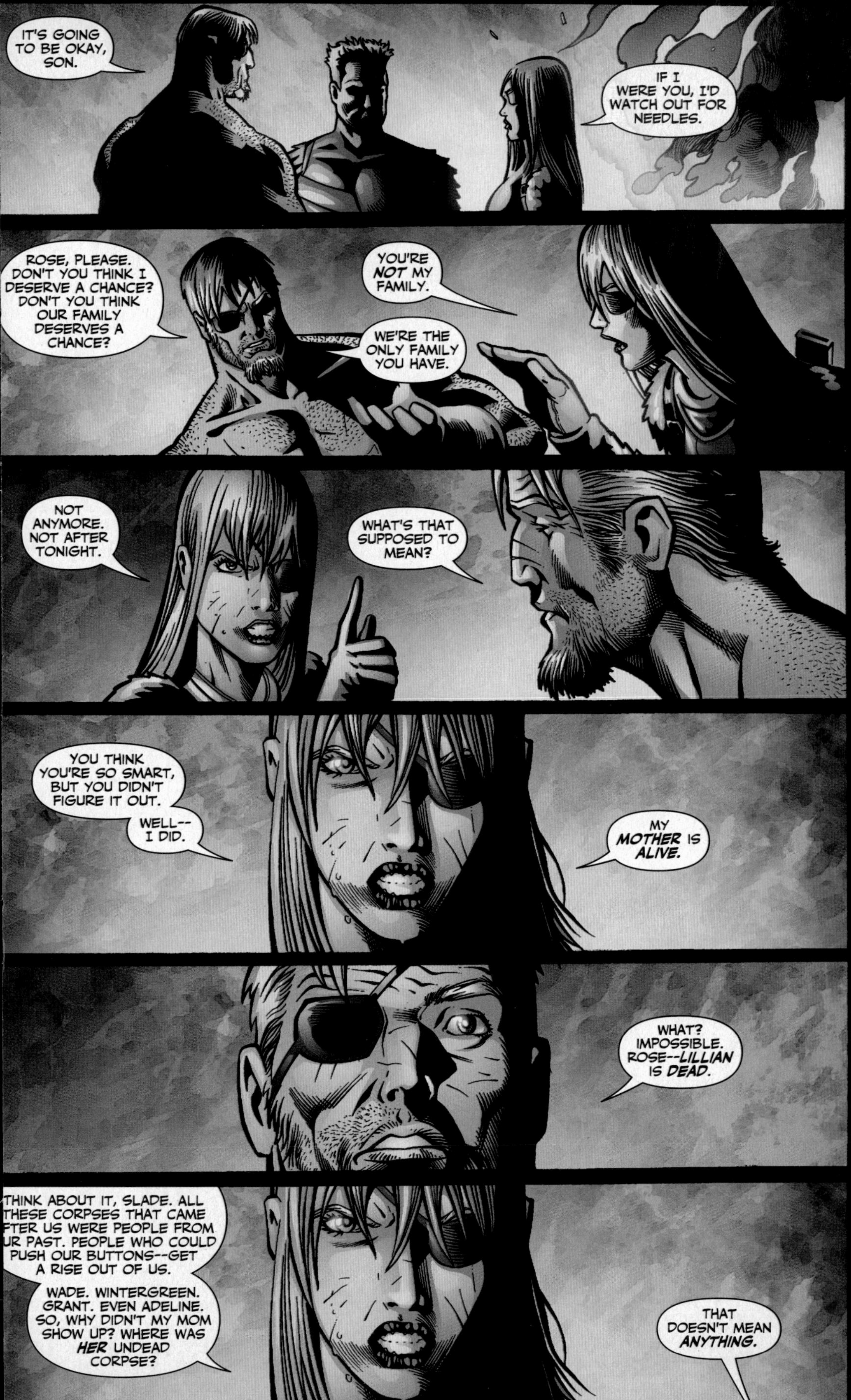
IT'S GOING TO BE OKAY, SON.
IF I WERE YOU, I'D WATCH OUT FOR NEEDLES.
ROSE, PLEASE. DON'T YOU THINK I DESERVE A CHANCE? DON'T YOU THINK OUR FAMILY DESERVES A CHANCE?
YOU'RE NOT MY FAMILY.
WE'RE THE ONLY FAMILY YOU HAVE.
NOT ANYMORE. NOT AFTER TONIGHT.
WHAT'S THAT SUPPOSED TO MEAN?
YOU THINK YOU'RE SO SMART, BUT YOU DIDN'T FIGURE IT OUT.
WELL-- I DID.
MY MOTHER IS ALIVE.
WHAT? IMPOSSIBLE. ROSE--LILLIAN IS DEAD.
THINK ABOUT IT, SLADE. ALL THESE CORPSES THAT CAME FTER US WERE PEOPLE FROM UR PAST. PEOPLE WHO COULD PUSH OUR BUTTONS--GET A RISE OUT OF US.
WADE. WINTERGREEN. GRANT. EVEN ADELINE. SO, WHY DIDN'T MY MOM SHOW UP? WHERE WAS HER UNDEAD CORPSE?
THAT DOESN'T MEAN ANYTHING.

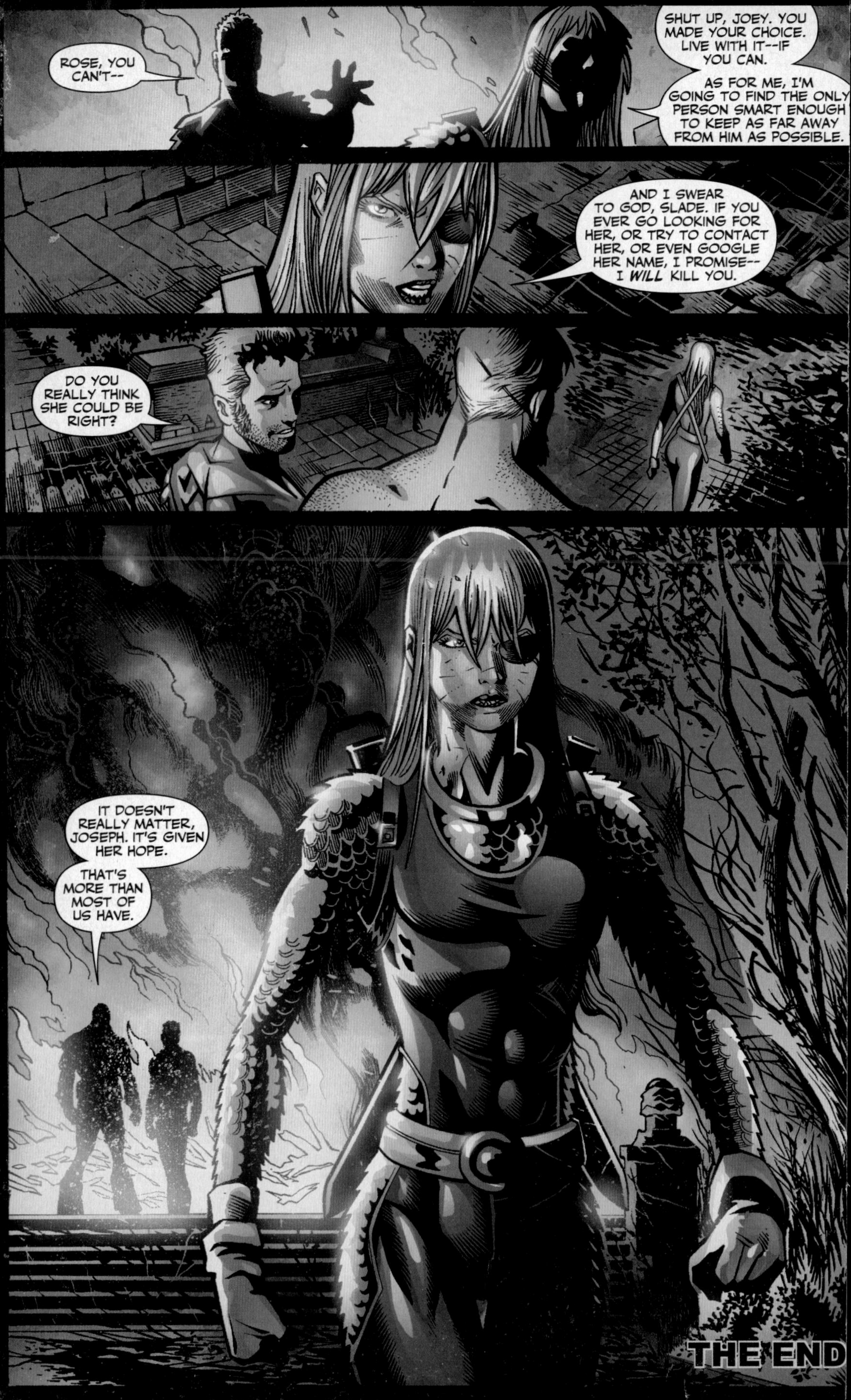
ROSE, YOU CAN'T--
SHUT UP, JOEY. YOU MADE YOUR CHOICE. LIVE WITH IT--IF YOU CAN.
AS FOR ME, I'M GOING TO FIND THE ONLY PERSON SMART ENOUGH TO KEEP AS FAR AWAY FROM HIM AS POSSIBLE.
AND I SWEAR TO GOD, SLADE. IF YOU EVER GO LOOKING FOR HER, OR TRY TO CONTACT HER, OR EVEN GOOGLE HER NAME, I PROMISE-- I *WILL* KILL YOU.
DO YOU REALLY THINK SHE COULD BE RIGHT?
IT DOESN'T REALLY MATTER, JOSEPH. IT'S GIVEN HER HOPE.
THAT'S MORE THAN MOST OF US HAVE.
THE END